The University of Cambridge in the Eighteenth Century

BY

D. A. WINSTANLEY, M.A.
FELLOW OF TRINITY COLLEGE

CAMBRIDGE
AT THE UNIVERSITY PRESS
1922

PREFACE

IT is sometimes assumed that the University of Cambridge in the eighteenth century led an isolated existence, remote from the stream of the national life; and that its numerous deficiencies were due to its immunity from external interference and its freedom to wallow in its sin. This generalisation is however more sweeping than accurate; and is certainly quite untrue of that part of the century when the Duke of Newcastle was Chancellor of the university. The following narrative, which can be briefly described as an account of Newcastle's activities as Chancellor, attempts to show that, at least as long as the Duke was a power in Cambridge, the connection between the academic and political worlds, instead of being non-existent, was in reality much too close and intimate to be salutary, and that the university was very far from being left to itself. The abuses were many, but they were not exclusively of home manufacture, and the politicians must shoulder their portion of the blame.

Use has been made of the Newcastle, Hardwicke, and Cole manuscripts in the British Museum; and in defence of the rather numerous extracts from these papers, it can be pleaded that events are generally most vividly described by those who have taken part in them. It is obvious that such a method does not make for brevity, but possibly the loss of conciseness may be compensated for by increase of interest.

I am glad to have this opportunity of expressing my great gratitude to my friends, Sir Geoffrey Butler, Fellow of Corpus Christi College, and Mr A. F. Scholfield, Librarian of Trinity College, for very much needed assistance most generously given; and for the sake of the few who may have read an appendix to an earlier work I should mention that a more careful and complete study of the manuscript authorities has shown me that my previous account of the contest between Lord Hardwicke and Lord Sandwich for the High Stewardship of the university was unfortunately not free from serious inaccuracies. It is to be hoped that the description given in the following pages of that fierce struggle more closely approximates to the truth.

D. A. W.

CAMBRIDGE,
September 1922

CONTENTS

CHAP.	PAGE
I. INTRODUCTION	1
II. THE UNIVERSITY AND POLITICIANS	34
III. THE CHANCELLOR AND THE UNIVERSITY	145
IV. THE CHANCELLOR AND THE COLLEGES	231
INDEX	331

LIST OF ILLUSTRATIONS

PLATE

I. THOMAS PELHAM-HOLLES . FRONTISPIECE
FIRST DUKE OF NEWCASTLE
From the portrait in the hall of Clare College, by permission of the Master and Fellows

II. JOHN MONTAGU . . . . . TO FACE 56
FOURTH EARL OF SANDWICH
From the portrait by Zoffany in the National Portrait Gallery

III. PHILIP YONGE 148
MASTER OF JESUS COLLEGE, CAMBRIDGE (1752–58)
BISHOP OF BRISTOL (1758–61)
BISHOP OF NORWICH (1761–83)

IV. LYNFORD CARYL 232
MASTER OF JESUS COLLEGE, CAMBRIDGE (1758–81)
Plates III and IV are from portraits in Jesus College Lodge, by permission of the Master

CHAPTER I

INTRODUCTION

MUCH has been written about the university of Cambridge in the eighteenth century, and it would be idle to attempt to do again what already has been done so well. The stormy years of Bentley's Mastership of Trinity are admirably and fully described in Monk's biography of that turbulent scholar[1], and Henry Gunning, in his *Reminiscences of the University, Town and County of Cambridge*, has given a vivid and entertaining account of university ways and manners at the close of the century. But Bentley died in 1742 and Gunning did not begin his undergraduate career until 1784; and between these two dates lies an unexplored tract of university history. It cannot be pretended that this middle period claims attention as being peculiarly rich in great scholars and striking characters; but the history of an university, like the history of a nation, is not exclusively a record of the achievements of great men. Mediocrities play their part in building up the whole; and it may at least be said of Cambridge during the middle years of the eighteenth century that, though not prolific of great scholars, it was peculiarly rich in university politicians. From 1748 until 1768 it had as its Chancellor that very typical eighteenth century politician, Thomas Pelham-Holles, Duke of Newcastle; and any society over which Newcastle presided was not likely to lack opportunities of exercising its talents in the direction of intrigue and wire-pulling. It is now the

[1] *Life of Richard Bentley*, by James Henry Monk, Bishop of Gloucester (1830).

fashion to deride those who spend their time and energy upon the ephemeral controversies which rage in an university, and possibly they might often be more profitably employed; but, while the moralist and scholar condemn, the student of human nature has cause to be grateful. It is neither uninteresting nor uninstructive to see men imitating on a small stage the warfare of the great world and striving to attain their petty ambitions with as much fury and as little scruple as if contending for empires; and the Cambridge combatants in the eighteenth century, though frequently contending for nothing greater than the satisfaction of their own ambitions, certainly carried on their struggles with an ingenuity and resource deserving of a better cause. But the period of university history under consideration does not present an unrelieved picture of sordid struggles for ignoble spoils. The lamp of learning was not burning with startling brightness but it was still burning; jobbery was rampant but honest merit came sometimes to its own; scandals were unpleasantly frequent but probably not as frequent as is popularly supposed. We indeed have often occasion to blush for our predecessors; but we possibly have been readier to blush than to enquire.

And enquiry is the more necessary as we are separated by a wide gulf from eighteenth century Cambridge. Much has changed in the university during the last two centuries; but in no respect has the change been greater than in the habits and outlook of its senior members. A present-day Fellow of a college is not very different in type from the ordinary professional man. His university career is a part and a very important part of his life, but it is not the whole. His interests are many and by no means exclusively academic. Almost as much at home in London as he is in Cambridge, he has friends and acquaintances in many paths of life, does not garnish his conversation with Greek and Latin quotations, and plays his part without conscious effort in general society. He takes a pride in his freedom from eccentricities and improves upon the Pharisee by thanking God that he is as other men. His eighteenth century predecessor had a far more limited outlook upon life and bore more visibly the marks of his calling. Generally in orders and often of comparatively lowly origin, he was a stranger to the exclusive social world of his time. When he visited the metropolis his manners and behaviour stamped him as a provincial, and he commonly had no higher ambition than to become a tutor to the son of an influential nobleman through whose assistance he might secure advancement in the church. If he was singularly fortunate he might obtain a bishopric which would place him on terms of equality with the great, but such good fortune was reserved for the few, and the average university 'don' only saw the polite world from the point of view of the humble dependent. His social experience was in consequence extremely limited. Removed from refining influences, and with few opportunities of measuring his conduct by any other standard than that prevailing in the university, he retained many of the characteristics of the class from which he had sprung. Servile towards his superiors and overbearing towards those he considered beneath him, he was frequently gross and boorish with his friends and equals; but it must in fairness be remembered that the seclusion, which kept him a boor, was productive of certain virtues. It is likely that he had a far deeper and more enduring love of his college and university than is at all common at the present day. To his education he was mainly indebted for whatever success he had achieved in life, and his college, if not his first, was at least his greatest patron. It was moreover his home in a way which it has nowadays ceased to be except for the few, and he therefore gave it the affection which men reserve for their homes. He may often have quarrelled with his colleagues and neglected his pupils; but he was seldom found wanting in loyalty to the society to which he belonged.

His virtues, however, have perished with him and he has come down in history with a sorry and tarnished reputation. It is popularly believed that he was lazy and self-indulgent; but there is good reason to think that his failings have been exaggerated. Though Cambridge in the eighteenth century was sadly lacking in eminent mathematicians[1], it was not wanting in great classical scholars; and a century of university history which can boast of Bentley, Porson, Dawes and Markland may be accounted to have paid its debt and more than its debt to classical scholarship. It can of course be contended that scholars of such merit were rare, that they were the exception rather than the rule, and that to derive from them the standard of industry prevailing in the university is to argue from the particular to the general; but, inasmuch as it is the inevitable consequence of the progress of learning that the greater part of the work of one generation is superseded by the next, and that only a comparatively few students are remembered for all time, it is particularly necessary to be cautious of assuming that idleness must have been almost universal because the proofs of industry are not very obvious. It is true that research was not quite so much the order of the day as it is at present; but the claims of learning and scholarship were certainly not completely disregarded. No one now troubles to investigate the high dusty shelves of college libraries on which repose the volumes on philosophy, divinity,

[1] As Sir Isaac Newton died in 1727 he can hardly be claimed as an eighteenth century mathematician.

mathematics and the classics, which, though now completely out of date, were greeted in their day as valuable contributions to learning. Dr Smith, Master of Trinity, is now chiefly remembered as the founder of the mathematical prizes named after him; but in his own day he was famous as a mathematician and his treatise on optics was translated into French and German. The *Essay on the Roman Senate*, written by Dr Chapman, Master of Magdalene, has fallen into still deeper oblivion; but yet the treatise, when published, was thought sufficiently important to be translated into French. Few moreover have ever heard of Dr Law, Master of Peterhouse, who, when a Fellow of Christ's, assisted to edit *Roberti Stephani Thesaurus Linguae Latinae*; and probably fewer still have heard of Professor Rutherforth, Fellow and Tutor of St John's, who was accounted one of the best scholars in the university and published in quick succession volumes upon the natural sciences, theology and international law.

This list of forgotten scholars could be indefinitely extended, and, as it takes some trouble to produce even a bad book, industry was presumably not an unknown virtue in the university. It must be admitted however that if scholarship was not so neglected as is often supposed, there is a great deal of truth in the traditional belief that the instruction given in the university was very far from satisfactory. It was by no means unknown for a newly appointed Professor to be unacquainted with the very rudiments of the subject he was supposed to teach, and for a college Tutor systematically to neglect the instruction of his pupils. Dr Richard Watson, Bishop of Llandaff, was in many ways a very favourable specimen of an eighteenth century Professor, and appears conscientiously to have discharged his duties as a teacher; but nothing is more astonishing than the courage with which he shouldered responsibilities for which he was most inadequately prepared. He has left on record that, when he was appointed Professor of Chemistry in 1764, 'he knew nothing at all of chemistry, had never read a syllable on the subject, nor seen a single experiment in it,' and that it was only by as much hard work as his 'other avocations would permit,' he was able, fifteen months after his election, to deliver a course of lectures. Seven years later he was appointed Regius Professor of Divinity, and again he frankly admits that he only knew as much divinity 'as could reasonably be expected from a man whose course of studies had been directed to, and whose time had been fully occupied in, other pursuits,' and that it was not until his election to the Regius Professorship that he embarked upon the study of theology[1]. There were probably many Professors who initially were as badly equipped as Dr Watson and never troubled to overcome their deficiencies, and others who possessed the requisite knowledge but preferred not to impart it by way of lectures. Edward Waring, who was Lucasian Professor of Mathematics from 1760 to 1798, did not lecture as his 'profound researches...were not adapted to any form of communication by lectures,' and Waring's case is only singular in the excuse given for the non-performance of his duties.

The average college Tutor does not appear to have been any more conscientious than the average Professor, and Richard Cumberland, who came up to Trinity as an undergraduate in 1747, has left a very unfavourable account of the instruction he received.

'When the time came for me to commence my residence in college' he wrote 'my father accompanied me and put me under the care of the Rev. Dr Morgan, an old friend of our family and a Senior Fellow of that society. My rooms were closely adjoining to his, belonging to that staircase which leads

[1] *Anecdotes of the life of Dr Richard Watson*, pp. 28, 29, 34.

INTRODUCTION

to the chapel bell; he was kind to me when we met, but as Tutor I had few communications with him, for the gout afforded him not many intervals of ease, and with the exception of a few trifling readings in Tully's Offices, by which I was little edified and to which I paid little or no attention, he left me and one other pupil...to choose and pursue our studies as we saw fit[1].'

There were however Tutors who conscientiously fulfilled their duties towards their pupils. The Rev. James Backhouse of Trinity is now only remembered as the victim of some scurrilous verses by Porson[2]; but he appears to have been an admirable Tutor, for we are told that he 'gave regular lectures and fulfilled the duties of his charge ably and conscientiously[3].' Another Tutor of Trinity, Thomas Jones, is still remembered in the college for which he laboured, and deserves to be remembered.

'During many years' it is recorded in his biography 'he continued to take an active part in the Senate House examinations; but latterly he confined himself to the duties of college Tutor. These indeed were sufficiently numerous to engage his whole attention; and he displayed in them an ability, which was rarely equalled, with an integrity which never was surpassed[4].'

Jones was too busy as a Tutor to win fame as a writer, and his only published writings are a sermon on duelling and an address to the volunteers of Montgomeryshire; but his biographer, while regretting that much of his learning died with him, finds consolation in the knowledge that

his lectures on philosophy will not be buried in oblivion: all his writings on those subjects have been delivered to his successor in the tuition, and, though less amply than by publication, will continue to benefit mankind[5].

[1] *Memoirs of Richard Cumberland*, p. 69.
[2] Gunning's *Reminiscences*, II. 113–114.
[3] *Memoirs of Richard Cumberland*, p. 69.
[4] Marsh's *Memoir of the Rev. Thomas Jones*, p. 7.
[5] *Memoir of the Rev. Thomas Jones*, p. 9.

There is little doubt however that we have improved upon our predecessors in regard to the education given in the university; and, though there are some who think that the improvement has gone too far, a return to the eighteenth century standard of efficiency has never been contemplated[1]. There has also been an improvement in the refinements and decencies of life. The eighteenth century was a time of heavy eating and copious drinking, and Cambridge, faithfully reflecting the characteristics of the age, was the home of rude plenty. Students of Gunning's *Reminiscences* are familiar with Dr Ogden's pathetic complaint that the goose was a silly bird, being too much for one person and not enough for two[2], and it is possible that some of Ogden's contemporaries were of the same opinion but lacked the ability to give it such epigrammatic expression. Excesses in eating and drinking were certainly not uncommon phenomena. Dr Chapman, Master of Magdalene, who died in 1760, probably shortened his life by gluttony, for we are told that, about a week before his death, 'he eat five large mackerel, full of roe, to his own share, but what gave the finishing stroke was a turbot on Trinity Sunday, of which he left but very little for the company[3].' Dr Ridlington, Fellow of Trinity Hall and Professor of Civil Law, was more

---

[1] 'It is interesting to note that whereas the earlier Royal Commissions were concerned with providing against the indifference and want of conscientiousness of some of the Fellows, the charge now made in some quarters is that the Fellows overwork themselves at teaching and administration.' *Report* of the Royal Commission on Oxford and Cambridge Universities (1922), p. 39.

[2] Dr Ogden was a Fellow of St John's and Professor of Geology. For twenty years he was vicar of St Sepulchre's Church in Cambridge. He published volumes of sermons and was warmly commended for his merits as a preacher by Dr Johnson who remarked: 'I should like to read all that Ogden has written.'

[3] Gray's *Letters* (edited by D. C. Tovey), II, 160.

INTRODUCTION 9

fortunate though not more temperate; for, when supposed to be dying of the dropsy, he 'prescribed himself a boiled chicken entire and five quarts of small beer[1],' and by aid of this unorthodox remedy recovered. Such Gargantuan feats must have been rare, but self-indulgence was only too common and sometimes had disastrous results. In the year 1779 the Rev. George Mounsey, Fellow and Tutor of Jesus College, accompanied some friends on a pleasure party on the river, and, having drunk too much,

got out of the boat at Ditton Plough, a public house on the waterside, and, kneeling down before a number of people who happened to be there, denied his faith, blasphemously reviled the Holy Ghost, and...cursed the King, the Queen and all the Royal Family[2].

In consequence of this escapade Mounsey was deprived of his Tutorship, but he continued to hold his Fellowship, and in 1780 officiated as Moderator in the Schools when, much to the indignation of the antiquarian, Cole, 'he seemed as unconcerned as if nothing had happened.'

There is however no reason to think that, even in the eighteenth century, college Tutors habitually imitated Ben-hadad, King of Syria[3]; but the general standard of conduct left much to be desired and the outlook on life was very often frankly materialistic. When the Rev. Dr Walker, Vice-Master of Trinity, lay dying in 1764, he heard one of his nurses say 'Ah, poor gentleman, he is going,' and his comment, though it would have been creditable to a philosopher, was disgraceful in a divine: 'Going, going,' he ejaculated, 'where am I going? I'm sure I know no more than the man in the moon[4].' The

---

[1] Gray's *Letters*, III, 61. [2] Add. MS. 5852, f. 119.
[3] 'And they went out at noon. But Ben-hadad was drinking himself drunk in the pavilions, he and the kings, the thirty and two kings that helped him.' I Kings, ch. xx. 16
[4] Gray's *Letters*, III, 61.

INTRODUCTION

doubts of the Vice-Master were probably shared by many, and it was perhaps because they felt so uncertain of the future that they sought to make the most of the present. For whatever be charged against the senior members of the university, they cannot be accused of neglecting their worldly interests, and Cambridge was not behindhand in that shameless hunt for places and preferments which is associated with the eighteenth century. As long as the Duke of Newcastle remained in the service of the king and dispensed the crown's ecclesiastical patronage, he was constantly being reminded by his academic supporters of their claims to recognition. When the Deanery of Ely fell vacant, both Dr Prescot, the Master of St Catharine's, and Dr Law, the Master of Peterhouse, applied to the Duke for the preferment, Dr Prescot urging that he had 'always retained and shewn some affection to the royal family[1],' and Dr Law imploring the Duke, whose displeasure he had incurred,

to give credit to this, my solemn and sincere profession, that as I never entertained the least thought of seeking any patronage beside that of your Grace, so neither was any application made either by me, or, to my knowledge, for me, to any person whatsoever, but in perfect concurrence with and proper subordination to your Grace's pleasure[2].

In 1759 another Head of a House, Dr Sumner, Provost of King's, requested Newcastle to advance him in the church; and, as he was already holding a canonry and two livings, he naïvely suggested

a method, perhaps the readiest, of carrying into execution in the most effectual manner your Grace's favourable intentions towards me; and that is, my Lord, to divest me at once of both my canonry and my livings by placing me upon the Bench[3].

Most of the applicants stated their wishes in plain

[1] Add. MS. 32877, f. 170.   [2] Add. MS. 32876, f. 508.
[3] Add. MS. 32896, f. 168.

INTRODUCTION

language, commendably free from ambiguity, but Dr Ogden practised the oblique mode of address. Gunning in his *Reminiscences* alludes to this peculiarity, and mentions having been told by his father of a letter from Ogden to a prime minister which began 'The great are always liable to importunity, those who are good and great to a double portion[1]'; and a letter, which has survived among the papers of the Duke of Newcastle, confirms Gunning's testimony. Though Ogden in 1759 held the livings of Damerham in Wiltshire and St Sepulchre's in Cambridge, he was not content and made an exceedingly characteristic appeal to the Duke.

'Winchester, my Lord,' he wrote in the April of that year, 'stands well for the vicar of your parish of Damerham, a few hours distance, almost in the road. Let me bespeak your Grace's pardon, but it is impossible to pass by and overlook so fine an object as that ancient cathedral. Your Grace, it is probable, will shortly place a new bishop in the only see almost which perhaps you have not filled. The prebends will be in his gift. I most humbly take my leave and am, etc.[2]'

It was inevitable that many of these seekers after preferment should be disappointed, but it can be confidently asserted that as long as Newcastle remained in office the claims of Cambridge were recognised in over-running measure. It was good to be a whig in those days, but still better to be a Cambridge whig, and best of all to be a whig who had been educated at Westminster and Clare, the Duke's school and college. In 1748 Edmund Castle, Master of Corpus, was made Dean of Hereford; and Dr John Green, who in 1750 succeeded Castle in his Mastership, became Dean and afterwards Bishop of Lincoln. In 1752 Edmund Keene, Master of Peterhouse, was given the Bishopric of Chester, and in 1758 Dr Yonge, Master of Jesus, be-

[1] Gunning's *Reminiscences*, I, 237.
[2] Add. MS. 32890, f. 292

came Bishop of Bristol and later Bishop of Norwich. Dr Newcome, Master of St John's, was Dean of Rochester, and Dr Thomas, Master of Christ's, was Dean of Ely. The Duke's Cambridge supporters certainly did not serve him for nought; and, if we blame them, it is for their shamelessness and not for their ignorance in asking.

This hunger for advancement in the church had unfortunate consequences. The university was not only familiarised with the most sordid side of contemporary political life but suffered in its independence. It was only natural that men, so anxious to receive, should be timorous of offending possible benefactors and unwilling to pay much attention to scruples which stood in the way of obedience to their patrons. Nice customs have to curtsey to great kings, and there is at least a suspicion that impartiality in university and college examinations had on occasions to be abandoned to comply with the wishes of the great. Thus in October 1757 the Duke of Newcastle wrote to Dr Green, Master of Corpus, and Dr Rutherforth, Regius Professor of Divinity, to recommend to their favourable attention Jonathan Davies, an undergraduate of King's, who was thinking of competing for the Craven scholarship[1].

'My Lord Hertford,' wrote the Duke, 'a particular friend of mine, having desired me, as you will see by the enclosed note, to recommend Mr Davies, who is represented to be a very ingenious young man, to your favour for the scholarship founded by Lord Craven, I should be much obliged to you if you would be so good as to assist him upon that occasion[2]';

and the request was most sympathetically received. It is true that Green pointed out that no Craven scholarship had yet been declared vacant, that, as the right of electing was confined to the Vice-Chancellor, the five

---

[1] Add. MS. 32875, f. 103, f. 105, f. 107.
[2] Add. MS. 32875, f. 103.

INTRODUCTION 13

Regius Professors and the Public Orator, he would not have a vote until he became Vice-Chancellor, and that

the candidates for this scholarship are examined with great care and it has been given, as far as I have been concerned in the disposal, to those who wanted it most and deserved it best;

but, having paid this tribute to the decencies, he proceeded to remark that

should this young man's character and improvements be found to answer, as I have no doubt but they will answer, the representation made to your Grace, I should with the utmost readiness and pleasure assist in choosing him[1].

Dr Rutherforth also laid stress upon the strictness of the examination and the keenness of the competition; but he too concluded by begging leave

to assure your Grace that I shall in this and every other instance act under the fullest sense of the duty which I owe to your Grace, and shall be ready to shew my Lord Hertford's friend all the favour that the nature of the examination will admit of[2].

A few weeks after these letters were written, Dr Green was elected Vice-Chancellor, and, two days before Christmas, he was able to inform Newcastle that Lord Hertford's candidate had been awarded the Craven scholarship.

'It is with great pleasure' he wrote 'I now acquaint your Grace that Mr Davies, a scholar of King's college, whom you were pleased to recommend at Lord Hertford's request, was this day elected into the Craven scholarship. There were six candidates who were examined with great care and all of whom appeared very well on the examination: a favourable sign, I should hope, that good letters are far from losing ground among us. There was a difference in their attainments, and it was judged a circumstance much in Davies' favour that, though he

---

[1] Add. MS. 32875, f. 165. The five Regius Professors were the Regius Professors of Physic, Civil Law, Divinity, Hebrew and Greek. The Regius Professor of History was not an elector as that Professorship had not been in existence when the scholarship was founded.

[2] Add. MS. 32875, f. 187.

was not of equall standing, he had made equall improvements with the best[1].'

As Jonathan Davies became in after life Headmaster and then Provost of Eton, it is possible that he deserved the scholarship[2]; but, while this is only a surmise, we know for certain that two of the examiners had been prejudiced in his favour, and that Davies, whether he needed it or not, had been given an unfair advantage over the other candidates. Nor was this the only occasion on which Newcastle successfully played the part of destiny shaping the wills of examiners. When in 1762 a certain John Fuller was a candidate for a Trinity Fellowship, his uncle, Rose Fuller, who was a member of parliament, asked Newcastle to use his influence, and the Duke, without hesitation and without delay, wrote to the Master, Dr Smith, the Vice-Master, Dr Walker and the two Tutors, Backhouse and Whisson[3]. His letter to Whisson is a fair example of his mode of approach.

'Though I hope for the pleasure of seeing you to-morrow with our address' he wrote 'I would not omit acquainting you that my friend, Mr Rose Fuller, has earnestly desired me to recommend his nephew, Mr Fuller, of your college, to be chose Fellow at your next election. I shall be very much obliged to you if you would favour him with your vote and assistance. I hear he is a very good young man[4].'

Of the four electors thus appealed to, the two Tutors were apparently most anxious to please. Backhouse

[1] Add. MS. 32876, f. 408.
[2] He apparently preserved a pleasant memory of having won the Craven, for by his will he left a thousand pounds to found a scholarship to be called 'Dr Davies' university scholarship,' and he specially mentioned in his will that he bequeathed this money 'remembering that he was so fortunate as to get one of the said university scholarships.'
[3] Add. MS. 32941, f. 335, f. 391, Add. MS. 32942, f. 33, f. 99, f. 131, f. 133.
[4] Add. MS. 32942, f. 131.

assured Newcastle that, as his greatest happiness was to serve him, 'I will certainly endeavour to serve that young gentleman as far as may be consistent with my indispensible (*sic*) duty to my own pupils[1],' and Whisson declared that 'Mr Fuller's nephew may depend upon my best services at our next election[2].' The Vice-Master was more cautious. He pointed out that there were more candidates than vacancies, that 'the Master and Seniors take a solemn oath to choose those that have made greatest proficiency in their studies,' and that much would depend upon Fuller acquitting himself well in the examination; but he significantly added 'where there is an equality there is room for favour[3].' The Master however remained silent. Not until after the election had taken place did he reply to the Duke and then he rebuked him:

'Your Grace, I hope, will excuse this late answer to your letter' he wrote 'as I could not sooner say anything satisfactory to it for want of knowing the number of vacancies and the merits of the candidates. For a long time we had but two vacancies, till last night I received a resignation of two more, and this morning we filled them up with these bachelors of arts—Fountaine, Hilton, Fuller and Zouch, elected out of twelve candidates[4].'

Thus, though the Master had kept his counsel and the Vice-Master had been guarded, Fuller secured his Fellowship; and it is possible that the Master would not have displayed such Roman virtue if Newcastle, a few months before, had not been driven from office and the cabinet. It is of course quite possible that the Duke's interference had not influenced the issue in the slightest degree; but it was clearly in the highest degree undesirable that there should be any interference at all. Yet, as long as many among the university authorities

[1] Add. MS. 32942, f. 277.   [2] Add. MS. 32942, f. 322.
[3] Add. MS. 32942, f. 99.   [4] Add. MS. 32943, f. 9.

were dependent upon the great, it was difficult to prevent the great from intervening; for it must not be imagined that the practice originated with or was confined to the Duke of Newcastle. As Chancellor he was closely in touch with the authorities of the university and therefore favourably situated to exercise an influence; but he was certainly not the only nobleman who commended a candidate for a scholarship or fellowship to the favourable consideration of the examiners and electors. But, even if the university had been immune from outside interference, it is unlikely that all would have been well; for jobbery had bitten deep into the age and was by no means a monopoly of politicians.

'I was the second Wrangler of my year' wrote Dr Watson in his memoirs 'the leading Moderator having made a person of his own college and one of his private pupils the first, in direct opposition to the general sense of the examiners in the Senate House who declared in my favour....Our old Master[1] sent for me and told me not to be discouraged, for that, when the Johnians had the disposal of the honours, the second Wrangler was always looked upon as the first[2].'

Enough has been said to show that a change has taken place in the morals and manners of the university since the eighteenth century; and the change has not been confined to the senior members. Two hundred years ago disorderly and riotous conduct was far more common among undergraduates than nowadays, and discipline was lax and ineffective. In 1716 a decree, issued by the Vice-Chancellor and Heads of Houses, called attention to the

late divers disorders among several scholars of the university, tumultuously meeting together, provoking and exasperating one another by invidious names, opprobrious words, hissing and

---

[1] Dr Smith.   [2] Watson's *Anecdotes*, p. 18.

shouting one against another, throwing of stones and other great irregularities[1];

and, twelve years later, another decree alluded to the disorder which had arisen 'to the manifest scandal of the university, the destruction of all good order and discipline, and to the great and sometimes irreparable injury of persons educated amongst us[2].' In 1749 two Fellow Commoners of Trinity were convicted in the Vice-Chancellor's court of being at an inn until 4 o'clock on Sunday morning June 4th, and then going to the Market Cross and 'in a riotous manner eating lobsters and drinking a bottle of wine there[3]'; and in an undated letter the poet Gray complains that

the Fellow Commoners (the Bucks) are run mad, they set women upon their heads in the streets at (noon) day, break open shops, game in the coffee houses on Sunday, and in short act after my heart[4].

Sometimes the disorder assumed serious proportions, and in April 1751 Dr Keene, Master of Peterhouse, was called upon as Vice-Chancellor to quell a riot which might easily have resulted in bloodshed.

'Major Folkes and Captain Shaftoe' he informed the Chancellor 'came to Cambridge on Sunday noon and Frederick Vane[5] accidentally met with them. They three went to Mr Ladd's room and drank seven bottles of claret. On the officers going away, Mr Ladd and Mr Vane went into the post-chaise with them in their habits and, as they say, with a design of going a mile on the Huntingdon road and then walking back. This was done about six o'clock on Sunday even, and when they came to the turnpike, just at the end of the town, they saw two young women drinking tea with some tradesmen; and Shaftoe and Vane got out of the chaise and went into the house, and, upon the young women retreating, they forced themselves upstairs,

[1] Cooper's *Annals*, IV, 143. [2] Cooper's *Annals*, IV, 204.
[3] Add. MS. 5852, f. 119. [4] Gray's *Letters*, I, 162.
[5] Vane was a Fellow Commoner of Peterhouse and afterwards represented the county of Durham in parliament.

broke the windows of the house, and beat the young men who had by this time secured the girls in the cellar. It appears that Folkes and Mr Ladd continued in the chaise and desired the others to desist. This disturbance occasioned the neighbours to collect themselves, and constables were sent for and blows ensued. After some time Mr Vane got upon a horse and rode into the town and endeavoured to summon the gownsmen by telling them that the townsmen were murdering some gentlemen of the university; and, had it happened that any number could have been collected, God knows what might have been the consequence, considering that the townspeople are greatly irritated by the last affair. The moment I heard of the affair I immediately ordered the college gates to be shut and went myself down to the coffee-house where I found Ladd and Vane with many gownsmen and strangers and much mob assembled about the door. I secured Vane and sent him home in my chariot attended by Brockett. I directed the rest of the gownsmen to go home forthwith, requested of the strangers that they would go to their inns, and I read the proclamation amongst the people who immediately dispersed, and so an end was put to this disturbance[1].'

This is not the only instance of a Vice-Chancellor being called upon to quell a riot; for in a letter written in March 1770 it is mentioned that

on one of the days of our late assizes there was a very great disturbance and tumult in the court between the gownsmen and the townsmen, insomuch that the Judge (Adams), after having tried other means of appeasing it, was at last forced to stop all business and to send for the Vice-Chancellor[2].

Disorder, indeed, was unpleasantly frequent, and in 1781 there was another disturbance on a serious scale. Six men of different colleges, after supping together at Emmanuel, were proceeding in the direction of St Catharine's

in two parties, four in one, two in the second, of which the last was about thirty yards behind the other. The four passed by

---

[1] Add. MS. 32724, f. 236.
[2] Add. MS. 32628, f. 102, f. 104, f. 105.

Mrs Jacob's house, who was then leaning over her hatch, without taking any notice of her. One of the two hindmost held out his hand to shake hands with her and she gave him hers; at the same instant almost, his companion gave either her or the hatch a push which threw her backwards in the passage; her son in law, Elkin, rushed out to seize the man, the old woman followed, a scuffle ensued, and a blow with a heavy stick, intended for Elkin, fell on Mrs Jacob's head who shrieked and cried 'murder.' At the cry of murder the four hastened back and also Prettyman of Pembroke[1], the Moderator, who was passing accidentally. I fancy one or two also from the neighbouring houses[2].

Thereupon a general scuffle ensued, and the unfortunate Pretyman, 'having no gown on and being in boots,' was mistaken for a townsman and 'received a violent blow on the face from an undergraduate[3].' Proceedings against the six offenders were taken in the Vice-Chancellor's court; and although four of them escaped with a fine and reprimand, the other two were fined and rusticated for a year[4].

It is of course quite true that young men will always incline to disorder, and that nowadays it is not unknown for undergraduates to overstep the limits of decorous behaviour. Nevertheless it is impossible to deny that discipline was lax and rioting far too common. Nor was it unknown for individuals among the authorities to be threatened with violence. About 1779 an undergraduate of Emmanuel was bound over to keep the peace for

[1] Pretyman, who afterwards took the name of Tomline, had a distinguished career in the church and for the last seven years of his life was Bishop of Winchester. In 1821 he published a biography of the younger Pitt.
[2] Add. MS. 35658, f. 53.   [3] *Ibid.*
[4] An account of the proceedings in the Vice-Chancellor's court is given in a manuscript in the University Library (MMV, 51). Among the witnesses was Rose Elkin, the fair Jewess, mentioned by Gunning. The story told by the witnesses does not agree in detail with the version given above; but the differences are not material.

20   INTRODUCTION

threatening to shoot Dr Hallifax, the Regius Professor of Civil Law, whom he accused of having slandered him; and though the charitably disposed were convinced that the young man was not right in the head, the Fellows of Emmanuel refused to admit that he was 'out of the way[1].' But a far more grievous fate befell Dr Rooke, Master of Christ's, who for some months went in fear of being chastised by John Hutton, an ex-Fellow Commoner of his college. It appears that Hutton, who had entered Christ's in November 1747, was admonished early in his university career by the Master for some gross irregularity; and, as he continued refractory, his family was requested in 1749 to remove him from the college. Rightly or wrongly, and probably wrongly, he considered himself a victim of tyranny and injustice; and the full weight of his anger fell upon the Master whom he regarded as principally, if not solely, responsible for his disgrace. He brooded over his wrongs, and when about Christmas 1750 he visited Cambridge, he called upon Dr Rooke, used insulting language to him and repeated his insults in the combination room. Two years later he was again in Cambridge, but on this occasion the Master was away; nevertheless Hutton went about the town declaring that he would insult and abuse Dr Rooke whenever and wherever he met him. He was clearly obsessed with the idea of revenge, and when on April 19th, 1753, which happened to be Maundy Thursday, the Master returned to spend Easter in college, he must have been alarmed to hear that Hutton had been some days in Cambridge, awaiting his return[2].

Until Easter Sunday nothing happened, but on the

[1] Add. MS. 35626, f. 100. Dr Hallifax was originally a Fellow of Jesus but migrated to Trinity Hall in 1760. In 1781 he became Bishop of Gloucester.
[2] Add. MS. 33061, f. 345.

afternoon of that day, when Dr Rooke was dining in hall with the Fellows and scholars, Hutton

came into the backgate of the said college on horseback with pistols...and riding along a passage, which is only a way from one part of the college to the other, and never used for a horseway or even by passengers on foot but by sufferance, and at the entrance into the screens, which is a covered and paved passage between the hall on one hand and the buttery and kitchen on the other, the porter of the college, meeting and desiring him not to ride through the said screens, especially as the Master and Fellows were then at dinner in the hall, he, the said John Hutton, threatened to blow out the said porter's brains or the brains of anyone who should offer to stop him; and accordingly, riding down the steps and through the said screens, he proceeded through the court of the said college,

cursing and vilifying the Master 'in a very outrageous manner[1].'

This was merely a foretaste of what was to happen later in the day. Between eight and nine o'clock that evening, Hutton came again into college, and on learning that the Master was at home, took his stand outside the Lodge and volleyed oaths and curses. When the Master's servant appeared, Hutton seized hold of him and began to beat him, and a porter, who rushed to the rescue of the unfortunate domestic, was in his turn knocked down and chastised. Disturbed in their studies by the noise in the court, two scholars of the college, John Tatham and John Bull, appeared on the scene and attempted to restore order, and, rather unwisely, the Master issued from the Lodge and began to expostulate with Hutton. What followed is related by the Master in a formal account of the proceedings which he afterwards compiled.

'He not only' declared Dr Rooke 'renewed his curses and abuse of and threats against this deponent but actually endeavoured to break from the persons, who withheld him, to come at this

[1] Add. MS. 33061, f. 345.

deponent. And that with a design and intention, as this deponent verily believes, to assault and do him some bodily harm; and was with great difficulty withheld from such assault, and at last put out of the said college by the assistance of two scholars and some of the college servants, though without any kind of violence either done or offered to him; and when he was out of the gates he still continued to abuse and threaten this deponent, and in particular said that if ever he saw him at Carlile (*sic*), where some of this deponent's friends live, that he would play the devil with him or words to that effect, and also further swore, as this deponent is informed and believes, that, if he met him on the road in his chaise at any time, he would run him into the ditch[1].'

And another witness testified that Hutton, after being ejected, stood outside the gate and loudly denounced the Master as a 'damned scrub and a scoundrel[2].'

After such an experience Dr Rooke cannot be blamed for seeking the protection of the law. He began proceedings in the court of King's Bench, and a grave public scandal was only averted by the intervention of Hutton's uncle, the Archbishop of York[3], who, as a former Fellow of the college, a friend of the Chancellor, and a great ecclesiastical dignitary, was in a position to exercise considerable influence. At the express wish of the Archbishop, the Master abandoned the legal proceedings and consented to abide by the judgment of the Chancellor who decreed that Hutton, in the presence of the Vice-Chancellor, the Master of Christ's and the two senior Fellows of the college, should confess to have acted wrongly, promise not to offend again, and enter 'into a recognisance in the penalty of five hundred

---

[1] Add. MS. 33061, f. 345. [2] *Ibid.*

[3] Matthew Hutton, who had been an undergraduate of Jesus before he became a Fellow of Christ's, was created Archbishop of York in 1747, and, ten years later, Archbishop of Canterbury. He is described as an amiable and cheerful person who 'never let himself down below

pounds to be of good behaviour towards Dr Rooke for the future.' The Master, thinking that the demand might 'excite some animosity,' waived his claim to the recognisance, but the rest of the sentence was carried out, though Hutton, refractory to the last, did not apparently make his apology with a very good grace[1].

Yet, though riotous and disorderly conduct was far too common, it is important to bear in mind that the offenders belonged to the comparatively small class of wealthy young men who came up to the university to amuse themselves and lacked the outlet of athletics for the dissipation of their energy. It is significant that the calm, which prevailed in the university early in the year 1752, was attributed by the then Vice-Chancellor to

the good conduct of Lord Euston, Lord John Cavendish, Lord Weymouth and his brother, Sir John Armitage, Mr Yorke, Mr Hervey, and some others that might be named of some distinction, whose example cannot fail of having the best effects[2];

and it is frequently forgotten that the gilded youth were comparatively few in number, and that there were many poor and industrious undergraduates who had neither the means nor the inclination to indulge in extravagance and disorder. Dr Watson, while specially

[1] Add. MS. 32731, f. 457; Add. MS. 32732, f. 97, f. 98, f. 160; Add. MS. 35640, f. 27.

[2] Add. MS. 32728, f. 127. About 1774 the usual annual allowance for a Fellow Commoner was three hundred pounds. Philip Yorke went into residence at Queens' in that year, and his uncle, Lord Hardwicke, inquired of the President what allowance the boy ought to have. 'As your Lordship' replied the President 'may wish to have your question concerning allowance for a Fellow Commoner satisfied, I will not defer writing any longer, though I have but little else to add. I have lately made enquiry at three other colleges, besides those which I had mentioned to your Lordship whilst at Wimple, viz. Clare Hall, Trinity Hall, and Caius. They all, as well as those which I had enquired of before, seem to agree in about £300 per annum, keeping a servant and horse, clothes and pocket money included.' Add. MS. 35628, f. 170.

INTRODUCTION

excepting noblemen and Fellow Commoners, declared that 'there is no seminary of learning in Europe in which youth are more zealous to excel during the first years of their education than in the university of Cambridge[1]'; and there is no reason to think that Dr Watson, who came up to Trinity as a sizar in 1754, was merely generalising from his own exemplary and industrious career as an undergraduate. In 1774 an undergraduate of St John's communicated to his friend, Philip Yorke, then a Fellow Commoner of Queens', a set of rules for university life which certainly suggests a strenuous existence. The victim of this code was commanded to

rise at six—chapel, walk, breakfast till eight—eight to nine, prepare for lecture private tutor rather, if within your expense —nine to ten the college lecture—ten to eleven, revision of lectures—eleven to twelve, logick or mathematics, college lecture—twelve to three correspondence, dress dinner, coffee-house or friend's rooms to drink wine—three to five Greek history or translation—five to six, visits, tea-drinking—six to seven, Locke (or private tutor rather —seven to eight, chapel, hall, classical part of examination college exercise extending sometimes beyond eight,—nine to eleven, friend's rooms or company at home—eleven to six, rest seven hours—wash before chapel, and take with you a small Greek testament in your pocket². 'I do suppose' commented Philip Yorke in a letter to his uncle, Lord Hardwicke, 'that the hours and some certain exercises may be immediately cast for that particular society and may require a different application in any other. I have consulted my young acquaintance how far he finds this good plan practicable. He very candidly confesses that he cannot bring himself to fill the whole circle which he allows to be excellent. With your Lordship's leave I will give you the journal of his practice. Rise at six, breakfast and walk till eight, lick her lectures till nine, got a lecture till ten, private tutor till eleven, lecture till twelve, ch ne, dress and write lectures, dinner, coffee-house and walk till four, to my rooms till five, coffee-house again till six, private tutor till seven, chapel and hall till half after eight, half an hour in my rooms, and from nine to eleven in company. He concludes by saying that this has hitherto been the regular plan of his time, sometimes broken into but not often, which he imagines will increase as the summer comes on[1].'

It will be noticed that Philip Yorke's 'young acquaintance' had considerably modified the original programme and anticipated having to make still further modifications; but, as he was possibly a Fellow Commoner, it is to his credit that he attempted as much as he did. He was perhaps assisted to be virtuous by the exceptional conditions prevailing at St John's, the Master, Dr Powell, having introduced the practice of annual college examinations; but it may be assumed that the ordinary boy, who came up to Cambridge to carve out a career, would not have had the same difficulties in conforming to a scheme of life which was presumably not impossible of practice. Industry was clearly not unknown among the junior members of the university; and, as we hear so much of the exploits of the 'Bucks,' we are apt to forget that then as now the idle rich were only a small though aggressive minority. But if eighteenth century Cambridge was not so black as it has been painted, it was certainly very different from what it is at the present day. Both 'dons' and undergraduates belonged to an old order which has passed away; and the change which has taken place is not only in respect of customs and manners. The machinery of government has been entirely transformed and the ancient constitution thrown upon the dustheap of antiquities.

An enquiry into the constitution of the university in the eighteenth century may be thought a waste of labour, but it at least serves to confirm the truth of the

[1] Add. MS. 35658, f. 32.

maxim that institutional progress is from complexity to simplicity. For whatever may be said of the machinery of university government two hundred years ago it cannot possibly be described as simple. The constitution was based partly on the Elizabethan statutes, partly on earlier statutes unrepealed by the Elizabethan code, partly on royal letters accepted by the university, and partly on ordinances or by-laws passed from time to time by Graces of the Senate; and thus it was not the work of one architect, uniform and symmetrical, but an edifice built up through the ages and reflecting many different styles. Nor were its different parts of equal sanction and authority; for though the Senate, acting alone, could repeal or modify its own by-laws and the ancient statutes, it was unable to make any change in the Elizabethan statutes or in that part of the constitution which was based upon the royal letters accepted by the university. Thus the independent authority of the Senate was strictly prescribed, and this tendency to inflexibility was still further increased by the growth of customs and conventions which, though without legal sanction, had in practice almost the same authority as law and materially diminished the elasticity of the constitution. Therefore for a full understanding of the actual system something more is needed than a knowledge of the Elizabethan statutes, for a freedom, which was permitted by law, was not infrequently forbidden by custom.

The highest office in the university, as at present, was that of Chancellor. Originally the Chancellor had been chosen for a term of two years from among the resident members of the university, but about the sixteenth century the custom began of conferring the office for life upon some eminent statesman or magnate who was expected to protect the university and to further its interests. The inevitable consequence of this innovation was that the Chancellor became a non-resident official, his duties and functions being discharged by the Vice-Chancellor who thus became for practical purposes the most important person in the university. It was provided by the statutes that the Vice-Chancellor should be annually elected by the undivided Senate[1] from two candidates nominated by the Heads of Houses; and it was further provided that in the event of the votes of the Heads being equally divided between several candidates, the Regius Professor of Divinity should determine 'which two of those who have equal voices shall be proposed to the body[2].' Thus the Senate was only permitted to choose between two candidates and still further restrictions were imposed by custom. In theory any graduate of a degree not inferior to that of master of arts was eligible for election as Vice-Chancellor; but by the eighteenth century it had become a well-established practice only to nominate Heads of Houses, and, indeed, to reduce the nomination and election to a mere form by invariably appointing the senior in degree among those Heads of Houses who had not already served as Vice-Chancellor[3].

There was much to be said for confining the most important office in the university to Heads of Houses, but the establishment of a regular rotation by seniority of degree is open to criticism. It not infrequently happened that a recently appointed Master of a college, who had long been absent from the university and was totally unacquainted with its business, found himself Vice-Chancellor within two or three months of be-

[1] For purposes of legislation the Senate was divided into two houses, regents and non-regents.

[2] Add. MS. 32960, f. 143. It was expressly provided that no one holding the office of Regius Professor of Divinity could serve as Vice-Chancellor.

[3] Monk's *Life of Bentley*, 1, 150.

coming a Head; while another Master, because he lacked sufficient seniority, might have to wait several years before he was called upon to serve as Vice-Chancellor. Dr John Sumner, Provost of King's, for instance, became Provost and Vice-Chancellor in the same year, 1756, because he happened to be a doctor of divinity; while Sir James Burrough, who was only a master of arts, was not elected Vice-Chancellor until he had been Master of Caius for five years. It is obvious that such a system placed a premium upon inexperience and might easily have militated against the efficient administration of business, especially as it was against the custom of the university, though not forbidden by the statutes, for a Vice-Chancellor to continue in office for longer than a year. The danger of inefficient administration however was less than it appears, as it was usual for a Vice-Chancellor, in the discharge of his administrative duties, to consult the other Heads of Houses; and though he does not seem to have been compelled to seek or take their advice, the tradition that he should do so was well established and faithfully observed. A Vice-Chancellor, new to his duties and unversed in university business, would be ready enough to take the opinion of a body which included several of his predecessors in office; and it is probable that the system of rotation, however unsound in theory, was not productive in practice of any serious inconvenience. There is certainly plenty of evidence that the Heads played a very active part in administration. In a letter written on January 20th, 1756, the Master of Peterhouse, then Vice-Chancellor, informed the Duke of Newcastle that he had summoned a meeting of the Heads to devise a way of breaking up a combination of 'ingrossers and forestallers[1],' and the sort of business dealt with at these meetings is well illustrated by a letter written by

[1] Add. MS. 32862, f. 163.

INTRODUCTION

Dr Caryl, Master of Jesus, when Vice-Chancellor, to Newcastle.

'Yesterday' he wrote on December 5th, 1758 'I desired a meeting of the Heads. The matters, which I had to propose to their consideration, were (1) how to recover some rent that seemed to be in danger of being lost, upon which we agreed to take advice; (2) the obligation which I apprehended we were under to the Solicitor-General for the great pains that he has taken in defending our printing of law-books, upon which I was directed to write him a letter of thanks in the name of myself and the Heads; (3) the prosecution of a surgeon for stealing the body of a person, who died of a malignant sort of the small-pox, and conveying it through the most public street of the town; ...(4) the case of the peddling Jews who do much mischief by exchanging their trinkets with young scholars for books, clothes or anything they can lay their hands on[1].'

In another letter Dr Caryl mentions having called a meeting of the Heads in order to take their opinion upon some matters which 'I was unwilling to transact upon my own judgment solely[2]'; and apparently all business, save possibly the purest routine, was discussed at these meetings. The Heads, in consultation with the Vice-Chancellor, settled the details of Newcastle's installation as Chancellor[3] and all university addresses were submitted to them before being brought before the Senate.

The influence of the Heads was not confined to the administrative sphere; for they were entitled by the statutes to assist the Vice-Chancellor in the discharge of his judicial functions. He could neither expel a student nor imprison a doctor or Head of a House without the concurrence of the majority of the Heads who also acted as his advisers and assessors in all matters affecting the conduct and discipline of the scholars[4].

[1] Add. MS. 32886, f. 173. [2] Add. MS. 32889, f. 215.
[3] Add. MS. 32718, f. 226.
[4] Peacock's *Observations on the Statutes of the University*, p. 46.

The same oligarchical tendency is noticeable in the machinery of legislation. Before a Grace could be submitted to the Senate for approval or rejection it had to be unanimously approved by a small committee of that body, known as the Caput and consisting of the Vice-Chancellor, sitting *ex officio*, three doctors representing respectively the faculties of divinity, medicine and law, a regent master of arts and a non-regent master of arts. A single member of the Caput had the right of vetoing a Grace, and this power of obstruction was the less defensible as belonging to a non-representative body. Though the Caput was annually elected, only Heads of Houses, doctors and the two Scrutators were entitled to vote; and, restricted as were the electors, they were not even allowed an unfettered choice. At the beginning of the Michaelmas term, which was the date appointed for the election of the Caput, the Vice-Chancellor and the two Proctors presented separate lists, each containing the names of three doctors in the different faculties, a regent and a non-regent, and the choice of the electors was confined to the fifteen persons thus named. Further restrictions were imposed by custom. 'Much depends in the election of a Caput on the prospect of the Vice-Chancellor for the ensuing year[1],' wrote the Master of Corpus in 1764, 'as by the usage of the university one is always of his own college and the rest usually such as are not thought disagreeable to him[2]'; and according to another authority it was customary to vote for those whose names appeared on the Vice-Chancellor's list[3].

The Caput could only claim to represent the more senior members of the university who thus indirectly

[1] The Caput was elected in October and the Vice-Chancellor in November.
[2] Add. MS. 35640, f. 158.
[3] Add. MS. 35628, f. 20; Peacock's *Observations*, p. 47, *n.* 2.

INTRODUCTION 31

possessed a veto upon all legislation. On a Grace being brought before the university assembled in congregation, the Vice-Chancellor called the Caput together to pass or reject it[1]; and, in the event of any member of this body being absent, his place was taken by the senior person present in the same faculty. If unanimously approved by the Caput, the Grace would be read for the first time in the two houses of regents and non-regents into which the Senate was divided; but in neither house would a vote be taken. If the Grace was at all controversial, it was usual to circulate copies of it among the colleges after the first reading in the Senate, and there was therefore generally an interval of a few days between the first and the second congregation[2]. At the second congregation the Grace was first voted upon in the non-regents' house, the votes being counted by the two Scrutators.

The Scrutators went both together and each of them marked the placet or non-placet of each voter who stood up when he gave it. At the end of each row they compared their papers and so went on from row to row...till they had gone through the whole[3].

If passed by the non-regents, the Grace would then be voted upon in the regents' house where exactly the same procedure was adopted except that the two Proctors acted as tellers.

The division of the Senate into two houses gave a decided advantage to age. Every master of arts, who had kept his name on the books of some college, was a regent during the first five years from his creation after which he became a non-regent; but doctors were

[1] The Vice-Chancellor could decline to summon the Caput, but this right was only exercised in very exceptional circumstances.

[2] Add. MS. 35628, f. 186. Both congregations could be held on the same day, but this was unusual.

[3] Add. MS. 5852, f. 147, f. 148.

able to sit and vote in either house except within two years of taking that degree when they sat in the regents' house[1]. It is obvious that the regents were at a double disadvantage. A Grace, which they approved, might be rejected by the non-regents before it reached them, and their opposition to a Grace, which they disapproved, might be overcome by flooding their house with doctors. But though age was at the helm it possibly was not able to use to the full the advantage it possessed. However strongly he might disapprove of a particular measure, a single member of the Caput probably hesitated to exercise his right of veto, and even if all the members of the Caput agreed in disapproving a Grace they would be slow to reject it if it was supported by a considerable body of opinion in the university. The Caput, indeed, suffered from the defects of its origin, and if it had been more representative it could have made a more liberal use of its autocratic power. It is also easy to exaggerate the importance of the fluidity of doctors. The game of distributing the doctors between the two houses, so as to secure a majority in both, was often played by university politicians; but it was a perilous enterprise, demanding a nice calculation of forces and might easily end in disaster. Nor is it likely that the doctors were ever sufficiently numerous or unanimous to be used to overcome a really formidable majority, and they were probably of the greatest assistance when the two houses were fairly equally divided.

Nevertheless, when all reservations have been made, the fact remains that the balance of power was with the more senior members of the university. Our modern creed that youth is wise and age foolish was not accepted

[1] Add. MS. 33061, f. 261. The Chancellor, the Vice-Chancellor, the Proctors, the Taxors, the Moderators, the Esquire Bedells, provided they were masters of arts, also sat in the regents' house.

in the eighteenth century which regarded juvenile intemperance as a greater danger than senile caution, and it was not thought a demerit in the constitution of the university to be an obstacle in the path of the reformer. But the age of reform had hardly begun to dawn, and it is foolish to assume that because a system of government was unsuited to the needs and requirements of the nineteenth century, it could never have served an useful purpose. And the same may be said of the university as a whole in the eighteenth century. Regarded from our point of view and judged by our standards it stands condemned; but, though possibly no better, it was at least no worse than its age. If it was lacking in idealism and self-sacrifice, if it sinned by self-indulgence and comfortable acquiescence in traditional abuses, it only faithfully reflected the contemporary code of morality, and much of the censure it has incurred should in fairness be given to the century.

CHAPTER II

THE UNIVERSITY AND POLITICIANS

THE internal affairs of the university in the eighteenth century cannot be fully understood without a knowledge of contemporary politics; for the academic and parliamentary worlds were closely connected and party divisions at Cambridge more or less corresponded with those at Westminster. Such a connection was almost inevitable as long as the power of a statesman depended to a great extent upon the amount of patronage at his disposal. It is not surprising that the average Cambridge 'don' was keenly desirous to be on the winning side in politics, for unless he was skilled in seeing which way the political wind was likely to blow and steering his course accordingly, he had little chance of obtaining the preferment he coveted; and it is as little surprising that politicians sought to enlarge the number of their followers by establishing a connection with the university which would enable them to influence the disposal of academic posts. Doubtless the prizes of university life were small and mean in comparison with the rich sinecures for which venal politicians competed; but eighteenth century statesmen were not particular in their methods of accumulating patronage. And as the obvious way of establishing an influence in the university was by becoming its Chancellor, eminent statesmen were frequently eager competitors for that office and for the office of High Steward which was regarded as a stepping stone to the Chancellorship. Consequently, when either of these places fell vacant, the parliamentary contest was apt to be

THE UNIVERSITY AND POLITICIANS 35

extended to Cambridge and academic peace to be rudely disturbed by the clash of rival political parties. Thus university and national politics were closely connected; and neither the nation nor the university profited. The higher interests of the university were not advanced by its Chancellor being a politician who would be tempted to be principally interested in extending the influence of his party, and no advantage accrued to the nation from an increase of the means of bribery and corruption at the disposal of statesmen.

The connection was certainly unfortunate and the responsibility for it partly rests upon that master in the art of corruption, Thomas Pelham-Holles, Duke of Newcastle. Until comparatively lately Newcastle has been usually depicted as an industrious nonentity whose only weapon was treachery; but a more complete analysis is needed to explain the fact that this seemingly contemptible person proved more than a match for many of the ablest politicians of his time, and, from the fall of Sir Robert Walpole until the death of George II, exercised a parliamentary influence which made his support indispensable to any administration. The secret of his success is not difficult to discover. Undistinguished as an orator, inefficient as an administrator, and deplorably deficient in all the higher arts of statesmanship, he triumphed by uniting a sincere and entirely disinterested passion for public life with a frank and cynical appreciation of the politics of his age[1]. Understanding that bribery and corruption were

[1] Newcastle was as financially disinterested as the elder Pitt, though he paraded his virtue less. He refused a pension when he resigned office in 1762, though he had materially reduced his own fortune in the service of the state; and he seems to have always been quite indifferent to money. In 1723 he refused a gift out of the secret service fund, offered him by Lord Townshend to meet financial difficulties caused by 'services to the Government'; and in a letter to the Bishop of Chichester he explains his refusal. 'You know' he wrote 'the great backwardness

36 THE UNIVERSITY AND POLITICIANS

the acknowledged weapons of politicians, he took full advantage of his position as a servant of the crown and used the vast resources of the royal patronage to win and maintain a personal following in parliament which made him independent of the favour of the king and the confidence of the country. He bestowed places in church and state with a lavish though discriminating hand, and became a power in the land by playing upon the weakness of his fellow creatures.

The work was disgusting but the workman was not disgusted, and Newcastle consistently laboured to increase the patronage at his disposal. Consequently, when on the death of the Earl of Anglesey in 1737 he came forward as a candidate for the office of High Steward of the university, it is unlikely that he was only influenced by a sentimental attachment to his Alma Mater. He undoubtedly had a very genuine affection for Cambridge, but he was, first and foremost, a politician, and it was as a politician that he was anxious to establish an official connection with the university. He hoped by becoming High Steward to establish a claim to succeed the Duke of Somerset as Chancellor of the university; and as Somerset was in his seventy-fifth year, Newcastle might reasonably expect that he would not have to wait long for the highest honour that the university could confer. But it was power as well as honour that he sought. He desired the Chancellorship in order that he might establish an unchallenged influence in Cambridge, hoping to further the interests of his party and the whig cause, and to teach the members of the university that political orthodoxy was more likely to lead to advancement than a reputation for learning.

I have always had to ask or receive any sums of money from the king, how I detest it in others, and consequently how unwilling I should be to do the like myself.'

THE UNIVERSITY AND POLITICIANS 37

There is no reason however to think that when in 1737 Newcastle appeared as a candidate for the office of High Steward, the university realised that it was being asked to place itself under the control of the greatest living exponent of the art of jobbery. Though Newcastle had been Secretary of State for thirteen years, he was overshadowed in the cabinet and the country by the Prime Minister, Sir Robert Walpole; and it was not until Walpole's fall from office, five years later, that his power became apparent. It was moreover natural and in the order of things that an university, which was predominantly, though not exclusively, whig, should desire to confer a distinction upon a prominent whig minister who was also a Cambridge man; and there does not seem to have been any serious opposition to the Duke's candidature. But as the High Steward was appointed by Grace of the Senate, it was necessary to ensure a safe passage for the Grace through the Caput where a single negative vote would be fatal, and this was not achieved without careful preliminary preparation.

'I also beg leave upon this occasion' wrote in 1751 Peter Goddard, Fellow and afterwards Master of Clare 'to inform your Grace that when you was chose High Steward of the university, I was the person who was principally, if not solely, employed by the present worthy Master of Clare Hall[1], to concert the proper methods and precautions to prevent a defeat; and particularly that it was owing to my applications and sollicitations that a proper Caput was procured the day that the Grace was proposed; otherwise it would very probably have been stopped in the first instance, such was then the state and temper of the university[2].'

As Goddard coupled with this reminder of his services a request for ecclesiastical preferment, he possibly

[1] Dr Wilcox who was the Vice-Chancellor when Newcastle was appointed High Steward.
[2] Add. MS. 32725, f. 382.

exaggerated the danger of disaster and the greatness of his achievement; and his testimony is therefore not above suspicion. There were probably however a certain number of tories in the university who would not be indisposed to prevent the election of a leading whig statesman; but as we hear nothing of their activities it may safely be concluded that they did not on this occasion constitute a serious menace. But if Newcastle thought that by becoming High Steward he had made sure of becoming Chancellor within a few years and without opposition, he was doomed to disappointment. In 1747 the Duke of Somerset was still alive, and, though his death could not be far distant, it was by no means certain that Newcastle would be permitted to succeed him. A rumour began to spread in Cambridge that Frederick, Prince of Wales, intended to stand for election as Chancellor on Somerset's death; and when Dr Richardson, the tory Master of Emmanuel, returned to Cambridge from London in February 1747, he informed the Vice-Chancellor that during his stay in London he had been introduced to the Prince who, after professing great regard to the university of Cambridge, said he should take it as a favour and honour to stand in a nearer relation to it whenever a vacancy...should happen[1].

The Prince was likely to prove a dangerous competitor. Having quarrelled with his father in accordance with the family tradition, he had gone into political opposition and placed himself at the head of a faction which was nicknamed the 'Leicester house party,' and recruited from whigs who had a grievance against the government, and tories who were prepared to compromise so far with their principles as to support a Hanoverian prince against a Hanoverian king. Thus it was as the leader of a parliamentary party that he came

[1] Add. MS. 35657, f. i.

THE UNIVERSITY AND POLITICIANS 39

forward as a candidate for the Chancellorship, and, if he succeeded in his venture, the prestige of the ministry, of which Newcastle was now the most influential member, would be seriously shaken. The Prince's success moreover was not at all improbable. There was no reason to anticipate that he would not survive the King; and cautious members of the Senate were certain to reflect upon the wisdom of neglecting the father and paying homage to the son. No disloyalty to the whig cause and the Hanoverian succession was involved in supporting him, and much might be thereby gained; and, if the university had been left to its own unguided instincts, the royal candidate could have counted upon a substantial following. Indeed Dr Rooke, Master of Christ's, who was one of Newcastle's most enthusiastic supporters, was seriously alarmed at the outlook; and, though he admitted that some of his 'brethren are extremely clear that the generality of the place will by no means come into it,' he confessed to an inability to share their optimism.

'I well know' he wrote 'that the Masters of Trinity and St John's are too sanguine in their calculations (the latter of whom has occasioned great matter of merriment by closetting his Fellows and being just as wise as he was about their sentiments after it). The corps of old Jones, though not large, is not despicable. The young men are apt to run riot[1].'

The Master of Christ's apprehensions were shared by Newcastle, and there was ground for alarm. Quite apart from the advantage enjoyed by the Prince as the heir to the throne, there was a danger of it being commonly assumed that his candidature had the approval of his father, and that therefore it should receive the support of all loyal subjects. Doubtless such a mistake was not likely to be made by those behind the political scene, but it might easily prevail in the university and

[1] Add. MS. 35657, f. i.

40 THE UNIVERSITY AND POLITICIANS

contribute to the Prince's triumph. Consequently Newcastle decided to convince the members of the Senate that they could not vote for the Prince without running counter to the King's wishes. In May 1747 Edmund Castle, Master of Corpus and Vice-Chancellor, was summoned to appear before a meeting of the Privy Council at which the Lord Chancellor Hardwicke read out a formal statement that

> the King having been informed that application has been made in the university of Cambridge for the election of His Royal Highness, the Prince of Wales, to be their Chancellor in case of a vacancy, we are commissioned by His Majesty to acquaint you that the said application was without his consent and privity; and that though His Majesty does by no means intend to interfere in their election, yet he is persuaded from the regard and affection which he has always shewed for the university, and from their duty to him, that they will not choose any one of his family for their Chancellor without his approbation[1].

After reading this declaration the Lord Chancellor gave a copy of it to the Vice-Chancellor, and at the same time informed him that

> he was not to communicate the said paper to the university assembled in congregation nor to any publick meeting of the Heads; but privately to as many persons as he pleased, not suffering anybody to take a copy of it. That he was particularly to insist upon that clause that His Majesty has no intention to interfere in the election[2].

The language of this royal message was commendably free from ambiguity; and, in order to insure that the university fully understood the situation, Newcastle's fellow Secretary of State, Lord Chesterfield, instructed the Master of Caius[3] in the King's name 'to signify to the university of Cambridge that His Majesty did not approve of their choosing either of his sons

---
[1] Add. MS. 33c61, f. 211.   [2] Add. MS. 5852, f. 114.
[3] Sir Thomas Gooch, Bishop of Ely.

Chancellor of the university[1].' The Vice-Chancellor and the Master of Caius circulated the information they had received, thus putting a speedy end to the legend that the King favoured his son rather than his minister; and, as only a minority would be prepared to cut themselves off from all hope of preferment by defying the wishes of the sovereign and the government, it is probable that if the Duke of Somerset had died about this time, Newcastle would have met with little or no opposition. But the octogenarian Chancellor continued to live, and in time the impression produced by the royal announcement faded away, and the Cambridge supporters of the Prince began to show signs of renewed activity. The rumour was spread that the King had changed his mind and was now willing for his son to become Chancellor[2]; and when in July 1748 it was reported that Somerset was dying, an informal canvass on behalf of the Prince was begun at Cambridge by the Master of Emmanuel and Thomas Rutherforth, Fellow and Tutor of St John's[3].

Unfortunately Newcastle was in Germany with the King; and the task of fighting his battle at Cambridge devolved upon his colleagues in the cabinet, and in particular upon his brother, Henry Pelham, the First Lord of the Treasury, and the Duke of Bedford, who had succeeded Chesterfield as Secretary of State. One alarming feature of the situation was that Dr Parris, Master of Sidney, was supposed to sympathise with the Prince of Wales' party; for Dr Parris was Vice-Chancellor and in this capacity could exercise considerable influence in the event of an election. By the statutes of the university a Chancellor had to be elected within fourteen days of the declaration of a vacancy; but the Vice-Chancellor, with whom it rested to deter-

[1] Add. MS. 5852, f. 114.   [2] Add. MS. 32715, f. 426.
[3] Add. MS. 32715, f. 428.

mine the date of the election, was free to abbreviate the prescribed period; and it was feared that Dr Parris might act as a partisan and name a day too early to allow Newcastle's supporters to rally to the fray. As it was the dead season of the academic year many residents were absent from the university; and, though the Prince's supporters were probably numerically insignificant, it was feared that they might prevail by being on the spot.

The occasion was critical, for Somerset might die at any moment; and the cabinet rose to the emergency. Instructed by the Duke of Bedford, who had sent his commands through a certain Mr Butcher of Peterborough, William Hetherington, the Rector of Dry-Drayton[1], came over to Cambridge on the morning of Saturday July 16th, and waited upon the Vice-Chancellor.

'I acquainted him' he informed the Duke of Bedford 'that I had received a message from your Grace by a special messenger, wherein you are pleased to order me to take some opportunity of assuring him in your name "that His Majesty had not altered his mind since he sent a message to the last Vice-Chancellor in relation to the choice of a Chancellor of the university upon a vacancy; and that it would be disagreeable to his Majesty to have any of his family elected without his consent and approbation." I likewise added that, as fourteen days were allowed by statute, it was hoped a sufficient time would be given that the election might be the more publick and general. The Vice-Chancellor asked me if I expected a particular answer to this message: I told him, no, I could not say I did; but only left it with him to consider of[2].'

After his interview with the Vice-Chancellor, Hetherington communicated his message to several Heads of Houses[3]; but if his embassy was intended to force the

---
[1] A village about five miles from Cambridge.
[2] Add. MS. 32715, f. 426.   [3] Ibid.

THE UNIVERSITY AND POLITICIANS 43

Vice-Chancellor to show his hand, it must be counted to have failed.

'After you called on me yesterday' wrote Dr Parris to Hetherington on July 17th 'with a message from his Grace, the Duke of Bedford, I had certain intelligence that the Lords of the Regency had been informed that Dr Richardson, Taylor, Rutherforth and the Vice-Chancellor had begun a stir here in favour of the P—; and that the Vice-Chancellor, to further the design, had engaged to bring on the election immediately. This is utterly false as far as it concerns me, and without any other foundation than that, as I have no particular attachments to either side, I have not been forward to make any declarations in a matter of great niceness, and when I perceived others, who had greater reason to be more zealous, expressed themselves with caution[1].'

The Vice-Chancellor was studiously vague with regard to his intentions; and, though Hetherington believed that he was really trying to be impartial and would 'act a very fair part in his public capacity[2],' the situation was too critical to justify incurring any risks. Consequently those of Newcastle's friends, who were not too far away, were summoned to Cambridge or the neighbourhood[3]; a party of voters was collected at Peterborough, ready to descend upon Cambridge[4]; and a 'stout body of fifty good men and true' was gathered together in London[5]. Moreover Lord Dupplin[6], who

[1] Add. MS. 32715, f. 428.
[2] Add. MS. 32715, f. 434; see also f. 430.
[3] Add. MS. 32715, f. 434.   [4] Add. MS. 32715, f. 430.
[5] Add. MS. 32715, f. 463.
[6] Lord Dupplin was the eldest son of the Earl of Kinnoull and one of Newcastle's staunchest supporters. On his father's death in 1758 he succeeded to the Earldom of Kinnoull, and, after Newcastle resigned office in 1762, abandoned political life. The Duke was aggrieved by Kinnoull's retirement from the parliamentary contest; and among the Newcastle papers is a copy of the following verses, dated 14th July 1763, and endorsed 'by a gentleman's servant.'

'Banish this picture, Hollis, from thy view,
For Dupplin from his heart has banished you.

had a very good effect in the university. The point is well understood, and the young men, who were most in danger of being dazzled with the glittering of reversionary preferment, see the opposition in a right light as a means calculated to distress the true friends of government, dishonourable to the great name which is made use of, and injurious to the university. The harmony, which appears among the king's friends,...gave me pleasure, and the spirit and determined firmness, which they have all shewn, has strengthened their own party and discouraged their adversaries. Those who came from a distance, far from repining at the journey they had taken, are pleased that their appearance contributed to give life and weight to the cause in which they are engaged. The majority exceeds all expectation, very very few of the whigs are in the opposition, and many of the tories, particularly those of Caius college, have declared their obedience to His Majesty's pleasure. The design of the opposers was undoubtedly to bring on the election by surprise; but whether the Vice-Chancellor would have taken so extraordinary a step I don't pretend to determine. So far is certain that the pressing and repeated applications of his brethren could not extort from him a declaration that he would give proper notice till it was evident to everybody that the superiority of the king's friends was such as could not be defeated by any act either of power or cunning. As he has now promised the Bishop of Ely not to bring on the election in less than ten or twelve days after the notice of the vacancy,...our friends are dispersing again[1].

The battle, indeed, had been won, though the fruits of victory could not be gathered until after Somerset's death. As he had pledged his word to the Bishop of Ely, there was now no fear of Dr Parris rushing an election; and his conversion seems to have been complete, for when in September 1748 a false report of Somerset's death reached Cambridge, he at once wrote to Thomas Townshend and the Duke of Bedford, informing the former of his readiness 'to execute any commands that you or any friend of the Duke of New-

[1] Add. MS. 32716, f. 17.

THE UNIVERSITY AND POLITICIANS 47

castle shall be pleased to honour me with through you[1],' and asking the latter to send 'any such directions as your Grace may think proper for me[2].' Nor was Dr Parris the only or the most notable convert. About October 1748 Dr Richardson, Master of Emmanuel, was officially informed by Dr Ayscough, one of the chaplains to the Prince, that, though His Royal Highness was grateful for the honour intended for him by his friends in the university, he must command them not to make 'any attempt to confer it upon him as he finds it would not be agreeable to the King, his father[3].' For a time the Master of Emmanuel kept this information to himself; but when the Duke of Somerset at last died in December 1748, the Master, who happened to be in London, communicated Ayscough's letter to Dr Rutherforth who immediately publicly announced in Cambridge that no opposition would be offered to Newcastle's election as Chancellor[4].

Thus the succession, for which the Duke had waited so long, came to him in the end undisputed; and on December 14th he was elected Chancellor. As there was no other candidate the proceedings were formal and uninteresting, but his friends succeeded in converting the occasion into a demonstration of the victory they had achieved over a disloyal and factious minority. The attendance was unusually large[5], one hundred and ninety members of the Senate recording their votes[6]; and when Dr Chapman, Master of Magdalene, who had succeeded Parris as Vice-Chancellor, declared the Duke elected, the Master of St John's, carried away by

[1] Add. MS. 32716, f. 201.   [2] Add. MS. 32716, f. 207.
[3] Add. MS. 32717, f. 417; Add. MS. 5852, ff. 116–118.
[4] Add. MS. 5852, f. 117, f. 427.
[5] Dr Rooke mentions that it was 'the fullest Senate I have ever seen upon such an occasion.' Add. MS. 32717, f. 435.
[6] Add. MS. 5852, f. 116, f. 427. Lord Dupplin gives the number of votes as one hundred and ninety one; Add. MS. 32717, f. 443.

50   THE UNIVERSITY AND POLITICIANS

as dearly as lesser men love a lord: and at one time it seemed likely that he would have an opportunity of marching in triumph through the streets of Cambridge accompanied by the two Primates and the Bishop of London. This hope was disappointed[1], but he at least succeeded in gathering together as distinguished a company as ever graced an installation.

Everything was done to emphasise the importance of the victory which had been won. The Chancellor arrived in Cambridge on the evening of Friday June 30th, having slept the previous night at his father-in-law's residence on the Gog-Magog hills[2]. It had been arranged that he should stay at his old college, Clare, and, in order to escape the fatigue of a public reception, he entered the college from the Backs[3]. Shortly after his arrival he was waited upon by the Heads of Houses; but he was otherwise left in peace for that night. Soon after eleven o'clock on the following morning a deputation arrived at Clare to escort him to the Senate house, at the steps of which he was met by Dr Chapman, the Vice-Chancellor, who walked up the Senate house at his left hand. They then ascended the chair of state, the Duke standing at the left hand thereof and the Vice-Chancellor on the right. A band of music having performed a short overture, the Vice-Chancellor made a congratulatory speech[4]

which is said to have been both long and fulsome[5]. At the conclusion of his speech Dr Chapman presented the Duke with a handsomely bound copy of the university statutes and his patent of election, illuminated by Sir

[1] 'But the Archbishop of Canterbury, to the disappointment of the university as well as mine, after having determined to do honour to it, on a sudden laid aside the thoughts of it, (as is said) some difficulty having arisen in his mind as to precedency on the occasion.' Samuel Kerrick to his wife, July 2nd, 1749, Pyle MSS. vol. vi.
[2] The Duke was married to a daughter of Lord Godolphin.
[3] Add. MS. 5852, f. 427.   [4] Cooper's *Annals*, iv, 268.
[5] Add. MS. 5852, f. 427.

THE UNIVERSITY AND POLITICIANS 51

Thomas Brand[1] and enclosed in a 'silver box gilt with the university arms engraved thereon on one side, the Chancellor's and Vice-Chancellor's on the other[2].' Then the Senior Proctor administered the oath of office to the Duke who thereupon sat down in the chair of state and listened to a Latin speech by the Public Orator who endeavoured

to take off from the obloquy which might have been thrown upon the university for the late proceedings of some of our youth, and threw those irregularities on the licentiousness of the age in general[3].

To this oration the Chancellor replied in English, and his speech was followed by the singing of an ode, composed by William Mason and set to music by William Boyce of the Chapel Royal.

This brought the ceremony in the Senate house to an end: and the next item in the day's programme was the installation banquet. It had been arranged that the banquet should be held in the hall of Trinity, no other college having a hall large enough to accommodate the number of guests[4]: and the procession from the Senate house to Trinity was probably, as far as the

---

[1] Sir Thomas Brand was illuminator to the king and a gentleman usher daily waiter.

[2] Add. MS. 5852, f. 427.

[3] *Ibid.* 'I had the honour,' wrote Samuel Kerrick on July 2nd, 1749, to his wife, 'to walk in both the processions: the one for the nobility and great personages from Clare Hall (where the Duke of Newcastle lodged) to the Senate house in order to his being installed. Everyone's name was taken down and called over before the procession began and everyone was placed according to his rank under the direction of Sir Clement Cotterell, High Master of the Ceremonies, the Duke walking first. After the installation...there was another procession from the Senate house to Trinity college where a most magnificent entertainment was provided.' Pyle MSS. vol. VI.

[4] Even the hall of Trinity was not sufficiently spacious and there was an overflow into the Master's Lodge: Add. MS. 32718, f. 204.

general public was concerned, the most attractive part of the day's proceedings. The order of the procession was as follows:

Fellow Commoners, properly habited, preceded by the Yeoman Bedel, the juniors first, batchelors of physick, batchelors of law, regent masters, non-regent masters, batchelors of divinity—all with their proper hoods and caps—Scrutators, Taxors, Proctors with their chained books, the Orator, inceptors in physick, inceptors in law, inceptors in divinity, non-gremial doctors in physick, law, divinity, without robes, all these two by two, the Vice-Chancellor alone, and His Grace, the Chancellor, in his robes, followed by the nobility, bishops, etc., and preceded by the three Esquire Bedels[1].

This stately procession wended its way along Trinity street and across the Trinity Great Court: but, on reaching the hall steps, the Yeoman Bedell, who was leading, halted in order to allow the junior members to withdraw. The procession then reformed, and 'the Chancellor, nobility, doctors, etc., passed through into the cloysters where the doctors put on their common scarlet gowns[2].'

After a short wait the company trooped into the hall for the banquet. The Chancellor sat in the middle of the upper table, facing the hall, and each of the other tables was presided over by a nobleman. There was however no general assignment of seats, though apparently a natural order of aristocracy asserted itself, as there were noticeably more Heads of Houses at the Chancellor's table than at any other. Probably the hall was uncomfortably crowded: and though Newcastle's cooks had been sent down to Cambridge to assist in the preparation of the meal, we learn, from one who was present, that the fare was 'plain and in the academical manner of entertaining[3].' The dignity of the proceedings

---

[1] Add. MS. 5852, f. 427. [2] *Ibid.*
[3] Harris' *Life of Hardwicke*, II, 387.

THE UNIVERSITY AND POLITICIANS 53

was somewhat marred by the behaviour of the Vice-Chancellor who acted as toastmaster, and so overdid his part as to shock the sensitive Cole who afterwards complained that

it appeared equally shocking and disgusting to see the second person of the university rising up from his place upon every fresh health and, with his cap elated, delivering it out in a stentorian voice to all the company in the hall[1].

But whatever were the shortcomings of the Vice-Chancellor and the fare, it is probable that there was no lack of that conviviality and good-fellowship which contribute more than ceremony to the success of an entertainment.

Having been installed and feasted, Newcastle was free to spend the remaining days of his visit in making himself known to the university: and he made the most of the opportunity. On Sunday July 2nd he attended both the morning and afternoon services at the university church, and on the following day officiated as Chancellor at an admission to honorary degrees, resigning at the conclusion of the ceremony the office of High Steward which he had held for twelve years[2]. On Tuesday he was again in the Senate house, witnessing the creation of doctors, and these official appearances were only a part, and not the most arduous part, of his activities. During his stay in Cambridge he visited every college in turn, 'and was met at the college gates by the respective Masters and Fellows, properly habited, and by them regaled with wine, etc.[3]' The Duke was indeed unsparing in his efforts to make a good impression: and when on Wednesday July 5th he left

[1] Add. MS. 5852, f. 427.
[2] 'The Duke, in an exceeding handsome speech which charmed everybody, desired they would accept his resignation of the office of High Steward of the university,' Samuel Kerrick to his wife, July 6th, 1749, Pyle MSS. vol. VI.   [3] Add. MS. 5852, f. 427.

Cambridge to visit the Duke of Grafton at Euston, he must have been in a slightly shattered condition and in need of a rest.

'Everyone, while it lasted,' wrote Gray to his friend, Wharton, 'was very gay and very busy in the morning, and very owlish and very tipsy at night: I make no exceptions from the Chancellor to Blew-Coat[1].'

But though fatigued, Newcastle had good reason to be content with his reception which proclaimed the loyalty of Cambridge to the whig and ministerial cause. He was now in a favourable position to make his influence predominant in the university: and it was significant that, on the day he departed, the office of High Steward was given by Grace of the Senate to his old friend and most intimate political associate, Lord Chancellor Hardwicke. As a Cambridgeshire magnate[2] and a leading member of the administration, Hardwicke was an extremely eligible candidate: but possibly the Grace for his appointment, which passed 'without the least objection or murmur[3],' would not have been carried so easily if it had not been known that Newcastle was particularly anxious for him to be High Steward. Jealous of any rival influence being established in the university, the Chancellor needed a High Steward whom he could absolutely trust, and if he could not trust Hardwicke he could trust nobody. Thus the university submitted to the ministry, confessing that whiggism was the only true faith and that Newcastle was its prophet.

It will be seen later that the Duke spared no effort to foster this faith, and that his sins towards Cambridge were not those of omission. Seldom has the university

---

[1] Gray's *Letters* (edited by D. C. Tovey), I. 201–203.

[2] Lord Hardwicke's country seat was Wimpole Hall which is about ten miles from Cambridge.

[3] Add. MS. 32718, f. 273.

had a more active Chancellor: and as long as he remained in the service of the crown and in control of the royal patronage, he was able to rely upon the loyalty of his academic subjects. It is true that his authority in the university, even when he was at the height of his power, was never quite unchallenged, but the wishes of a Chancellor, who could so richly reward obedience, were not to be lightly disregarded. But when, eighteen months after the accession of George III, Newcastle fell from office, he found that he had built his greatness, both academical and political, upon a foundation of sand. From being the statesman whom the king delighted to honour, the maker and marrer of destinies, and the object of servile adulation, he became the leader of an impotent and discredited opposition party, doomed to failure from its inception. The weapon of patronage, which he had wielded for so long and so skilfully, was now turned against him by men who had learned its use from him. He paid to the uttermost farthing the penalty for having founded his political power upon human greed and avarice, and suffered the mortification of finding himself deserted by those who had been most obedient to his will in his days of greatness. Nor was it only in the political world that his influence declined. The change in his fortunes was not long in making itself felt in Cambridge: for there was little material inducement to remain faithful to a Chancellor who had only gratitude to give. The time was ripe for a rival banner to be planted in the university, and all that was needed was a favourable opportunity.

The opportunity came in the autumn of 1763 when Lord Hardwicke was overtaken by what proved to be his last illness. Though he lingered until March 6th, 1764, and at one time so far rallied his strength as to encourage hopes of a complete recovery, it was commonly assumed from the first that he would not survive, and the question of his successor as High Steward began to be canvassed almost as soon as he fell ill. Neither the young King nor the Grenville ministry, then in office, would have acted in accordance with the political traditions of the age if they had not contemplated utilising the occasion to overthrow the influence in the university of their antagonist, Newcastle; and when about November 22nd Lord Sandwich, one of the Secretaries of State, informed the King that in the event of Hardwicke's death he wished to succeed him as High Steward, the announcement was probably not unexpected. Sandwich had undoubtedly strong claims to recognition by the university of Cambridge. He had passed two years of his boyhood at Trinity, his country seat, Hinchingbrooke, was only a few miles distant from Cambridge, and he had always taken an interest in the affairs of the university. Moreover as a patron of the fine arts he was not unworthy of high academic office, and as a servant of the crown he might legitimately appeal for loyal support. Unfortunately, however, the scandals of his private life were such as to shock an age which was not easily put out of countenance. When every allowance has been made for the exaggeration of gossip and the malice of his enemies, enough remains to stamp Sandwich as an abandoned profligate sunk in sensual enjoyment. A distinguished member of the infamous hell-fire club which met at Medmenham Abbey, and the boon companion of some of the worst men of his time, he had chosen evil for his good; and his only innocent passion was a love of music. The morality of the eighteenth century however was not rigid, and it was apparently not until he added hypocrisy to his other vices that he became an object of public scorn. But when on November 15th, 1763, he rose in the house of lords and denounced his friend, John Wilkes, as the author of an indecent

PLATE II

JOHN MONTAGU

58 THE UNIVERSITY AND POLITICIANS

and might therefore fail: and he was fortified in this opinion by Keene, Bishop of Chester, who as a former Master of Peterhouse could speak for the university[1]. Grenville therefore urged strongly upon the King that Sandwich would disgrace the royal and ministerial recommendation, and suggested that Lord Halifax, who had also been educated at Cambridge, should be the government candidate. This was undoubtedly a very wise proposal, for Halifax, though not distinguished, was at least respectable: but on making further enquiries Grenville discovered that Sandwich, realising his own deficiencies as a candidate, had adroitly

[1] Edmund Keene, Bishop of Chester, was a younger brother of Sir Benjamin Keene, the diplomatist. He had been a follower of Newcastle in the days of the Duke's prosperity, but on the accession of George III he deserted his patron for the court. He had the reputation of being a 'cheerful, generous, and good-tempered man': but he lies under the suspicion of being a very abandoned time server. In 1774 the antiquary, Cole, met a lady at Horace Walpole's table, and after she had retired, Walpole told him a tale about her which Cole afterwards wrote down. 'She is' he wrote 'the natural daughter of Sir Robert Walpole, first Earl of Orford: and that she might not be left destitute when her father was no more, bought a living for £600 and proposed marrying her to Mr Keene....Accordingly, Mr Keene was put into possession of this living and enjoyed it as his first preferment for some time. In the interim Lord Orford dies, and when the lady was marriageable, it was proposed to Mr Keene to fulfil his engagement: but as he had by this time made other connections, and the lady, I suppose, not over-tempting, though of this Mr Walpole said not a word, and I only judge so from her present squat, short, gummy appearance, though by no means deformed or mishaped but rather under-sized and snub-faced, which probably might have been better when she was younger. When this was determined on, the lady had nothing to do but to retire and live as well as she could with her mother in a starving condition, as no further provision was made for her and the family knew nothing about her....Now I have related the story...I must needs add this caution about it. Mr Walpole is one of the most sanguine friends or enemies that I know. He has had a long pique, I well know, against the bishop and indeed his being a bishop is a sufficient reason for his spleen and satire.' Add. MS. 5847, f. 402, f. 403.

dissuaded Halifax from standing by dangling before him the prospect of succeeding Newcastle as Chancellor.

'In the evening' noted Grenville in his diary 'Mr Grenville mentioned to Lord Halifax, under the seal of secrecy, the difficulty Lord Sandwich would meet with at Cambridge, that the nomination would be much easier for his Lordship. He told Mr Grenville that Lord Sandwich and he had agreed between themselves that the first should be Steward and the last Chancellor[1].'

Sandwich had truly played his cards with skill: for as Grenville and the Lord Chancellor, Northington, hailed from the university of Oxford, and the Duke of Bedford, the Lord President, had not been educated at either university, Sandwich and Halifax were the only representatives of Cambridge among the leading members of the government; and, by persuading Halifax to stand aside, Sandwich practically forced the King and Grenville to choose between running him as their candidate or foregoing an opportunity of establishing the ministerial influence in Cambridge. In such circumstances neither the King nor Grenville was prepared to forbid his candidature, much as they disliked and feared it, and Sandwich was able to congratulate himself upon having surmounted the initial difficulty. He doubtless hoped that the university might forget his shortcomings as a man and remember his power as a minister.

Sandwich had not been singular however in perceiving that a new High Steward might soon be needed: and Newcastle, while yet unaware of the plot being hatched against him, had decided that Hardwicke should be succeeded by his son, Lord Royston[2]. Ever

[1] Grenville Papers, II, 227, 228. It is also possible that Halifax, who was on friendly terms with Newcastle, felt a certain delicacy in opposing him at Cambridge.
[2] Add. MS. 32953, f. 55.

fearful of a rival influence being established in the university, the Duke was naturally anxious to maintain a close connection between Cambridge and the Hardwicke family: and though Royston was not an eminent politician, he was a man of scholarly tastes and respectable life, and in many ways very well suited for academic office. He had been educated at Corpus, had always taken an interest in the university, and was well known to several of its leading members: and it is probable that Newcastle did not anticipate any serious opposition to his candidature. Had the Duke realised that he was embarking upon one of the fiercest and most hardly fought contests that either university has ever known, he might have selected another candidate: for though Royston was able to boast a moral superiority over Sandwich, he was conspicuously lacking in the love of battle and disinclined to support his claims with vigour. Something of a recluse and deficient in charm of manner, he had none of the attributes of a popular candidate: and though not unwilling to accept the office of High Steward, he was not prepared to fight for it. In after years he peevishly complained that he had been the victim of his brother, Charles Yorke, and Newcastle who had used him for their own ends and involved him in a wearisome and profitless struggle.

'I can never' he wrote 'think with pleasure of this affair. It gave me at the time a great deal of trouble, laid me under several obligations for an object which was in itself a trifle, and, unless made an unanimous compliment, not very acceptable[1].'

The decision however was taken before the need of a fighting candidate was realised, and for a few days Newcastle apparently thought that all would be plain sailing. But he was too experienced a campaigner not to take precautions: and on November 26th he issued instructions to his friend, Yonge, Bishop of

[1] Add. MS. 35657, f. 42.

THE UNIVERSITY AND POLITICIANS 61

Norwich, who, having formerly been Master of Jesus, was in touch with university politics and politicians.

'The Bishop of Lincoln[1]' he wrote 'received a most favourable letter last night from the Vice-Chancellor that I could have expected: and I really think, if this fatal event should happen, which I hope in God it may not, if proper care is taken in time my Lord Royston will meet with little or no difficulty. The management must be left entirely to the Bishop of Lincoln, the Bishop of Litchfield[2], and yourself. Proper notice should be given to all our friends in the university of the disposition of the Vice-Chancellor....I wish you would write a proper letter to my friend, Dr Sumner[3], and to Dr Sandby[4]. My honest friend, Mr Hughes of Queens', is now in town: he and all our friends in town should be applied to. Dr Barnard of Eton School should be spoke to. You best know what to do with the Masters of Trinity and St John's[5].'

Newcastle was sanguine and perhaps over-sanguine. He was confident of the support of the Vice-Chancellor, who, he declared, would 'make the nomination we desire[6]'; though it is doubtful whether the Vice-Chancellor, who was William Elliston, Master of Sidney, had gone further in his letter to the Bishop of Lincoln than the expression of vague and non-committal sentiments of loyalty to the whig cause[7]. Nor is

[1] Dr John Green, Bishop of Lincoln and Master of Corpus, was one of the most active supporters of the Newcastle and Hardwicke interest at Cambridge: but he seems to have been more closely connected with Hardwicke than Newcastle.

[2] Frederick Cornwallis who afterwards became Archbishop of Canterbury. He was for a time a Fellow of Christ's: and of the many bishops created by Newcastle, he was the only one who attended the first levée held by the Duke after his fall from office in 1762. It was on this occasion that Newcastle remarked with equal wit and truth that 'bishops, like other men, are apt to forget their Maker.'

[3] The Provost of King's.   [4] The Master of Magdalene.
[5] Add. MS. 32953, f. 73.   [6] Add. MS. 32953, f. 55.
[7] Elliston was elected Master of Sidney in 1760, being then a master of arts of less than two years' standing. It was remarked at the time that he was probably the youngest man ever made a Head of a House. Add. MS. 32905, f. 343.

there any suggestion that the Duke suspected a ministerial onslaught upon his sphere of influence: and he seems to have thought that nothing more was needed than a little management and a good deal of flattery. He was speedily aroused from this pleasant dream. To his disgust and annoyance he heard that the Masters of Magdalene and Peterhouse, though they had stoutly declined to desert their old friends, had been asked to pledge themselves to vote for Sandwich in the event of a vacancy in the High Stewardship[1]; and that the Master and Vice-Master of Trinity had both declared for Sandwich and begun actively to canvass their college on his behalf[2]. The news was bad both in itself and as an indication of evil in store. It was in no way surprising that Dr Smith, Master of Trinity, should espouse the cause of Sandwich, for his relations with Newcastle had never been cordial: but the Duke must have been deeply chagrined by the desertion of his old friend and ally, the Vice-Master, Dr Walker: and there was reason to fear, with all that Sandwich had to offer, that the Masters of Magdalene and Peterhouse would be the exceptions in their fidelity and Walker the rule in his treachery. If moreover the Master and Vice-Master of Trinity succeeded in their canvass of the college, Sandwich would gain a decisive advantage at the outset, for the Trinity vote might decide the contest.

Clearly the situation was fraught with danger, and Newcastle was compelled to revise his plan of campaign. It had been his original intention to avoid a public canvass, for a lengthy experience of politics had not killed all his finer feelings, and there was an obvious indecency in treating Lord Hardwicke's death as a foregone conclusion. Decency and Lord Sandwich however were complete strangers: and if Newcastle waited for Hardwicke's death as the signal for a public

[1] Add. MS. 32953, f. 85, f. 127, f. 145.   [2] Add. MS. 32953, f. 129.

THE UNIVERSITY AND POLITICIANS 63

appeal to the university, it was tolerably certain that he would find that many members of the Senate had pledged themselves to Sandwich in ignorance of any other candidate. Consequently he was advised by his friends to abandon his delicate reserve.

'Your Grace knows well' wrote John Chevallier of St John's[1] on November 30th 'that Lord Sandwich has offered himself a candidate, under favour of the court, for the office of High Steward of this university. His friends, some of them men of authority, are now busy in canvassing for him. Should it be agreeable to your Grace, as I hope it is, to give us an High Steward, I beg leave to lay before you this particular, namely that great part of the Senate would be very glad, if it be consistent with your Grace's views, to be informed of your intention. We are apprehensive that many absent and young masters of arts will engage themselves hastily to his Lordship because they will have heard of no opposition[2].'

The advice was sound and was accepted by Newcastle.

'So many of my friends' he informed the Vice-Chancellor on December 1st 'having pressed me to be no longer silent upon a subject, which I cannot think of without the utmost concern, I take the liberty to acquaint you that if it should please God to deprive the university of their most excellent patron, and myself of my most dear friend, Lord Hardwicke, I shall heartily wish that he may be succeeded as High Steward in the university by the truly worthy heir to his virtues and titles. My Lord Royston was educated with us, and does honour to his education by his character viewed in every light, as a nobleman of distinguished virtue, and as a scholar and a friend to religion and learning. He is your neighbour, Lord Lieutenant, and representative of your county: but above all he is the son of my Lord Hardwicke. I still hope it will please God to preserve the valuable life of that great and good man: if not, you have here my sentiments in relation to his successor, which you will be so good as to communicate to such members of the university as you may think

[1] Fellow and afterwards Master of St John's.
[2] Add. MS. 32953, f. 131.

proper. But I am desirous that this letter may not be read to them[1].'

Newcastle wrote similar letters to the Masters of Pembroke and St John's[2], and thus accepted the challenge thrown down by Sandwich. From this time onwards it was a fight to the death between two rival interests in the university: and though Royston remained in the background and displayed but a languid interest in the fray, his deficiencies as a combatant were more than compensated for by the vigour of the Duke. Reluctant though Newcastle had been to begin the contest, having once begun it he rightly thought of nothing but victory; and he knew that victory could only be achieved by careful and systematic organisation. It was imperative that as many members of the Senate as possible should be asked without delay to pledge themselves to vote for Royston if Hardwicke died; and that the canvass should not be confined to merely the resident voters, but extended so as to include the large number of members of the Senate scattered over the country. Such a task needed skill, knowledge and thoroughness for its successful accomplishment; and the general plan seems to have been for lists of voters to be sent from Cambridge to the Duke and the Bishops of Norwich and Lincoln who scrutinised them with a view of discovering the proper avenue of approach to each individual voter. Thus it is noted on one such list among the Duke's papers that Lord Dartmouth is to be asked to solicit Berridge of Clare and Wadeson, Fellow of St John's, that the Archbishop of York is to be entrusted with the task of sounding another Fellow of St John's, William Plucknett, who was a curate at Gainsborough, that the Bishop of Exeter is to be called upon to influence the son of one of his Canons: and

[1] Add. MS. 32953, f. 154.
[2] Add. MS. 32953, f. 158, f. 166.

THE UNIVERSITY AND POLITICIANS 65

that the Duke himself is to write to four other voters[1]. The task was tedious and tiresome; but Newcastle was determined upon victory and unsparing in his efforts. He could not have taken more trouble if the fate of England had been at stake. He wrote to Dr Markham, the headmaster of his old school, Westminster, to request him to use his influence with a Fellow of Trinity who had been at Westminster[2]; he asked Lord Edgecumbe to appeal to Dr Sumner, Provost of King's, pointing out that 'your Lordship has a right to command Dr Sumner as he owes the best of his preferments (two livings) to your father[3]'; he called upon Lord Folkestone to bring pressure to bear upon a Fellow of Queens'[4]; and sent to the Archbishop of Canterbury 'the names of those gentlemen of our university who, it is said, will be influenced by your Grace[5].' Nor was this work unattended with danger.

'When I saw your Grace's name on the direction of a letter to me' Dr Warner replied to the Duke 'I was in hopes it was in answer to one with which I had troubled your Grace, some little time ago, in favour of a charitable institution for the widows and children of the clergy in that part of the county of Surrey in which your Grace resides, and which I have had the principal part in getting established. I now enclose your Grace a copy of our rules and constitution, in hope that the Society will be honoured with your Grace's subscription[6].'

Like many other enthusiasts, however, Newcastle found, or thought he found, that his supporters were not as energetic as he considered they ought to be. About the end of December he complained with some bitterness that his friends at Cambridge were not exerting themselves, and insisted that the Bishop of Lincoln should speak to all our sure friends amongst the Heads,...and propose

[1] Add. MS. 32953, f. 283.   [2] Add. MS. 32953, f. 210.
[3] Add. MS. 32954, f. 256.   [4] Add. MS. 32955, f. 5.
[5] Add. MS. 32955, f. 3.   [6] Add. MS. 32953, f. 223.

to them to meet together every three or four days and bring in the accounts of their several colleges as well as of their re-admissions: and so make out the whole list[1].

Doubtless the Duke was exacting, and he was possibly the more exacting by reason of having to move in a world imperfectly known to him. Despite the attention he had lavished upon the business of the university, he had never really mastered the academic labyrinth: and to the end of his life he was never completely at home in Cambridge politics. Consequently his touch was not unfailing, and he was sometimes led by his ignorance into serious errors and miscalculations. For instance he requested his friend, Sir Edward Simpson, Master of Trinity Hall, to persuade his Fellows to vote for Lord Royston: and, on hearing from the Master that he had talked with five of his Fellows who seemed willing to vote as requested, he concluded that, as far as Trinity Hall was concerned, all was going well. He was undeceived by James Marriott, a Fellow of the college.

'I have been here but a few days' wrote Marriott from Trinity Hall on January 10th, 1764, 'and came over on purpose to confer with your Grace's friends, and to give what little countenance and assistance I can, understanding that Lord Sandwich does not relax of his violent applications, notwithstanding the great hopes of the Earl of Hardwicke's recovery. I desired Dr Caryl[2] to apprise the Bishop of Norwich of such circumstances as seemed to me somewhat necessary to secure your Grace's interest in a society so entirely independent of its Master as ours is. The members of it will undoubtedly expect, all of them, the compliment of separate applications. For besides Dr Wynne, Dr Dale, Dr Calvert and the Professor[3], none of whom positively declare themselves, I greatly doubt whether Sir Edward Simpson can fully answer for his own nephew, Dr Simpson[4], who too well knows his uncle's situation to expect

[1] Add. MS. 32954, f. 278.   [2] Master of Jesus.
[3] William Ridlington, Regius Professor of Civil Law.
[4] The Master's nephew, Frank Simpson, had been elected to a Fellowship of Trinity Hall in 1751.

THE UNIVERSITY AND POLITICIANS

anything at his death, and has just now engaged his vote to a candidate for a much sollicited Fellowship against his uncle's man....In this college the Master divides only as a thirteenth man[1], with small profits of absentees at Christmas: so that this Mastership, or almost Fellowship, is not better than that of one of our chaplains. He has no vote at any election of a Fellow or Scholar, and it is a mere complaisance that he is permitted to name college servants[2].'

Newcastle can hardly be blamed for failing to know that the Master of Trinity Hall was Master in little more than name, and he must have been ignorant of many other essential facts. He was however aware of his own deficiencies and wisely allowed himself to be guided by the Bishops of Norwich and Lincoln and by Caryl, Master of Jesus; for they possessed the knowledge of the university which he lacked. The Bishop of Norwich seems to have laboured with exemplary zeal, and it is to be hoped that he served God as faithfully as he served the Duke. Writing to Newcastle on December 5th from Grosvenor Square, he mentions that he is expecting letters from Cambridge and that he and the Bishop of Lincoln

design to be (having agreed it this morning) at Newcastle House by 10 o'clock to-morrow morning, and there to be preparing such minutes from the lists, which we both expect, as may be proper for your Grace's consideration when you shall be at leisure to see us[3].

Three days later he writes again to report that he has heard that the Master of Caius has half engaged himself to vote against Lord Royston, that the Master of Peterhouse has 'declined promising absolutely that he will not stop Lord Sandwich in the Caput,' and that Lord Rockingham was about to write to Sir T. Wentworth[4]. On December 9th he reported that he had had

[1] The Trinity Hall Fellowships were twelve in number.
[2] Add. MS. 32955, f. 134; see also f. 66, f. 80, f. 101.
[3] Add. MS. 32953, f. 208. [4] Add. MS. 32954, f. 136.

another conference with the Bishop of Lincoln, of which the result was 'the taking out of the lists several names to be written to by us and the enclosed for your Grace[1]': and, ten days later, he is still struggling with lists and lamenting that those he had recently received 'do not enable me to do quite what I wished in the transcript of them which I proposed sending to your Grace[2].'

It is difficult not to be impressed by the thoroughness with which the Bishop executed his task, and he combined with great powers of application a sound judgment. He fully appreciated the importance of the personal element, and realised how much might turn in winning votes upon a knowledge of petty and apparently trivial details. Hearing for instance that a certain Mr Barker, who was a son of a steward of the Duke of Rutland, desired to be approached by the Duke of Devonshire, he suggested a doubt whether 'the Duke of Devonshire will think it proper in him to apply to the son of one of the Duke of Rutland's stewards[3]': and sometimes he supplied what was little short of a family history of a particular member of the Senate.

'Mr Ekins, tutor at Eton to Lord Carlisle' he informed Newcastle 'is Fellow of King's, as is his brother. They are sons of Mr Ekins, Rector of Barton in Northamptonshire, the estate of the late Bishop of Rochester's son, Mr Wilcocks (Joseph Esq.) in Queen Street, Westminster, and I this instant recollect that he wrote to them or their father in favour of Dr Ewer[4] to oblige your Grace. The new Dean of Bristol's brother, Captain Barton, married their sister, which is a bad circumstance, for he and the other new Dean of Carlisle are the most active agents in this town for the Earl. If your Grace would send immediately

---

[1] Add. MS. 32953, f. 263.   [2] Add. MS. 32954, f. 96.
[3] Add. MS. 32954, f. 136.
[4] Dr Ewer was an unsuccessful candidate for the Provostship of King's in 1756.

THE UNIVERSITY AND POLITICIANS 69

to the Bishop of Worcester, who, I believe, goes into Sussex on Tuesday, he is a much better channel to Mr Wilcocks than I am[1].'

The Bishop's fears were justified, for both the Ekin brothers supported Lord Sandwich: but this was not due to any failure on his part to take trouble[2]. He was more successful in his suggestion that Samuel Peck, Fellow of Trinity[3], should be approached by the Duke of Grafton whose acquaintance he claimed: for though Grafton, when appealed to by Newcastle, denied any knowledge of Peck, the Bishop proved to be in the right.

'It is very possible' wrote James Backhouse, Tutor of Trinity, 'the Duke of Grafton may not recollect Mr Peck, but he certainly supposes himself known to his Grace, and has often said to me if the Duke of Grafton should apply for his vote he could not refuse him. Mr Peck comes from a place named Weston or Weston Green in the neighbourhood of Euston, and had once the honour of shewing the chapel, library, etc., to the Duke and Dutchess. If his Grace will be pleased to write as if he knew Mr P., I think I may be answerable for the success of such application[4],'

and possibly His Grace was pleased to write, for Peck certainly voted for Lord Royston.

Dr Caryl, Master of Jesus, was equally unflagging in his zeal. At one time he was writing daily to the Bishop of Norwich[5] who was doubtless deeply indebted to him for much valuable information, and without his

---

[1] Add. MS. 32954, f. 203.
[2] The Bishop of Worcester wrote to Wilcocks who replied to Lord Royston that he had no influence with the Ekin brothers and no wish to work against Lord Sandwich. Add. MS. 35657, f. 44.
[3] Gunning gives an amusing account of Peck in his *Reminiscences*, II, 114–116.
[4] Add. MS. 32954, f. 140; see also f. 7, f. 168.
[5] Add. MS. 32955, f. 9.

co-operation the Bishop and Newcastle would have been very much in the dark with regard to the situation at Cambridge.

'Pray write to your brother immediately' he instructed a certain Mr Twells in December 1763, 'and secure him for my Lord Royston, and desire him to let me know where he may be found at a minute's warning. And acquaint my Lord Duke that there is one Mr Johnson of St John's, who is preferred by his Grace, the Duke of Grafton, and that we hope that the Duke of Grafton will write to him. I have just now heard, and I depend upon it as true, that, the moment the vacancy happens, my Lord Sandwich will set out for Cambridge. Communicate this also to my Lord Duke[1].'

But, if Caryl and the Bishop of Norwich gave satisfaction by their enthusiasm and industry, this was not the case with John Green, Bishop of Lincoln and Master of Corpus.

'I am amazed' wrote Newcastle on January 4th, 1764, 'at the indifference and indolence of the Bishop of Lincoln: it looks really as if his friends and governors, the Yorkes, were not in earnest about it: for I should think his Lordship would never shew any backwardness in their affairs[2].'

Too much emphasis should not be placed upon what might only be a sudden outburst of temper on the part of Newcastle, overwrought by anxiety and a prey to fears: but it is also possible that the Bishop of Lincoln was infected by Lord Royston's apathy, and disinclined to take much trouble in preparing for a contest which might never occur.

Whatever credit however is given to those who organised the campaign, it must be remembered that their efforts would have been vain if they had not been able to depend upon the co-operation of those to whom they appealed to win votes. They must often have appealed in vain, but on the whole they met with an

[1] Add. MS. 32953, f. 207.   [2] Add. MS. 32955, f. 66.

THE UNIVERSITY AND POLITICIANS 71

encouraging response. The Archbishop of Canterbury had not waited to hear from Newcastle before espousing Lord Royston's cause.

'I should have thought myself much to blame' he informed the Duke 'if I had not, as soon as ever I knew the wishes of your Grace and Lord Hardwicke's family, endeavoured to second them. Accordingly I spoke and wrote, and got proper persons to write or speak, to as many as I could, and not without success[1].'

The Archbishop of York was also a willing and active worker in the same interest[2], and valuable services were rendered by the Duke of Grafton, Charles Townshend, and the latter's namesake and cousin who was distinguished from his more famous kinsman by the nickname of 'Spanish Charles[3].' 'Your Grace may depend,' wrote Grafton on January 5th, 1764, 'that I have spared no pains nor persuasions to have such friends of mine at Cambridge (as I could apply to) act in the manner you could wish them[4]': and on returning to his home, Honingham in Norfolk, towards the end of December 1763, Spanish Charles lost no time in reporting to Newcastle that

Mr Duquesne, having heard that there was likely to be a competition for the High Stewardship of Cambridge between Lord Sandwich and Lord Royston, and taking it for granted that your Grace wished well to the latter, had already applied to House and Herring of King's and May of Pembroke: he has since received answers from them, and they have all three given absolute promises to be for Lord Royston[5].

Spanish Charles had been educated at Clare College, as had also his more famous cousin; and the latter was

[1] Add. MS. 32955, f. 31.
[2] Add. MS. 32953, f. 212, f. 326, f. 338.
[3] The famous Charles Townshend was a younger son of the third Lord Townshend and a great-nephew of Newcastle; 'Spanish Charles' was the son of a younger brother of the third Lord Townshend.
[4] Add. MS. 32955, f. 76.   [5] Add. MS. 32954, f. 190.

able to be of service through his friendship with William Samuel Powell who had for a time been his private tutor. For many years Powell had occupied the position of principal Tutor of St John's College: and though in 1761 he left Cambridge for London, and, two years later, vacated his Fellowship, he retained considerable influence in his college and in time became its Master. Powell was also on friendly terms with the Vice-Chancellor, Elliston: and therefore in every way a person whose interest should be secured for Royston. The task of approaching him was very properly assigned by Newcastle to Charles Townshend.

'The Vice-Chancellor, I have reason to think' urged the Duke 'is not ill disposed to me, but Dr Powel can fix him if he pleases: besides Dr Powel has so much interest in St John's College that that would determine the election in our favour.... If therefore you would have the goodness to engage Dr Powel to use his interest with the Vice-Chancellor to nominate my Lord Royston, I am almost sure the Vice-Chancellor will do it: and if the Vice-Chancellor names my Lord Royston to the body, I will defy all that Lord Sandwich can do[1].'

The Duke did not make this appeal in vain. 'I have this morning' replied Townshend on December 1st 'seen Dr Powell who has engaged himself to me in the fullest manner. He will exert his interest with the Vice-Chancellor and in St John's college[2]': and having done this good turn, Townshend followed it up with another, reporting on December 10th that he had interviewed Professor Disney, 'who has engaged himself to Lord Royston and will do our cause further service[3].'

Newcastle and his friends had certainly good reason

[1] Add. MS. 32953, f. 123.
[2] Add. MS. 32953, f. 168; see also f. 145.
[3] Add. MS. 32953, f. 285; see also f. 184. Disney was Professor of Hebrew and a Fellow of Trinity.

THE UNIVERSITY AND POLITICIANS 73

to be unremitting in their applications: for their adversary was industrious and unscrupulous. Sandwich was both intelligent and well practised in the game of eighteenth century politics: and he realised, quite as fully as Newcastle, that victory could not be achieved without hard work. He did not under-rate the difficulties confronting him, and used to the full the advantages he possessed. In certain respects he was in a far stronger position than his adversary. As the candidate supported by the court and the government, he was able to promise those who were prepared to assist him that they would enjoy the material benefits of the favour of the crown, and to intimidate those who refused him their votes with the threat of being excluded from participating in the royal and ministerial patronage. He could also rely upon the active assistance of at least some of his colleagues in the cabinet. Before the end of the first week of December a certain Trinity master of arts had received two letters from the Duke of Bedford and one from the Lord Chancellor, urging him to vote for Sandwich[1]. In January 1764 it was reported that Sir James Lowther had written to the Master of Peterhouse to inform him 'that the King has ordered Sir James to write to Dr Law in favour of Lord Sandwich, and to tell him that the King will certainly take care of Dr Law[2].' Edward Barnard, Headmaster and later Provost of Eton, who nowadays is remembered as the only man who ever did justice to Dr Johnson's good breeding, is reported as resisting 'repeated applications and remonstrances with a manly spirit that does him honour[3],' and we hear that the Bishop of London, who was working for Sandwich, 'applied strongly to the Whitehall Preachers, and Dr Gisbourn, the Physician of the Household, has been told that his

[1] Add. MS. 32953, f. 223.   [2] Add. MS. 32955, f. 259.
[3] Add. MS. 32955, f. 84.

refusal to vote as commanded might have disagreeable consequences[1].' It was also rumoured that 'poor Kelly (of Jesus college and the late Mr Pointz's nephew) is turned out of a small but to him necessary employment for engaging for Lord Royston[2],' and that Mr Lushington of Peterhouse, who had also declared in favour of Royston, had been summoned, as a punishment, to join the regiment in Ireland of which he was the chaplain[3].

These stories must be accepted with reserve as they come from those who were anxious to think the very worst of Sandwich, but it is unlikely that the betrayer of Wilkes was morbidly scrupulous in his electioneering methods. Newcastle probably had some justification for complaining, early in December, that 'such shameful measures are taken that ought not to be practised in the meanest, most ignorant borough in the kingdom[4]': but the Duke might not have been so shocked if the shameful measures had not seemed so likely to be successful.

'I am sorry to say' he wrote on December 8th 'that some of the oldest and, I thought, most virtuous part of the university say that my Lord Sandwich might make a very good High Steward, though he would make a very bad bishop[5],'
and the Duke had good reason to be dismayed at the progress Sandwich was making. Like Newcastle he had procured lists 'not only of all the voters but likewise of most of their connections[6],' and having been the first to begin an active canvass, it was often found that he had anticipated his rival in an application for a vote. One of Sandwich's most active supporters in Cambridge was the Master of Trinity who eagerly canvassed his college on his patron's behalf. There is no doubt that

[1] Add. MS. 32955, f. 84.   [2] Add. MS. 32954, f. 313.
[3] Add. MS. 32955, f. 259. [4] Add. MS. 32953, f. 227.
[5] *Ibid.*   [6] Add. MS. 32953, f. 240.

THE UNIVERSITY AND POLITICIANS 75

he was extremely active[1]; and though John Pigott, one of the Fellows, was guilty of exaggeration in declaring on November 30th that the Master had already engaged 'most of the votes in this house[2],' there was a serious danger of this statement becoming true. But Trinity has always been inclined to resent being ruled from the Lodge, and a Newcastle party arose in the college with the Tutor, James Backhouse, at its head. Between the two camps feeling ran so high that Pigott suspected a brother Fellow of an intention to search the college letter-box in order to discover the address of an absentee[3]; and it seems that a good deal of this bitterness was caused by the Master's tyrannical methods. Indeed only a ludicrous blunder, made by the Vice-Master, saved one of the Fellows, William Preston, from being punished for his principles by financial loss.

'The Master' wrote the Bishop of Norwich on December 19th 'is confined by gout to his bed, and he sent for Preston thither on Thursday night to try once more if the loss of his stewardship would frighten him out of his integrity. In vain. So Dr Walker was directed to elect another person the next morning. Poor Walker's head was too weak for this business, and so, instead of declaring the Master's resentment against Preston, he actually proposed him to the Seniority to be elected steward. They in their obsequiousness supposed either that Preston had yielded or the Master altered his mind: and accordingly he was unanimously chosen. The Master blustered and

---

[1] John Fuller and Fountaine, who had been elected into Fellowships in 1762 but were no longer in residence, both received letters from the Master asking them to vote for Sandwich. Add. MS. 32953, f. 196, f. 210.

[2] Add. MS. 32953, f. 133.

[3] Pigott communicated his suspicion to George Onslow, but the paper on which the letter is written is very worn and some words have disappeared. Enough remains however to make it possible to understand the general drift of the communication. Add. MS. 32953, f. 222.

76 THE UNIVERSITY AND POLITICIANS

declared he should not be sworn into his office, but that was impossible as he was statutably elected. So poor Frog[1] is in infinite disgrace at the Lodge. It happened that the whole society resolved to meet that day after dinner to drink Mr Luther's health[2]; and in the course of the afternoon much indignation arose against the Master's violence. Meredith said he had indeed promised, but his hand should rot off before it wrote a suffrage for Sandwich. Powell and others blustered to the same purpose: and one, whose name I have not, to shew what his conduct would be, notwithstanding his forced engagement, actually betted five guineas that Lord Sandwich would not be High Steward[3].'

Hence there was war in Trinity, and the Master, who had done his cause no good by his violent and high-handed methods, still further alienated the sympathy of the college by committing a bad tactical mistake.

'Indeed' reported the Bishop of Norwich 'they are all disposed to go back, the Master and his Vice-Master having in their great prudence chosen this particular season to propose lowering their dividends, in which proposal they did not succeed[4].'

But undaunted by the opposition he was evoking, Dr Smith continued his campaign: and when he was commanded by Sir Edward Walpole[5], to whom he had dedicated one of his books, to 'recall all the force and

[1] Dr Walker was known as 'Frog Walker' from having once held a curacy in the Fens.

[2] Luther was a Trinity master of arts who had recently been elected to parliament for the county of Essex. 'The effect of Lord Sandwich's conduct began already to be felt. He, having to thwart the Duke of Cumberland who espoused Mr Luther, taken the opposite side on the election for the county of Essex, the court lost the election by dint of Sandwich's unpopularity.' Walpole's *Memoirs of the Reign of George III* (edited by G. F. Russell Barker), p. 267.

[3] Add. MS. 32954, f. 96. It is recorded in the Admission Book of the college that Preston was admitted into the office of Steward on December 17th, 1763.   [4] Add. MS. 32954, f. 136.

[5] A younger son of Sir Robert Walpole.

THE UNIVERSITY AND POLITICIANS 77

constraint he had put upon his Fellows[1],' he only gave an evasive answer[2].

As far as one can tell, however, Dr Smith seems to have confined his operations to his own college and to have done little outside it. Sandwich's leading supporters and organisers in the university were Dr Long, Master of Pembroke, Dr Brooke, Tutor of St John's, and Lawrence Brockett, Fellow of Trinity and Regius Professor of Modern History[3]: but as the Master of Pembroke was over eighty, it is likely that Brockett and Brooke bore the burden of the work. The Masters of Clare and Caius and the Provost of King's were also supporters of Sandwich, though the Master of Caius was by no means enthusiastic in the cause[4]; but among Heads of Houses Newcastle possessed and retained to the end a small majority. The Masters of St John's, Jesus, Magdalene, Corpus, Christ's, Peterhouse, Trinity Hall and the President of Queens' had all pledged themselves to support Royston, and Dr Richardson, the Master of Emmanuel, though his sympathies were with the government, had given a similar undertaking, in acknowledgment of valuable legal services rendered him by Royston's brother, Charles Yorke; though he was unable to go so far as to canvass for the candidate for whom he had promised to vote[5]. The Vice-Chan-

[1] Add. MS. 32954, f. 96.   [2] Add. MS. 32954, f. 136.
[3] Gray's *Letters* III, 31–34.   [4] Add. MS. 32953, f. 238.
[5] 'When the precentorship of Lincoln...became vacant on 18 May 1756, Richardson claimed it and filed a bill in chancery against Archdeacon John Chapman, another claimant. Henley, the Lord Keeper, gave a decision in November 1759 against Richardson who, under the advice of Charles Yorke, appealed to the house of lords. On 18 February 1760, after a trial lasting three days, the case was decided, mainly through the influence of Lord Mansfield, in his favour.' *Dictionary of National Biography*. In a letter to Newcastle, dated December 19th, 1763, the Bishop of Norwich refers to the 'coldness and indifference of the Master of Emmanuel who contents himself

cellor had not pledged himself to support either candidate, but at the beginning of the year 1764 the general opinion in the university was that he was anxious for Royston's success. It was reported that 'at dinner on Christmas day the Vice-Chancellor added to the usual healths "may the university know its own interests." Somebody desired leave (I don't know who) to correct it by altering one word and making it "its old interests" and the amendment was accepted, and so it went round[1].'

Yet though he was able to count upon a majority among Heads of Houses, and though the Vice-Chancellor seemed to be inclining in his favour, Newcastle was very far from being satisfied or confident of victory. He did not consider that his friends at Cambridge were as active as they might and should be, and he probably was disappointed in Lord Royston as a candidate. It is true that Royston was in a difficult position, for he naturally did not wish to lay himself open to the accusation of heartlessly anticipating his father's death; but he might have displayed more enthusiasm without incurring the charge of unfilial conduct. It was not until December 3rd that he communicated to the university his desire to succeed his father as High Steward; and it was unfortunate that this communication was made not to the Vice-Chancellor but to Dr Plumptre, President of Queens', who as rector of Wimpole was on intimate terms with the Hardwicke family[2]. At the instigation of Dr Plumptre, who pointed out that the Vice-Chancellor 'seemed to me to expect to hear from your Lordship on the occasion[3],' Royston with giving his own vote in return for Mr Yorke's securing him the whole house of lords'; and two days later the Bishop reports that 'Mr Backhouse confirms the Master of Emmanuel's coldness, and tells me he has told him (Backhouse) that he has not asked one of his Fellows.' Add. MS. 32954, f. 96, f. 136.

[1] Add. MS. 32955, f. 64. [2] Add. MS. 35628, f. 2.
[3] *Ibid.*

THE UNIVERSITY AND POLITICIANS 79

later repaired his error and formally communicated his intentions to Elliston[1]; but this was not an auspicious beginning of his candidature. He was moreover inclined to take for granted that men should labour in his interests; and it is characteristic of him that he omitted to recognise the very valuable assistance rendered by the Bishop of Norwich. 'As to the Yorke family' wrote the Bishop to Newcastle on January 4th, 1764, 'it has so happened that I never in my life had the honour of a visit from any one of them, no, not even a congratulation upon my first promotion to the Bench[2]'; and though the Duke succeeded in extracting something approaching an expression of gratitude from Royston, the Bishop refused to be pacified.

'I have read' he wrote to Newcastle on January 9th, 1764, 'your Grace's most affectionate letter to my Lord Royston and I have read his Lordship's answer, in which I have sought in vain for many things which I thought should have been there, and in particular for some idea of thankfulness to your Grace. ...This, I say, I have sought in vain, having, in my diligent scrutiny for it, only found a few words in the stile of a kingly answer to an address, declaring that his Lordship "has no doubt of the zeal, sincerity and services of all those persons" of whom your Grace was pleased to make such honourable mention[3].'

Newcastle had anxieties beyond the deficiencies of Royston as a candidate, and he was probably more disturbed by the cunning of his adversaries than by the shortcomings of his friends. He knew that those against whom he was matched would stick at nothing to gain their end, and it was not long before he discovered how little they were hampered by restrictive prejudices. Shortly after the beginning of the contest the Sand-

[1] Add. MS. 35657, f. 42.
[2] The Bishop excepted from this condemnation 'the illustrious head of that family, whose condescension has always been as conspicuous as his abilities.' Add. MS. 32955, f. 64.
[3] Add. MS. 32955, f. 126.

80 THE UNIVERSITY AND POLITICIANS

wich party made an attempt to swell its number by a device which Newcastle and his friends regarded as unfair. The constitution of the university provided that only those doctors and masters of arts whose names were on the books of a college could vote in the Senate, and though it was always possible for a former member of the university to replace his name on his college books, no master of arts thus re-admitted was entitled to a vote in the Senate until three months after the date of his re-admission[1]. As university struggles were commonly brief in duration, it was unusual for masters of arts, who had removed their names, to be asked to replace them in order to qualify for a vote; and doubtless the three months rule was designed to prevent the practice. But realising perhaps that Lord Hardwicke was not so near death as at one time had been thought, and that the election of a new High Steward might not take place for some months, the leaders of the Sandwich party decided to encourage the re-admission of masters of arts. Consequently on November 30th Lord Carysfort, who was a friend of Sandwich, replaced his name on the books of his college; and although for some days afterwards no other master of arts was re-admitted, the alarm was given.

'Spanish Charles Townsend' wrote Thomas Townshend on December 18th 'desires me to acquaint your Grace that he has offered himself to be admitted at Clare Hall but has been refused by Dr Goddard[2] who refuses all admissions at this time indiscriminately. The Master of Queens' has offered to admit him. He wishes to know your Grace's opinion whether he should accept that offer or not[3].'

This was not an easy question for Newcastle to answer. There was a difficulty in determining whether

[1] Doctors, who replaced their names on the college books, became at once entitled to a vote.
[2] The Master of Clare.   [3] Add. MS. 32954, f. 84.

THE UNIVERSITY AND POLITICIANS 81

Carysfort's re-admission was an isolated incident or the first of a series, and a policy of retaliation presented the obvious danger of driving the Sandwich party to further extremes. Consequently the Duke hesitated to express an opinion, but there was no hesitation with the Bishop of Norwich who was strongly opposed to the adoption of a re-admission policy. 'Lord Carysfort' he urged 'began the unfair business of re-admissions, but it has gone no farther on their side and I think should not be attempted on ours[1].' Unfortunately however Spanish Charles had not waited for an answer, having placed his name on the books of Queens' on December 16th[2]; and within the next few days four followers of Sandwich were re-admitted[3]. Both parties were therefore committed to the policy, and though it is possible to argue that, if it had not been for Townshend's precipitate action, Carysfort's admission would not have been followed up, this is no more than an assumption; and it is more probable that Sandwich and his friends were either waiting to see how much they were likely to gain by the adoption of such measures or intended to obtain the re-admission of their friends gradually and by degrees, in the hope of what they were doing passing unnoticed. It is at least certain that the Newcastle party would have willingly refrained. 'I am sorry for the re-admissions,' wrote the Duke on December 28th, 'I am sure they will turn out against us; but however, as the others go on, we must in our own defence go on too[4].'

It is a sign of weakness to allow your rival to dictate your policy; but though Newcastle might succumb to what he deemed the logic of hard facts, his friends at Cambridge were more resourceful. They declined to be

[1] Add. MS. 32954, f. 136.   [2] Add. MS. 32956, f. 260.
[3] *Ibid.*   [4] Add. MS. 32954, f. 278.

82 THE UNIVERSITY AND POLITICIANS

impaled upon either horn of the dilemma presented by the enemy, and devised a means of escape.

'Amongst other means used on both sides to increase their numbers,' wrote the President of Queens' to Royston on December 29th, 'one has been to re-admit masters of arts who have left the university and taken their names out, and then in three months after such re-admission they enjoy again the privilege of a vote in the Senate. This was about being carried to such a length that it was thought much confusion and detriment would ensue to the university from it; and much trouble and expence would certainly have been occasioned to those who were to have been brought up from all parts. A Grace therefore was yesterday proposed by some of our friends at St John's[1] to prolong the time for a twelvemonth for all who should be readmitted, after the passing of that Grace, before they should have a right of voting. Some altercation followed thereupon on the first reading, but a little before the second reading this day proposals were made that whereas it appeared that in the whole of these admissions, which amounted then in all to twenty-three, your Lordship had five more than Lord Sandwich, there should be five more admitted on his side to make a ballance, and then that this Grace should pass. The Bishop of Lincoln, who is here at present, was consulted on this head, and, as they did me the honour of consulting me also, I said that the proposal was in my opinion a very equitable one and for the peace and good of the university, and ventured to say I did not doubt your Lordship's approbation of it. On conferring afterwards with the Bishop of Lincoln and others of your Lordship's friends, we all agreed that it ought to be embraced, and, being thus settled, the Grace passed without any opposition, and is I think a very salutary measure upon the whole and I believe rather advantageous to us, as orders were issued from the enemy's quarter to pour in all the recruits of this sort which could be raised. Mr Ludlam of St John's, a fast friend of your Lordship, was the principal negotiator of this treaty[2].'

[1] The Grace was brought forward by William Abbot who is described by Newcastle as 'the great Tutor at St John's.' Add. MS. 32954, f. 307. He became Tutor in 1761.
[2] Add. MS. 35628, f. 3; Add. MS. 32954, f. 288. Writing on

This readiness on the part of Lord Royston's supporters to treat with their opponents suggests that they were by no means in a position of commanding strength, and it is probable that they were unable to count with any confidence upon a numerical superiority among the resident members of the Senate. They must have been still more doubtful of their strength among the non-resident voters. Indeed by the end of the year 1763 the canvass had not really made substantial progress. A list sent by the President of Queens' to Lord Royston on December 29th gives one hundred and nineteen votes to Royston, seventy-nine to Sandwich, and nearly two hundred and fifty as unknown[1]; and with such a wide margin of uncertainty clearly anything like an accurate calculation was impossible. The President moreover does not discriminate between regents and non-regents or between doctors and masters of arts; but, inasmuch as a High Steward was not elected by the undivided Senate but appointed by a Grace passed by the two houses, such a discrimination was essential for a reliable forecast. The omission is repaired in three lists submitted to Newcastle by the Bishop of Norwich about the same time. The first list contains the names of fifty-four 'doctors of more than two years standing and therefore regents or non-regents at pleasure'; and of these twenty-five are marked as voting for Royston, twelve as voting for Sandwich, and seventeen as uncertain[2]. The second list contains the names of two hundred and twenty non-regent masters; and though Royston is given a majority of about twenty over Sandwich, nearly half the voters named on the list are

December 28th the Bishop of Norwich mentions that the Grace was to be read for the first time on the following day; but this appears to be wrong. Add. MS. 32954, f. 274. For a list of re-admissions see Add. MS. 32956, f. 260.

[1] Add. MS. 32954, f. 290. [2] Add. MS. 32954, f. 178.

84   THE UNIVERSITY AND POLITICIANS

marked as uncertain[1]. The third list contains the names of one hundred and seventy regent doctors and masters, and of these one hundred and two are given as uncertain[2].

There is no reason to think that Sandwich was any better informed; and probably a good many voters were shy of committing themselves before seeing clearly which way victory was inclining. But about the beginning of the year 1764 it seemed as though the toil of the canvass had been undergone in vain, and that Sandwich's hope of becoming High Steward was to be dashed to the ground by Lord Hardwicke's recovery. 'There is the greatest reason to hope' wrote Newcastle on January 5th 'that by the blessing of God the vacancy will not happen[3]'; and by the beginning of February Hardwicke had so far rallied as to be allowed to receive a visit from his old friend.

'I saw yesterday' wrote Newcastle on February 2nd 'a most surprizing but most agreeable sight. My great and valuable friend, my Lord Hardwicke, who, after four months confinement for a most painful and dangerous disease, is at his age so far recovered as to be able to come down stairs; his looks and voice almost the same they ever were, his spirits and vigour of speech almost the same; and no other complaint at present but great weakness of body and inability to walk without assistance, which by the advance of the season and proper exercise I hope in God will soon be removed[4].'

Convinced that Lord Hardwicke had been snatched from the jaws of death, Newcastle came to the conclusion that the Cambridge contest was over, and testified to his belief by writing letters of thanks to his leading supporters and the Vice-Chancellor[5]. He soon found however that Sandwich was very pessimistic about

[1] Add. MS. 32954, f. 181.   [2] Add. MS. 32954, f. 186.
[3] Add. MS. 32955, f. 82.   [4] Add. MS. 32955, f. 474.
[5] Add. MS. 32955, f. 148, f. 156, f. 158, f. 160, f. 162, f. 180, f. 182, f. 184.

Hardwicke's chance of complete recovery and was therefore carrying on his campaign for the High Stewardship. Consequently the Duke was compelled to call upon his friends in the university to renew their efforts.

Upon the great and happy recovery of my most valuable friend, my Lord Hardwicke, our present High Steward, I was in hopes that that would have put an entire stop to the present contest at Cambridge and have restored peace and good harmony amongst us; but as I am well informed that on the contrary the opposite party are still pursuing with more violence, warmth and activity than ever, I must recommend it most earnestly to my friends, and those who have a regard to my Lord Hardwicke and his family, to redouble their application and to exert all honourable means of adding strength to that cause, to which so many of them have to their everlasting honour manifested so zealous and so truly virtuous an attachment[1].

It was well these instructions were issued, for about a week later Lord Hardwicke had a relapse from which he never recovered. On March 4th he was reported to be sinking, and two days later he died[2]. There is no doubt that Newcastle was genuinely distressed by the death of one who had been his friend and counsellor for many years, but he did not permit his private grief to diminish his public activities. It was now certain that the university must appoint a new High Steward, and Newcastle was as determined as ever to secure the succession for the son of his old friend. Yet he well knew that success was uncertain and that he was matched against a mightier antagonist than he had ever before encountered in an university contest. 'My judgment upon the whole' wrote the Master of Jesus on March 7th 'is that it will be a very difficult point to carry, as we outnumber them by so few and are in the dark about so many[3]'; but the Duke was too experi-

[1] Add. MS. 32955, f. 474. [2] Add. MS. 32956, f. 206.
[3] Add. MS. 32956, f. 256.

enced a politician to allow despair to damp his ardour. Directly he heard of Hardwicke's death he despatched two letters to the Vice-Chancellor by a special messenger who was instructed 'to ride all night, to be at Cambridge to-morrow morning by seven o'clock[1].' In one letter he asked that the date of the election might be so fixed as to allow 'those of the members of the university, who are at a great distance, to attend, and expressed a hope that the Vice-Chancellor would prove 'a friend to me and to the interests of the son of that incomparable person whose loss I can never sufficiently lament[2].' The other letter has not survived, but its contents can be gathered from a subsequent epistle of the Duke. 'I cannot' he wrote to the Vice-Chancellor 'express the sense I have of your kind intention to nominate the present Earl of Hardwicke to succeed that great and valuable man, his father, in the High Stewardship of our university[3]'; and there is no doubt that he was genuinely delighted with the success of his application. Hitherto the Vice-Chancellor had refrained from identifying himself with either party; and although he was suspected of antagonism to Sandwich, he had not given clear proof of such a sentiment. It was however his duty as Vice-Chancellor to bring forward the Grace for the appointment of a new High Steward[4]; and, by deciding that the Grace should be for the appointment of the new Lord Hardwicke, he undoubtedly gave that candidate an advantage. To be first in nomination was not to make certain of victory but, like winning the toss in the boat-race, it might just turn the scale in an

---

[1] Add. MS. 32956, f. 234. On March 5th Newcastle had conferred with the Bishops of Lincoln and Norwich; and probably the measures, to be taken immediately after Hardwicke's death, were decided upon at this meeting.
[2] Add. MS. 32956, f. 232.   [3] Add. MS. 32956, f. 254.
[4] Add. MS. 35657, f. 75.

THE UNIVERSITY AND POLITICIANS 87

even contest. Though convinced supporters of Sandwich would oppose the Grace, those members of the Senate who inclined to neutrality would be disposed to support it in the hope of avoiding a prolongation of the struggle; and Newcastle by no means under-rated the favour conferred.

'The Vice-Chancellor' he declared 'a young gentleman of character and merit, unpensioned, undignified, unbiassed by promises or threats, has acted the greatest part that ever man did, kept his resolution to himself, none of us knew what it would be; and, when the vacancy was made, then declared publicly that he intended (as is our form) to nominate the present Earl of Hardwicke to succeed his great and meritorious father[1].'

It also rested with the Vice-Chancellor to name the day for the Grace to be voted upon by the Senate; and Newcastle was particularly anxious that his friends in distant parts of the country should be allowed sufficient time to reach Cambridge, and that the day chosen should not clash with an ordination which the Bishop of Lincoln had arranged to hold at his palace at Buckden[2]. After consulting Lord Hardwicke's supporters, the Vice-Chancellor announced the election for Thursday March 22nd, but though this date was apparently quite convenient to the Bishop of Lincoln[3], it was too near in point of time to meet with the approval of Newcastle who complained that 'it will be impossible for us to give timely notice to our friends of the election[4].' It was in vain however that he appealed for an extension of time; the Vice-Chancellor pointed out that the day he had selected had been approved by Hardwicke's supporters, that the announcement had been communicated to the Masters and Tutors of the

[1] Add. MS. 32957, f. 5.
[2] Add. MS. 32956, f. 254. Buckden is about four miles from Huntingdon.
[3] Add. MS. 32956, f. 277.   [4] Add. MS. 32956, f. 312.

colleges, and through them to the absent electors, and that

if after this any alteration should be made in the time, it would certainly give those persons who are in the interest of Lord Sandwich an occasion, whether just or not, to complain of my conduct as a magistrate[1].

In spite therefore of his anxiety for Hardwicke's success, the Vice-Chancellor was not prepared to sacrifice everything to partisanship; and though, as will be seen later, the election was ultimately postponed for a week, this was not the result of Newcastle's plea but of a grave tactical blunder on the part of Lord Sandwich's friends.

The situation, though not desperate, was by no means favourable[2]; and it was apparently Dr Powell, Charles Townshend's old tutor, who expressed the opinion that the time had come for the despatch of a special emissary to Cambridge to assist in the canvass. In communicating the suggestion to Newcastle, Townshend quoted Powell as saying

how absolutely necessary it is your Grace should have a friend, considerable in himself and acceptable to the university, and a person of activity and quickness, present at the university to animate, conduct, and lead your party[3],

and the Duke, taking the hint, asked Charles Townshend to go himself[4]. Charles needed no pressing. Ever on the look out for a fresh excitement, he was happy to take a holiday from his duties at Westminster and disport himself among university politicians; but it is open to doubt whether Newcastle was justified in allowing him to go. The parliamentary opposition, of

[1] Add. MS. 32956, f. 369.
[2] The Master of Jesus reported on March 8th 'we have had a most discomfortable time for these last twenty-four hours. Every minute brings to light something bad.' Add. MS. 32956, f. 281.
[3] Add. MS. 32956, f. 246. [4] Add. MS. 32956, f. 250.

THE UNIVERSITY AND POLITICIANS 89

which the Duke was the leader and Townshend, for the time being, a member, was engaged in a fierce and critical struggle with the ministry; and it was not a time for it to dissipate its strength by indulging in side shows. Valuable as Townshend might be at Cambridge, he would be still more valuable in the house of commons as a critic of George Grenville's financial measures; and in sending him to Cambridge Newcastle was guilty of faulty generalship. He had however persuaded himself that the contest at Cambridge was of equal importance with the contest in parliament, and that the success of Sandwich would be as fatal to the opposition as to himself. 'Unless it may be made a publick measure and that all chief persons in the minority will set it in that light, and act in it as such,' he told the Duke of Devonshire on March 7th, 'I shall despair of success....Indeed, my dear Lord, it is necessary that we should all act together or we shall be all blown up[1].'

On March 8th Charles Townshend, accompanied by Dr Powell, left for Cambridge. On the following morning he waited upon the Vice-Chancellor who received him cordially and gave him permission to say that he, the Vice-Chancellor, had undertaken to nominate Lord Hardwicke to the Senate[2]. Then without further delay Townshend started to work upon the university.

'I began my canvass this morning' he informed Newcastle on March 9th 'and have had great success where it was least expected. Your Grace will perhaps be anxious to hear with exactness in what manner and upon what general grounds I have made my applications. In the first place then I have assumed the honour of being employed by your Grace with the

---

[1] Add. MS. 32956, f. 252. It seems that Newcastle was under the impression, which proved to be wrong, that Sandwich himself had gone or was going to Cambridge.
[2] Add. MS. 32956, f. 310, f. 318.

92 THE UNIVERSITY AND POLITICIANS

must arise from illness, absence from home, great distance and other causes[1],' and the Master of Jesus expressed a similar opinion[2].

Yet the experiment of sending a special emissary to Cambridge had been justified; and when Charles Townshend left the university about March 12th, his place was taken by his kinsman, Thomas Townshend, junior[3], who in his turn was succeeded by Lord Hardwicke's two brothers, the Dean of Lincoln and John Yorke[4]. By the date of Charles Townshend's departure the work of canvassing the university had been more or less completed; but the parties were too evenly balanced to allow of any relaxation of effort. 'No pains should be spared' wrote Thomas Townshend 'where we have the least chance of a vote. Things run very near indeed[5].' They ran so near as to make the whims and fancies of a single member of the Senate a matter of vital moment, and a reliable forecast an impossibility. A note by the Master of Jesus, dated March 18th, marks the ever changing character of the scene. He mentions that Evans and Bennet, two supporters of Sandwich, had arrived in Cambridge, though it had been anticipated that they would not come, that Castley, another member of the same party, had also unexpectedly arrived from the Isle of Man, and that Bacon of Caius had been 'carried off mad this morning[6].'

---

[1] Add. MS. 32956, f. 375.   [2] Add. MS. 32956, f. 308.

[3] Charles Townshend's first cousin.

[4] Add. MS. 32957, f. 133. It was Charles Townshend who urged that some members of Lord Hardwicke's family should come to Cambridge; and it is characteristic of Hardwicke's whole attitude towards the election that he only reluctantly accepted the suggestion. Add. MS. 32956, f. 310, f. 361, f. 363.

[5] Add. MS. 32957, f. 149.

[6] Add. MS. 32957, f. 165. In an undated list of absentees six persons are described as insane. Add. MS. 32954, f. 213. Castley was a Fellow of Jesus and Master of Castletown School, Isle of Man.

THE UNIVERSITY AND POLITICIANS 93

Much alarm and trouble was also caused by the behaviour of Dr Charles Berridge of Clare. After voluntarily undertaking to vote for Hardwicke, Dr Berridge began to fear that he had made himself a little too cheap; and his suspicions were confirmed by a letter he had written to Newcastle being left unanswered. In a thoroughly bad humour he came to the conclusion that his pledge to support Hardwicke was not being counted to him for righteousness but attributed to the electioneering skill of the Master of Jesus; and he therefore arranged to pair with a certain William Ellis and departed for Bath. As Berridge was a doctor whose vote could be cast in either house of the Senate, and Ellis was only a master of arts, the arrangement was a material loss to the Hardwicke party, and on learning from the Master of Jesus what had happened, Newcastle acted promptly. Hearing that Berridge was breaking the journey to Bath by a stay in London, he contrived to see him; and so far succeeded in placating him as to induce him to request Ellis to cancel the engagement between them. Ellis readily consented; and though, after arriving at Bath, Berridge pleaded he was too ill to travel to Cambridge, he was finally persuaded to make the journey and vote for Hardwicke[1].

Such difficulties were almost of daily occurrence, for Dr Berridge was by no means singular in being quick to take offence.

'On my return to college this morning' wrote a certain Mr Bigg of Clare to Newcastle 'I found myself honoured with a letter from your Grace through Mr Talbot[2]. I only observe that this was the first application I have had from that quarter, though several days passed after the melancholly event of my good Lord Hardwicke's death before I left college, and, what

[1] Add. MS. 32957, f. 99, f. 139, f. 155, f. 156, f. 158, f. 255.
[2] Talbot was a Fellow of Clare and the Chancellor's secretary for

is somewhat extraordinary, some of the managers on that side passed by my door to the juniors, though I had particularly offered to write to the absentees of our college[1].'

Bigg did not carry his resentment so far as not to vote for Hardwicke, but it is appalling to think of the time which must have been spent in healing the wounds unwittingly inflicted on pride and dignity. Nor was there any time to spare; for on both sides there was feverish activity until the end.

'I am informed' wrote Thomas Townshend 'that a letter from Lord Sondes to Mr Barton of Clare Hall might chance to be productive of a good effect. His engagement at present is to another Fellow of the same college, and there is great reason to think that an application from Lord Sondes would stagger him[2].'

Possibly it was of the same Barton it was suggested that as Lady Gainsborough allowed his mother a hundred pounds a year she might be able to persuade him to vote for Hardwicke[3]; but the services of Lord Sondes and Lady Gainsborough, if requisitioned, failed to wean him from Lord Sandwich. A few days before the election the President of Queens' reported that Carr of Clare, who was a follower of Sandwich and, as a member of the Caput, able to reject the Grace by his single vote, had been promised a valuable living by the Archbishop of York and Lord Rockingham[4]; and, whatever may be said of the methods employed, they were at least based upon a frank acknowledgment of the predominance of self-interest. Mr Mease, Fellow of St John's and curate at Halesworth in Suffolk, was to be approached by Sir Joshua Vanneck from whom he had hopes of advancement in the church[5]; and a certain Samuel Hill of the same college was successfully solicited by Newcastle who, though he did not

[1] Add. MS. 32957, f. 216; see also f. 52.
[2] Add. MS. 32957, f. 149.   [3] Add. MS. 32957, f. 165.
[4] Add. MS. 32957, f. 153.   [5] Add. MS. 32956, f. 393.

THE UNIVERSITY AND POLITICIANS 95

know him, pleaded that he had 'had the pleasure to contribute to your obtaining the degree of master of arts in our university[1].'

It was certainly a keen and unscrupulous game with a very sordid and unattractive side to it; and, as might be expected in such a hard fought contest, there was little that either party would not do to secure a vote.

'I have been earnestly pressed by my neighbour, Mr Wortham of Royston,' wrote Hardwicke to Newcastle on March 18th, 'to beg the favour of your Grace to recommend the pretentions of his nephew, Mr Ferris, to a Fellowship of St John's by a line from your Grace to Dr Ogden. I have already wrote to the Dean of Rochester[2] on the subject, but on no other footing than the merit of the young man, and to desire that a junior competitor may not bear him down by superior interest. Mr Wortham says he would not have had recourse to this sort of application if the other candidate had not set the example. Your Grace may be very sure that I shall shut the door as much as possible against these sort of interpositions, but at this juncture I would not have my friends in the county think that I neglect anything in which they are concerned[3].'

Sometimes an attempt was made to intimidate a voter from adhering to a promise he had given. Mr Story of Magdalene for instance pleaded hard to be excused from fulfilling his pledge to vote for Hardwicke as 'it will in all probability deprive me of my curacy and whole support at present[4]'; and William Gawthrop of Trinity was persuaded by Backhouse to foreswear the allegiance he had sworn to Sandwich.

'I have sent twice this week' wrote Backhouse on March 11th 'to Mr Gawthrop by special messengers but cannot yet obtain an explicit answer that he will vote for us, the Master

[1] Add. MS. 32956, f. 316; see also f. 292.
[2] The Master of St John's.
[3] Add. MS. 32957, f. 167. Ferris was elected to a Fellowship on the 9th April 1764.
[4] Add. MS. 32957, f. 103.

having sent his own servant to claim and insist on his first promise however unwarily made. This has so horrified him that he knows not what to do; however he has promised to let me see him before any other of the college[1].'

Though we know far less of the activities of the Sandwich party, it is quite certain that they were making a desperate bid for victory. 'Lord Sandwich is indefatigable in his applications,' wrote a supporter of Lord Hardwicke from Wakefield, 'his expresses are daily coming down to the North[2]'; and we also hear of Lord Chancellor Northington being so enraged with a young clergyman for supporting Hardwicke that he refused to give him a living which he had promised him[3]. Moreover a personal canvass of the university in the Sandwich interest was undertaken by Lord Carysfort, Colonel Draper and Charles Townshend's elder brother, George, who all arrived in Cambridge about the middle of March. George Townshend was soon called away, by the death of his father whom he succeeded in the peerage; but his two companions remained behind and solicited votes.

'Draper and Carysfort' wrote Thomas Townshend 'go round the university, make civil bows and civil speeches to everybody, and affect to shew a difference between their conduct and the eagerness of Charles Townshend[4].'

The industry of Lord Sandwich's friends was doubtless very commendable but their tactics were open to criticism. Interpreting the rule, by which re-admitted masters of arts were not entitled to vote until three months had elapsed from the date of re-admission, as meaning three lunar months, the Vice-Chancellor had purposely delayed the election of a High Steward until

---

[1] Add. MS. 32956, f. 394. Gawthrop finally voted for Hardwicke.
[2] Add. MS. 32956, f. 420.   [3] Add. MS. 32957, f. 67.
[4] Add. MS. 32957, f. 57; see also Add. MS. 32957, f. 35; Add. MS. 35640, f. 110.

THE UNIVERSITY AND POLITICIANS

March 22nd in order that all those re-admitted before December 30th should be able to vote. In so doing he had acted with perfect impartiality; for as the Grace, passed on December 29th and extending the period of three months to a year, had not been passed by the Senate until an equal number of masters of arts had been re-admitted on both sides, neither party was placed at a disadvantage. He must therefore have been both surprised and chagrined when he was presented on March 13th with a memorial from the Provost of King's and the Masters of Pembroke, Clare and St Catharine's[1], which stated that the three months should be interpreted as calendar months, and that therefore by the Grace in 1698 (confirmed by the King and Council in 1728) no person re-admitted after December 22nd has a legal right to vote in the Senate on March 22nd, nor can a new Grace of the Senate give him that right unless it could alter the law of the land[2].

The motive of this manœuvre was not difficult to detect. There had been seven re-admissions before December 23rd, of which five were in Lord Sandwich's favour[3]; and consequently, if the contention of the memorialists was accepted, Hardwicke would be at a serious disadvantage. The move, though savouring of sharp practice, was adroit, and undoubtedly caused a good deal of alarm in the Hardwicke camp. At a meeting on March 13th between Talbot, Thomas Townshend, the Master of Christ's and the Bishop of Lincoln, it was decided to take counsel's opinion: and without loss of time Townshend sought out Mr Sergeant White who happened to be in Cambridge for the assizes. This legal luminary announced the comforting

---

[1] The memorial was drawn up by the Master of Trinity and had the support of the Master of Caius. Add. MS. 32957, f. 53; Add. MS. 5852, f. 147.
[2] Add. MS. 35657, f. 57.   [3] Add. MS. 32956, f. 260.

doctrine that 'in all cases where calendar months were not particularly mentioned, twelve weeks were to be deemed "integrum spatium trium mensium"; but another authority on being consulted declared that 'as we are a kind of ecclesiastical constitution, we are to understand the words "trium mensium spatium" in an ecclesiastical way and as meaning three calendar months[1].' It was not for the Vice-Chancellor to decide a legal question upon which lawyers disagreed; and he adopted the only possible course in the circumstances.

The Vice-Chancellor had a meeting of some Heads at his Lodge on Thursday 15th March in the morning, to which none of the six Heads were called, and in consequence of this meeting sent a paper in the afternoon to each of the six Heads, signifying that upon this dispute he thought himself obliged to put off the election till Friday 30th March[2].

He could hardly have done otherwise; for the question having once been raised, the obvious way out of the difficulty was to appoint such a date for the election as would divest the doubt of any practical importance. Newcastle was of course delighted[3], having previously petitioned in vain for a postponement; and though no fault can be found with the Vice-Chancellor's action by an impartial critic, it was naturally resented by those who, in an attempt to score an unfair advantage, had badly over-reached themselves.

'I own' wrote Lord Sandwich to the Vice-Chancellor 'I expected much more candour from you than what I have lately met with; for I am not a little surprised and concerned at the news I yesterday received of your having put off the day of the election of the High Steward. You cannot but be sensible that this proceeding must greatly distress several of my friends who are come from a great distance with much expence and incon-

[1] Add. MS. 32957, f. 101; see also f. 53.
[2] Add. MS. 5852, f. 147; see also Add. MS. 35657, f. 54, f. 56 Add. MS. 32957, f. 95, f. 97.
[3] Add. MS. 32957, f. 133.

THE UNIVERSITY AND POLITICIANS 99

venience to their affairs, and who probably will not easily be prevailed on, if they go home, to take a second journey. I am not at present thoroughly apprized of the power of a Vice-Chancellor in this election; but you must not be surprized if I make strict enquiry into that matter; and that, if I find it is contrary to the laws or usage of the university to put off a day of election after publick notice has been given, I apply to superior powers for justice[1].'

This however was mere bluster, and, in accordance with the Vice-Chancellor's decision, the election did not take place until March 30th. It may be assumed that Newcastle knew his own interests, and that the postponement was to his advantage; but it does not certainly appear that he was able to gain any material addition to his strength. On the eve of the election he was extremely despondent.

'Lord Sandwich's talk' he declared 'is that he has a majority in the regent house, not so in the non-regent. It is feared he has in both, but perhaps he knows some weaknesses on his own side to which we are strangers[2].'

Clearly neither side had anything approaching an adequate margin of safety, and in these circumstances it was incumbent upon Hardwicke's supporters to be ready with a policy in the event of the defeat of their candidate. They did not however find this task at all easy. Though they were in general agreement that, if Lord Hardwicke's Grace failed to pass the Senate, the Vice-Chancellor must, either at the same or at a subsequent congregation, submit a Grace for the appointment of Sandwich, they were by no means united in opinion as to what should be done if both candidates were rejected. It was the Bishop of Lincoln who first suggested that it might be well to be prepared for such a contingency, and that, if both Hardwicke and Sandwich failed to secure election, the Vice-Chancellor

[1] Add. MS. 32957, f. 137. [2] Add. MS. 32957, f. 376.

should bring forward a Grace for the appointment of the Duke of Grafton[1]. Much could be urged in favour of this proposal. It would undoubtedly be easier to persuade members of the Senate to vote against Lord Sandwich's Grace if they knew that another candidate was in readiness: and there was also reason to fear that, unless he was forestalled, Sandwich, if both he and Hardwicke were defeated, might place his adversaries in a very difficult position by arranging for the new Lord Townshend to be proposed to the Senate for election as High Steward. It was known that Charles Townshend would not canvass against his brother, and Newcastle expressed himself extremely doubtful 'how far the other Townshends would act[2].' Thus the supporters of Hardwicke would be divided amongst themselves; and this disaster might easily happen if they did not safeguard against it by agreeing to support the Duke of Grafton.

As Grafton was quite willing to be thus used[3], and as the Vice-Chancellor gave a private assurance of his readiness to nominate him[4], the Bishop of Lincoln's proposal was approved by most of the party[5], and would almost certainly have been accepted if it had not been for the opposition of Lord Hardwicke and Charles Yorke. Despite his indifference and lack of interest, Hardwicke desired to be nominated again if he and Sandwich were rejected at the first trial[6], though it was quite obvious that a new candidate would have a much

[1] Add. MS. 32956, f. 279.   [2] Add. MS. 32957, f. 87.
[3] Add. MS. 32957, f. 55.   [4] Add. MS. 32956, f. 310.
[5] Add. MS. 32957, f. 55, f. 87. 'I am greatly embarrassed about this second man' wrote Newcastle on March 14th. 'I find all our university friends here, Dr Powel, Spanish Charles, etc. think that without we have a second man ready and known to be so, if once Lord Hardwicke is stopt in either house, Lord Sandwich will certainly be chose.' Add. MS. 32957, f. 55.
[6] Add. MS. 32957, f. 55.

THE UNIVERSITY AND POLITICIANS

better chance of success. Charles Yorke equally objected to the proposal. He argued that no third candidate was needed as, if Hardwicke was defeated, Sandwich would certainly be elected; and that, even if both Hardwicke and Sandwich were rejected, the third candidate should be a person in favour with the court and ministry and not like Grafton an active member of the parliamentary opposition[1]. It is true that Charles Yorke admitted that 'this matter must be settled by the Vice-Chancellor and the rest of our principal friends at Cambridge in confidence, just at the eve of the election[2]'; but it was perfectly clear that both he and his brother very much disliked the proposal[3] which was consequently dropped. As late as March 25th the Bishop of Lincoln was urging that

it is highly necessary that another person on our side should be ready, that our friends should all be apprized of this, and that he should be immediately proposed as one whom we are determined to support in the second trial of our strength[4];

but no steps were taken, and the Hardwicke party went into action unprepared to meet a situation which was not unlikely to arise. That no such situation arose, and that therefore no ill consequences ensued from failing to prepare for it, cannot be pleaded in excuse of Hardwicke and his brother. They were not more farsighted than their friends but only more selfish.

Fortunately there was not the same difficulty in

---

[1] Add. MS. 32957, f. 85.   [2] *Ibid*.

[3] In an undated letter to his brother, Charles Yorke described a conversation he had had with Newcastle. 'Then the Duke mentioned (what he called a thing undecided and an absolute secret) whether the Duke of Grafton would not be a proper nominee. I spoke with great regard of the Duke of Grafton but said, if it failed in your case, it was likely to fail more strongly in his case, because his nomination would be seen more in the light of opposition as things now are.' Add. MS. 35631, f. 9.

[4] Add. MS. 32957, f. 263.

102 THE UNIVERSITY AND POLITICIANS

settling certain other points. At a meeting on March 27th, attended by the Vice-Chancellor, Talbot, and Hardwicke's leading supporters, it was agreed that, if the Grace was rejected, the Vice-Chancellor should delay bringing forward a Grace for Lord Sandwich's appointment until the following day, and that if

the Scrutators in the non-regent house should make different returns, which might happen if one of them admitted those votes that the other rejected as bad or disputable,...the Vice-Chancellor ought to dissolve the congregation and defer the election till the legality of the votes in question should be determined by proper authority[1].

There was also general agreement that it would be unwise to veto Sandwich's Grace in the Caput for fear of provoking anger; and though Talbot urged that 'the employing a negative in the Caput as a last resource would be less invidious and exceptionable if a majority or at least a moiety of the Caput could be induced to join in the negative,' the suggestion was not warmly received[2].

Excitement ran high in Cambridge on the eve of the election. From five o'clock on the afternoon of Thursday March 29th, a committee of the Hardwicke party 'sat at the Rose, receiving intelligence from those who had been appointed in each college to bring in accurate lists of all who were then arrived[3],' and it is easy to imagine the eagerness with which these lists were scanned. As late as the morning of the appointed day, a certain number of voters, whose absence had been counted upon, arrived to support Lord Sandwich[4]; and

[1] Add. MS. 32957, f. 301.
[2] Add. MS. 32957, f. 301. Talbot's proposal was deferred for consideration at a meeting on the following day; and though we do not know what happened at this second conference, it is improbable that the suggestion was accepted.
[3] Add. MS. 35657, f. 150.   [4] Add. MS. 35657, f. 150.

THE UNIVERSITY AND POLITICIANS 103

it was doubtful up to the last moment whether the Master of Trinity intended to vote. Pleading ill-health, but more probably afraid of being maltreated by the undergraduates of his own college, Dr Smith announced on March 29th that he did not propose to attend the congregation; and, though he adhered to this resolution, his adversaries not unnaturally suspected that he was seeking to deceive them, and thought it unsafe to count upon his absence[1]. There were also a certain number of members of the Senate who, after professing to be neutral, finally decided to vote for one or other of the candidates[2]. Consequently it was not until the last moment that the Hardwicke party was able to decide the very important question of the proper distribution of the doctors between the two houses. Despite earlier gloomy prophecies to the contrary, Hardwicke preserved the advantage he had always had in doctors, counting thirty-one among his supporters to Sandwich's twenty-two. It was calculated that Sandwich would need to place all his doctors but one in the regents' house; and, working on this assumption, the leaders of the Hardwicke party reckoned that Sandwich would have in the regents' house one hundred and seven or one hundred and eight votes, including his twenty-one doctors; and that therefore, to ensure the passing of the Grace, twenty-six of Hardwicke's doctors must be added to the eighty-three masters of arts in that house who had pledged themselves to vote for the Grace. This however would only leave Hardwicke with five doctors to use in the non-regents' house; and though it was calculated that this would be sufficient if the Master of Trinity absented himself, Hardwicke's

---

[1] Add. MS. 32957, f. 398; Add. MS. 35657, f. 150. Their suspicions of the Master of Trinity were strengthened by seeing his carriage at his door on the morning of March 30th.

[2] Add. MS. 32957, f. 398.

friends were too suspicious of the Master's sincerity to take the risk. They therefore decided to keep six doctors in the non-regents' house, thus only leaving twenty-five for use among the regents[1]; and in so doing made a blunder which was to have most unfortunate consequences. They certainly would have done better to have risked the appearance of the Master of Trinity; but they can hardly be blamed for refusing to believe that such an ardent supporter of Sandwich would be found wanting at the last.

It was indeed impossible to foretell the victor, for seldom have the combatants in a university contest been more evenly matched. In Trinity, King's, Pembroke and Caius, Sandwich had many more supporters than his rival, and not a single vote from St Catharine's was cast against him. But in Peterhouse, Clare, Queens', Jesus, and Christ's, Hardwicke's adherents were in a large majority, and his own college, Corpus, was almost to a man on his side[2]. There was however very much less difference of opinion among the undergraduates who were for the most part very enthusiastic supporters of Lord Hardwicke, and their enthusiasm was not always displayed in a decorous fashion. 'The lads, I hear,' wrote the Master of Magdalene on March 20th, 'assembled about King's Lodge on Thursday night last, made a riot, and cried aloud "Bring out your daughters, Jemmy Twitcher is come[3]."' Fearing a disturbance on the election day, the Vice-Chancellor forbade undergraduates admission to the Senate house and enrolled special constables for the maintenance of

[1] There is one list (Add. MS. 32957, f. 326) which gives twenty-four doctors voting for the Grace and twenty against it in the regents' house; but the account in the text is based upon a letter from the Bishop of Lincoln who was likely to know what really happened.

[2] Add. MS. 35657, f. 69. St John's, Magdalene, Emmanuel and Sidney were more or less equally divided in their sympathies.

[3] Add. MS. 32957, f. 193.

order[1]. He also took the precaution of conferring with the Scrutators and Proctors 'about the manner of taking the votes[2].' He suggested that the senior Scrutator in the non-regent house and the senior Proctor in the regent house should, as each vote was given, mark it down on his paper in the presence of his colleague and the voter, that the junior Scrutator and Proctor should then do the same; and that, at the end of each row, the two Scrutators and the two Proctors should compare their totals[3]. It cannot be said that these precautions were unnecessary, for the traditional method of recording the votes was extremely unsatisfactory. It was the custom for each Scrutator and Proctor to be provided with a long scroll of paper on which were drawn two lines, against which were written placet and non-placet respectively; and a vote was recorded by a stroke across either one or other of the two lines[4]. It is clear that an unscrupulous or careless person might easily mark a vote on the wrong line; and as the parties were so evenly matched, and the Scrutators and Proctors themselves supporters of one or other of the candidates, it was clearly expedient to guard against error or fraud.

The best laid plans however are often those which most easily go astray; but it is improbable that the most gloomy prophet of disaster ever anticipated that they would go as sadly astray as they did. The proceedings on March 30th were singularly rich in sensational incidents. At the morning congregation Lord Hardwicke's Grace was read for the first time and passed by the Caput, after which the Vice-Chancellor dissolved the congregation[5]. At two o'clock in the afternoon the members of the Senate again assembled in congrega-

[1] Add. MS. 5852, f. 147, f. 148; Add. MS. 32957, f. 396.
[2] Add. MS. 32957, f. 265.   [3] Add. MS. 35657, f. 81.
[4] Terrae Filius, no. 5.   [5] Add. MS. 5852, f. 147, f. 148.

tion; and it was noticed that the undergraduates, who crowded the approaches to the Senate house, cheered the supporters of Lord Hardwicke as they arrived[1]. After the voters had taken their seats in their respective houses the Grace was read for the second time; and then began the scrutiny by the two Scrutators in the non-regents' house. They adopted the method suggested by the Vice-Chancellor, comparing their figures at the end of each row; and, having completed the scrutiny, declared the Grace carried by one hundred and three placets to one hundred and one non-placets. The announcement was greeted by loud cheers which were taken up by the undergraduates outside[2]. Then began the scrutiny in the regents' house by the two Proctors, Longmire of Peterhouse and Forster of St John's. They started like the Scrutators by comparing their numbers at the end of each row; but it is important to note that they made no such comparison at the end of the last row of all, and that while Longmire, the senior Proctor, recorded the votes in the usual and approved fashion, Forster practised 'a strange manner of marking in a method unknown to the Schools[3].' At the end of the last row, when all votes had been taken except those of the Proctors themselves, Longmire glanced at his paper and calculated that an equal number of placets and non-placets had been given for and against the Grace. He then declared his own vote, which was placet, in a loud tone, and marked it down on his paper; and, as he noticed the junior Proctor simultaneously record a vote, he concluded that his placet had been overheard and marked on the junior Proctor's list. But unfortunately Forster was hard of

[1] Add. MS. 35657, f. 150.
[2] Add. MS. 5852, f. 147, f. 148; Add. MS. 32957, f. 318, f. 398; Add. MS. 35657, f. 64, f. 150.
[3] Add. MS. 35640, f. 117; Add. MS. 35657, f. 181.

THE UNIVERSITY AND POLITICIANS 107

hearing, and the vote he had entered was his own which was non-placet.

Thus each Proctor had recorded his own vote and omitted to record the vote of his colleague; and, if they had at once compared their papers, they would have discovered their error and seen that the votes were equal. But they failed to take this precaution, and began to add up the votes. Their totals of course disagreed, Longmire making one hundred and eight placets to one hundred and seven non-placets, while according to Forster the placets were one hundred and seven and the non-placets one hundred and eight. While they were engaged in puzzling over their difference, one of the Bedells, who had taken a look at their papers, proceeded to inform the Vice-Chancellor that the two Proctors disagreed; and at once the rumour spread that Forster had marked Longmire as voting non-placet. This was unfortunate as it helped to confuse the issue; but it was plausible enough to gain easy acceptance and was of course readily believed by Hardwicke's followers, two of whom came forward to testify that they had seen Forster mark Longmire as voting non-placet.

While the parties were wrangling, the two Proctors discovered that each had omitted to record the other's vote, and thereupon agreed that both the placet and non-placet votes numbered one hundred and eight. They then appeared before the Vice-Chancellor who enquired whether they were able to declare placet or non-placet, adding that, if they could not make either return, they must proceed to a second scrutiny. It was unfortunate that the Vice-Chancellor at this stage suggested another scrutiny, as it encouraged Sandwich's followers in the belief that he was acting in Hardwicke's interest. There was no doubt that a second scrutiny was necessary if the Proctors disagreed; and probably the Vice-Chancellor, misled by the Bedell, honestly believed that there was a disagreement. But the two Proctors now concurred in returning the votes as equal; and it does not seem to have been known for certain whether an equality of votes involved the loss of a Grace or a second scrutiny. It is noteworthy that a follower of Hardwicke privately expressed the opinion that, if the votes were equal, the Grace was lost[1]; though on the other hand it was contended that

if the votes are equal, it is agreeable to the constitution of the said university in similar cases that the votes should be numbered a second or even a third time before a negative is declared or reported on the Grace proposed[2].

Clearly it was a disputable point; and no sooner had the Vice-Chancellor mentioned the possibility of a second scrutiny than certain of Sandwich's friends declared that no second scrutiny ought to be held, as the votes were equal and the Grace therefore lost. In reply to the Vice-Chancellor, Longmire declared that as the votes were equal he could make no return, but that he was ready to go to a second scrutiny; while Forster answered that, though prepared to make a return, he could not do so without the concurrence of his fellow Proctor, and that in no circumstances would he go to a second scrutiny. Meanwhile the followers of Hardwicke were loudly calling for a second scrutiny, and the followers of Sandwich equally loudly urging Forster not to comply with the demand. When the confusion was at its height, knocking was heard on the Senate house door; and it was believed that the Master of Trinity was seeking admission. Dr Smith had taken a drive in the morning, but, being visited on his return by Lord Townshend and Lord Weymouth, he had promised them that he would attend the second congregation. Yet he had not appeared, though urgent

[1] Add. MS. 32957, f. 318.
[2] Add. MS. 35657, f. 75; see also Add. MS. 35640, f. 117.

THE UNIVERSITY AND POLITICIANS 109

reminders had been sent him; and therefore when the knocking was heard, it was hoped by the one party and feared by the other that he had at last summoned up courage to come. If admitted, his vote would decide the election in favour of Sandwich if there was a second scrutiny; and therefore, while the Provost of King's called upon the Vice-Chancellor to admit Dr Smith, the Master of Magdalene declared that 'the mistake which was made amongst the numbers then present, was not to be rectified by the admission of a new vote[1].' The Vice-Chancellor ruled that the door could not be opened, and it was then discovered that the wrangle had been purposeless, as the seeker for admission was not the Master of Trinity but Beilby Porteous, a future Bishop of London, who, having voted as a non-regent for Hardwicke, had left the Senate house to obtain refreshment and now desired to return[2].

The Vice-Chancellor having decided that the doors of the Senate house should not be opened, the dispute over a second scrutiny was vigorously resumed. Sir Edward Simpson, Master of Trinity Hall, who as a lawyer was entitled to express an opinion, supported the Vice-Chancellor in the contention that there should be a second scrutiny; but the junior Proctor obstinately refused to be either commanded or persuaded, and, as it was now nearly six o'clock in the evening, the Vice-Chancellor dissolved the congregation. It is reported that 'he sent for the Registrary and Mr Bennet, Esquire Bedel, Notary Public, up to his table and before them asked the senior Proctor, Mr Longmire, if he was ready to make a declaration with regard to the scrutiny for an High Steward in the regent house. He answered to this effect: that he did not see how he could declare it but was ready to take another scrutiny. Then the Vice-Chancellor put the same question to the

[1] Add. MS. 32957, f. 394.   [2] Add. MS. 35640, f. 117.

other Proctor, Mr Forster, who answered he was ready to make a declaration if the senior Proctor would join with him but did not see how he could do it by himself. Being asked if he would assist in taking a second scrutiny, said he would not or words to that effect. Then the Vice-Chancellor immediately said: "I admonish you for this omission in your duty." The Vice-Chancellor then said: "I suppose I have power to continue or dissolve this congregation"; and some persons near him saying he certainly had, said: "Then I will dissolve it," and accordingly went to the chair at the foot pace and dissolved it[1].' The doors were then opened, and, as the members of the Senate passed out, the undergraduates rushed in and

proceeded immediately to an election without one discordant voice, and, after having chaired Lord Hardwicke's proxy and fixed the name of Hardwicke above the Chancellor's chair, dispersed quietly to their respective homes[2].

The proceedings reflect no little discredit upon the university. Nothing could have been more undignified than the futile and unseemly wrangle between men who were hopelessly confused as to what had actually happened; and the Vice-Chancellor is blameworthy for his failure to maintain order. It is moreover very surprising that there should have been any doubt as to the proper action to be taken if there was an equality of votes. Both parties were well aware that the contest was going to be extremely close, and surely no great foresight was needed to envisage the possibility of the candidates receiving an equal number of votes in one

[1] Add. MS. 5852, f. 147, f. 148.
[2] Add. MS. 35657, f. 150. Accounts of the proceedings will be found in Add. MS. 32957, f. 310, f. 312, f. 316, f. 318, f. 343, f. 355, f. 394, f. 396, f. 398, f. 425; Add. MS. 35640, f. 117; Add. MS. 35657, f. 64, f. 66, f. 75, f. 81, f. 150; Add. MS. 5852, f. 147, f. 148.

THE UNIVERSITY AND POLITICIANS 111

or other of the two houses. Yet, when the possibility actually happened, no one was in a position to say authoritatively what procedure should be adopted.

The earliest information received by Newcastle of the great event came from Charles Townshend who wrongly reported that Forster had blundered in marking Longmire as voting against the Grace, that the placets therefore exceeded the non-placets by one, and that Longmire refused to admit that the votes were equal[1]. Consequently the Duke concluded that the battle was won, and that it only remained to settle 'how to put my Lord Hardwicke in possession of the office to which he is elected[2]'; but he soon heard the true story and was deeply distressed to learn that another election might be necessary. He was an old man and felt unequal to the strain of resuming the struggle with Sandwich.

'For God's sake' he implored 'don't let us have all this trouble over again if it can be avoided. Dr Smith will come to the next congregation, and we shall have all the votes in North and South of Europe and America brought upon us[3].'

The trouble however could not be warded off by Newcastle's passionate desire to avoid it; and he became still more despondent on hearing from Charles Yorke that the Vice-Chancellor, by dissolving the congregation before the Proctors had made a declaration, had annulled the proceedings, and that 'no remedy is to be had either at law or anywhere else, and consequently we must proceed to a new election[4].' Newcastle however was not prepared to face a new election if it could be possibly avoided, and as the only alternative policy was an appeal to the courts of law, he was forced to advocate legal proceedings. On learning that the Vice-Chancellor was not prepared 'to suffer any Grace to be read or to pass, relating to the late or any future election

[1] Add. MS. 32957, f. 310. [2] Add. MS. 32957, f. 347.
[3] Ibid. [4] Add. MS. 32957, f. 404.

of an High Steward, until Lord Hardwicke shall have determined what course he shall take for the support of his election,' the Duke interviewed Hardwicke, called a meeting of the 'four Mr Townshends and Mr Charles Yorke,' and issued instructions for the collection of material for a law-suit[1].

'The great point' he told the Master of Magdalene 'is to ascertain the number...present and how each man voted, if it can be done, and to know the constitution of the university and the method of their proceedings in these cases, particularly with regard to the refusal of the junior Proctor to consent to a scrutiny or telling over again, which is always the practice and was now denied[2].'

While Newcastle and his friends were preparing a plan of campaign, Sandwich was considering his position which was indeed as dubious as that of his rival. The King and George Grenville were probably anxious for him to withdraw from a contest upon which they had never wanted him to enter[3], but it was asking not a little that he should acknowledge defeat and desert his friends when it still remained possible that he might emerge triumphant. Adopting the standpoint that Lord Hardwicke's Grace had been lost in the regents' house as the votes were equal, he contended that the Vice-Chancellor was now in duty bound to bring forward a Grace for his appointment as High Steward; and that, in the event of the Vice-Chancellor refusing to do so, recourse must be had to the law. Yet he did not desire to use coercion if gentler means could be effective; and he cautiously felt his way before definitely deciding upon a course of action. In the letters of thanks which he issued to his supporters, he mentioned that he still regarded himself as a candidate

---

[1] Add. MS. 32957, f. 417.   [2] Add. MS. 32957, f. 419.
[3] Add. MS. 32957, f. 430.

THE UNIVERSITY AND POLITICIANS 113

for the High Stewardship[1]; and he followed up this announcement by a visit to Cambridge. The professed object of this visit was personally to thank his friends for their assistance and support[2]; but he had other and more important designs which it was as well not to publish abroad. He hoped to persuade the Vice-Chancellor to bring forward a Grace for his appointment as High Steward; but, if his arguments failed to convince, he thought of petitioning the King in Council for redress of his wrongs, and was anxious to discover what his adherents in the university thought of such a petition and how many were prepared to sign it[3].

Accompanied by his friends, Lord Townshend and Lord Carysfort, he arrived in Cambridge on the evening of Thursday April 5th and stayed at Trinity Lodge. By accepting Dr Smith's hospitality he doubtless intended to show him that his conduct on the day of the election had been forgiven; but it is doubtful whether Sandwich was wise to honour by his presence a college of which the undergraduates were such enthusiastic supporters of his rival. On the evening he arrived, an effigy, decorated with a wig belonging to one of the Tutors, was flung across the lamp over the Lodge door[4]; but he was well-hardened by this time to manifestations of public disapproval and was unlikely to be worried by the insults of voteless undergraduates. He spent his first evening in Cambridge in conferring with his leading supporters[5]; and on the following morning started on

[1] Add. MS. 32958, f. 3; Add. MS. 32957, f. 425.
[2] Add. MS. 32958, f. 7.   [3] Add. MS. 32958, f. 5, f. 15, f. 49.
[4] Add. MS. 32958, f. 15. *The Scrutator*, No. 3: 'I am afraid' wrote the author of the *Scrutator* 'there is more than one Tutor in the world who ought to be hanged up, not by proxy but in propria persona; for I am sure, as it is sometimes managed, it is a very infamous and pickpocket employment.'
[5] Dr Brooke of St John's, Brockett of Trinity, the junior Proctor and others; Add. MS. 32958, f. 49.

WUC

114 THE UNIVERSITY AND POLITICIANS

a round of visits. He first waited on the Vice-Chancellor to whom he presented both an olive-branch and a sword. While professing greatly to desire the restoration of peace to the university, he made it perfectly clear that he was not prepared to secure that peace by tamely submitting to defeat; and, though he asked the Vice-Chancellor to suggest a way of ending the dispute, he was at pains to say that he had 'prepared materials for a ligitation.' 'I should have made some reply,' reported the Vice-Chancellor to Hardwicke, 'but his Lordship said he did not expect an immediate answer, and then left me[1].'

After leaving the Vice-Chancellor, Sandwich went to Peterhouse, where he called upon the Master, Dr Law, and Longmire, the senior Proctor. The Master had loyally supported Hardwicke, though he was a poor man and anxious for advancement in the church; and doubtless Sandwich had hopes of winning him over. But Dr Law was not to be won; and to Sandwich's declaration that he had come to Cambridge to restore peace, he retorted that

he had heard that his Lordship was come down with a petition to be signed by his friends here and to be presented to the King and Council, in order to oblige the Vice-Chancellor or Proctors to do more than they thought they ought to do[2].

There was clearly nothing to be done with the Master, and the visit to the senior Proctor was equally disappointing. He hoped to extract from Longmire useful information about what had happened on March 30th,

[1] Add. MS. 35657, f. 155; Add. MS. 32958, f. 13. Newcastle was puzzled whether Sandwich meant 'the settling some method for finishing the present dispute and proceeding to another election (which I rather think was his meaning) or the finding out some third person who might be agreeable to both parties and come in without any opposition.' Add. MS. 32958, f. 86.
[2] Add. MS. 32958, f. 51.

THE UNIVERSITY AND POLITICIANS

and possibly might have done so if Lord Townshend, who accompanied him, had not badly blundered.

'From Dr Law' reported the Master of Jesus 'they went to Mr Longmire where they stayed not long; for somebody rapping at the door, and Mr Longmire, leaving his inner door open whilst he stepped out to the outer one, he heard Lord Townshend say "My Lord, you are wrong, you should not talk but hear him," upon which Mr Longmire on his return thought proper to shut up his mouth, and they soon left him[1].'

On the same day Sandwich and his two companions dined in the hall of Trinity; and, to mark their disapproval, the undergraduates, with the single exception of a certain William Lowther, not only absented themselves from hall but collected in the court outside and serenaded the diners with cheers for Lord Hardwicke[2]. It says much for Sandwich's perseverance that, in spite of these many rebuffs, he remained in Cambridge until the afternoon of Monday April 8th, hard at work the whole time. He was entertained in Caius, dined with the Provost of King's, supped with the Master of St Catharine's, and 'endeavoured to see everyone of those who voted against Lord Hardwicke's Grace and a few more.' Yet he was certainly disappointed by his visit. He had seen no sign of wavering among Hardwicke's friends, and his idea of proceeding by petition to the King in Council was so unfavourably received that he abandoned it[3].

[1] Add. MS. 32958, f. 49.
[2] Add. MS. 32958, f. 7, f. 15, f. 21. Lowther was a kinsman of Sir William Lowther who was a supporter of the government and Sandwich; and therefore his presence in hall may have been due more to political conviction than to greed.
[3] Possibly Sandwich discovered that, as the university did not recognise the crown as visitor, an appeal for redress against a Vice-Chancellor must go to the court of King's Bench and not to the King in Council. Newcastle, writing to Charles Yorke on April 19th, 1764, says 'The Bishop of Ely also wishes to see you on the subject of the

116 THE UNIVERSITY AND POLITICIANS

Yet though his visit had been a failure, it was rich in consequences for a certain college of the university. The Master of Trinity was greatly annoyed by the conduct of the undergraduates on the occasion when Sandwich dined in hall, and was determined that they should feel the weight of his displeasure. He desired that they should be commanded to sign a declaration, confessing that by their conduct they had debased themselves, dishonoured the college, and merited the penalty of expulsion[1]; but as he could take no action without the Seniority, consisting of the eight senior Fellows, it was by no means certain that he could execute his project. Of the eight seniors six were supporters of Hardwicke and therefore certain to oppose power of visitation in the crown; and, particularly, as to the declaration of my Lord Chief Justice Pratt in Dr Bentley's case to Dr Snape, then Vice-Chancellor, and the members of the university who attended the King's Bench with him. He asked the Vice-Chancellor whether they claimed or admitted any local visitor or acknowledged the power of the crown to visit. Dr Snape answered no, neither, that they insisted that the trial of those complaints was to be only in the Vice-Chancellor's court. Upon which the Chief Justice replied, 'If you have no visitor, the court of King's Bench shall take cognizance of this complaint.' Add. MS. 32958, f. 172. See also Add. MS. 32958, f. 84, and Monk's *Life of Bentley*, II, 204.

[1] The document ran as follows: 'It being notorious that not one of the scholars of the house, and but one of the pensioners, did appear in the college hall on Friday, the 6th April last, when, by invitation from the Master and seniors, the Earl of Sandwich, Lord Townshend and Lord Carysfort were entertained there; we, whose names are underwritten, do confess that, being then in commons, we did knowingly and wilfully conspire to be absent from the hall, as above mentioned, in open contempt and defiance of all decency, discipline and government; and having thus debased ourselves and dishonoured the college by branding it with disgrace and infamy, we confess we have incurred the penalty of expulsion by the 38th statute, de poena majorum criminum et minorum; and do receive from our governours this admonition in order to expulsion instead of expulsion itself which we have justly deserved.' Trinity College Admission Book; Add. MS. 32958, f. 383.

THE UNIVERSITY AND POLITICIANS 117

any punishment of the undergraduates for demonstrating against Sandwich; but nevertheless Dr Smith, in spite of all difficulties, succeeded in attaining his end. It was provided that if, when the Seniority was summoned, any members of that body were absent, their places should be taken by those who came immediately after the seniors on the roll of Fellows; and, by biding his time, the Master was able to obtain a majority for his proposal. He waited until three of the seniors opposed to him were away, and then summoned a meeting of the Seniority, knowing quite well that the places of two at least of the three absent members would be taken by his own personal adherents, and that he would thus have a majority.

'On Friday last,' wrote Backhouse to Newcastle on Sunday May 13th, 'when Davis, Meredith and Newbon (our friends in the present cause) were out of college, the Master, having previously converted Powell and Place, summoned the seniors to confirm the sentence he had drawn up for the undergraduates, which at last, after a sort, he effected....Mr Brockett was of the Seniority, and, I need scarce tell your Lordship, most violent in his counsels. The next day he declared in a public coffee-house that, now the sword was drawn in Trinity college, it should never be sheathed whilst there was one left standing in the field. To give your Lordship a specimen of the Master's behaviour at the meeting, I mention the following circumstance, viz., when he was pressed to a non-plus about the true sense and meaning of a clause in the statute, de pona (*sic*) majorum criminum, he commanded me in a magisterial strain to be silent, alledging this reason for it, that the interpretation of the statutes belonged to the Master alone and the seniors had nothing to do with it[1].'

[1] Add. MS. 32958, f. 382. 'The four seniors who concurred with the Master (whose concurrence made a majority) were Dr Walker, Mr Powell, Mr Place, Mr Brockett. The Master availed himself of the absence of Dr Davis and Mr Newbon; for, by their going out of college, Place and Brockett came into the number of the eight resident seniors.' Add. MS. 32958, f. 429.

The Master however found it easier to subdue the seniors than the undergraduates, of whom only four signed the admonition when first called upon to do so. The remainder, knowing that if expelled they would be readily taken in at other colleges, raised the flag of rebellion and defied the authorities[1]. The Master and seniors, confronted by such resistance, could not immediately capitulate and withdraw the admonition, but it was equally certain that they could not proceed to a wholesale expulsion and reduce the college to four undergraduates. As a compromise they decreed on May 14th that 'none of the pensioners, who will not subscribe the admonition to-morrow evening after chapel, shall be permitted to offer himself a candidate for scholarships'; and, as only a portion of the undergraduates were affected by this order, it was agreed to defer the punishment of the scholars and those pensioners, not competing for scholarships, for future consideration[2].

Only a single undergraduate, James Carrington, was induced, by anxiety for a scholarship, to sign the admonition: the others continued impenitent and doubtless thoroughly enjoyed combining the rôles of rebel and martyr. They were moreover encouraged to continue their resistance by the knowledge that the action of the authorities was widely condemned. It was reported that legal proceedings were threatened by the father of an undergraduate who was denied admission to his Westminster scholarship[3]; and Lord Chief Justice Pratt marked his disapproval by removing his nephew, Harding, from the college.

'Lord Chief Justice Pratt' wrote the Master of Jesus to Newcastle on June 23rd 'has at length taken away his nephew, Harding, from Trinity college and from the university: there

[1] Add. MS. 32958, f. 382, f. 476.   [2] Add. MS. 32958, f. 386.
[3] Add. MS. 35640, f. 129.

has been much altercation about it. The Master has been pressed to declare what punishment of the scholars will satisfy him but cannot be brought to speak plain. The Chief Justice therefore, in his last letter to Mr Whisson, says that he cannot wish his nephew to sign so base a submission as is proposed, nor suffer him to stay in the college exposed to the future vengeance of the Master and seniors, to be wreaked upon him at a time when they can most essentially hurt him[1].'

On the same day that Dr Caryl communicated this information to Newcastle, the Master of Trinity, at last realising that he was contending against insuperable odds, surrendered; and at his suggestion the Seniority passed an act of oblivion.

'In order to restore tranquillity and time for study,' runs the entry in the college Admission Book, 'the Master and seniors have pardoned all the offenders in the case above mentioned, or any way relating to it, even those who refused to sign the admonition[2].'

The surrender was thus complete and unconditional, and the episode is of a piece with all Dr Smith's activities on behalf of Sandwich. As a mathematician he was not particularly distinguished and as a politician he was beneath contempt. By bullying his Fellows to vote for Sandwich he had made many converts to Hardwicke, and by attempting to punish the undergraduates for an offence which a wise man would have left unnoticed, he seriously undermined the discipline of the college. He can perhaps be most fittingly described as a pinchbeck Bentley[3].

[1] Add. MS. 32960, f. 46.   [2] Trinity College Admission Book.
[3] In spite of the act of oblivion the Master and his allies appear to have continued a petty persecution. 'The act of oblivion' wrote the Master of Jesus on June 30th 'is not so absolute as it was given out to be; for one of the young gentlemen has since asked for a bene discessit to remove to Queens' and been refused; though it was what he intended before Lord Sandwich came down, and no objection, I am told, can be made to him but his absence from hall on that night.' Add. MS. 32960, f. 143.

While Dr Smith had been quarrelling with his undergraduates, Newcastle and his friends had been collecting evidence in support of Hardwicke's election; and the task was not an easy one. If a second election was to be avoided, it was necessary to show that one or more of those who had voted in the regents' house for Sandwich, were either disqualified from voting or had voted in the wrong house; and it was therefore with great joy that the Bishop of Norwich told Newcastle that Thomas Pitt, who had non-placeted the Grace in the regents' house on March 30th, was already at that time a non-regent. Thomas Pitt[1], who had been a Fellow Commoner at Clare, was admitted to his degree of master of arts on July 18th, 1758, and, save for exceptional circumstances, he would still have been a regent on the day of the voting upon Lord Hardwicke's Grace, as the five years of regency were dated not from the admission to the degree but from the creation at the subsequent 'Commencement.' Pitt however had received his degree by royal mandate, and those who received mandate degrees were 'created immediately and their creation makes their commencement[2].' He had therefore ceased to be a regent by July 18th, 1763.

It seems improbable that Sandwich's supporters were unaware of this distinction between mandate and other degrees; and it is more likely that either they did not know that Pitt had taken his degree by mandate or knew that he had done so and took the risk of the truth being discovered by their adversaries. But whether they were careless or cunning, they were delivered into the hands of their opponents. Newcastle, ever haunted by the fear that there might have to be another election,

[1] He was a nephew of William Pitt, Earl of Chatham, and was later created Lord Camelford.
[2] Add. MS. 32958, f. 23; see also Add. MS. 32879, f. 463.

rose at once to the heights of optimism and jumped to the conclusion that Hardwicke's election was already to all intents and purposes established.

'For, as I conceive it,' he wrote, 'the election is already over and the demonstration we have...that Mr Pitt's vote must be set aside, we have a clear majority in both houses in support of your nomination of the Earl of Hardwicke, and God forbid that in this country there should be anywhere a right and no remedy. But where that remedy is properly to be applied for, whether to you as Vice-Chancellor, to your court, or to a congregation to be summoned by you for that purpose, or, as I rather fancy will be the case, to the court of King's Bench for a mandamus to carry the election of my Lord Hardwicke into execution and to put his Lordship into his office to which he is duly elected —you, sir, and our friends in the university, and Mr Yorke and Mr Wilbraham (who are my Lord Hardwicke's council) must determine[1].'

The Duke however was to discover that lawyers decline to be hurried, and that it is their business to see obstacles and difficulties not apparent to the lay mind. Charles Yorke was inclined at first to think that the wisest course would be to allow Sandwich to make the first move[2]; but in any case he refused to commit himself to a plan of campaign[3] without knowing 'the rules, customs and laws of the university.' When this information had been collected, he pointed out that there was no evidence that Pitt had non-placeted the Grace, and that until this evidence was forthcoming it was useless to proceed. It was by no means certain however that this very necessary piece of evidence could be produced. The Proctors were bound by oath and statute not to reveal a vote, and Pitt could not be compelled to declare how he had voted. Charles Yorke was even doubtful if a court of law would admit his

[1] Add. MS. 32958, f. 86.   [2] Add. MS. 32958, f. 303.
[3] Add. MS. 32958, f. 182, f. 192.

122 THE UNIVERSITY AND POLITICIANS

evidence if he offered it of his own accord[1]; but, as this was at least doubtful, it was agreed that Talbot should write and ask Pitt to 'make an affidavit of his having given a non-placet in the regents' house on the 30th of March[2].' Nearly three weeks elapsed before Talbot received Pitt's reply which was a firm refusal.

'I must say' he answered 'I should look upon myself as guilty of very great injustice if I could be prevailed upon, in so ligitable a point, to furnish weapons to one party against the other, before it is determined whether I can properly be called upon to give evidence at all in this affair[3].'

His delay in answering had made his refusal a foregone conclusion, and, before his reply had been received, another expedient was under consideration. With the subtlety of a theologian the Bishop of Lincoln pointed out that, though a Proctor was bound by oath and statute not to reveal a vote, this prohibition could not apply to a vote illegally given, which was indeed no vote at all. The Bishop therefore arranged that Longmire should be asked whether he would reveal Pitt's vote if convinced that it was invalid; and the senior Proctor replied that if it could be proved to him, beyond all shadow of doubt, that Pitt was a non-regent on the day that Lord Hardwicke's Grace was voted upon, he would regard himself as not bound by his oath. Consequently the Master of Jesus and others set to work to collect 'evidence, as far as we can, for Mr Longmire's satisfaction[4]'; and their labours were successful, for by about the middle of June the senior Proctor had undertaken to reveal the important secret.

The conversion of Longmire enabled immediate action to be taken. It was arranged that a patent of

---
[1] Add. MS. 32958, f. 359; Add. MS. 32959, f. 3, f. 75.
[2] Add. MS. 35640, f. 138; Add. MS. 32958, f. 376, f. 392.
[3] Add. MS. 35640, f. 140; see also f. 138, f. 470.
[4] Add. MS. 35640, f. 142.

THE UNIVERSITY AND POLITICIANS 123

Hardwicke's election as High Steward should be drawn up, and that the Vice-Chancellor, the two Scrutators and the two Proctors, as the seal-keepers of the university, should be asked to fix the seal of the university to it. But as the five seal-keepers had to be unanimous, it was certain that the request would be refused, the junior Scrutator and the junior Proctor both being supporters of Sandwich; and, in consequence of this refusal, the court of King's Bench could be petitioned for a writ of mandamus[1]. In accordance with this plan Lord Hardwicke's solicitor, Vernon, arrived in Cambridge, and, assisted by the Master of Jesus, drew up a patent of Hardwicke's election and then demanded of the five chest-keepers severally the seal to be put to it and wrote down their several answers. The Vice-Chancellor thought that my Lord Hardwicke had been fairly elected but, as he had not been duly declared so, he could not think himself at liberty to seal the patent. The senior Proctor and senior Scrutator answered in some such qualified manner: the other Proctor and Scrutator more bluntly. Mr Vernon afterwards waited upon them all together, assembled at the Vice-Chancellor's, tendered the patent and his commission from Lord Hardwicke, and then retired: in a few minutes he was called in and the Vice-Chancellor told him, in the name of them all, that they had considered his Lordship's demand but could not comply with it[2].

The refusal had of course been foreseen and anticipated; and during his stay in Cambridge Vernon had collected seven affidavits, including one from Longmire stating that Pitt had voted non-placet in the regents' house[3].

All was now ready for the case to be taken to the courts, and on June 28th the Solicitor-General, William De Grey, moved on behalf of Hardwicke in the court of King's Bench that the seal-keepers should show

---

[1] Add. MS. 32959, f. 304. [2] Add. MS. 32960, f. 56.
[3] Add. MS. 32960, f. 46.

cause for refusing to seal Lord Hardwicke's patent. At the suggestion of Lord Chief Justice Mansfield, who pointed out that the seal-keepers might fairly retort that, as the Proctors had made no return, they could not affix the seal, De Grey extended his motion; and finally,

the rule was granted by the court for showing cause on Monday se'nnight why three writs of mandamus should not issue; one to the Vice-Chancellor to hold a congregation, another to the Proctors to make a return of the Grace, and the third to the keepers of the chest to seal the patent[1].

On 'Monday se'nnight,' which was July 9th, Sandwich's counsel asked that his client should be allowed until the Michaelmas term to show cause, alleging that time was required for the collection of the necessary evidence; and the plea was allowed. 'This is the common way of proceeding in like cases[2],' wrote Dr Powell to Newcastle who however was too disappointed to accept comfort. Though he had always feared the proverbial delay of the law, he had continued to hope for a speedy settlement; and his anxiety was justified. He had to reckon with the possibility of Hardwicke losing his case and consequently another election being held; and if the second election was not held until the Michaelmas term was well on its way, it might possibly have to be fought under unfavourable conditions. With the new academical year there would be a new Vice-Chancellor, a new Caput, new Scrutators, and new Proctors; and until these new brooms were known, it was impossible to tell how they would sweep. Newcastle had therefore desired a speedy end to the lawsuit[3]; but when it became clear that this was not to be, he plunged again into the troubled sea of university politics, and sought

---

[1] Add. MS. 32960, f. 112; see also f. 99, f. 125, f. 143.
[2] Add. MS. 32960, f. 229; see also f. 226.
[3] Add. MS. 32958, f. 103, f. 423, f. 476.

THE UNIVERSITY AND POLITICIANS 125

to secure that the changes, incidental to the new academical year, worked for the good of his party. As the Vice-Chancellor continued in office until the beginning of November, the question of finding a suitable successor to Elliston was not of such pressing urgency as the election of a new Caput, which was fixed by statute for October 12th, and the admission of new Proctors and Scrutators which occurred two days earlier. The Duke was indeed completely powerless with regard to the appointment of Proctors and Scrutators who were nominated by the different colleges in a prescribed order of rotation; but he was served by good fortune and had no cause to regret his impotence. On October 10th Longmire and Forster were succeeded as Proctors by Murhall of Christ's and Martyn of Sidney, who were both supporters of Hardwicke; and though one of the new Scrutators was a member of the Sandwich party, the other was Peck of Trinity, who had voted for the Grace on March 30th[1]. Thus three out of the four new officers were Newcastle's friends; and, as they would play a leading part with the Vice-Chancellor in the election of the new Caput, the gain was material. It was clearly necessary, as there was a possibility of a second election, to secure the exclusion of all supporters of Sandwich from the new Caput; and with the Vice-Chancellor and the two Proctors as supporters of Hardwicke, the task was comparatively easy. Only Heads of Houses, doctors, and the two Scrutators were entitled to vote at election of a Caput; and their choice was limited to the fifteen candidates named in the three lists presented by the Vice-Chancellor and the two Proctors, each list containing five names. It was therefore easy to arrange that not a single adherent of Sandwich should be among the fifteen candidates nominated for election. 'Now as the three nominators are all of them our

[1] Add. MS. 32960, f. 143.

friends,' wrote the Master of Jesus to Newcastle, 'we may hope that all the fifteen will be nominated from amongst our friends also, and consequently we cannot well fail of having a good Caput[1].'

The hopes of the Master of Jesus were fully realised. As it was customary to vote for the candidates nominated by the Vice-Chancellor, it was arranged that Elliston's list should contain the names of those persons whose election was most desired by the Newcastle party; but no risks were run and none but trustworthy persons were placed on the lists of the two Proctors[2]. No anxiety was therefore felt, and the success of the Vice-Chancellor's nominees was taken as certain until the eve of the election when it became known that certain friends of Sandwich among the doctors had arrived unexpectedly in Cambridge[3]. These late-comers held a meeting at which it was agreed that 'the Master of Clare Hall should take the lead and the rest of the party observe to act as he did[4]'; and, though it is by no means clear what lead the Master of Clare was intended to take, it is possible that his idea was to vote for the candidates nominated by the junior Proctor as being probably those whose election was least desired by Hardwicke's supporters[5]. If this however was the

[1] Add. MS. 32960, f. 143.
[2] Newcastle only reluctantly agreed to the inclusion of Dr Hallifax of Trinity Hall among those nominated, and stipulated that he should 'previously give some assurance as to his behaviour, as far at least as regards the election of the High Steward.' Dr Hallifax had failed to support the Duke's candidate in a recent election of a Master of Trinity Hall, and Newcastle therefore regarded him with suspicion. Add. MS. 32960, f. 94; Add. MS. 32961, f. 293.
[3] Add. MS. 32962, f. 284.   [4] *Ibid.*
[5] 'Yesterday' wrote the Master of Jesus on October 13th 'we assembled in the Senate house before two, and the first intelligence I had there was from Mr Backhouse who told me that the Vice-Master had been with him from the Master to recommend the junior Proctor's list, and that he had sent word to the Master that he thought himself

THE UNIVERSITY AND POLITICIANS 127

design, it failed dismally in execution. The followers of Sandwich, either from lack of preparation or rendered reckless by knowing how little they could do, appear to have voted at random; and the candidates on the Vice-Chancellor's list were 'chosen by twenty-two out of thirty-two[1].'

Up to this point Newcastle had undoubtedly been very successful and he realised that fortune had been kind to him. 'I hear' he commented 'the enemy is very angry at our having secured the whole Caput. How could they expect otherwise when the election or nomination was entirely in our friends and none else[2].' But he knew that his task was not completed and that he now had to secure the appointment of a suitable successor to Elliston who would resign the office of Vice-Chancellor early in November. Unless he was successful in this also, it would avail him little to have secured a compliant Caput; and it was by no means certain that he would be able to crown his work in the way he desired.

It has been previously mentioned that the election by the Senate of a Vice-Chancellor from among the two candidates nominated by the Heads of Houses had become little more than a form; and that it was customary to elect the senior by degree among the Heads of Houses who had never held the office. If it happened, as it occasionally did, that all the Heads had been Vice-Chancellor in their turn, it was usual to re-appoint the one who had least recently served. Consequently it was impossible to predict the order of succession which was

old enough to judge how to give his vote in that and in all other cases. Upon this we concluded that they had agreed all to vote for the junior Proctor's list, and therefore changed our own plan by putting Dr Wynne and Dr Glynn into the junior Proctor's list, whom we had before designed for the senior Proctor's.' Add. MS. 32962, f. 294.

[1] Add. MS. 32962, f. 284; see also f. 280, f. 294.
[2] Add. MS. 32963, f. 74.

always liable to be changed by the death or resignation of a Head; and although this uncertainty was of little moment in ordinary times, it was particularly menacing to Newcastle's plans at this particular juncture. It was of the greatest importance that the new Vice-Chancellor should be a friend; but, if the usual procedure was followed, the Duke could not tell until the last moment upon whom the lot would fall. He therefore contemplated finding salvation by persuading Dr Elliston to continue Vice-Chancellor for another year. He would thereby free himself from a considerable burden of anxiety; and the continuance of a Vice-Chancellor for a second year of office could be supported by recent precedents. In the early days of his Chancellorship the Duke had actively encouraged such prolongations, and had twice succeeded in obtaining the re-election of a Vice-Chancellor particularly pleasing to him; but when a cry had been raised against such a breach of established custom, he had wisely deferred to public opinion and abandoned the practice. That he now thought of reviving it is a measure of his anxiety; but fortunately he was dissuaded by the Bishop of Lincoln from resorting to a desperate expedient which would almost certainly have caused considerable offence in the university[1].

It was wise of the Duke to refrain from taking a short but dangerous cut out of his difficulties, and certainly his best policy was to wait upon events. The unforeseen was the predominating element in the situation; and it was clearly impossible to formulate a definite policy until Elliston's resignation was imminent. It happened that in April 1764 there was not a single Head of a House who had not been Vice-Chancellor, and, unless there was a change before the following

[1] Add. MS. 32958, f. 103; Add. MS. 32959, f. 304, f. 423. See Chap. III.

THE UNIVERSITY AND POLITICIANS 129

November, the successor to Elliston would be Dr Long, Master of Pembroke, who was one of Sandwich's most loyal followers. The Duke however had it in his power to avert this disaster by calling upon the Bishop of Lincoln to resign the mastership of Corpus; for the Bishop's successor in the mastership would precede Dr Long in the Vice-Chancellorship; and, as the Bishop had long been anxious to confine himself to his episcopal duties, Newcastle could count upon his ready acquiescence[1]. But he knew too well the value of the Bishop lightly to discard him, and rightly refused to be panic-driven into immediate action. He judged that there was nothing to be lost by waiting, and that before November the death or resignation of a Head might exclude Dr Long from the Vice-Chancellorship and make it unnecessary for the Bishop to retire. And the opportunity, for which he was waiting, came sooner than he expected; for in May occurred the death of Sir Edward Simpson, Master of Trinity Hall. Without loss of time Newcastle threw himself into the fray and laboured hard to secure the appointment of a friend as Simpson's successor; but on this occasion he toiled in vain. James Marriott, who, after being for many years in close and intimate relations with the Duke, had recently deserted to Sandwich, was elected Master of Trinity Hall, and consequently, unless there was a change in the situation before November, would succeed Elliston as Vice-Chancellor.

Thus the last state was worse than the first, and the Duke was driven to do that which he was loath to do. 'The only sure way' he wrote a few days after Marriott's election 'of having a Vice-Chancellor we can depend upon, I am afraid must be by the Bishop of Lincoln's resignation. It is a sad expedient and will be found so[2].' But the expedient, though sad, was not difficult of execu-

[1] Master's *History of Corpus Christi College*, with additional notes by John Lamb, p. 251.   [2] Add. MS. 32960, f. 94.

tion, as there was an understanding between the Bishop and his Fellows that they should elect as his successor, John Barnardiston, a follower of Hardwicke[1]. As Barnardiston however was only a master of arts and Marriott a doctor of laws, the latter, as the senior by degree, would have the first claim upon the Vice-Chancellorship; and it was therefore arranged that Barnardiston should take the degree of doctor of divinity and thereby obtain precedence over Marriott[2]. This programme was carried out shortly after Marriott had succeeded Simpson at Trinity Hall. On June 30th Barnardiston was admitted to the degree of doctor of divinity, and on July 12th was elected to the mastership of Corpus which had been resigned by the Bishop of Lincoln a few days before[3].

Thus the situation was redressed; but the battle was by no means over or the issue certain. If the usual procedure was followed, Barnardiston and Marriott would be nominated by the Heads and the former elected by the Senate; but it was at least doubtful whether this constitutional convention would be respected. Party feeling was running high in the university, men were in the mood to violate time-honoured traditions, and the Master of Corpus' claim to be appointed Vice-Chancellor rested upon nothing more substantial than custom. Such a foundation might well prove unable to withstand the clash of warring parties; and as of the sixteen Heads of Houses seven were avowed supporters of Sandwich, and one, the Master of Emmanuel, had only reluctantly voted for Lord Hardwicke's Grace[4], Barnardiston's nomination could not be

[1] Master's *History of Corpus Christi College*, p. 251; Add. MS. 32959, f. 423.
[2] Doctors of divinity ranked above doctors of laws.
[3] Add. MS. 35640, f. 156; Add. MS. 32960, f. 256.
[4] The seven certain supporters of Sandwich among the Heads of

treated as a certainty. The Heads were too equally divided to allow either party to be confident of victory; but the balance of advantage rested with the supporters of Hardwicke, as it was provided by the statutes that, in the event of the candidates tying for nomination to the Senate, the Regius Professor of Divinity should decide between them; and the Regius Professor at this time was Dr Rutherforth who was warmly supporting Hardwicke.

Such was the situation immediately after Barnardiston became Master of Corpus; and it was naturally feared that Sandwich would not tamely submit to the exclusion of his friend, Marriott, from the Vice-Chancellorship. But a further complication was introduced by the death on August 7th of Sir James Burrough, Master of Caius. Ten days after Burrough's death the Fellows of Caius elected John Smith as their Master; and as Smith was only a master of arts he could not be preferred to either Barnardiston or Marriott for the Vice-Chancellorship. But shortly after his election he applied to the Vice-Chancellor for the degree of doctor of divinity by royal mandate, and Hardwicke's supporters were quick to see how much they stood to gain by complying with his wish. 'This event will bid fair for securing a quiet election of a Vice-Chancellor,' wrote Dr Caryl to the Duke, 'for there will be two doctors of divinity to be nominated by the Heads. Dr Marriott, as only doctor of laws, will be excluded[1].' Moreover there were good grounds for hoping that the substitution of the Master of Caius for the Master of Trinity Hall, as the second

---

Houses were the Provost of King's and the Masters of Trinity, Caius, Clare, Pembroke, St Catharine's and Trinity Hall. 'Emmanuel' wrote Dr Caryl on June 30th 'could not for shame but be with us in Lord Hardwicke's affair; but I do not expect his assistance on any other occasion.' Add. MS. 32960, f. 143.

[1] Add. MS. 32961, f. 354.

132 THE UNIVERSITY AND POLITICIANS

candidate for the Vice-Chancellorship, might prevent a contested election; as in his anxiety to obtain a mandate degree, Smith went so far as to deny that he had any intention of disturbing 'the usual course of election into that office[1].' Consequently his request was granted and he became a doctor of divinity by royal mandate[2].

Though a supporter of Sandwich the Master of Caius had undoubtedly played into the hands of the Hardwicke party; but as the day of election drew near, Newcastle began to fear that all might not go according to programme. Dr Smith's engagement not to disturb the usual course of election was personal to himself; and it was significant that his friends and the Fellows of his college declined to limit their liberty of action[3]. Moreover, though Marriott had apparently taken his exclusion in good part, and had declared that he did not intend to interfere in the election, he had given warning that he meant 'to be on the spot at the election for Vice-Chancellor,' and it was feared that 'if he can gain any point for himself, he will not...much mind the loose and somewhat general expressions he has dropt on that subject[4].' A certain amount of uneasiness was also caused by so little being known of the intentions of the Sandwich party; and, though it was tolerably certain that the Masters of Corpus and Caius would be nominated, it was feared that the latter might be elected by the Senate. Both candidates had only very recently become doctors, and Barnardiston's seniority over Smith was slight enough to afford a pretext for disregarding it.

Aware of this danger Newcastle contemplated the possibility of persuading his friends among the Heads to pass over the Master of Caius and nominate one of

[1] Add. MS. 32961, f. 354, f. 366. [2] Add. MS. 32961, f. 368.
[3] Add. MS. 32963, f. 6. [4] Add. MS. 32962, f. 177.

THE UNIVERSITY AND POLITICIANS 133

themselves with the Master of Corpus; and, though he abandoned the scheme when it was pointed out that such a violation of constitutional custom would cause widespread offence in the university, he was obviously very unwilling to run the hazard involved in the Master of Caius' nomination[1]. His reluctance was justified, for though the Senate had hitherto presented a greater menace than the Heads, there suddenly appeared a danger of the Sandwich party being able to prevent the nomination of Barnardiston. Newcastle had always confidently reckoned upon the support of eight Masters of colleges out of the sixteen; and he was greatly alarmed to learn that the Master of St John's was wavering in his allegiance, and that the Master of Magdalene refused to return to Cambridge because his wife was about to have a child[2]. 'You surprize me' wrote the Duke on October 30th 'about Dr Sandby[3]; for God's sake get him to come. I am sure if he knew how the enemy have used us and what we want of him, nothing could keep him away[4].' But in spite of urgent appeals[5], Sandby insisted on playing the part of a good husband, and Newcastle saw disaster looming ahead. The situation however was far less serious than he imagined it to be. By a Grace of June 11th, 1580, Heads of Houses were enabled to appoint a representative to vote at the nomination of a Vice-Chancellor; and there was therefore no need for the Master of Magdalene to lacerate his feelings by hurriedly returning to Cambridge. The difficulty caused by the unexpected conduct of the Master of St John's was also successfully overcome. The Bishop of Lincoln undertook to convince the Master of the error of his ways; and, though he failed to induce him to

[1] Add. MS. 32963, f. 6, f. 84, f. 86, f. 98, f. 101, f. 117, f. 128, f. 161, f. 205.
[2] Add. MS. 32963, f. 86.   [3] The Master of Magdalene.
[4] Add. MS. 32963, f. 114.   [5] Add. MS. 32963, f. 86.

134 THE UNIVERSITY AND POLITICIANS

vote for Barnardiston, he succeeded in persuading him to retire from Cambridge and to appoint as his representative, Dr Ogden, who was a supporter of Hardwicke[1].

But the problem of the Senate still remained, and Newcastle was very seriously alarmed as to what might happen there. He was urgent in calling upon those of his friends, who were members of the Senate, to appear in Cambridge on the election day, and he appealed without ceasing to his supporters in the university to whip up as many voters as they possibly could[2]. Nor did he ask of others more than he was prepared to do himself.

'I immediately sent' he informed the Master of Jesus on October 30th 'to some of the great line of our friends, the doctors of law; Calvert and Simpson will go down, Wynne makes a difficulty, but I am sure Burrel will go. I have sent also to desire the Duke of Cumberland to send Dr Biddle and the Windsor voters....The Yorkes must take care of Soame Jenyns[3], Jack Yorke, the Dean of Lincoln[4], etc. You should write to the Bishop of Norwich for the Dean, Charles Townshend of Yarmouth, and the Norfolk or Norwich voters. Henry Pelham I will send to, and find some channel to Dr Gisborne....I will write to Dr Barnard for the Eton men but I doubt they are most against us. Dr Smith, Master of Westminster school, has no vote. Dr Hinchliffe has a vote. There is an usher at Westminster who voted with us. Pray send to Backhouse of Trinity to take care of these Westminster people[5].'

Though Newcastle was ably seconded in these efforts by the Master of Jesus, the President of Queens', and

[1] Add. MS. 32962, f. 148; Add. MS. 32963, f. 205.
[2] Add. MS. 32963, f. 38, f. 40, f. 54, f. 56, f. 78, f. 82, f. 90, f. 138, f. 140, f. 142, f. 144, f. 150.
[3] Member for Cambridgeshire and the son of Sir Roger Jenyns of Bottisham Hall near Cambridge.
[4] James Yorke, a brother of Lord Hardwicke.
[5] Add. MS. 32963, f. 114; see also f. 62, f. 161.

other Cambridge friends[1], he as usual complained that he was not receiving the support he might fairly demand:

'I am very angry with you all' he told Dr Caryl on November 1st 'that you take no notice of my letters nor ever acknowledge the receipt of them. I have given myself much trouble to write and send to everybody that I can think of; and you will see by their answers that they all go down, almost to a man. What have the Yorkes done? What has the Bishop of Norwich done with his Dean and Norwich voters?...Now is the time for our friends to exert. If we lose our Vice-Chancellor all is lost[2].'

The Duke was as usual very excited and alarmed, and he apparently anticipated that Sandwich would offer battle. This however was only a surmise, for he knew next to nothing of his adversary's plans. All he knew was that, about a week after the Caput had been elected, the Bishop of Chester, representing Sandwich, had informed the Master of Christ's that they were willing to allow Barnardiston to become Vice-Chancellor if he would give an undertaking 'that if another election for a High Steward should come on in his Vice-Chancellorship, it should not be brought on by supprise (*sic*)[3].' On the advice of his friends and with Newcastle's formal approval, the Master of Corpus at once undertook not to hold an election without at least three weeks' notice[4]; but, encouraged by this concession, Sandwich then proceeded further and wrecked the negotiation by imposing the additional demand that the Caput should agree 'that if Lord Hardwicke shall be rejected by the majority of the Senate, they will let my Grace pass their body and come to the electors at large[5].' It was clearly impossible for the friends of Hardwicke to restrict their liberty of action in this fashion, and the Master of Jesus

[1] Add. MS. 32963, f. 62, f. 86.   [2] Add. MS. 32963, f. 173.
[3] Add. MS. 32963, f. 8, f. 156.   [4] Add. MS. 32963, f. 8, f. 29.
[5] Add. MS. 32963, f. 88.

voiced the sentiments of the party when he said 'we have now nothing left but to fight as good a battle as we can[1].'

Newcastle may therefore be forgiven for believing that a contest was inevitable, for certainly all the signs pointed in that direction; and yet it is possible that Sandwich and his followers were only playing a game of bluff and never intended to oppose Barnardiston's election. They probably realised the difficulty of persuading the moderate members of the party to concur 'in so extravagant a measure as that of setting aside the senior[2]'; and although they may have vaguely contemplated the idea of securing the Vice-Chancellorship for the Master of Caius, they do not appear to have taken any steps towards the execution of the design, and finally to have abandoned it. On Saturday November 3rd the Heads unanimously nominated the Masters of Corpus and Caius, and on the following day the former was unanimously elected Vice-Chancellor[3].

Newcastle had good reason to rejoice. By securing a reliable Caput and a trustworthy Vice-Chancellor he had safeguarded himself against having to fight at a disadvantage in the event of a second election. He could not have done more; and the value he placed upon his achievement is best attested by his intentions in the event of failure.

'I believe' he told Dr Caryl 'I am not thought one who would rashly do an improper or indiscreet thing; but, if they had carried it for Dr Smith, I had taken my resolution. I would have come to Cambridge, acted myself as Chancellor, have re-

---

[1] Add. MS. 32963, f. 60.   [2] Add. MS. 32963, f. 223.
[3] *Ibid.* The Master of Emmanuel did not appear on the nomination day, having taken to his bed on the plea of illness. It is possible that he was upset by receiving from Charles Yorke 'a thundering letter with so much civility but yet urged with so much force, as must be enough to stun if it were not able to satisfy him.' Add. MS. 32963, f. 227.

THE UNIVERSITY AND POLITICIANS 137

mained in the university as long as necessary, and have declared in Senate to Dr Smith that he had no power or authority nor had anything to do during my residence in the university. And I am not at all unwilling that it should be known that this was my intention[1].'

It was fortunately unnecessary for him to adopt such drastic measures; and, freed from all anxiety with regard to the immediate future at Cambridge, he was able to watch with comparative calm the slow and stately progress of the law-suit. Lord Sandwich had been given until the Michaelmas term to show cause why the writs of mandamus should not be granted; and on November 16th his counsel submitted seven affidavits. These documents endeavoured to show that Pitt had been duly qualified to vote in the regents' house, that six regents had voted for the Grace in the non-regents' house, and that 'no second scrutiny ought to be made when the votes are equal, nor the validity of any vote examined afterwards[2]'; but it does not appear that Lord Hardwicke's friends were at all alarmed. Indeed they were much relieved to find that Sandwich was unable to put up a better case, and, feeling confident of the issue, ceased to take much interest in the legal proceedings. Their optimism was justified, for in April 1765 the court gave judgment in Lord Hardwicke's favour.

'I have great pleasure in acquainting your Grace' wrote Dr Caryl to Newcastle on May 7th, 1765, 'that all our trouble about the office of High Steward is now at an end. The mandamus was obeyed without any hesitation; my Lord Hardwicke's patent is sealed; and the bells are now ringing merrily to close the whole[3].'

[1] Add. MS. 32963, f. 251. Dr Caryl kept the Duke's intentions to himself. Add. MS. 32963, f. 312.
[2] Add. MS. 32964, f. 1; see also Add. MS. 32963, f. 356, f. 397.
[3] Add. MS. 32966, f. 343; see also f. 273 and Gray's *Letters* (edited by D. C. Tovey), III, 69–72.

Thus after many months and much labour Hardwicke succeeded his father as High Steward of the university, and Newcastle could congratulate himself upon having victoriously repelled the assault of the enemy. Never before had he been compelled to fight so fiercely for his predominance in the university; and, inasmuch as he had prevailed and routed the forces which had overthrown him in parliament, his success was doubly sweet. He enjoyed the satisfaction of having soundly beaten a redoubtable antagonist, and the furious and prolonged character of the struggle added prestige to the victory. Sandwich indeed was too decisively defeated not to be compelled to admit it; and in 1767 he referred in a letter to the Duke to 'that unlucky contest in the university which I was so silly as to be drawn into[1].' Yet Newcastle's triumph was not complete and not unattended with disappointment. He had induced himself to believe that success at Cambridge would react favourably upon the fortunes of the parliamentary opposition; and truly, unless he so believed, he was hardly justified in raising an academic dispute to the dignity of a great political issue. Yet there was no such favourable reaction; and the decline in the strength of the opposition was in no way stayed by Sandwich's defeat at Cambridge. Newcastle moreover must have been deeply mortified to find that both Hardwicke and Charles Yorke failed to recognise that they were under any obligation to him. From the very outset Hardwicke had behaved with studied indifference, allowing others to work for him and taking their services for granted; but he was at least consistent and never evinced any interest in the proceedings. Charles Yorke behaved in a still more despicable fashion. Being extremely anxious for his brother to become High Steward, he had encouraged the Duke to be unsparing in effort; and as in November

[1] Add. MS. 32982, f. 435.

THE UNIVERSITY AND POLITICIANS 139

1763 he had resigned the office of Attorney-General and thrown in his lot with the opposition party, he was favourably situated to demand a service of Newcastle. Yet in December 1764, when the Duke had accomplished his work at Cambridge and it could be taken for granted that Hardwicke would be declared High Steward, Charles Yorke deserted the opposition and came to terms with the court and ministry, and his desertion must have considerably detracted from Newcastle's pleasure in his victory over Sandwich. The personal triumph remained; but it was difficult after the desertion of Charles Yorke to pretend that it was a triumph of the opposition over the government.

Thus what seemed about to be the crowning glory of Newcastle's career as Chancellor turned to something like dust and ashes; and at times he must have reflected that it was hardly worth while to have taken so much trouble for so little result. He was however to be avenged, though not until after his death. Though apparently so indifferent to the honour conferred upon him, Hardwicke was not unwilling to hold office in the university as long as he was not expected to take any trouble; and there is reason to think that he was glad enough to be High Steward and regarded himself as the natural successor to Newcastle in the Chancellorship. He characteristically however was not prepared to exert himself in paving the way to the accession to the higher dignity; and apparently lightly assumed that the greater prize would come to him in the natural order of things, and that therefore it was quite unnecessary for him to display the slightest interest in the affairs of the university. And by a curious irony of circumstance the place which he coveted, and to gain which he had taken the High Stewardship, was to be wrested from him by the Duke of Grafton who had been one of his supporters in the previous contest. In

140   THE UNIVERSITY AND POLITICIANS

July 1766 Grafton had severed his connection with the opposition and taken office as First Lord of the Treasury; and when in January 1767 he re-entered his name on the books of his old college, Peterhouse[1], it was probably with a view of standing for the Chancellorship in the event of Newcastle's death.

'I suspect my old friend, the Bishop of Chester, to be at the bottom of this affair,' remarked Newcastle to the Master of Jesus, 'though no one was more offended at his Lordship's conduct, in deserting us as he did, than the Duke of Grafton was at that time. But, dear Caryl, almost everybody changes but you and I[2].'

The Duke however could hardly be expected to take much interest in a struggle which would not begin until he was on his deathbed, and though he certainly did not desire the court to control the university through Grafton, he never indicated that he wished Hardwicke to be his successor. He probably realised that his preferences and wishes would carry little weight when he was in the grave, and that it was not for him to regulate a future he would not see. He had only to give the signal for operations to begin, and this duty he fulfilled. When he fell seriously ill about the end of the year 1767, academic politicians at once began to stir. The question whether Hardwicke or Grafton should be his successor was eagerly discussed in the university; and the President of Queens' was informed by a friend that Grafton 'means to offer himself as a candidate for the Chancellorship whenever it becomes vacant, and that

[1] Add. MS. 32979. It seems fairly clear that Grafton could not have replaced his name on the college books with a view of obtaining a vote in the Senate, as a Grace, passed in January, 1766, provided that no re-admitted person was entitled to vote, 'unless he shall be chosen into an academical office or a professorship or into the foundation of some college or shall reside here three terms.' Add. MS. 32973, f. 271. See also Add. MS. 35628, f. 53.

[2] Add. MS. 32980, f. 42.

THE UNIVERSITY AND POLITICIANS 141

he seems to be preparing for it[1].' The President also drew his own conclusions from the butler of his college having received from a Fellow of Peterhouse 'a paper containing a list of names of several of the absent members of this college, to which he was desired to affix their respective addresses[2]. It was also significant that during the Christmas vacation the Vice-Chancellor, who was Marriott of Trinity Hall, 'sent to the butler of Benet for a list of all the members of the Senate who had their names upon the boards in that college[3]'; and it is possible that he made similar enquiries at other colleges. Though there is no definite proof that the Vice-Chancellor and the Fellows of Peterhouse were acting on Grafton's behalf, it is at least quite likely that they were; and Hardwicke was advised by a friend that Grafton was stirring.

It will hardly be a matter of surprise to your Lordship to hear that many of those, who gave your Lordship so much trouble about the High Stewardship, are disposed to support this interest. And I am sorry to add I am not without some fears that some of those, who were your Lordship's friends upon that occasion, will show themselves in different colours on any others. Indeed, my Lord, to speak the plain truth, there is a general complaint of your Lordship's shyness and inattention to the interests of those who distinguished themselves in support of your Lordship's interest on that occasion, a circumstance which I must entirely rely upon your Lordship's candour and good understanding to pardon me for mentioning. But I cannot discharge my duty without it. Whether your Lordship means to do us the honour offering (sic) yourself a candidate for the Chancellorship or not in case of a vacancy, it would ill become me to presume to judge; but, as I have your Lordship's interest really much at heart, I cannot but in the most earnest manner recommend it to your Lordship, in case you have any such design, to make yourself more known to your friends in the university, and by a proper application to them to secure them in time[4].'

[1] Add. MS. 35628, f. 71.   [2] Add. MS. 35628, f. 70.
[3] Add. MS. 35628, f. 71.   [4] Add. MS. 35657, f. 292.

This was very plain speaking, and as Newcastle rallied and survived until November 1768, the High Steward could not complain that he had not received timely warning. There is no evidence however that he took any action beyond informing the President of Queens' that, in the question of his conduct when the Chancellorship fell vacant, he must be guided by the advice of his friends at Cambridge. As it was hardly possible to ask men to support a candidature which might never materialise, nothing was done to urge his claims, though probably the supporters of Grafton were not idle. Thus the months passed away until the death of the Duke of Newcastle, which took place in the early hours of Thursday November 17th. The news was received in Cambridge by noon on the same day; and without loss of time the Vice-Chancellor, who was Dr Hinchliffe, Master of Trinity, summoned a meeting of Heads of Houses for the following morning[1]. At this meeting the Vice-Chancellor read a letter from the Duke of Grafton, announcing that if he could be elected Chancellor without a canvass of the university he would be much honoured; and, after this letter had been read, the President of Queens' communicated to the meeting 'Lord Hardwicke's sentiments on the same subject[2].' We unfortunately do not know the exact nature of the President's communication, but it is probable that he made it understood that Hardwicke was contemplating standing for election, without however having definitely decided to do so[3]. As it was therefore possible that the Senate might have to choose between two candidates, it was decided to hold the election on Tuesday November 29th, though the Vice-

[1] Add. MS. 35657, f. 307.   [2] Add. MS. 35640, f. 299.
[3] In a letter to Charles Yorke, Rutherforth uses the phrase 'that as Lord Hardwicke had thought proper to declare his readiness to accept of the Chancellorship.' Add. MS. 35640, f. 303.

THE UNIVERSITY AND POLITICIANS 143

Chancellor had originally suggested Monday November 21st as a suitable and convenient date.

It was now the business of Lord Hardwicke's advisers at Cambridge to form an estimate of the support that their candidate was likely to receive; and the President of Queens' and Professor Rutherforth undertook the task of conducting a discreet enquiry. The information they collected was decidedly discouraging. They discovered that Dr Powell, now become Master of St John's, who had so strenuously assisted Hardwicke against Lord Sandwich, was in favour of Grafton and could count upon the support of the majority of his Fellows, that Trinity, led by its Master, was overwhelmingly on the same side, that the Master and Fellows of Peterhouse were united 'in support of the Duke of Grafton as a college cause,' that both in Christ's and King's Grafton was certain of a considerable following, and that even Dr Caryl of Jesus, though prepared to vote for Hardwicke, declined to canvass 'his Fellows as he did in the case of the High Stewardship, for he then laid himself open to such claims from them as he has found very inconvenient, and as he never has been able to answer[1].' It was roughly calculated that about two hundred and forty persons would vote, and that of these Hardwicke could not possibly count upon more than eighty[2]. In these circumstances it would be both useless and ridiculous for him to come forward as a candidate; and when the President of Queens', the Masters of Corpus, Jesus, and Emmanuel, and Professor Rutherforth met in conference on Tuesday November 22nd, they had little difficulty in deciding the character of the communication they should address to Hardwicke.

'Upon consideration of the state of the university, after the best inquiry that can be made in the several colleges,' they stated, 'and reflecting on the disadvantages of entering so late

[1] Add. MS. 35640, f. 303.   [2] *Ibid.*

into an opposition, we are of opinion that there is no reasonable expectation of making a respectable minority in favour of Lord Hardwicke, and therefore, for the honour of his Lordship and to avoid inconvenience and distress to the members of the university, we think it best that his Lordship's name should not be made any farther use of on this occasion[1].'

Acting upon this very sound advice Hardwicke decided not to stand for election; and on Tuesday November 29th the Duke of Grafton was unanimously chosen Chancellor. It was well that the university was spared another contest, for it had already suffered enough from the strife of politicians. Twice in twenty years Cambridge had been the scene of a fierce party struggle; and on both occasions victory had rested with Newcastle. In the closing years of his life, when he was commonly regarded as an impotent old dotard, he had the happiness of finding that at least he could prevail in Cambridge, and that there, if only there, he could repel the attack of the tories and renegade whigs who elsewhere had completely triumphed over him. As he closed his eyes in death upon the wreck of his former greatness, it is possible that he thought with peculiar affection of the university where he had remained a power until the end.

[1] Add. MS. 35628, f. 78; see also, f. 76.

CHAPTER III

THE CHANCELLOR AND THE UNIVERSITY

WHATEVER measure of success Newcastle achieved in life was owing almost exclusively to his amazing industry. This is the secret of the rise of a mediocrity to political greatness. With no serious interest in life except work, he found his only happiness in the transaction of business, and outstripped far abler men in the race for power by modelling himself upon the tortoise and leaving them to imitate the hare. Instinctively and almost unconsciously he extended the sphere and increased the importance of every office he filled; and as a cabinet minister his tendency was to reduce his colleagues to cyphers by retaining in his own hands much more business than he could efficiently manage. He was certainly ambitious and loved power; but it is doubtful whether that infirmity of noble mind was the dominant trait in his character. It is possible that he loved the means by which power is attained more than the power itself, that the race not the goal was the attraction, and that, before it was preached, he practised the maxim that 'to travel hopefully is a better thing than to arrive, and the true success is to labour.' Had he been solely actuated by ambition he would probably have displayed a more discriminating industry and more deftly proportioned his zeal to the importance of the task; but, loving labour for its own sake, he obeyed with slavish fidelity the command to do with your might all that your hand finds to do, and often spent his energy upon trifles at the expense of more weighty and urgent

146 THE CHANCELLOR AND THE UNIVERSITY

matters. No blame could have attached to him if he had elected to treat the office of Chancellor as a sinecure, for it was as such that his immediate predecessors had regarded it, and a hard-worked statesman could hardly be expected to immerse himself in academic affairs. But he had no inclination to avail himself of an excuse at which nine persons out of ten in his position would have eagerly snatched. He desired to keep in the closest possible touch with the university, to know and influence all that happened there; and to attain this end he was willing to endure an almost intolerable burden of drudgery. It is true that his activity was not disinterested, and that he hoped to increase his political influence by converting Cambridge into a stronghold of that section of the whig party which he controlled; but the trouble he took was out of all proportion to the gain; and, even if the gain had been less, it is unlikely that he would have been appreciably less active.

As an absentee however he was not favourably situated to establish a dominant influence in the university, and as a servant of the crown he could only devote a portion of his time to academic business. It was consequently necessary for him to depend to a certain extent upon subordinates, of whom not the least important was Doctor Samuel Squire. A nephew of the wife of Dr Newcome, Master of St John's, of which college he was for some years a Fellow, Squire in 1748 became the Duke's chaplain and his secretary for the business of the university. It was his duty as secretary to keep Newcastle informed of any academic events of importance, to deal with the large Cambridge correspondence, and on occasions to serve as the medium of communication between the Chancellor and the university. On his promotion to the Bench in 1761 as Bishop of St David's, he was succeeded in the office of the Chancellor's university secretary by William

THE CHANCELLOR AND THE UNIVERSITY

Talbot, Fellow of Clare[1]. As Talbot continued to reside in Cambridge the management of the Duke's Cambridge correspondence passed into other hands; but the new secretary was clearly more favourably situated than Squire for acting as a conveyer of news and a medium of communication.

In addition to the Chancellor's secretary, who occupied an official and recognised position, Newcastle had always a few trusted agents at Cambridge whose business it was to let him know when anything was stirring, and on the occasion of controversy or dispute to organise a party in support of his wishes. Such were the functions fulfilled at different times by Dr Keene, Master of Peterhouse, Dr Green, Master of Corpus, Dr Yonge, Master of Jesus, and his successor in the mastership, Dr Caryl. It was clearly expedient to employ upon such work Heads of Houses who by virtue of their position possessed considerable influence in the university; and it is to be noticed that Yonge continued to be so employed even after he had become a bishop and resigned his mastership. Without such assistance Newcastle could have exercised but a faint control over university affairs. Having no official relations with him they served to cloak his interference; and appeared to be following their own inclinations while acting in accordance with his secret instructions. They were of course well known to enjoy the Chancellor's confidence, but the extent of that confidence could only be guessed; and they seem to have been scrupulously careful, unless a contrary policy was either advisable or inevitable, to refrain from committing the Duke. The task was such

[1] In a letter, dated May 25th, 1761, Talbot mentions that 'a letter from My Lord Bishop of Bristol acquaints me that your Grace had done me the high honour of appointing me your Grace's secretary for the business of the university in the room of Dr Squire, now Bishop of St David's.' Add. MS. 32923, f. 255.

as could only be performed by trusted friends; and Newcastle was no easy task-master. On one occasion Dr Yonge, after he had become Bishop of Norwich, fell below the exacting standard demanded; and received a letter from the Duke which can only be described as terrific:

'I never was so much surprised or indeed offended' wrote Newcastle 'with any letter that I have ever received as with that which I have received from your Lordship this night. Everyone which I have had from you this summer has been full of reproaches to me. The present Bishop of Norwich reproach me with leaving his diocese to obey me. Had he not common charity or christian compassion to come to his benefactors when they had been and were under such distress and affliction as we were this whole summer. Reproach me with being some hours at my house upon business by no means agreeable to him. What business? The support of that cause and that fortune, the which he would have had no Clapham to go to, and might have been a junior Fellow of Trinity college to this hour. The present Bishop of Norwich to reproach me for having put off an engagement to come to dine with me. I shall give your Lordship no further trouble I can assure you. You may remain at your diocese at Clapham and I will never call you from thence. One favour I have to ask of your Lordship, and that is that you would shew our correspondence of this summer to every bishop upon the Bench, and I will venture to say that, except the Bishops of Chester and St David's, there will not be a single bishop who will approve the ungrateful part you have acted towards me, and those, who put you upon it, do not consult your character and reputation[1].'

Yet, however perfect the organisation, it was imperative for the success of Newcastle's plans that he should be personally known to as many members of the university as possible. Though in the sphere of private life affection may be stimulated by absence, public

[1] Add. MS. 32955, f. 125. Keene was Bishop of Chester and Squire was Bishop of St David's. When this letter was written both these divines had ceased to be supporters of Newcastle.

PHILIP YONGE
MASTER OF JESUS COLLEGE, CAMBRIDGE (1752-58)
BISHOP OF BRISTOL (1758-61)

THE CHANCELLOR AND THE UNIVERSITY 149

characters are apt to be out of mind when out of sight; and a Chancellor, who was only known by name to the university, would never find a party ready to his call. Hence the frequency of Newcastle's visits to Cambridge. Few Chancellors have been so conscientious or so thorough in the discharge of this part of their duties. Whenever he was at Cambridge which, considering his other engagements, was not seldom, he was careful to see as many people as possible, and consequently was far better known than most of his predecessors. To the undiscerning he might appear to be wasting his time upon social trivialities, and the poet, Gray, was loudly contemptuous of the 'fizzling Duke'; but Newcastle was wise in his generation and knew the value of aristocratic condescension.

It is indeed probable that he would have visited the university even more frequently if he had not been so much engaged with affairs of state and so often in attendance upon the King in Hanover. Thus he was obliged to postpone his first appearance in Cambridge after his installation until June 1753 when he visited the university to admit Lord Hardwicke to the degree of doctor of laws. A present day Chancellor, when called upon to perform some such duty, generally only spends a few hours among his academic subjects, and seldom exchanges a word with more than a handful of them; but that was not the Duke's way. His stay extended over four days, and in addition to officiating as Chancellor in the Senate house, he held a levée at Clare, presided over a meeting of Heads and Tutors which had been called 'to consider how to remedy the mischiefs arising from peddling Jews dealing with scholars, and the inconvenience of the long non-residence of scholars, particularly in the long vacation,' dined or supped with six Heads of Houses, and dined on Trinity Sunday, which fell within his stay, in the hall

150 THE CHANCELLOR AND THE UNIVERSITY

of Trinity college[1]. Between 1753 and 1768 he seems to have visited the university six times in all, and though on one occasion he did not stay more than a night, he usually remained at least three or four days and kept high festival the whole time.

'Everything has passed here, since my coming down, extreamly well,' he wrote to Lord Hardwicke from Cambridge in July 1761, 'the performances of the young men yesterday were extreamly good and gave great satisfaction, particularly your friend, Mr Flitcroft's son of Benet. We had last night a very fine entertainment at the new Master's of Queens'. We have constantly drunk your Lordship's health twice a day, as I told you we would[2].'

Indeed, so anxious were the members of the university to give their Chancellor a rousing welcome, and so anxious was the Chancellor to accept their hospitality, that it was perhaps as well for all parties that these visits were not more frequent.

'I had the favour of your letter' wrote Newcastle to the Master of Corpus in June 1760 'and hope to have the pleasure of taking a slight supper with you at your Lodge on Saturday evening. I dine at Therfield[3], so can't say exactly what time I shall come to Clare Hall, but I hope by eight o'clock. The Vice-Chancellor has wrote to me very obligingly to sup with him that night, but I have excused myself, having been engaged to you. I think you would do well to ask him to your Lodge. I can't possibly wait upon Dr Beridge and I beg you would make my excuse. My engagements are Master of Benet, Saturday supper, Vice-Chancellor, Commencement Sunday dinner, Master of Jesus, supper that night, Provost of King's, Monday dinner, Master of Christ's, supper that night, Trinity college, dinner Commencement Tuesday, Clare Hall, supper that night; and on Wednesday morning I propose to return to London[4].'

It was customary on the occasion of these dinners and

[1] Add. MS. 5852, f. 69, f. 70.
[2] Add. MS. 32924, f. 441. Henry Flitcroft was admitted to Corpus in 1759 and took his M.A. in 1763.
[3] Therfield is near Royston.   [4] Add. MS. 32907, f. 351.

THE CHANCELLOR AND THE UNIVERSITY 151

suppers to invite a large number of guests[1], and consequently the Duke had ample opportunities of enlarging the circle of his acquaintances. The strain was doubtless severe but he had to endure it. It was necessary for him to court the university as a parliamentary candidate courts a constituency, to be accessible to all, and to win friends by kindly words and genial attentions. He certainly cannot be accused of having acted on the assumption that the members of the university, like parsnips, could not be buttered with fine words; for he was prodigal of his blandishments. After dining on one occasion in the hall of Trinity he despatched an enthusiastic letter to the Master who had unavoidably been absent.

'I am too sensible' he wrote 'of the honour that was done me at Trinity college, and of the very agreeable entertainment which I had there on the Commencement Tuesday, not to take the first opportunity of acquainting you with it, and returning you my most sincere thanks for it. The very great improvements that are made to the buildings and the revenues of the finest college in England, owing entirely to your care, ability and attention to the real advantage of that great society, and the flourishing condition of it owing also to the good order and discipline established there by you, give me, who have so much the honour and reputation of our university at heart, the greatest satisfaction, and require from me the best return which I can make to shew my gratitude for it and sense of it. Independently of my attachment to the university I have always had a particular affection for Trinity college, and as Chancellor I am now truly proud of it in every respect. I hope you will forgive my taking this liberty which proceeds entirely from what I thought but justice to say to you upon the subject. I have acquainted the King with it as well as with the dutiful and loyal behaviour of the university upon all occasions[2].'

[1] When Newcastle supped with the Master of Christ's the company numbered twenty in all, and when he dined with the Provost of King's, nearly thirty persons were present. Add. MS. 5852, f. 145.

[2] Add. MS. 32908, f. 104. For the details of the Chancellor's visits

Newcastle probably wrote many such letters after departing from Cambridge; and although his compliments were wasted upon Dr Smith who never became one of his ardent supporters, he was more successful in other quarters. By assiduously applying himself to the task and by a prodigal expenditure of his time and energy, he acquired a personal following in the university and thereby laid a solid foundation for his power. It is true that as long as he was in the service of the crown he was able richly to reward devotion; but it would be wrong to imagine that his influence as Chancellor solely depended upon the means of corruption at his disposal. When the evil days came and he retired from the king's service into the ranks of a discredited and ineffective opposition, he still retained a measure of control over the university and thus reaped the harvest he had sown. There were of course some who left him when he ceased to have anything to give, but there were many who remained true, remembering how closely he had identified himself with the university and how solicitous he was for its welfare.

The question of the extent of his influence and the degree to which he interfered in the affairs of Cambridge, is not easy to answer in a general fashion. His authority certainly never approached anything like despotic sway, and more than once he met with a serious rebuff; but on the other hand there is no doubt that he was until the end a power in the university and, if he prudently refrained from offending academic susceptibilities, could generally prevail. He was a constitutional ruler in the sense that he could do little or nothing unless supported by a majority of the Senate; but, as has been previously

see Add. MS. 5852, f. 69, f. 70, f. 137, f. 139, f. 145; Add. MS. 32907, f. 255, f. 257, f. 280, f. 282, f. 292, f. 351; Add. MS. 32908, f. 104, f. 144; Add. MS. 32923, f. 245; Add. MS. 32924, f. 384, f. 410, f. 441; Cooper's *Annals of Cambridge*, IV.

THE CHANCELLOR AND THE UNIVERSITY 153

explained, he had means, not strictly constitutional, of organising the necessary popular support. But though it is possible to differ over the extent of the control he exercised, it would be generally admitted that there have been very few Chancellors who have taken their duties so seriously or have attempted to exercise so minute a supervision over the details of university business. This supervision and interest extended to even such a matter of pure routine as the drafting and presentation of addresses. When an event of national importance occured it was usual for the university to present a loyal address to the crown; and the customary procedure was for the address to be drafted by the Vice-Chancellor, approved by the Heads, passed by the Senate after two readings, and then presented to the sovereign by the Chancellor who was usually attended by a deputation from the university. As the Chancellor made himself responsible for the address by presenting it, he certainly had some claim to be consulted; but some surprise and on occasions resentment, was caused by Newcastle behaving in what was considered to be an arbitrary fashion. For instance, when in the late summer of 1758 the news reached England of the fall of Louisburg, Dr Richardson, Master of Emmanuel, proposed to Dr Law, Master of Peterhouse, who was acting as deputy Vice-Chancellor in the absence of the Master of Corpus, that the university should present an address to the crown; and though without loss of time Dr Law informed the Chancellor, mentioning that he regarded himself as obliged 'to consult your Grace before any publick step be taken in an affair concerning which we here seem to be no very competent judges[1],' the Duke was very seriously annoyed.

'I send you' he wrote to Lord Hardwicke 'a silly letter from poor Dr Law: I call it silly, for, poor man, he should

[1] Add. MS. 32883, f. 269.

have told this officious Master of Emmanuel that he had heard nothing from the Chancellor who was the proper person to tell them if an address was proper or expected[1].'

According to this doctrine it was for the Chancellor to tell the university when to address the crown; but even Newcastle admitted on this occasion that, as the suggestion had been made, it must be acted upon. He was careful however to see that the address should be such as he could approve. He arranged that it should be drafted by Law and revised by Lord Hardwicke; and when Hardwicke sent the address to the Duke, he generously gave the Master of Peterhouse the credit for any merit it might have.

'If your Grace should happen to approve of this address' he wrote 'I suspect that your usual partiality to me may ascribe what is good in it to your faithful servant; but, if you do, you will in truth wrong Dr Law, for his draught (*sic*) was a very good one, the topics well chosen and well expressed in my apprehension[2]';

and, softened perhaps by Hardwicke's pleading, the Duke repented of his harshness.

'There is nothing omitted' he wrote to Law on receiving the address, 'which the most zealous servant of His Majesty and friend to his country could wish to have had inserted, and the various points are mentioned so properly that I don't know which to admire most, the propriety of the matter or the elegance of the manner[3].'

This was giving praise in unstinting measure; but there was one phrase in the draft which the Duke could not allow to pass. Dr Law had expressed the hope that the King might 'enjoy the calm evening of a glorious reign,' but as that evening was already far advanced, Newcastle, who knew the ways of kings and courts, remarked that 'though that is undoubtedly the fact, I would submit to

[1] Add. MS. 32883, f. 273.   [2] Add. MS. 32883, f. 297.
[3] Add. MS. 32882, f. 333.

you whether in an address of congratulation you would just name it[1].' For the unfortunate phrase therefore was substituted: 'may in perfect tranquillity enjoy a long and glorious reign' and the King was spared being reminded that he was on the verge of the grave.

The address, thus amended, having been submitted to the Heads and passed by the Senate[2], was presented to the King on September 12th, 1758, by the Chancellor who was accompanied by the Masters of Corpus and Peterhouse. The numerous deputation from the university, usual on such occasions, was dispensed with, as fatiguing ceremonies were considered bad for the King at his age[3]. It may be presumed that the absence of Dr Richardson was a punishment for his forwardness in suggesting an address; and, though all had turned out well, it is evident that Newcastle considered that he had not altogether been treated with proper respect. On this particular occasion it had been comparatively easy for him to nip rebellion in the bud and regain effective control, as both the Vice-Chancellor, Dr Green, and the deputy Vice-Chancellor, Dr Law, were his loyal supporters; but he could not rely upon being always so favourably situated. There was ever the danger that an independent spirit might resent his interference; and at times he must have been sorely torn between a desire for the university to present an address and a fear that the particular moment was not favourable to the exercise of his influence. Generally however the occasions demanding an university address were too well defined to allow the Chancellor much discretion. Thus when in October 1759 the news of the capture of Quebec reached England, Newcastle was compelled to direct the university to address the King; and, as Dr Caryl was Vice-Chancellor, the Duke probably did

[1] Add. MS. 32883, f. 333.   [2] Add. MS. 32883, f. 349, f. 376.
[3] Add. MS. 32883, f. 333.

not anticipate that there would be any difficulty. But Caryl's term of office was drawing to a close; and when on November 4th he was succeeded as Vice-Chancellor by James Burrough, Master of Caius, he had not even completed the draft of the address. This was particularly unfortunate, as Burrough, being tory in his sympathies, might not be obedient to the Chancellor's wishes; but Caryl was equal to the emergency. By November 5th he had completed the address and communicated it to Newcastle; but he purposely delayed handing a copy of it to the new Vice-Chancellor until late on the following day, his object being, as he informed the Duke, to prevent any meeting of the Heads being summoned to consider it before November 7th, by which time he and his friends would have had 'an opportunity of receiving any commands your Grace may please to honour us with before it will become difficult to pay a proper regard to them[1]'.

The Master of Caius was probably unjustly suspected of wishing to cause annoyance; for when it came to the point he proved himself unexpectedly compliant. Though he had been anxious for a numerous deputation from the university to attend the presentation of the address, he at once abandoned the idea when it was pointed out that the King would be thereby caused unnecessary trouble[2], and in no respect had Newcastle any reason to complain of his conduct. He earned his reward.

'On the 12th of November' states Cooper in his Annals of Cambridge 'the following address was presented to the King at St James's by the Duke of Newcastle, Chancellor of the university, attended by James Burrough, Esq., Vice-Chancellor, Dr Richardson, Master of Emmanuel College, Dr Law, Master of Peterhouse and Dr Caryl, Master of Jesus College, which address His Majesty was pleased to receive very graciously. They all had the honour to kiss His Majesty's hand, and His

[1] Add. MS. 32898, f. 105. [2] Add. MS. 32898, f. 86.

THE CHANCELLOR AND THE UNIVERSITY 157

Majesty was pleased to confer the honour of knighthood upon James Burrough, Esq., Vice-Chancellor[1].'

Ten days before the expiration of Sir James Burrough's Vice-Chancellorship, George II died; and it was of course necessary for the university to address the new King. Burrough's successor as Vice-Chancellor was Sandby, the recently appointed Master of Magdalene, who was an Oxford man and entirely unacquainted with the university over which he was called upon to preside; and Newcastle not unreasonably feared that he might be too new to his duties to produce an address worthy of the occasion. He therefore calmly decided that the Vice-Chancellor should not be allowed to draft the address, and instructed Dr Yonge to write immediately to the Dean of Lincoln[2] and Dr Caryl, and acquaint them that the university must address and come up in a body. That the Duke of Newcastle desires they would take care that the address may be a well drawn and a proper one. That the late King's amiable and great character should be drawn. The happiness his subjects enjoyed under his long and glorious reign should be mentioned as well as the particular marks of his grace and favour to the university of Cambridge. Then something as strong as possible upon the present King—his amiable character and good setting out, and assurances of the same duty to him and attention in the university to bring up their youth in principles of zeal for his royal person and government. That as the Duke of Newcastle is to read this address to the King, His Grace wishes that the draft might be sent up to him. It will be a work of but twenty four hours....That they will certainly take care to shew all proper respect and regard to the new Vice-Chancellor; but not leave to him the forming of the address[3].

Dr Sandby was, therefore, to be politely though firmly shoved aside, and both he and the university would have been poor-spirited to submit to the affront. But on this occasion Newcastle's zeal out-ran his dis-

[1] Cooper's *Annals*, IV, 302.   [2] Dr Green, Master of Corpus.
[3] Add. MS. 32914, f. 9.

158 THE CHANCELLOR AND THE UNIVERSITY

cretion; and he was rebuked by the Master of Corpus who told him that, as it lay with the Vice-Chancellor 'to make any address which may happen during his year, we could not without great offence take that matter out of his hands[1].' Nor indeed was there any real need for such a violation of custom, as Dr Sandby, fully conscious of his inexperience, was willing and anxious to take expert advice. 'As he was pleased to request my assistance in drawing it up,' continued Dr Green, 'and the draft will be submitted to the review and judgment of your Grace's friends here, I hope it may in some measure be executed agreeably to your advice and directions[2].' Newcastle however proved more exacting than the Master of Corpus had anticipated, and was sufficiently dissatisfied with Dr Sandby's draft to return it for re-consideration.

'I have the favour' he wrote 'of your letter by your servant with the draught (*sic*) of an address from the university to the King enclosed. As you are so good as to desire my opinion of it, and as I (as Chancellor) shall have the honour of reading it to the King, I hope you will forgive the liberty I take in wishing that you and the Heads, whom you have consulted, would reconsider this draught which, though I am persuaded it was not intended, seems to me not quite to come up to those demonstrations of duty and gratitude to my late royal master which a constant avowed countenance and protection and a series of unprecedented favours have deserved from us. Some more explicit declarations with regard to the loss which we with the whole nation have suffered, and some more specifick assurances of our firm resolution to breed up the youth under our care in principles and practice of duty and loyalty to his present Majesty, on whom the hopes of the whole nation and particularly of our university now devolve, I humbly conceive are necessary[3].'

The Vice-Chancellor must have felt very much like a schoolboy who had done his task badly; but, pocketing

---

[1] Add. MS. 32914, f. 94.   [2] *Ibid.*
[3] Add. MS. 32914, f. 143.

THE CHANCELLOR AND THE UNIVERSITY 159

his pride, he acquiesced in the rebuke and set to work at once upon another draft which, with one slight alteration, Newcastle cordially approved[1]. Sandby was sensibly relieved, for the worst was now over.

'I rose very early this morning' he informed the Duke on November 9th 'and wrote out the address again from your Grace's copy and presented it before the Heads in the vestry at St Mary's. It was well liked there, and this afternoon I called a congregation and read it in the Senate house. To-morrow morning at nine it will be read a second time[2].'

Thus all was well; but Sandby must have wondered whether the Vice-Chancellor was not the Chancellor's deputy in fact as well as in name. Possibly Newcastle was more than usually worrying on this occasion as it was important to represent the university in a favourable light to a young king who was suspected of cherishing tory sympathies; and certainly the presentation of the address, which took place on November 12th, 1760, was attended with a great deal of pomp and ceremony. The necessity of keeping the deputation as small as possible existed no longer; and the Duke went to Court accompanied by the High Steward, the Vice-Chancellor, 'several of the nobility, students in the university,' and a bevy of bishops, heads of houses, doctors and masters of arts[3].

Enough has been said to show that Newcastle took his duty with regard to university addresses with almost unbecoming seriousness; and his fussiness must have been extremely irritating to his victims. His interference was due in great measure to over-anxiety for the dignity of the university and a morbid fear of being treated as a cipher; and it certainly was not inspired by any ulterior political motive. It cannot however be said that his conduct was always equally innocent, for there

[1] Add. MS. 32914, f. 183, f. 197. [2] Add. MS. 32914, f. 221.
[3] Cooper's *Annals of Cambridge*, IV, 305, 306.

were occasions when he laid himself open to the charge of sacrificing the university to his requirements as a party leader. This tendency was perhaps most marked in the matter of mandate degrees which assumed an unfortunate importance during his Chancellorship and occasionally placed him in an embarrassing situation. It must be explained that though the statutes of the university forbade the granting of degrees, except to noblemen and quasi nobiles[1], unless the proper exercises had been performed at the proper time, and declared all dispensations from this regulation to be null and void, it had always been permissible for the crown to issue letters mandatory for a degree to be granted to an unqualified person notwithstanding any statute to the contrary. Such action on the part of the crown, as long as it was kept within due limits and only taken when there was urgent cause, might clearly be the most easy and convenient way of circumventing the rigidity of the university constitution, but in the latter half of the seventeenth century this royal privilege began to be abused. In the first year of his reign Charles II ordered the creation of one hundred and twenty-one doctors of divinity, twelve doctors of civil law, twelve doctors of physic, twelve bachelors of divinity, two masters of arts and one bachelor of civil law; and though this wholesale issue of letters mandatory can be excused on the ground that several persons had been prevented by the troubles of the Commonwealth period from taking their degrees at the proper time and in the proper way, it seems that throughout the reign of Charles II mandate degrees were more frequently granted than they ever had been before[2]. It must have been obvious,

[1] Quasi nobiles included all those allied to the sovereign by consanguinity or affinity, as well as all those commonly called 'honourable personages, sive men, women or maids of honour and their sons being their nearest heirs.' [2] Cooper's *Annals of Cambridge*, III, 481.

THE CHANCELLOR AND THE UNIVERSITY 161

even to the most prejudiced tories, that a frequent exercise of this right by the sovereign threatened both the independence and the prestige of the university, placing it between the dilemma of incurring the consequences of resistance to the royal will and allowing degrees to be habitually granted to unfit and unqualified persons; and the system received its deathblow when James II issued letters mandatory for a degree to be conferred upon Alban Francis, a Benedictine monk. Consequently, shortly after the Revolution, it was agreed between the crown and university that only on the receipt of a petition from the Chancellor should letters mandatory be issued by the crown, and that the Chancellor should not petition until he had received a certificate, signed by a majority of Heads of Houses, that the applicant was a 'person of good learning[1].'

By this arrangement the initiative was left with the university. Letters mandatory could not be issued except upon the receipt of a petition from the Chancellor, and

[1] The Certificate of the Heads was generally in the following form. 'We, the Vice-Chancellor and the Heads of colleges in the university of Cambridge, whose names are underwritten, humbly beg leave to certify to his Grace, Thomas Holles, Duke of Newcastle, Chancellor of the university aforesaid, that Robert Roper hath been recommended to us as a person of good learning, and as desirous of proceeding to the degree of doctor in laws in this university; but that he cannot be admitted to the same without His Majesty's most gracious letters mandatory dispensing with our statutes in that behalf. And we do further certify that such His Majesty's letters mandatory in favour of the said Robert Roper will be no ways prejudicial either to the university in general or to any college in particular, he paying the accustomed fees and performing the usual exercises, or giving a sufficient caution for the performance of the same.' The Chancellor's petition embodied the certificate, and concluded with a request for the issue of 'His Majesty's most gracious letters mandatory in this behalf.' Add. MS. 36001, f. 275, Add. MS. 32933, f. 314. See also Add. MS. 32950, f. 142, Add. MS. 35629, f. 73.

162 THE CHANCELLOR AND THE UNIVERSITY

the Chancellor could not present a petition until he had received a certificate from the Heads of Houses. Thus adequate protection was granted, and for a time the system appears to have worked well. During the Chancellorship of the Duke of Somerset about seventy mandate degrees were conferred, which does not seem to be an excessive number for a period of nearly sixty years[1]; and when in the reign of George I the College of Physicians, jealous of the honour of their profession, objected to mandate degrees in medicine, the university graciously undertook 'not to confer degrees in Physick, out of the ordinary and regular course, but with a very sparing hand and unless there was something very particular and urgent in the case[2].' There were doubtless abuses, but the Heads seem to have commonly acted with care and discrimination, and to have generally demanded, before signing the certificate, that the applicant should either be recommended by the Master of his college or present testimonials from persons of standing and reputation who were prepared to testify from personal knowledge that he was 'of good learning' and fully qualified for the degree to which he aspired[3]. It is not surprising that the university was unwilling to cheapen its degrees by bestowing them upon the unworthy; and as long as the initiative was left to those who were interested in making a sparing use of the privilege, the practice of resorting to the royal mandate was not only innocuous but positively useful. It sometimes happened that a thoroughly well equipped candi-

---

[1] Add. MS. 32949, f. 435. Of these seventy, ten were created doctors of divinity, twelve doctors of physic, three doctors of laws, five bachelors of divinity, one bachelor of physic, two bachelors of laws, and thirty-seven masters of arts.

[2] Add. MS. 32945, f. 31; Cooper's *Annals of Cambridge*, IV, 168.

[3] Add. MS. 32936, f. 112; Add. MS. 32941, f. 114; Add. MS. 32952, f. 328, f. 330.

THE CHANCELLOR AND THE UNIVERSITY 163

date for a professorship lacked the degree requisite to qualify him for election; and the deficiency could only be remedied by the intervention of the crown. It was also not unknown for those, who for some reason or another had been obliged to leave the university without taking a degree, to find in later life that they could not advance in their profession without becoming graduates. This was frequently the case among schoolmasters; and it was generally felt that if such persons could show that they had continued their studies after leaving the university, no harm would be done by allowing them to receive a mandate degree.

It was impossible however to eliminate completely the danger of abuse; and during Newcastle's Chancellorship the defects in the system were revealed. It was quickly noticed that more than the usual number of mandate degrees were being granted, and that this increase was accompanied by a very hazardous innovation. In 1757 Frederick Montagu, a Fellow-Commoner of Trinity college, received a master of arts degree by royal mandate, being the first Fellow-Commoner to be so distinguished, and though he seems thoroughly to have deserved the compliment by his learning and scholarship, an unfortunate precedent was thereby established. It was difficult to refuse the same privilege to other Fellow-Commoners; and thus what had originally been intended as an exception became the rule.

'I was sorry' wrote Dr Yonge in 1767 'when this practise (*sic*) of giving degrees to the Fellow-Commoners began, even though the first person so honoured was Mr Montagu, for whom the university could not do more than enough. But I saw the opening and the danger of it[1].'

There is no doubt that Newcastle was partly responsible for this undesirable increase, and that he particularly encouraged the practice of conferring man-

[1] Add. MS. 32980, f. 112; Add. MS. 35629, f. 73.

date degrees upon Fellow-Commoners. In so doing he certainly endangered the independence and prestige of the university. It was clearly the business of the Chancellor to act as a check upon the Heads, in the granting of mandate degrees, by refusing to petition the crown unless satisfied that there was good cause; and it had never been intended that he should take the initiative and call upon the Heads to produce the necessary certificates for the candidates he recommended. The recommendation of a Chancellor might be as difficult to resist as a royal command; and the case for the university was well put on one occasion by Dr Yonge.

'I take the liberty' he told the Duke 'of acquainting your Grace that whenever the Heads are disposed to make compliments of masters' degrees to the young gentlemen who are educated at Cambridge, I see no reason why your Grace should obstruct their designs. They are very good judges of the propriety of the cases before them, and will, I am persuaded, not recommend any person but such as they think will not be disagreeable to your Grace. In general I cannot but think it would be best for your Grace not to recommend but to approve their recommendation when it shall be (as this is) previously made known to your Grace[1].'

The advice was sound enough but it was very difficult for Newcastle to follow it. He would have probably frankly admitted that he was not well qualified to judge the learning and attainments of the candidates; but he might fairly have pleaded in defence of his conduct that he was obliged to consider the question from a point of view not exclusively academic. It was part of his business as a party leader to secure favours for his supporters and their friends, and his success in politics was largely due to his thorough execution of this duty. He had encouraged men to ask for things both great

[1] Add. MS. 32980, f. 112.

THE CHANCELLOR AND THE UNIVERSITY 165

and small, so as to advertise his power as a patron; and it was therefore to him that applicants for mandate degrees or their friends naturally turned. Consistently to refuse such applications, especially when they came from influential quarters, might re-act unfavourably upon his power in parliament, and yet he was well aware that it would be dangerous to affront the pride of the university by converting its degrees into mere rewards for political services.

There was doubtless a half-way house between these two extremes but the Duke had some difficulty in finding it. He was far too ready to press the claims of applicants who besought him to use his influence, and to assume the initiative instead of waiting for the university to take action. In June 1760 he directed the Master of Corpus to take the proper steps for securing a master of arts degree by royal mandate for Samuel Hill, a Fellow-Commoner of St John's[1], who was only seventeen years old and had been at Cambridge for little more than a year[2]. The command on this occasion was executed without hesitation[3]; but when in 1762 the Duke demanded mandate degrees for two persons, one of whom had been recommended to him by Lord Hertford, the request, though obeyed, was not much liked. 'The proposal of a second degree immediately as soon as the first had been granted,' remarked the Master of Corpus, 'occasioned, as the Vice-Chancellor sends me word, some little demur among the Heads[4].' There is no doubt that the Duke's demands were apt to be excessive, and he was at last obliged to promise the Heads to be more moderate for

[1] Add. MS. 32907, f. 373.
[2] *Admissions to St John's College*, Part III, p. 155.
[3] Add. MS. 32907, f. 373.
[4] Add. MS. 32936, f. 112; see also Add. MS. 32936, f. 86; Add. MS. 32939, f. 146.

166 THE CHANCELLOR AND THE UNIVERSITY

the future[1]. It was not easy for him however to keep such a promise, and in fairness it must be remembered that he was continually being importuned by those whom it would be hazardous to refuse. Thus in June 1763 he was approached by Lord Huntingdon to obtain a master of arts degree for a certain Mr Ragdale, and by Lord Clive to obtain a bachelor of arts degree for Thomas Humphreys, a former member of St John's[2]. Both Lord Huntingdon and Lord Clive were clearly desirable persons for Newcastle to oblige, and their candidates were able to advance valid claims for consideration. Ragdale was a clergyman who needed a degree in order to hold a certain living in Leicestershire for which he was an applicant, and Humphreys, who had been obliged by his father's death to leave the university after four terms residence, was a candidate for a mastership at Shrewsbury school. Yet though both applications were reasonable and had influential support, Newcastle was careful on this occasion not to act precipitately. He was aware of the danger of exhausting the patience of the university, and was further aware that it was not a favourable moment for him to ask a favour. The Vice-Chancellor at the time was Dr Goddard, Master of Clare, who was the Duke's declared enemy; and it might be taken for certain that he would seize any opportunity of inflicting a rebuff upon the Chancellor. Newcastle therefore acted with far more caution than usual. He told Lord Huntingdon that he could not at present comply with his demand and gave a similar answer to Lord Clive who applied a little later.

'I hope' he wrote to Lord Clive on June 30th 'your Lordship thinks that it is the greatest concern to me that I am not at present able to obey your commands for obtaining a mandate for a degree for Mr Humphreys. I have explained the whole

[1] Add. MS. 32949, f. 244.
[2] Add. MS. 32949, f. 263; Add. MS. 32952, f. 330

matter to him, that I had promised the university to be more cautious than I had been in permitting these degrees; and, what is worst of all, it happens very unluckily that, in consequence of that promise, I did actually refuse, the day before yesterday only, to obtain a degree for a friend of my Lord Huntingdon in Nottinghamshire; and wrote him word I could not do it consistently with my promise to the university. Should I so soon after do the thing for another it would not have a good appearance for me; and therefore I am sure your Lordship will forgive me. I have desired Mr Humphreys would stay a little, which I hope would be no inconvenience to him[1].'

By thus playing off Ragdale against Humphreys and Lord Huntingdon against Lord Clive, Newcastle had extricated himself from a difficult situation; and, had he been content to do no more, all would probably have been well. But, anxious to oblige and to demonstrate his influence, he could not resist making an attempt to secure the two mandate degrees, even though he had announced that it was impossible for him to do anything. Consequently he instructed Dr Caryl and his other friends at Cambridge to find out whether it would be possible to satisfy the two applicants.

'Mr Ragdale's character' wrote Hurdis, the Duke's secretary, to Dr Caryl 'is an exceedingly good one. His testimonial is signed by very respectable persons and everybody speaks extremely well of him. He has very considerable connections amongst His Grace's friends in Nottinghamshire; himself and his relations have been staunch friends for many years; and his case seems to be so particular and indeed so compassionate that His Grace cannot but wish to oblige them, and that it may be one of those that would be agreeable to the university to admit.' Hurdis in the same letter enlarged upon the claims of Humphreys, urging that

if this should be an admissible case and can be complied with, consistently with his promise to the Heads of the university, His Grace would be glad to oblige his Lordship upon this occasion[2].

[1] Add. MS. 32949, f. 244. [2] Add. MS. 32949, f. 263.

168 THE CHANCELLOR AND THE UNIVERSITY

Unfortunately however it was not made perfectly clear in this letter that both or neither of the mandate degrees must be granted; and the omission was the cause of a good deal of trouble. On Monday July 4th Ragdale visited Cambridge and waited upon the Vice-Chancellor. It is possible that he prejudiced Dr Goddard in his favour by mentioning that his application had been refused by the Chancellor; for his suit was successful. Moved either by compassion or malice the Vice-Chancellor espoused his cause and proposed at a meeting of the Heads that he should be given a mandate degree. The proposal was naturally supported by the Duke's friends among the Heads, and Ragdale was presented with the necessary certificate to take to the Chancellor. But as Dr Caryl and his allies were convinced that it would be a fatal mistake to suggest the granting of two mandate degrees simultaneously, they purposely refrained from bringing forward the case of Humphreys. Their policy was intelligible but it was extremely inconvenient to the Duke who was dismayed on learning what had happened.

'My Lord Duke' wrote Hurdis to Dr Caryl on July 8th 'received the favour of your letter by Mr Ragdale who came here this morning to give an account of his success at Cambridge, and to beg His Grace would be so good as to sign the certificate, usual in such cases, for the king's mandate. His Grace was very much concerned to find that nothing had been done for Mr Humphreys, Lord Clive's friend. You must be sensible from what passed when you was here that His Grace does not like to recommend to such degrees, that he is resolved to keep his promise to the Heads of the university to be very cautious in that respect; but as these cases were very particular and therefore thought to be admissible, and so circumstanced (as appears from the letters you have) that one could not be consented to without the other (for His Grace in answer to Lord Clive had made that a principal reason for not granting his Lordship's request that he had refused to do the same thing for Lord Huntingdon's

THE CHANCELLOR AND THE UNIVERSITY 169

friend a few days before) it was therefore hoped that both would be complied with; and His Grace does not a little wonder that the one should be granted and not the other, which puts him under greater difficulties now than ever, and has suspended signing Mr Ragdale's certificate till he hears further from you and his friends upon this occasion, and what can be done for Lord Clive's friend which His Grace has equally at heart with the other. Mr Ragdale is very much pressed for time; he has none to lose, for the living has now been vacant upward of four months, and, till Mr Humphreys affair is determined, his must be in suspense, and therefore it is hoped the answer will come soon[1].'

After making every allowance for the difficulties of the situation in which the Duke found himself, there does not appear to be any sufficient excuse for his highhanded action in refusing to proceed with Ragdale's application until he was satisfied that Humphrey's application would also be granted. The two cases were unconnected except in point of time, Ragdale had been beforehand with Humphreys in applying, and it was unreasonable that he should suffer because another applicant was disappointed. The Chancellor moreover was not justified in refusing to petition the crown for a mandate degree, upon receipt of a certificate from the Heads, unless he was able to show that the certificate had been granted on insufficient grounds. He had grievously blundered in attempting simultaneously to secure two mandate degrees, and his secretary had blundered still deeper in failing to make Dr Caryl understand that Ragdale and Humphreys must stand or fall together.

'In excuse of what is already passed' wrote the Master of Jesus 'I can only say that I and your Grace's friends here were verily persuaded that if we had tried for both the degrees we had certainly lost both; and we made no question but that your Grace gave the preference to Mr Ragdale's case, as it was

[1] Add. MS. 32949, f. 290.

mentioned in the first place, was the most compassionate, of the greatest consequence, and the most amply recommended to your Grace[1].'

Newcastle would have acted wisely if he had allowed Ragdale to proceed to his degree and held out hopes to Humphreys of satisfaction in the near future. He was however determined that one should not be taken and the other left; and as Humphreys' case could not be proceeded with until the autumn when the university re-assembled after the long vacation, he decided that Ragdale must wait until then for his degree[2]. Both Humphreys and his patron, having no option, acquiesced in this arrangement[3]; but Dr Goddard did not prove so complaisant. He had no occasion to love the Chancellor and very good reason heartily to dislike him[4], and he adroitly used Ragdale as a stick with which to beat him. It was customary for the Chancellor, on receipt of a certificate from the Heads, to petition the crown through one of the Secretaries of State; and in August 1763 Newcastle was astonished and aghast to learn that the certificate for Ragdale's degree had been sent, presumably by the Vice-Chancellor, direct to Lord Egremont, one of the Secretaries of State, that thereupon Egremont had applied to the crown for letters mandatory which had been granted, and that on Saturday August 13th Ragdale had been admitted to his degree. To excuse such an insult to the Chancellor and such a violation of the customary procedure, it was alleged that Newcastle had requested that Ragdale's certificate 'should be sent in to the Secretary's office[5]'; but he certainly had not given any such instructions,

[1] Add. MS. 32949, f. 324.   [2] *Ibid.*
[3] Add. MS. 32949, f. 431, f. 438; Add. MS. 32950, f. 53.
[4] For an account of relations between Dr Goddard and the Duke, see Chapter IV.
[5] Add. MS. 32950, f. 158.

THE CHANCELLOR AND THE UNIVERSITY 171

and it can only be concluded that Dr Goddard, annoyed by the Duke's procrastinating policy, intentionally passed him over. Furious at the insult and the triumph of his enemy, Newcastle threatened legal proceedings, consulted with the Attorney-General, and called upon Lord Hardwicke as High Steward 'to support and defend the rights of the Chancellor[1]'; but he soon found that he was helpless to avenge himself and that the Master of Clare had completely outwitted him.

The punishment, though severe, was hardly undeserved; for Newcastle had blundered badly in placing his own personal inconvenience before the respect which he owed to the university. He had however no redress; and though immediately after Goddard had ceased to be Vice-Chancellor, Humphreys obtained his mandate degree, this was but scanty consolation[2]. It must be admitted that, though in many ways an admirable Chancellor and genuinely anxious to further the interests of the university, the Duke sadly mismanaged the question of mandate degrees. Despite his good resolutions he was not content to be a mere channel of communication between the university and the crown, and allowed his necessities as a party leader to influence his policy as Chancellor. Such conduct bred a justifiable resentment in the university; and it may have been partly due to his unwise activity that in 1781 a Grace was passed which required the assent of the Senate, as well as the Heads, to petitions for mandate degrees[3].

Unfortunately this was not the only question on which Newcastle found himself at cross purposes with the university. It had for long been a well established

[1] Add. MS. 32950, f. 142.
[2] Add. MS. 32951, f. 379; Add. MS. 32952, f. 223, f. 256, f. 268, f. 328, f. 330, f. 347, f. 399, f. 401, f. 411.
[3] Add. MS. 35629, f. 73; Cooper's *Annals of Cambridge*, IV, 400.

custom that a Vice-Chancellor should not be re-elected on the expiration of his year of office; and though in exceptional circumstances a Vice-Chancellor had been continued for a second year, the practice was not popular and had not been encouraged. It could of course be urged that the rule of enforcing retirement at the end of a year was essentially wasteful, and that a Vice-Chancellor would probably be far more useful after twelve months experience of office; but the dignity was coveted, and it was obvious that if a two years tenure of the office became usual, many Heads of Houses would either never attain the honour or be obliged to wait for it longer than was thought desirable. Therefore, whatever might be ideally best, it was probably well from the point of view of the general contentment of the university that the old custom should be maintained; but Newcastle was not convinced by the argument for peace and goodwill. He was well aware that it was extremely important for him to be on friendly and intimate terms with the most influential resident member of the university; and he was therefore always anxious that a Vice-Chancellor, of whom he approved, should be continued in office for a second year. This attitude was reasonable, especially in a Chancellor who intended to play an active part; but it was almost certain to provoke trouble.

But for a time the Duke was extremely successful in converting what had been an exception into an established rule. Thus when Dr Keene, Master of Peterhouse, who had been appointed Vice-Chancellor in November 1749 and proved himself extremely useful to the Duke, was nearing the end of his first year of office, Newcastle urged his re-election. Circumstances favoured the design, for it happened that all existing Heads of Houses had served their turn as Vice-Chancellor, and that if Keene retired he would be suc-

THE CHANCELLOR AND THE UNIVERSITY 173

ceeded by Dr Wilcox, Master of Clare, who was elderly and not desirous of office. Hence no resentment was aroused by the proposal and the Master of Peterhouse was duly re-elected[1]. It is possible that Newcastle was misled by the ease with which his wishes had been obeyed, and omitted to notice that the circumstances were peculiar and not likely to recur often. Yet he was warned that 'the Heads in general may look with jealousy upon this particular mark of distinction[2].' The temptation however proved irresistible; and in October 1753 he urged the prolongation of his friend, Dr Yonge, Master of Jesus, who was just completing his year of office as Vice-Chancellor.

'There is nothing so natural' he informed Dr Keene who had recently been appointed Bishop of Chester 'as to continue Dr Yonge, and nobody will so well answer the end or be so agreeable to me. I know my appearing publickly is improper and perhaps might do more hurt than good. But with your Lordship and my real friends I flatter myself that my inclinations will have weight[3].'

The Duke's inclinations indeed had so much weight that his friends had anticipated them.

'The day before I received your Grace's letter' replied the Bishop of Chester 'I had invited to dinner the Vice-Chancellor, the Masters of St John's, Trinity, Christ's and Magdalene; and took occasion, in the absence of the Vice-Chancellor, to mention the affair and it is but justice to those gentlemen that I assure your Grace their only question was what your sentiments were, and on my telling them they determined to assist. I do not hear of any objection to the measure amongst the body, and I am verily persuaded that it will be effected and in the handsomest manner[4].'

The Bishop proved a true prophet, and the Master of Jesus was continued as Vice-Chancellor for another year. When he finally resigned in November 1754 he

[1] Add. MS. 32722, f. 418. [2] Add. MS. 32722, f. 418.
[3] Add. MS. 32733, f. 135. [4] Add. MS. 32733, f. 148.

was succeeded by Dr Thomas, Master of Christ's; and as Dr Thomas was also an ardent supporter, Newcastle assumed, almost as a matter of course, that he too would be continued for a second year. But there were limits to the patience of the university, and the Chancellor had succeeded in reaching them.

'His Grace, as your Lordship may remember,' wrote Dr Thomas to Lord Dupplin in October 1755, 'desired me to continue another year in the office of Vice-Chancellor which, in obedience to his commands, I readily submitted to. And when I returned to college I found that many of our friends here took it for granted that I was to continue in office a second year. But I find now that Dr Walker, Vice-Master of Trinity college, and several in that college declare they will, if they can, prevent the office from being continued two years in my hands or in the hands of any other person. And the tories and the friends of the Master of Caius college are grown very jealous and suspicious of a design of keeping him out of the Vice-Chancellorship, and will doubtless be very ready to join the Trinity people[1].'

The revolt of Trinity was an ugly phenomenon. It was not inspired by any dislike of Dr Thomas, who had proved a successful and tactful Vice-Chancellor[2], but intended as a protest against the Chancellor's attack upon the established traditions of the university. Dr Thomas believed that not only was he personally popular in Trinity but that

several in that college, if they had not known that it was agreeable to our Chancellor to have had me continued in office another year, would have voted for me sooner than any other person in the university[3];

[1] Add. MS. 32860, f. 118.
[2] 'They cannot have any objection to me' wrote Dr Thomas 'unless they be tired with peace and quietness. For everything has been carried on all the year in the most quiet manner without one non-placet in the Senate house and without the least disturbance in the university.' Add. MS. 32860, f. 118.
[3] *Ibid.*

THE CHANCELLOR AND THE UNIVERSITY 175

and this opinion was probably based upon something more substantial than personal vanity. It was clearly the Chancellor who was the object of the attack, and Trinity, as one of the largest and most influential of the colleges, was able to make an effective protest and to count upon considerable support in the university at large. The rebels moreover were able to contend with some show of reason that they had law as well as tradition on their side, and that for a Vice-Chancellor to remain in office for two successive years was not only inexpedient and irregular but illegal. By an act passed in the ninth year of Queen Anne's reign, it was provided that

no person who has been in an annual office in any borough or town corporate, to which person it belongs to preside at the election and to make return for any member to serve in parliament, shall be capable of being chosen in the same office for the year immediately ensuing[1];

and it was argued that as the university members were elected under the title of burgesses, the university was consequently a borough, and that therefore the Vice-Chancellor, as the returning officer, was not eligible for re-election[2].

Though the argument may have been unsound, it was good enough to convince men willing to be convinced; and, threatened by what might turn out to be a rebellion on a large scale, Newcastle beat a timely retreat, and in November 1755 Dr Law, Master of Peterhouse, succeeded the Master of Christ's as Vice-Chancellor. Like everybody else in the university the new Vice-Chancellor was well aware that he was an unwelcome intruder as far as Newcastle was concerned,

[1] Add. MS. 32860, f. 195. Those are not the exact words of the act, for which see 'Statutes at Large,' ninth year of Queen Anne, *c.* 20.
[2] Add. MS. 32860, f. 195.

and that his election represented a victory for the party of resistance.

'I think myself obliged' he wrote 'to take the first opportunity of acquainting your Grace that the university has this day conferred an honour upon me, very much against my own inclination and endeavour, in electing me Vice-Chancellor for the ensuing year. An office which is now made the less agreeable as going contrary both to your Grace's judgment and the general good[1].'

The Duke was doubtless deeply mortified by what he must have deemed factious resistance; but he had only himself to blame. He had been warned that the policy he was pursuing was likely to cause resentment; and though it was natural that he should desire to continue a friendly Vice-Chancellor, he had no excuse for neglecting the force of public opinion. As in the matter of mandate degrees he allowed his own personal convenience to outweigh more important considerations; and so strong was this inclination that it was some time before he drew the proper conclusions from the Trinity rebellion. A few weeks before Dr Law completed his first year of office, Dr Summer was elected Provost of King's; and if the customary order of succession was observed, the newly elected Provost would follow the Master of Peterhouse as Vice-Chancellor. The prospect was displeasing to Newcastle who had opposed Sumner's election as Provost, and he therefore began to consider ways and means of preventing what he doubtless regarded as a catastrophe. It is not likely that he contemplated the prolongation of Law, for, apart from the danger of such a scheme, he appears to have held the Master of Peterhouse in unjustifiably low esteem; but it is possible that he might have been driven to this extremity if a happier solution of the difficulty had not been suggested. With an ingenuity for which

[1] Add. MS. 32860, f. 357.

THE CHANCELLOR AND THE UNIVERSITY 177

he is deserving of much credit, Dr Keene pointed out that Dr Green, who had been Master of Corpus since 1750, had never served as Vice-Chancellor, being disqualified by holding the Regius Professorship of Divinity[1]; but that, as he had already announced his intention of resigning his professorship[2], it was expedient that he should execute his intention without delay, and thereby establish a claim to succeed Law as Vice-Chancellor[3]. The scheme was certainly ingenious but it had one serious defect. Dr Sumner was senior by degree to Dr Green and consequently entitled to precede him as Vice-Chancellor, but it was hoped that as the Provost had long been absent from the university and was entirely unacquainted with its business, he might be happy to be allowed to delay undertaking a task for which he lacked the necessary experience. This expectation however was not fulfilled. In answer to Dr Green, who had broached the question with him, the Provost with Roman fortitude replied that he was deeply obliged

for the civility of the offer, but that by accepting the Headship he thought he ought not to decline any trouble that fell to his share, that he understood the office would by the rules of the university come to him the following year[4], and that it would not become any person of resolution to postpone the discharging it on account of some little inconvenience, and that another year might perhaps be as inconvenient to him as the next[5].

When Dr Green inquired if this was his final answer, he replied that it was.

It is extremely likely that Dr Sumner was well aware that Newcastle distrusted him, and that a plot was on foot to prevent his election as Vice-Chancellor. He not

---
[1] Chapter 1, p. 27, *n.* 2.
[2] Green had recently been made Dean of Lincoln.
[3] Add. MS. 32868, f. 106.   [4] That is the next academic year.
[5] Add. MS. 32868, f. 370.

unnaturally declined to be a party to the intrigue of which he was to be the victim; and if he chose to stand out for what was certainly his right by custom, he could count upon considerable support in the university. Dr Yonge and Dr Thomas agreed with the Master of Corpus in believing that if the Provost 'persists in this resolution, he can't be attempted to be sett aside without many and great inconveniences or without throwing this place into a great ferment[1]'; and this was no groundless fear. It would be comparatively easy to raise once again the cry that the Chancellor was tampering with the independence of the university; and it seemed not at all improbable that Trinity would take up the cudgels for Sumner as they had taken them up for Law[2]. The fear of what might happen served as a sufficient deterrent; and although the Master of Corpus resigned his professorship in order to be ready for any emergency, it was finally decided, that as the Provost had indicated he was ready to adopt a friendly attitude towards Newcastle[3], it would be wise to allow him to become Vice-Chancellor[4]. Consequently he succeeded Law in November 1756; and the Duke was particularly careful to give him a cordial welcome.

'The university' he declared 'could not have made a better choice, and I shall be extremely happy if during the time of your Vice-Chancellorship it may be in my power to be of any use or service to you in the execution of your office. Allow me also to thank you for some particular marks of regard which I have received from you, and to assure you that, though from a previous engagement I had it not in my power upon a late occasion to show you the due regard I had for you, nobody is more sensible of your merit than myself or shall be more desirous

[1] Add. MS. 32868, f. 370.   [2] *Ibid.*
[3] The Provost had undertaken to support Newcastle's candidate for the Regius Professorship of Divinity which Dr Green was vacating.
[4] Add. MS. 32868, f. 410; see also, f. 382, f. 464.

THE CHANCELLOR AND THE UNIVERSITY

to show you, and the learned society of which you are the head, all marks of my esteem and regard[1].'

This was an extremely courtly welcome, but the Duke was probably much annoyed at his failure. It must have seemed intolerable to him that the university should think more of custom than of his wishes; and until the very end he fretted against the restrictions imposed by the dead hand of tradition. Had it not been for the wise advice tendered by his friends at Cambridge, it is possible that he would have ventured upon further trials of strength. When Dr Green, who had succeeded the Provost as Vice-Chancellor, was approaching the end of his year of office, he was urged by the Duke to stand for re-election; but he wisely declined to embark upon an enterprise which if it failed would be extremely damaging to the Chancellor's prestige, and if it succeeded would bequeath a legacy of hatred.

'I beg leave to acquaint your Grace' he wrote on November 3rd, 1758, 'that this morning I resigned the office of Vice-Chancellor in the usual form. As I was well apprized of your sentiments as to the expediency of continuing for two years, and think it would be much for the advantage of this place, I used the precaution of calling together your Grace's friends to consult about this matter and to offer my service for another year if it should be thought an advisable measure. After a due consideration of the affair it was not judged proper to attempt it at present, as it would not probably be done without an opposition[2].'

Dr Green's refusal to stand for re-election seems to have convinced Newcastle that, whatever he might think of university traditions and however inconvenient he found them, he must at least pay them the homage of outward respect. It is significant that the much trusted Dr Caryl, who succeeded the Master of Corpus as Vice-Chancellor, retired from office at the end of a year; and though at the height of the High

[1] Add. MS. 32869, f. 55.   [2] Add. MS. 32885, f. 212.

Steward controversy the Duke contemplated a return to his old policy, he was dissuaded from embarking upon such a perilous venture by the Master of Corpus, and manfully resisted the proposal when it was put forward by the Bishop of Ely.

'I objected to his Lordship' he declared 'the supposed illegality of a returning officer, the Vice-Chancellor,...serving his office two years successively. The Bishop would not imagine that that could be so, as the contrary had been so often practised; but whether the objection in law be founded or not I am not prepared to say; but the objection in fact is sufficient to lay aside any thought of that kind. For under the present doubts and in the present situation of things, the university would certainly not consent to it; and, if we were to attempt it, we should (I am afraid) try our strength upon a very weak and unpromising point[1].'

This was something of the nature of a death-bed repentance; and it is evident that Newcastle had mismanaged the questions of mandate degrees and the Vice-Chancellor's tenure of office. By the attitude he had adopted in both cases he had given rise to the suspicion that he was seeking to play the part of a dictator, and thus done himself an injustice; for he had no desire to convert the Chancellorship into a despotism. He was well aware that the university was jealous of its independence and resented dictation; and his aim was therefore to guide rather than direct, and to establish an influence which would be more felt than seen. Such a policy was difficult to put in practice, and it is evident that he was not always successful, especially where his own immediate interests were concerned, in exercising the necessary restraint; but he was aware of the danger and occasionally displayed a most commendable caution.

His caution is most noticeable in the matter of professorial elections. It was extremely important for the

[1] Add. MS. 32959, f. 249.

THE CHANCELLOR AND THE UNIVERSITY 181

maintenance of his influence that not only his friends should occupy the high places in the university but that the aspirants to such places should understand that they could not afford to be indifferent to the goodwill of the Chancellor. If his avowed opponents succeeded in securing all the prizes of academic life, it would be difficult for him to win followers except among that very small minority which preferred a losing cause and disclaimed worldly advancement. On the other hand it would be extremely dangerous for him to interfere openly in such elections. The electors were under a moral obligation to judge fairly and impartially between the candidates; and though it must be admitted that this obligation sat particularly lightly upon many of them, it would be probably remembered and evoked with due solemnity if the Chancellor attempted anything like dictation. Moreover, if he openly espoused the cause of one particular candidate, he could hardly avoid incurring the hostility of all the other competitors, and thus make many enemies in order to win a single friend. Generally speaking however he seems to have successfully steered a course between the two dangerous extremes. He undoubtedly took a very intimate interest in professorial elections and encouraged the candidates to appeal for his favour; but, unless it was absolutely necessary, he refrained from committing himself deeply in support of any single competitor, and remained as much as possible in the background. There is no doubt that this was the right policy for him to pursue. It would certainly be inexpedient for him to express a preference if all the candidates were his loyal supporters; and, if it was necessary to prevent the election of an enemy, this task could be best performed by his agents at Cambridge who, while carrying out his instructions, would be careful to give an appearance of acting independently.

From the very first Newcastle seems to have pursued this policy which, though it involved him in a net of intrigue and entailed endless correspondence, was probably the best means he had of keeping a control over professorial appointments without incurring the charge of encroaching upon the independence of the university. At about the same time as he became Chancellor, the Regius Professorship of Divinity fell vacant through the death of Dr Whalley, Master of Peterhouse; and before Dr Whalley was actually dead, Dr Smith, Master of Trinity appealed to Newcastle to support Philip Yonge, a Fellow of Trinity, who was thinking of standing for the professorship. Dr Smith was extremely pressing and engagingly frank.

'On my return to Cambridge' he wrote on December 11th, 1748, 'I found our Divinity Professor in so weak a condition that his death is expected every hour. That professorship most properly belongs to Trinity college as being founded by King Henry VIII who has obliged us to pay the Professor a salary of forty pounds per annum out of the estates he gave us; to this King James I annexed the rectory of Summersham, valued at about £300 per annum. In consideration of the salary being paid by us, the founder has given us three votes out of seven for electing the Professor, viz. the Master and the two maxime seniores who are Dr Walker and Mr Whitehall. The other four out of the college are the Vice-Chancellor, Dr George, Dr Newcome and Dr Rook as Heads of King's, St John's and Christ's College. By this it appears that the founder has almost appropriated the professorship to a Trinity college man, seeing that one more vote than our three will carry it for him. Our present candidate is Mr Yonge, a very amiable man, a true friend to the government, an excellent scholar from Westminster school, and esteemed by us as the greatest ornament of it. So that for the honour of Westminster school, which your Grace has frequently put me in mind of and which I have much at heart, I must beg the favour of your Grace to assist Mr Yonge, particularly by applying to Dr George[1]....Mr Yonge is well

[1] Provost of King's.

THE CHANCELLOR AND THE UNIVERSITY 183

acquainted with Dr George who has told him to-day that he is not yet engaged[1].'

Philip Yonge, who has already figured prominently in this narrative as Dr Yonge, Master of Jesus and later Bishop of Norwich, was already a person of established reputation in the university. In 1746 he had been appointed to the office of Public Orator, and he was well known to Newcastle whose interest he had steadily supported. He doubtless counted upon his patron's favour in this venture, for otherwise it is unlikely that he would have thought of standing. To be eligible for election it was necessary to be either a doctor or bachelor of divinity; and as Yonge was only a master of arts, he would have to qualify for election by taking the degree of doctor of divinity, *per saltum*[2], which however he could not do without removing his name from the books of his college and forfeiting his Fellowship[3]. Thus he ran the risk of losing his Fellowship without gaining the professorship; and it was not

[1] Add. MS. 32717, f. 421.
[2] 'If he be a master of arts and not a gremial, he may take the degree of doctor of divinity, per saltum, provided he be of twelve years standing from the degree of master of arts.' Gunning's *Ceremonies*, pp. 180–181. Yonge took his M.A. degree in 1735.
[3] The custom by which it was necessary to remove your name from the books of your college before taking a degree, *per saltum*, was based upon a misunderstanding. By an interpretation given in 1575 of the 21st chapter of the Elizabethan statutes, the privilege of taking a degree, *per saltum*, was confined to non-gremials which properly and originally meant non-resident members of the university. In course of time, however, the term gremial came to be applied to all members of the Senate, whether resident or not, and therefore non-gremial came to denote non-membership of the Senate. See Appendix A, p. xvii, n. 1, of Peacock's *Observations on the statutes of the University*. It should be noted that Yonge could not get over the difficulty by obtaining the degree of doctor of divinity by royal mandate, as probably a good many of the Heads would have been unwilling in the circumstances to approve the necessary certificate.

even possible for him to be re-elected to his Fellowship after having resigned it. If he had been possessed of the gaming instinct he might have been attracted by the hazard of the game; but he was not a gambler by nature, and had not the slightest intention of relinquishing a comfortable competence unless he could make certain of securing something better. His election was sure if four out of the seven electors pledged themselves to support him; and, having engaged the votes of the three Trinity electors, he naturally looked to Newcastle to win over the Provost of King's and thereby make his success certain[1].

It might have been expected that Newcastle would have rushed to the support of his follower and secured the Provost's vote without delay, but he was far too experienced in such matters to allow himself to be hurried, and knew that it was always best to play for time. He replied to Dr Smith in an extremely non-committal fashion, lavishing compliments upon Trinity and Yonge but at the same time carefully pointing out that the other electors were 'persons for whom I cannot but have the greatest regard, and that they may with reason expect of me that I should not take a determined part in this affair without first knowing their sentiments upon it[2].' This was a polite way of intimating that he would not pledge himself before ascertaining who were likely to be candidates; and it was well that he waited. In addition to Yonge, Dr Rutherforth, Fellow and Tutor of St John's, John Green, then a comparatively unknown Fellow of St John's but afterwards Master of Corpus and Bishop of Lincoln, and Dr Rooke, Master of Christ's, announced their intention of standing; and though from the first Rutherforth had no chance of

[1] Yonge and Dr Walker also wrote to the Duke. Add. MS. 32717, f. 423, f. 426.
[2] Add. MS. 32717, f. 431.

THE CHANCELLOR AND THE UNIVERSITY 185

succeeding, as he had been one of the leaders of the faction which had favoured the Prince of Wales' candidature for the Chancellorship and was unsupported by any of the electors, the two other competitors were likely to prove very serious rivals to Yonge. Both Green and Rooke were stalwart supporters of Newcastle and had claims upon his favour which could not possibly be disregarded. It is possible, and certainly not incongruous with his character, that Dr Smith, knowing that Green and Rooke were about to come forward, hoped to surprise the Duke and induce him prematurely to commit himself to Yonge. As a politician however the Chancellor was quite a match for the Master of Trinity who gained nothing by his early application. 'I take it for granted' wrote the Vice-Chancellor to Lord Dupplin 'that his Grace will be cautious of interposing[1]'; and the Duke stood in no need of the warning. It was hazardous for him to discriminate between the three candidates who were his friends; and, as there was no danger of Rutherforth being successful, the right policy for the Chancellor was at least to make a show of standing aside and leaving the issue to be decided by the electors.

How far he really stood aside it is difficult to say; and it may be that his neutrality was more nominal than real. It is certain however that he refused to intervene on behalf of Yonge who abandoned his candidature on discovering that the Vice-Chancellor and the Provost of King's were pledged to support Dr Rooke, that the Master of St John's had engaged himself to vote for Green, and that Dr Rooke, who was an elector in his capacity of Master of Christ's, would either vote for himself or not vote at all[2]. By with-

[1] Add. MS. 32717, f. 443. The Vice-Chancellor was Dr Chapman, Master of Magdalene.
[2] Add. MS. 32717, f. 435, f. 465, f. 481. It was provided that in

drawing from the contest he not only saved his Fellowship of Trinity but increased in favour with the Duke by not playing the part of an importunate suitor.

'I don't enter into the reasons that induced you to it' wrote Newcastle to Yonge 'but am persuaded that you are so reasonable and must know the delicacy of my present situation so well that, however I may have wished your success from the great good opinion I have of you and long acquaintance I have had with you, you could not expect that I should have gone further than I have done, at least as yet, in your favour. All the electors without distinction and all the candidates but one are equally my friends, and would have had just cause to complain of me if in my present circumstances I had at once declared in favour of any one candidate, before I either knew who the other candidates might be or what were the sentiments of the particular electors[1].'

Yonge's withdrawal eased but did not remove the Duke's difficulties. He was appealed to by Dr Rooke to persuade the Master of St John's to abandon his support of Green[2], and was urged by the Master of St John's to espouse Green's cause:

'Mr Green' wrote the Master 'is a most excellent preacher, a very good scholar and divine, and has presided in our divinity disputes in the chapel with great credit. He is a true friend to your Grace and to the Royal Family....In short, and to be plain, amongst your Grace's friends I think none of the competitors equal to Mr Green[3].'

But this opinion of the Master of St John's was not shared by the Vice-Chancellor and the Provost of King's who thought none of the competitors equal to Dr Rooke, and presumably Dr Rooke was in agreement with

the event of no candidate obtaining at least four votes, the Vice-Chancellor and the Master of Trinity should elect, and if they failed to agree, the Chancellor, if he was a Bishop, or otherwise the Archbishop of Canterbury, was to appoint to the professorship.

[1] Add. MS. 32717, f. 478.   [2] Add. MS. 32717, f. 435.
[3] Add. MS. 32717, f. 472.

THE CHANCELLOR AND THE UNIVERSITY 187

them. The uncertain but decisive factor was of course the Trinity vote, and both Green and Rooke hoped that the Duke would intervene to secure that vote for them. Newcastle however was no more prepared to intervene for them than he had been for Yonge; and though it was tolerably certain that the three Trinity electors would all vote the same way, it was difficult to forecast which way it would be. As Dr Rooke had been a scholar of Trinity in his time, he expected their support, especially against a Johnian[1]; but, as he was one of the most unpopular characters in the university, it is possible that he was too well known in his old college to find much favour there. It is at least significant that Yonge privately told Green, some days before the news was published abroad, that he did not intend to stand for the professorship, thereby allowing Green to anticipate Rooke in applying for the Trinity vote[2]; and the Master of St John's expressed the belief that Green was well thought of in Trinity[3]. Nevertheless Dr Smith and his two senior Fellows kept their own counsel; and the issue remained uncertain until the eve of Christmas when it was announced that the Master of Christ's had withdrawn from the contest[4]. Dr Rooke's example was quickly followed by Rutherforth who must have known from the first that he was engaged upon a forlorn hope[5]; and in due course Green, the only surviving candidate, was elected to the Regius Professorship.

Dr Rooke's sudden retreat is somewhat inexplicable. In a formal letter to the Duke he explained that he had been over-persuaded by his friends to stand, and that on finding that 'the publick voice rather allotted this province to a person in all respects equal to it,

[1] There was bitter rivalry between Trinity and St John's in the eighteenth century.
[2] Add. MS. 32717, f. 470.   [3] Add. MS. 32717, f. 497.
[4] Add. MS. 32717, f. 530.   [5] Add. MS. 32717, f. 470.

Mr Green of St John's College, I made no hesitation in conforming to this opinion, and with much more readiness do now decline than I at first sollicited this office[1].' This profession of deference to public opinion smacks somewhat of unreality; and it may be that the Master of Christ's was influenced by less avowable motives. It is possible that he either surmised or knew that the Trinity electors were going to vote for Green; but it seems unlikely that he would take a final decision upon mere surmise, and there is nothing to suggest that anyone knew for certain, not even perhaps the Trinity electors themselves, which way their votes would be cast. There is no doubt however that Dr Rooke knew that Green was under the patronage of Lord Hardwicke who was anxious for his success[2]; and, as it was common knowledge that Hardwicke and Newcastle were knit together in the closest bonds of friendship, no great insight was needed to perceive that, though Newcastle might refuse to express a preference, he was probably anxious that Lord Hardwicke's candidate should be successful. It is therefore possible that Rooke, understanding that his success was at least uncertain and not really desired by the Duke, came to the conclusion that his most politic course would be to retire with a magnanimous gesture; and, at the cost of relinquishing all hope of the professorship, establish a claim upon Newcastle's gratitude. There is nothing inherently improbable in such a theory; and it was certainly believed at the time that the Master of Christ's had been influenced by other considerations than the welfare of the university and the advancement of learning.

[1] Add. MS. 32717, f. 546.
[2] In a letter to Newcastle of December 16th, 1748, the Vice-Chancellor remarked of Green that 'the interest of my Lord Chancellor would be employed in his behalf.' Add. MS. 32717, f. 462.

'Dr Rooke' wrote a contemporary 'made interest and secured such a number of votes that Green could not obtain it without making interest above to get a promise made to Rooke that pleased him as well as the professorship, for which he is not fit[1].'

We are not told with whom the interest was made, but the reference is almost certainly to Hardwicke and indirectly to Newcastle; and though no details are given of the 'promise,' it is not improbable that the Prebendaryship of Lincoln, given to Rooke in 1751, was a consolation prize for the professorship he had lost. If this be the true story of how Green came to be Regius Professor of Divinity, it is clear that Newcastle exercised an indirect but very potent influence over the course of affairs, and that much happened behind the scenes at which we can only guess. But even if there was no reason to think that the withdrawal of the Master of Christ's was not quite so spontaneous as he represented it to be, it is obvious that the Duke's wishes were very carefully considered. If the electors had been solely influenced by the merits of the candidates, it is probable that the prize would have gone to Rutherforth who had the reputation of being a remarkably good scholar[2], and in after years was described as 'the great and unrivalled ornament of the divinity scholes[3].' Yet, because he was known to be an enemy of the Chancellor, his claims were disregarded, and not a single elector was prepared to vote for him.

The lesson was not thrown away upon Rutherforth who quickly saw that something more was needed for advancement in the university than a reputation for learning, and that, unless he repented and sought forgiveness, his ambition would remain unsatisfied. Through

[1] *Memoirs of a Royal Chaplain*, p. 158.
[2] *Anecdotes of the Life of Bishop Watson*, p. 5.
[3] *Admissions to St John's College*, Part III, p. 396.

the good offices of Dr Keene he was reconciled with the Chancellor, and it is said that he was encouraged in the hope of becoming Regius Professor of Divinity if ever Green was promoted to a higher dignity[1]. It is not at all unlikely that some such prospect was held out to him, for Newcastle was always ready to forgive the repentant sinner; but Rutherforth was not particular as to the exact professorship, and when in July 1756 it was falsely reported that Dr Long, Master of Pembroke and Lowndean Professor of Astronomy, was either dead or dying, he was quick in applying to the Duke.

'The notice that your Grace has been pleased to take of me' he wrote 'encourages me to request the favour of your interest, if it is not already engaged to any other person, to succeed to Lowndes' professorship in your Grace's university....I have no other pretentions to ask for such a favour besides your Grace's great humanity, and the assurance, which I beg leave to give you, of my sincere attachment to His Majesty's person and government, and of a steady regard for your Grace and for the interest of your friends[2].'

These loyal professions were thrown away as Dr Long lived and enjoyed his professorship for another fourteen years; but Rutherforth was not long kept waiting for an opportunity of testing the sincerity of the Duke's friendship. Two months later Dr George, Provost of King's, died; and as it was common knowledge that Green, who in the interval had become Master of Corpus, would receive the Deanery of Lincoln, vacated by the Provost's death, and resign the Regius Professorship of Divinity, Rutherforth once more appealed to the Duke for his assistance and protection[3].

[1] *Memoirs of a Royal Chaplain*, p. 271.
[2] Add. MS. 32866, f. 308. In 1748 Rutherforth had published a two volume work entitled *A System of Natural Philosophy, being a Course of Lectures in Mechanics, Optics, Hydrostatics and Astronomy, which were read at St John's College, Cambridge.*
[3] Add. MS. 32867, f. 444.

THE CHANCELLOR AND THE UNIVERSITY 191

Nor did he appeal in vain, for the Duke was sincerely anxious for his success and pledged himself to support his candidature. He intended to tread warily however and was not prepared to allow Rutherforth to use his name to the electors[1]. As on the previous occasion the uncertain factor was the Trinity vote; for though there was no candidate from that college, it was believed that the Trinity electors would willingly vote for Dr Law, Master of Peterhouse, if he could be persuaded to stand. As Law was Vice-Chancellor and therefore himself an elector, and moreover could confidently count upon the vote of his old friend, Dr Thomas, Master of Christ's, it was within his power to secure the professorship; and as he was a poor man with a large family, he was undoubtedly anxious to succeed Dr Green[2]. It would have been clearly very unwise for Newcastle to intervene and impose a veto upon Law's candidature; but Dr Keene, who had preceded Law in the Mastership of Peterhouse, and was aware that Newcastle intended Rutherforth to be Regius Professor, was equal to the emergency.

'As soon as it appeared' he wrote to the Duke on October 6th 'that Dr Green was secure of the Deanery of Lincoln and was disposed to resign the divinity chair, I wrote to the Vice-Chancellor that Dr Rutherforth would be a candidate, and that I hoped he would receive him as a friend of the Duke of Newcastle and of mine. This he has done already in a handsome manner, though the expectations of many of the university, and of some of great weight in the election, were in his favour if he had offered himself. This is not to be wondered at as his character and behaviour have already rendered him very acceptable to the body of that place. It is impossible to judge what part the Trinity people will take, or what the event may be; but it appears plain that if Dr Law had declared himself he would stand the best chance of having the Trinity votes if they have not a candi-

[1] Add. MS. 32868, f. 20, f. 76.
[2] Add. MS. 32868, f. 106; *Memoirs of a Royal Chaplain*, p. 271.

date of their own. In that case I hope it will appear to His Grace a matter of great self-denial for a man of his character, with a family of nine children, to renounce his pretentions to prospects of so advantageous a preferment, out of deference to the prior inclinations of His Grace to Dr Rutherforth, and I persuade myself that His Grace will form a more favourable sentiment of him from this instance of his conduct, and dispose him to support him in any future openings in the university, more particularly the Margaret Professorship[1].'

It is evident from this letter that Dr Keene either told or plainly hinted to the Vice-Chancellor that he would disoblige Newcastle by standing for election; and Law, who was a loyal though not a favoured follower of the Duke, was obedient to the command. No better instance could be given of the influence which Newcastle exercised over professorial elections without appearing to take any part at all in them. Yet Rutherforth's success was not made certain by Law's act of self denial. The Chancellor was by no means popular in Trinity[2], and it was not at all improbable that the Master and the senior Fellows of that college would run another candidate against Rutherforth, and that Dr Sumner, the newly elected Provost of King's, who had no cause to love Newcastle, would throw in his lot with the opposition, and consequently secure for the Trinity candidate the four votes which would ensure his election. If the Trinity electors harboured any such design, the best way of defeating it was for the Newcastle party to secure the Provost's vote for Rutherforth; for w thout the Provost Trinity was impotent, the remaining three e'ectors, having engaged themselves to vote for Newcastle's candidate. Consequently the Provost was approached by Dr Green, but for some time without success. Dr Sumner refused to commit

[1] Add. MS. 32868, f. 106.
[2] *Memoirs of a Royal Chaplain*, p. 271.

himself, even when Green, throwing caution to the winds in the belief that a desperate situation demanded desperate remedies, frankly told him that Rutherforth's candidature was favoured by the Duke[1].

For some days the issue remained in suspense, and it is possible that the Trinity electors were trying to find a candidate to oppose to Rutherforth. If this was really their quest they failed in it: for about the middle of October Dr Hooper told Green that he was prepared to vote for Rutherforth, and hinted that the Master and the other senior Fellow would probably do likewise[2]. Dr Hooper's vote alone however made Rutherforth certain of the professorship: and when towards the end of the month the Provost of King's promised to support the Duke's candidate[3], the announcement, though of interest to Newcastle as indicating a friendly disposition on the Provost's part, was of small importance as far as the election went. On October 31st, 1756, Rutherforth was elected to the Regius Professorship[4], and by his subsequent conduct acknowledged his debt to the Chancellor.

It is clear that Newcastle was able to exercise considerable influence in these professorial elections: but it is equally clear that he was cautious in using the power he possessed, and that, though prepared to intervene in order to defeat an enemy or keep a promise to a friend, he was always particularly careful to remain in the background, and to refrain as far as possible from

[1] 'The Provost' wrote Green 'asked me among other things whether Dr Rutherforth's election into the Professor's office would be agreeable to your Grace. I told him Your Grace, I believed, was cautious of having your name made use of on this occasion, but as he thought proper to enquire particularly into that matter, I had great reason to suppose that it would be agreeable to your Grace.' Add. MS. 32868, f. 370.

[2] Add. MS. 32868, f. 370.   [3] Add. MS. 32868, f. 464.
[4] Add. MS. 32868, f. 509.

openly expressing a preference for any one particular candidate. When not compelled by reasons of policy to take a side in these contests, he apparently left the decision to the electors: and it would be to wrong him to believe that he systematically used the professorships of the university as prizes for good conduct. He was often content, and probably preferred, to hold his hand and leave the decision to the experts: and though he may have assisted Green, and certainly assisted Rutherforth, both these candidates had claims upon him which he could not afford to neglect. His attitude was very different, and possibly more typical, when the Lucasian professorship of mathematics was vacated in 1759 by the death of John Colson. On the day Colson died, Edward Waring, a junior Fellow of Magdalene, communicated to Newcastle his intention of being a candidate for the professorship, and petitioned for his 'Grace's favour and protection upon this occasion[1].' Though only twenty-five years old, and not even of sufficient standing to take his master of arts degree, Waring had gained a great reputation in the university as a mathematician, and was already engaged upon his *Miscellania Analytica* which was to make his name famous throughout Europe. At the time of Colson's death, however, he was only known as a young man of great promise, and in the eighteenth century the dignity of age was more highly appreciated than the vigour of youth. All the Heads of Houses were electors to the professorship, and as Waring required a master of arts degree by royal mandate, in order to qualify as a candidate, it was within the power of the Heads not only not to elect him but to prevent him from even standing. He was therefore in urgent need of all the assistance he could obtain: but Newcastle was not pre-

---

[1] Add. MS. 32900, f. 109.

THE CHANCELLOR AND THE UNIVERSITY 195

pared to take him under his protection without due inquiry into his merits.

'I have the favour of your letter' he wrote to Dr Caryl 'and send you enclosed a letter which I have received from Mr Waring. I have heard a very good character of him, and have not had any application from any other person. But as the Master of Trinity is from his superior knowledge in the science of mathematicks the best judge of the qualifications of those who either wish to be, or we should wish to have, our professor, I must beg that you would wait upon Dr Smith and in my name desire to know his thoughts who would be the most proper person. In all these elections I have no other view but to promote the interest of those who are the best qualified. This is for the honour of the university which is and ever shall be my principal object[1].'

Newcastle was wrong in believing that no other consideration but the intellectual qualifications of the candidates had ever weighed with him: and like many of us he suffered from the delusion that his ideal was his practice. But as on this occasion he was neither fettered by any promise nor threatened by any enemy, he could indulge his impartiality: and his conduct was studiously correct. Having received his instructions Dr Caryl waited upon the Master of Trinity who however declined on the ground of propriety to suggest the names of other possible candidates, and only spoke of Waring with very tempered enthusiasm.

'Having seen part of the book which Mr Waring is going to publish,' reported Caryl, 'he says that Mr Waring shews a deal of fire and some invention, but seems to have given too little attention to the proper manner of expressing his thoughts, and is therefore sometimes not easy to be understood. This however he considers as a fault that time will probably correct, and as the young man has discovered an earnest desire to excell, it is likely that he will improve himself into a degree of eminence[2].'

[1] Add. MS. 32900, f. 216. [2] Add. MS. 32900, f. 229.

196 THE CHANCELLOR AND THE UNIVERSITY

This was damnation with faint praise, and in the light of what happened later, it seems not improbable that Dr Smith was anxious for his friend, Ludlam, to obtain the professorship, and therefore intentionally depreciated Waring. But as, for the time being, Waring was the only candidate, it was agreed between Newcastle and the Heads that he should receive a mandate degree, with the clear understanding however that the Heads were not thereby committed to vote for his election as professor[1].

Shortly after this decision had been taken, two other candidates appeared, William Ludlam and Francis Maseres. Ludlam was a Fellow of St John's where for many years he had been a lecturer on algebra and taken an active part in administering the affairs of the college. He was considerably senior to either Waring or Maseres, and, though he had published nothing more substantial than occasional papers, he was an intimate friend of Dr Smith who in the second edition of his *Harmonics* had described him as one of the two 'most ingenious and learned gentlemen in this university.' Maseres, a far younger man, after being a Scholar and Fellow of Clare and gaining the first Chancellor's classical medal[2], had left the university and been called to the Bar. He had not however allowed law to monopolise his attention, and in 1758 had published a *Dissertation on the Use of the Negative Sign in Algebra* with a dedication to the Duke of Newcastle. As a mathematician he was certainly inferior to either Waring or Ludlam, but he was believed to be their superior in general ability[3]; and doubtless he and many others thought that as a Clare man he could confidently count upon Newcastle's support.

[1] Add. MS. 32900, f. 231, f. 325; Add. MS. 32901, f. 395.
[2] Maseres gained the first Chancellor's medal in 1752, the year in which those prizes were instituted.
[3] Add. MS. 32901, f. 395.

Maseres lost no time in appealing to the Chancellor, and both he and Waring personally waited upon him[1]. Their example was not followed by Ludlam who possibly thought the assistance of the Master of Trinity sufficient; but as all three candidates were unobjectionable from Newcastle's point of view, he wisely decided not to interfere, even indirectly, and to leave the decision to the electors. Thus if Maseres thought that his connection with Clare would cover his shortcomings, he was disappointed: and it soon became evident that his candidature was not regarded with any favour in the university, and that his chances were negligible. The Lucasian Professor was strictly bound to residence, and it was not until it was too late for the announcement to exercise any influence that Maseres made perfectly clear that he intended, if elected, to sacrifice his career at the Bar and reside in Cambridge[2]. Ludlam on the other hand was a very serious competitor. In addition to the support of the Master of Trinity, whose opinion as a mathematician of repute would have considerable weight with the other electors[3], Ludlam was favoured by the Masters of Corpus and St John's, and 'several more of the older Heads[4].' Moreover one of his most ardent champions was Dr Powell, Tutor of St John's, who published anonymously a very bitter attack upon the first chapter of the *Miscellania Analytica* which Waring had circulated 'in order that the electors and the uni-

[1] Add. MS. 32900, f. 339; Add. MS. 32901, f. 395.
[2] On January 21st, 1760, the Master of Corpus wrote of Maseres that 'the notion of his design to follow the study and profession of the law, which seems incompatible with the strict residence that the founder of the professorship has injoined, makes many not so well disposed to assist him on this occasion, however well they may think of his talents'; and after the election the Master remarked 'Mr Mazeres, though very able, was too late in declaring his intention to reside here.' Add. MS. 32901, f. 500.
[3] Add. MS. 32901, f. 500.   [4] Add. MS. 32901, f. 395.

versity at large might judge of the nature of his pursuits and his qualifications for the high office which he solicited.[1]'

Thus the fight was between the elderly competent teacher and the young man of genius: and, though genius prevailed, the victory was a very narrow one.

'I beg leave to take this early opportunity of acquainting your Grace' reported the Master of Corpus on January 28th, 1760, 'that the election for the mathematical professorship came on at three o'clock this afternoon and was determined in favour of Mr Waring: six voted for him, five were disposed to serve Mr Ludlam, and the other Heads were absent through illness or by inclination. It was conducted very amicably and without the least ill-will on any side. The Master of Trinity was not well enough to attend, but was inclined, as far as he chose to say anything, to favour Mr Ludlam[2].'

It reflects little credit upon the university that Waring, who was one of the few eminent mathematicians produced by Cambridge in the eighteenth century, should have so narrowly escaped defeat, but no blame attaches to Newcastle who never swerved from the impartial attitude he adopted from the first. It is fairly obvious that the Duke, partly because he really desired the prosperity of the university, and partly because he was aware of the danger of an opposite course, preferred, if he possibly could, to leave the university to elect its own professors, and it is not surprising that he should not have been over-willing to intervene. Throughout his Chancellorship there was always a party in Cambridge which was anxious to seize any favourable opportunity of challenging his authority; and he could render this party no greater service than by affording a pretext for an agitation against his despotic power. Experience had taught him that though the

[1] Baker's *History of St John's College* (edited by J. E. Mayor), II, 1069.   [2] Add. MS. 32901, f. 500.

THE CHANCELLOR AND THE UNIVERSITY 199

disaffected were normally few in number, they constituted a nucleus of a formidable agitation, and that there were very definite limits to the influence he could safely exercise.

In the early days of his Chancellorship, indeed, he had been confronted with a revolt which for many months occupied his attention and distracted the university. The original cause of the disturbance was the question, which age has not withered nor custom staled, of university reform. Early in the year 1749 certain members of the government, seriously alarmed by the prevalence of Jacobite sentiments at Oxford, began to consider the establishment of a commission of enquiry into that university[1]; and though, on hearing of this proposal, Newcastle was careful to emphasise that, in contrast with Oxford, Cambridge was distinguished by its loyalty to the crown[2], he was probably well aware that the discipline in his university was very far from satisfactory, and that, however correct its politics, it needed over-hauling quite as much as Oxford[3]. He further must have seen that an enquiry begun at one university might easily be extended to the other; and it is therefore not unlikely that he deemed it advisable to anticipate the action of the ministry and to hint to the Vice-Chancellor, Dr Chapman, that, as the government was preparing to take action against Oxford, it would be well for Cambridge to set its house in order. But whether or not it was the Chancellor who gave the signal, it is certain that in March 1749 the Vice-Chancellor and Heads, with the Duke's approval, were busily engaged 'in drawing up several necessary

[1] Add. MS. 32718, f. 29. [2] Add. MS. 32718, f. 31.
[3] In a pamphlet attributed to Dr Green it is stated that in 1749 more than twenty members of the university were 'sentenced to an entire or temporary banishment.' See *Considerations on the expediency of making and the manner of conducting the late Regulations at Cambridge.*

regulations for restoring good order and discipline in the university[1]'; but they were not allowed to perform their task unaided. The Duke, assisted by Herring, Archbishop of Canterbury, who had been a Fellow and Tutor of Corpus, and Sherlock, Bishop of London, who had been Master of St Catharine's, revised and amended the regulations proposed by the Heads; and, though it is difficult to apportion the labour, there is no doubt that Newcastle and the two Bishops played an active part, and that the regulations in their final form were very far from being the exclusive work of the Heads[2].

Progress could not be otherwise than slow in the circumstances, and tardiness was not the only or the most serious objection to the method of procedure adopted. It soon became known in Cambridge that something was on foot, and considerable resentment was caused by what was thought to be an attempt on the part of the Chancellor and the Heads to dictate to the university. It was contended that inasmuch as any regulations framed must be passed by the Senate, a committee of that body should have been constituted to assist in drafting them[3], and that in matters of discipline Tutors and Deans were far better qualified to express an opinion than Heads of Houses reposing on Olympian heights. There was much substance in these objections, and Newcastle and the Heads were guilty of a bad error of judgment. They fell under the delusion, common to reformers, that mankind willingly submits to improvement, and for months they continued their labours without taking public opinion into account. By the spring of 1750 their task was completed, and probably any impartial critic would have admitted that the

[1] Add. MS. 32718, f. 117.
[2] Add. MS. 32718, f. 117, f. 119; Add. MS. 35657, f. 12.
[3] *An occasional letter to the Rev. Dr Keene,* attributed to Peter Chester, Fellow of St Catharine's.

code they had framed was on the whole a praiseworthy achievement. It applied for the most part to persons *in statu pupillari*, and cannot be described as particularly drastic. Valid objection might be taken to the articles which enforced the keeping of the whole term and the transmission to the Chancellor of the names of offenders against the new regulations[1]; but for the most part only a reasonable degree of discipline was enforced. Undergraduates and bachelor of arts were forbidden to be out of college after eleven o'clock at night, to keep a servant or a horse without permission, to frequent coffee-houses or places of amusement in the morning, or to dice and play cards in taverns; and they were further commanded to hear sermons at St Mary's church, and to refrain from rioting and extravagance in dress. Various penalties, ranging from the payment of a fine to expulsion from the university, were imposed for violations of these regulations, and the Chancellor and the Heads doubtless believed that their reasonable attempt to reform the lax and ineffective discipline of the university would receive a warm welcome[2].

Academic politicians however are very human; and are quite as liable as the ordinary uneducated man to be swayed by passion more than by reason. The new code was not judged on its merits but condemned by its origin. It was construed as an attempt at arbitrary government; and there was a widespread feeling that if the Senate tamely submitted and passed the regulations, a dangerous and most unfortunate precedent would be established. The mainstay of this opposition were doubtless certain lovers of faction who liked nothing more than a fight, and certain hide-bound tories who disliked nothing more than reform; but associated with these

[1] The Heads were not responsible for the regulation that the Chancellor should be sent the names of offenders. Add. MS. 35657, f. 16.
[2] Cooper's *Annals of Cambridge*, IV, 278–280.

malcontents were many honest and sagacious men who were not prepared to purchase the reform of the university by the sacrifice of its liberty. Confronted with an opposition which was too respectable and too dangerous to be regarded with contempt, and fearful of what might happen when the regulations were submitted to the Senate, Dr Keene, the Vice-Chancellor, thought to repair the original blunder by consulting 'with some leading men in each college, with a view to take off a popular objection that had been made against us for not having consulted some of the body[1]'; but the remedy was applied too late to be effective.

On May 5th, 1750, the regulations were brought before the Senate, and it had previously been arranged between the Vice-Chancellor and the Heads that the proceedings should begin with the reading of a letter from the Chancellor, that the regulations should then be passed by the Caput and given a first reading in the two houses; and that, before they were voted upon at a later congregation, they should be sent 'to each college for their consideration[2].' The Chancellor's letter was duly read; and, though couched in a somewhat dictatorial tone, no objection was taken to it[3]. But when

[1] Add. MS. 32720, f. 383.   [2] Add. MS. 35657, f. 16.

[3] Newcastle's letter to the university, which was dated April 26th, 1750, ran as follows. 'The situation I am in gives me the frequent opportunities of hearing the sentiments of others on the state of our university; and although many things alledged against us are without foundation, and others greatly aggravated and misrepresented, and much may be said in some sort of excuse for what is really true from the general depravity of manners that too much prevail everywhere, yet the most sanguine of our friends cannot be so far prejudiced in our favour as to think that there is no want of reformation or further restraint amongst us. The corruption of the times will account for the inroad that luxury has made into places where temperance and frugality ought chiefly to reside, and will discourage in some degree, but ought not to prevent, our endeavours to prevent its increase.... To accomplish so desirable an end much time and deliberation is required; but that we

THE CHANCELLOR AND THE UNIVERSITY 203

Dr Keene began to read the regulations to the Caput, a member of that body suggested that before they were read, and consequently passed or rejected, the Caput should be allowed to consider them at their leisure. Such a proposal was revolutionary and against all custom and tradition, but it nevertheless found considerable support.

'You will imagine' wrote Dr Rooke 'that as this was contrary to the constant method of proceeding and indeed impracticable, (as it is seldom known who are to make the Caput till they are actually called up for that purpose,) the Vice-Chancellor and I did not fail to put them in mind of this....But notwithstanding all that could be said (which was put with the utmost temper) the above gentlemen continued to wish and desire that they might not be read till another day, and they, as well as the rest of the body, have time to consider of them. To which the Vice-Chancellor was at last forced to consent, from an apprehension that, if they had been then published, they might have been in the first instance and out of hand rejected, and accordingly put it off till next Friday. You may imagine that this has thrown us into some little hurry, and we are not without fears that an obstruction, though perhaps not ill-designed in the beginning, started in this manner may encourage a more general opposition[1].'

This was a very ominous beginning, and Dr Rooke's might make some progress towards it, I have recommended it to those, whose experience and constant residence in the university have rendered them proper judges of the state of discipline amongst you, to specify such particular irregularities as call for a more immediate attention and to point out the best method of correcting and suppressing them. Those observations have since been sent to me which (after being revised and fully considered by the Archbishop and Bishop who have been bred up amongst us, and after being digested under the form of regulations,) I herewith transmit to you for your approbation, that they may have all the force necessary for obtaining their just effect.' Add. MS. 35657, f. 14. Newcastle's language rather implied that the Senate must obediently approve what he and the Heads had agreed upon, and the letter was not likely to remove the grievance of the opposition.

[1] Add. MS. 35657, f. 16; see also Add. MS. 32720, f. 383.

204 THE CHANCELLOR AND THE UNIVERSITY

fears were fully justified. The action of the Caput, in demanding that they should be allowed time to consider the regulations before voting upon them, was a very thinly veiled protest against the method of procedure adopted by the Chancellor and Heads, and in that lay its significance. A crisis was clearly at hand and it was impossible to foretell the course of events. The first reading of the regulations having been postponed to Friday, May 11th, it was arranged that the second reading should be taken at a congregation on the afternoon of the same day; and in the short time at his disposal Dr Keene made a valiant attempt to stem the rising tide of hostility. Perceiving that the opposition included a certain number of moderate men who sincerely believed that it was their duty to resist what they deemed to be tyranny, he decided to attempt to detach them from the extremists in the party by making a display of deference to public opinion. With this end in view he dropped the two regulations which ordered the full term to be kept and the names of offenders to be sent to the Chancellor[1]; and hoped that by a sacrifice of the articles, to which most objection had been taken, he had saved the rest.

The opening proceedings at the morning congregation on Friday, May 11th, breathed peace and goodwill, and encouraged the hope of a happy issue. Before beginning the business of the day, the Vice-Chancellor summoned the two houses before him, and delivered a short speech in which he explained that he intended to omit certain regulations which had been adversely criticised, and was so well aware of the imperfect character of what remained that he was willing to consider any suggestions for their improvement. The regulations were then passed by the Caput and read for the first time in the two houses; and such a favourable im-

[1] Add. MS. 32720, f. 383.

pression had been created by the Vice-Chancellor's address that it was generally believed that opposition was at an end, and that the regulations would be passed at the congregation in the afternoon. This interpretation of the situation proved too optimistic, for the extremists were not to be so easily outmanœuvred. They realised that by his policy of conciliation Dr Keene had deprived them of a considerable measure of moderate support and materially diminished their chances of success, and that their only hope lay in revealing the Vice-Chancellor and Heads as the implacable enemies to the liberties of the university, and thereby reuniting the opposition. Therefore, before the morning congregation came to an end, Jonathan Lipyeatt[1], of St John's, a member of the opposition, brought forward a Grace which provided that in all cases where penalties were incurred by a breach of the regulations the offender should have a right of appeal from the Vice-Chancellor to the Senate. Lipyeatt urged that this Grace, if passed, would remove the objections felt by him and his friends to the regulations, which would therefore be approved without opposition; and he seems to have been at some pains to pose as an honest man sincerely anxious for a compromise[2].

It was however only a pose, for it is not uncharitable to believe that he desired to fan opposition once more to fever height, and to wreck the Vice-Chancellor's attempt at conciliation. If a right of appeal was allowed, the regulations would become unworkable and discipline in the university be still further undermined; and yet, absurd as was this Grace, it was admirably designed to attain its promoter's purpose. For some years an angry dispute had raged in the university whether doctors and masters of arts, convicted of a

[1] This name is also given as Lyppeat and Lypeat.
[2] Add. MS. 32720, f. 383; Add. MS. 35657, f. 16.

disciplinary offence in the Vice-Chancellor's court, could claim the right to appeal to delegates appointed by the university, which they certainly had in cases other than disciplinary; and, as was perhaps inevitable in the circumstances, the controversy tended to become a struggle between the Heads and the rest of the university. The popular cry that liberty was being destroyed by a self-appointed oligarchy was used with effect, and the right of appeal was claimed not so much as of value in itself but as an emblem of freedom and independence[1]. The sting of Lipyeatt's Grace therefore lay in reviving the embers of an ancient controversy; and the Vice-Chancellor was driven between the horns of a dilemma. He believed that if he allowed the Grace to pass, it would be useless to proceed with the regulations, and he knew if he arranged for the Grace to be rejected by the Caput, Lipyeatt and his friends, purposely confusing the issue, would persuade the regents and non-regents that, despite a show of conciliation, the Heads were intent as ever upon creating a despotism, and determined as ever to limit the right of appeal; and that, therefore, just as in the days when the liberty of the nation was at stake, the house of commons had refused to vote supplies until grievances had been redressed, the Senate must refuse to approve the regulations until the right of appeal in its full extent had been secured.

Somewhat at a loss to know what to do, the Vice-Chancellor, instead of at once submitting the Grace

[1] The controversy was mainly concerned with the proper interpretation of the 42nd and the 48th statutes of the Elizabethan code. The right of appeal was specially provided for by the 48th statute but not mentioned in the 42nd; and those who maintained that there was no appeal in disciplinary cases supported their contention with the argument that the 48th statute was exclusively concerned with the non-disciplinary jurisdiction of the Vice-Chancellor.

to the Caput, put it in his pocket and dissolved the congregation. This was an unusual procedure and calculated to arouse antagonism by making it impossible for the Grace to be finally passed with the regulations at the afternoon congregation. The delay was unfortunate; and although Dr Keene probably felt that he needed time to consider his policy and consult his friends, it can be urged that, as there was really no alternative to the rejection of the Grace by the Caput, it might have been better if this step had been taken at the morning congregation, and time allowed for the resulting animosity to cool before the regulations were voted upon. It is unlikely however that anything that Dr Keene might have done could have saved the situation; and there was really nothing left for him but to meet his fate with becoming dignity. At an early stage in the afternoon congregation Lipyeatt's Grace was submitted to the Caput and vetoed by the Master of Caius. The expected followed. Men, reasonable enough in ordinary circumstances, fell a prey to the extremists who convinced them that 'the liberties of the university were in danger and the Heads were aiming at new powers in these regulations[1]'; and though there was little or no justification for such an accusation, it was accepted as true in the excitement of the moment.

'It proved as we apprehended' wrote Dr Rooke 'that upon a pretext of the above mentioned Grace not being read in the morning, and being read but stopt in the Caput in the afternoon, they fought through every one of the regulations and stopt just half of them[2].'

It was a notable victory and the Vice-Chancellor had been completely outmanœuvred. The disaffected party had only allowed the less important regulations to pass; and rejected all that the framers of the code considered most valuable. The bitterness of defeat was moreover

[1] Add. MS. 32720, f. 383. [2] Add. MS. 35657, f. 18.

208 THE CHANCELLOR AND THE UNIVERSITY

intensified by the attack having been inspired by a dislike of the power of the Chancellor and the Heads, and supported by many whom it was impossible to accuse of a love of faction. Though the Master of Christ's declared that the tory party was at the bottom of the mischief, he admitted that the tories 'under the show of guarding against oppression, drew in many honest, well meaning men to side with them[1]'; and both Trinity and King's were well represented in the opposition[2]. That the revolt had been directed against the Chancellor as well as the Heads was apparent; for though Dr Keene assured Newcastle that 'few, very few, my Lord, objected to them on account of your Grace's recommendation[3]' the Duke was far too closely identified with the regulations to escape his share in the condemnation. He had co-operated with the Heads in the attempt to improve the discipline of the university, and had apparently only succeeded in providing an excuse for a revolt[4].

The failure indeed was too complete to be endured, and the defeated party was united in a determination to continue the struggle. It is possible that Newcastle, incensed by the ingratitude of the university, was tempted to resort to the last weapon in the arsenal of academic reformers and impose the regulations upon the university by act of parliament[5]; but he wisely refrained from a course of action which would have diminished his popularity in the university, and for

[1] Add. MS. 35657, f. 18.   [2] Add. MS. 32720, f. 383.
[3] Add. MS. 32721, f. 200.
[4] For the accounts of the congregations on May 11th, see Add. MS. 35657, f. 18; Add. MS. 32720, f. 383.
[5] 'I would however submit it to your Grace's consideration' wrote Lord Dupplin on June 9th, 1750 'whether you will not give them one instance more of your paternal affection by forbearing to do any act of your own for some time, and thereby leaving them full room for better thoughts and amendments.' Add. MS. 32721, f. 91.

THE CHANCELLOR AND THE UNIVERSITY

which there was no necessity. It was perfectly obvious that the Senate had acted under the impulse of anger and the excitement of the moment, and might in time be converted to a better frame of mind. This policy of appealing from a Senate drunk to a Senate sober commended itself to Dr Keene who pressed to be allowed to make another attempt to secure the passage of the rejected regulations[1]. Aware however that a second defeat would probably be final, Keene was prepared to bide his time and not to return to the breach until he could confidently count upon success.

'From the first defeat' he informed Newcastle 'I have exerted all my spirits and devoted my whole time to secure a second attempt. To this purpose I solicited a small number of trusty friends, such as the new Master of Benet[2], the Master of Magdalene[3], Mr Garnet[4], Courtail[5], Caryl, and Backhouse, who gave me the best information of the disposition of their respective colleges[6].'

An active propaganda was thus set on foot; and it is possible that a good many members of the Senate were reminded that their chance of advancement in the church was not independent of the goodwill of the Chancellor. But it did not prove at all easy to win converts in sufficient numbers; and, in order to make more certain of the victory, the Vice-Chancellor was obliged to make important changes and modifications in the regulations. He was of course accused of having conceded so much as to deprive what remained of any value[7]; but there are always those who scent weakness in every compromise; and as the extremists were still winning converts by representing the regulations as an encroachment upon liberty under the guise of reform, Dr Keene

[1] Add. MS. 32720, f. 383.
[2] Dr John Green.
[3] Dr Chapman.
[4] Of Sidney.
[5] Of Clare.
[6] Add. MS. 32721, f. 200.
[7] Add. MS. 35657, f. 21.

was doubtless well advised to defer to public opinion and thus deprive the enemy of its most potent argument.

The battle was fought in the Senate on June 26th, 1750; and though the opposition had mustered all their strength[1] and strove hard for victory, the regulations, rejected on May 11th, were passed in their modified form by the Caput and the two houses. The victory, though decisive, was narrow, for the majorities were slender, never amounting to more than twelve and sometimes falling as low as four[2]. Pursuing the same tactics as on the previous occasion, the opposition again brought forward their Grace about the right of appeal which was promptly vetoed in the Caput; but, in order to neutralise the possible ill effects of its action, the Caput immediately afterwards passed another Grace 'importing that no alteration was made or intended to be made in the article of appealing where it was allowed by the statutes[3].' Thus the Vice-Chancellor spared no effort to conciliate his opponents, and though he failed to soften the hearts of many, he succeeded in persuading a certain number that the struggle was not between liberty and tyranny but between faction and order. He was not an admirable character and was conspicuously lacking in the virtue of loyalty; but he appears to have possessed a very sound political sense and many statesmanlike attributes[4].

But, though the regulations had been passed, they had yet to be enforced; and there was likely to be trouble in this connection. It might be anticipated that the undergraduates, aware of the controversy which had divided the university, and never over-anxious to obey authority, would under the pretext of resisting tyranny indulge their passion for disorder; and there was the

[1] Add. MS. 35657, f. 21.   [2] Ibid.   [3] Ibid.
[4] For the proceedings in the Senate House on June 26th, see Cooper's Annals, iv, 278–281.

THE CHANCELLOR AND THE UNIVERSITY

further danger that they might be encouraged by certain members of the Senate who, though defeated in their attempt to reject the regulations, were anxious to continue the struggle. Stormy times were thought to be ahead; and in November 1750 Dr Keene was continued as Vice-Chancellor for another year, as it was believed that 'his temper and firmness joined together will enforce the execution of the regulations better than it could be done by any other[1].' A strong man was certainly needed; for about a fortnight after Keene had been re-elected Vice-Chancellor, there occurred a very scandalous breach of that article of the new code which forbade bachelors of arts and undergraduates to be out of college after eleven o'clock at night.

'On Monday the 19th instant' reported the Vice-Chancellor to Newcastle in November 1750 'Mr Brown, Fellow of Pembroke Hall and senior Proctor of this university, came to me and acquainted me that on Saturday night he visited the Tunns tavern[2], that he found there the gentlemen educated at Westminster school, celebrating the anniversary of their royal Foundress, and that Pembroke clock had struck eleven before he set out from his college to visit. The master of the tavern attended him into the room and then retired. The Proctor being told by some one in the room that masters of arts were in the company, he went to the head of the table where he found Mr Professor Francklyn, President, Mr Crew, Fellow of Trinity, and Mr Ansell, LL.B. Fellow of Trinity Hall. He told them that he came thither to require that every person under the degree of M.A. should immediately retire to their respective colleges. On having said this Mr Ansell told him he hoped he would observe that every person was sober in the room, which immediately produced a loud huzza from the whole company. The Proctor said he thought that was an insult upon him; Mr Ansell replied that he (the Proctor) mistook what was meant as applause to him, for vindicating the regularity of the club, for

[1] Add. MS. 32722, f. 418.
[2] The Three Tuns Tavern stood at the corner of the market and St Edward's Passage.

an insult on him (the Proctor). The Proctor's charge against Mr Ansell was not founded so much on the words themselves as the manner of expressing them, which he said was with an air of triumph and with a sneer. Mr Francklyn expostulated with the Proctor about the propriety of visiting a room where there were M.A. That when the Proctor urged the necessity of doing his duty, and that the Professor knew that there were laws against clubs in general, and that this step of the Proctor was not a rigorous execution of the new regulations, the Professor laughed in his face and said with an air of contempt, "this he calls a mild execution of the laws." The Proctor asserts that Mr Francklyn expressed great indignation at being visited that night, and moreover at the close of the dispute Mr Francklyn drank "to our next meeting without interruption from Proctors." The Proctor charges Mr Crew with telling him that it was rude and uncivil to visit where M.A. are in company, and said the Proctor might have concluded that they, the M.A. in company, would take proper care of the young part of the club. That Mr Crew insisted that it was strange that the execution of these orders should be begun with the Westminster club, and that we scarce knew which were to be observed, which not, and that some were executed, some not. On these accounts the Proctor charged Mr Professor Francklyn, Mr Crew, and Mr Ansell with interrupting and insulting him in the execution of his office. Mr Proctor did likewise charge Mr Vernon, Fellow Commoner of Trinity college, with rude and insolent behaviour to him both at the club and after at his chamber. Mr Proctor charged also Mr Vane, Fellow Commoner of Peterhouse, that, over and above the general charge of insult in the room, he behaved disrespectfully to him in his chamber. The ill-behaviour was expressed by each of them talking to him of their independence in the university, Mr Vernon laughed in his face, and Mr Vane told him at his room that what he did was in approbation of what Francklyn had said, and that, if he was to be pitched upon, he would gladly suffer for his school-fellows. The younger part of the company, consisting of about forty, were accused of making the noise which was frequently repeated during the litigation between the Proctor and the M.A.; and consequently of insulting him in the execution of his duty[1].'

[1] Add. MS. 32723, f. 333.

THE CHANCELLOR AND THE UNIVERSITY 213

The most serious feature of this incident was that three masters of arts, all of whom were Fellows and one, the Regius Professor of Greek, had in the presence of a crowd of undergraduates cast ridicule upon the Proctor for attempting to enforce one of the new regulations. It was impossible not to suspect premeditation. Before the dinner was held the Proctor had given notice that 'he intended to visit the Westminster club that night[1]' and it was not unreasonably assumed that the masters of arts were aware of the intended visit, and purposely allowed the festivities to continue until eleven o'clock in order to compel the Proctor to enforce an article of the new code. But whether what had happened was due to design or accident, the Vice-Chancellor felt called upon to intervene in support of the Proctor; and he cannot be accused of having acted in haste.

'I was struck, my Lord,' he told Newcastle, 'with the importance of the accusation and immediately determined to proceed upon it; but, as it is very rare that any accusation is made against M.A. in matters of discipline, I summoned a meeting of the Heads to consult with them, and they all agreed that the whole must be brought into my court and publicly heard[2].'

The citations having been sent out in the usual form, the Vice-Chancellor, attended by his assessors, the Heads of Houses, opened his court in the Law Schools at three o'clock on the afternoon of Saturday November 24th. There was a large attendance of undergraduates who of course were overwhelmingly in sympathy with the culprits. The proceedings began with a lengthy statement by the senior Proctor which was taken down by the Registrary. The Proctor, who delivered his statement in a 'cool, deliberate, and precise manner[3],' gave almost identically the same account as he had already

[1] *An Enquiry into the Right of Appeal*, attributed to Dr Chapman.
[2] Add. MS. 32723, f. 333.   [3] *Ibid.*

214 THE CHANCELLOR AND THE UNIVERSITY

given the Vice-Chancellor; but he withdrew his charge against Vane of indecorous behaviour at the dinner, while still maintaining that at the subsequent interview Vane had not conducted himself respectfully. Before the Proctor had concluded his statement dusk had fallen, and the court was obliged to adjourn to the Senate house. When the Proctor had completed his evidence, Ansell was called upon to make his defence, and he appears to have been extremely offensive.

'He began' wrote the Vice-Chancellor 'and addressed himself to me and "Gentlemen of the university," looking up to the gallery where the scholars were permitted to go. I stopped him and said that the scholars made not part of the court, were not my assessors. He then changed his address and went on in a warm and indecent speech, appealing to the passions of the boys, and venturing to accuse my conduct in hearing the accusation, in consulting with the Heads, and in sending out my citations[1].'

Ansell's speech concluded the proceedings of the day and the court was adjourned until nine o'clock on the morning of Tuesday November 27th. As the dignity of the first session had been marred by the unruly behaviour of the undergraduates who had interrupted the Proctor and applauded Ansell, the Vice-Chancellor ordered the Law Schools to be fenced off, enrolled thirteen vice-Proctors to maintain order, and publicly declared that he would expel 'on the spot any one that should give the least disturbance[2].' These precautions were effective, for the proceedings on the Tuesday were far more orderly. Moreover none of the accused imitated Ansell's insolence. Professor Francklin succeeded in proving to the satisfaction of the court that the Proctor's entry had not been greeted with a shout, and that his account was inaccurate in certain minor details; and though the Vice-Chancellor thought the

[1] Add. MS. 32723, f. 333.   [2] *Ibid.*

THE CHANCELLOR AND THE UNIVERSITY 215

Professor's speech 'light and ludicrous, and principally intended to render the Proctor's evidence contradictory and expose him to the crowd[1],' it was admittedly free from any sign of disrespect to the court. But if Francklin was an improvement upon Ansell, Francklin was improved upon by Crew who

made a speech which, with the agreeable manner of delivering it, prejudiced everybody in his favour. He gave the best turn that could be to the charge made against him, and omitted to take notice of some of the allegations when he was pressed[2].

Both the Fellow-Commoners also acquitted themselves well, especially Vane who made a very favourable impression upon the court by his 'manner of speaking which was attended with an ingenuous trepidation[3].'

Sentence was passed on Thursday, November 29th. Francklin, Crew, Vernon and Vane escaped with a reprimand, and the last three were particularly complimented upon the modesty of their defence, but Ansell, for his 'rude, contemptuous and disobedient behaviour' to the Vice-Chancellor, was sentenced to be suspended 'ab omni gradu suscepto et suscipiendo.' 'I do accordingly' added the Vice-Chancellor 'suspend you from your degree[4],' explaining at the same time however that the sentence would be revoked directly Ansell made his submission and acknowledged his offence[5]. The punishment, though severe, was thoroughly well deserved. Ansell had conducted himself in court in an extremely offensive and unbecoming fashion; and the assessors were in complete agreement with the Vice-Chancellor's sentence. Moreover, on the morning of the day on which sentence was passed, the Vice-Chancellor had sent a message to Ansell to the effect that 'if he would make an acknowledgement of his fault,

[1] Add. MS. 32723, f. 333.   [2] *Ibid.*
[3] *Ibid.*   [4] Add. MS. 32723, f. 339.
[5] *An Enquiry into the Right of Appeal.*

before sentence was delivered, the Vice-Chancellor would not proceed to that part of the sentence which related to the suspension[1]'; and Ansell had deliberately refused to take this means of escape[2].

He cannot therefore in any way be regarded as the victim of tyranny; and it is possible that his provocative attitude was due more to political design than to native insolence and obstinacy. His subsequent conduct certainly suggests that he was asking for trouble with a definite object in view. Shortly after sentence had been passed upon him, he claimed the right to appeal against it, and thereby raised again the much disputed and vexatious question whether in cases of discipline there was any appeal from the Vice-Chancellor's court. Dr Keene could not allow the appeal without retreating from the position which he and the Heads had taken up, and yet it was certain that by refusing it he would revive an unfortunate controversy, and restore to the extremists the advantage of which he had deprived them by his conciliatory tactics. Ansell, who was probably the agent of a party, thus threw down a definite challenge; and the Vice-Chancellor, driven into a corner, had no option but to accept it.

'The Heads at a meeting yesterday' he wrote on December 4th 'were of opinion that I should persevere in refusing the appeal, in order to have that great question finally settled about the right of appealing with which we are so frequently annoyed, and which, if granted in the unlimited manner so much contended for by many people, utterly destroys all government in this university[3].'

[1] *An Enquiry into the Right of Appeal.*
[2] The court also reprimanded the undergraduates for applauding the Proctor, and expressed the opinion that 'all persons concerned, under the degree of master of arts, batchelor of law or batchelor of physick, did incur the penalty of six shillings and eightpence for being out of his college after eleven of the clock.'
[3] Add. MS. 32723, f. 357.

It is worthy of note that Dr Keene was prepared to admit an inquiry into the right of appeal, and only declined to take such action as would prejudge the question; and no fault can be found with his attitude. Therefore when at a congregation on December 16th William Ridlington, Fellow of Trinity Hall and afterwards Regius Professor of Civil Law, asked for a Caput to be summoned, in order that delegates might be appointed to hear Ansell's appeal, the Vice-Chancellor very properly refused to summon the Caput, and announced that early in the following term he intended to bring forward a Grace dealing with the question in dispute. Ridlington and his friends vented their spite by stopping in the non-regents' house a supplicat for a bachelor of arts degree[1]; and when on the 18th January 1751, the Vice-Chancellor, in fulfilment of his pledge, proposed his Grace for the appointment of a syndicate 'to consult the statutes and archives of the university, and from thence draw out a state of the case about appeals to be laid before the king and council,' it was rejected in the non-regents' house by fifty-two votes to eleven[2].

The opposition contended that there was no necessity for a syndicate, as the question should be decided by the Senate; and they therefore in their turn proposed a Grace by which all members of the university were to enjoy an unlimited right of appeal, though persons *in statu pupillari* must act through their Tutors. This Grace was withdrawn in order to allow the Chancellor to be consulted[3]; but there is no doubt that, had it been persevered with, it would have been vetoed in the Caput. The Heads were the authorised interpreters of the

[1] Add. MS. 5852, f. 125, f. 126; Cooper's *Annals*, IV, 282–283.
[2] *Ibid.*
[3] Add. MS. 35657, f. 26. *A letter to the Author of a further Inquiry.*

statutes, and though prepared on this occasion to accept a decision of the king in council, they could not allow their functions to be usurped by the Senate, nor could a Grace over-ride a statute. Hence there was a deadlock with regard to the mode of procedure, and Newcastle was as helpless as Dr Keene. For a time indeed there was a hope that the question might be decided by the courts of law, as Ansell was preparing to seek a remedy in the court of King's Bench; and both the Chancellor and Vice-Chancellor would have welcomed such a solution of the difficulty[1]. Ansell was however obliged to abandon his suit, and any hope of a settlement receded into the background. In July 1751 Dr Keene told the Duke that he would endeavour 'this summer to form a plan by which the disputes on appeals may entirely be prevented for the future[2]'; but he had no plan ready when the Michaelmas term began.

The delay in a settlement played into the hands of the opposition by allowing them time to air their grievances and fan an agitation. An association was formed in defence of the right of appeal, which consisted of about thirty-six masters of arts and met at the Tunns tavern under the presidency of Dr Banson, Fellow of Trinity Hall[3]. There was also a shower of pamphlets. Both parties rushed into print, quoting authority against authority and statute against statute, and contributing more heat than illumination to the controversy[4]. Even the undergraduates joined in the fray, and from this quarter came an amusing production entitled *An Expostulatory Address of the Undergraduates*

[1] Add. MS. 32724, f. 290.   [2] Add. MS. 32724, f. 445.
[3] In February 1751 Dr Rooke gave the number of 'associators in favour of liberty' as forty-four; Add. MS. 35657, f. 26.
[4] A list of these pamphlets will be found in Cooper's *Annals*, IV, 280, n. 2.

of the University of Cambridge to the Doctor and thirty-six Masters of Arts met together at the Tunns Tavern. The author or authors of this squib contended that though, as to the matter of appeal we confess at present we neither understand the old nor the new statutes....we do, with great submission and a due deference to your better judgment, suggest that if there be an appeal from the Vice-Chancellor to the masters of arts, there should be one from the masters of arts to the undergraduates....We cannot be so unjust to you as ever to imagine that you will desert a body of youth ever serviceable in carrying on all popular schemes, and who so loudly supported you in all the late trying occasions. Recollect the hazards we ran when we were threatened with tolbooths, prisons, and expulsions. Call to mind the bravery of that young heroe who dared in the midst of the crowd to scatter his aqua fortis. Think of that humourous person that imitated an ass with such native similitude, and who is scarce yet recovered from the violent agitation such a performance must necessarily throw him into. But enough of this, stand firm, reverend friends, a select body of men, firmly united, must at length prevail and bear down a corrupt multitude. You may depend on our joint and sincere endeavours till that natural liberty and equality, to which we were born, be again restored, and government, that creature of policy and ambition, be dissolved[1].

The undergraduates were undoubtedly extremely amused at the bickerings of their seniors; but the state of affairs in the university was really more an occasion for sorrow than amusement. When in November 1751 Dr Wilcox, Master of Clare, succeeded Dr Keene as Vice-Chancellor, the controversy was still raging and apparently as far off an end as ever. As a demonstration of hostility the opposition had voted against Dr Wilcox's election[2], and three weeks later they brought forward their Grace for an unlimited right of appeal. The Grace was rejected by the Caput, and when it was again

[1] Add. MS. 33061, f. 343.
[2] They voted for the Provost of King's who had been nominated with Dr Wilcox.

brought forward in January 1752, Dr Wilcox declined to summon the Caput to consider it[1]. The opposition retaliated for these defeats by voting against supplicats for degrees, though they were not always successful in preventing them from passing.

In any prolonged contest, however, there comes a stage when the desire for peace is stronger than the passion for victory; and in spite of the controversy seeming likely to continue indefinitely, the end was really near at hand. During the Christmas vacation of 1750–1751 the Vice-Chancellor conferred with the representatives of the opposition party, and though they failed to agree upon a settlement, it was something that the antagonists had been able to meet; and doubtless an atmosphere favourable to peace was generated[2]. Probably there were subsequent meetings of which we know nothing; for on the 13th March 1752 the Senate unanimously passed a Grace requesting Newcastle, Hardwicke, the Archbishop of Canterbury, the Bishop of London, Lord Chief Justice Lee, and his brother, Sir George Lee[3], to act as referees in the dispute, and stipulating that whatever they or a majority of them decided to be 'consentaneum statutis, privilegiis et consuetudinibus academiae' should be accepted by the university as a final judgment. It was further provided by the same Grace that the Heads should be represented by the Vice-Chancellor and the Masters of Corpus and Magdalene, and the opposition by Bickham of Emmanuel, Smith of King's and Thomas Balguy of St John's[4].

All of those asked to be referees consented to act

[1] Add. MS. 5852, f. 129, f. 130; Cooper's *Annals*, IV, 285–286.
[2] Add. MS. 35657, f. 31. *A letter to the author of a further Inquiry.*
[3] Sir William Lee was Chief Justice of the King's Bench, and his brother, George, had recently been appointed Dean of Arches.
[4] Cooper's *Annals*, IV, 285–286. Add. MS. 35657, f. 33; Add. MS. 35591, f. 299.

THE CHANCELLOR AND THE UNIVERSITY

with the exception of Newcastle who declined as a party interested in the dispute, and as about to leave for the continent with the King[1]. It had probably been understood from the first that the Duke would refuse, and his co-operation was not essential to the success of the scheme. It is however remarkable, in view of the angry passions aroused, that not only was the proposal to refer the dispute to arbitration greeted with enthusiasm, but that it alone sufficed to restore peace and harmony to a distracted university. 'If there be any contentions left amongst us at present' wrote Dr Squire in April 1752 'it seems to be which side was most willing to come into reference[2],' and another testifies that 'if there should be anyone who repine at peace being restored to us, they dare not so much as utter it in a murmur[3].' When in June 1752 Dr Keene returned to Cambridge after an absence, he was able to report that he 'found it in that state of tranquillity which I foresaw would take place on the reference being unanimously complied with[4]'; and thus, as though by a wave of a magician's wand, peace was restored at the moment when the outlook was darkest. We know very little as to how this happy state of things was brought about; but there is no doubt that both parties welcomed the truce, and were well content to wait in patience for the decision of the referees. Whatever that decision had been it is unlikely that discord would have broken out again; but, curiously enough, the referees apparently never pronounced a verdict. When in November 1752 Dr Yonge, Master of Jesus, became Vice-Chancellor, he told Newcastle that there was little reason

to apprehend a revival of our late dissensions, since duty and

[1] Cooper's *Annals*, IV, 286; Add. MS. 5852, f. 130; Add. MS. 32726, f. 424.   [2] Add. MS. 32726, f. 424.
[3] Add. MS. 32726, f. 427; see also, f. 481.
[4] Add. MS. 32728, f. 127.

gratitude to the great persons, who have so kindly undertaken to hear and determine our dispute, must dispose all parties to wait their leisure with an entire acquiescence[1];

and, so well were the parties disposed that they allowed the dispute to be shelved altogether. It is possible that the referees came to the conclusion that it might be hazardous to the recently restored peace to promulgate a decision; and it was doubtless far better to allow the controversy to perish of inanition, even though the story is thus deprived of an end.

It is clear that the relations between Newcastle and the university were very far from being consistently harmonious, and that he was often compelled to struggle for the maintenance of his power. There is however another and a pleasanter side to his Chancellorship, and a side which tends to be forgotten. A generous benefactor, it was he who set a good example to his successors by instituting the custom of the Chancellor annually awarding two gold medals to those 'who, having obtained senior optimes in philosophical learning, shall pass the best examination in classical learning[2]'; and by so doing he certainly encouraged the study of the classics. From the very first these medals attracted the best brains in the university; and the examination seems to have been conducted with commendable thoroughness. On one occasion, when the votes of the examiners were equally divided between two of the candidates, the Vice-Chancellor appealed to the Duke who decided 'that where there is an equality of voices in the disposal of the medals, the casting vote ought to be in the Vice-Chancellor,

---

[1] Add. MS. 32730, f. 212.
[2] Add. MS. 32936, f. 99. In the nineteenth century the restriction of the competition to those who had attained a certain standard in mathematics was abolished.

THE CHANCELLOR AND THE UNIVERSITY 223

and I should desire that it might always be so determined[1].' In 1765 only two competitors appeared, and this unusual lack of candidates so grieved the Vice-Chancellor, Dr Barnardiston, Master of Corpus, that he postponed the examination for a fortnight, and went 'to everyone of the young gentlemen, who were capable of appearing as candidates, that the victors, by increasing the number, might receive the greater honour'; and, though his solicitations failed, he was able to report to Newcastle after the examination that 'the two young candidates were very deserving of your Grace's favour, and, though the contest was only for precedence, they were examined with the same accuracy as if the number had been greater[2].'

It was also during his time as Chancellor that the present east front of the Library was erected; and though he did not originate the idea which had long been under consideration, he took an active and leading part in its execution. There were indeed some who thought that it would have been better if he had been less active and left more to the initiative of the university; and possibly James Burrough, afterwards Master of Caius, was of this opinion. Burrough, who was an amateur architect of some merit[3], produced in 1752, a design for an east front of the Library, uniform in style with the Senate house which had been recently erected. If left to itself the university would probably have accepted Burrough's scheme without demur; but at this point Newcastle intervened and took the matter into his own hands.

'I have directed Mr Wright' he informed Dr Keene in October 1753 'to prepare forthwith a complete design for building a wing to answer the Senate house in front, and to the

[1] Add. MS. 32903, f. 307.   [2] Add. MS. 32966, f. 61.
[3] According to tradition Burrough designed the Senate house, but probably he did no more than give general suggestions.

Regent Walk. And also of a new front to the Library and Schools to front the Regent Walk, with arcades to Caius college and King's college to join the Schools with the other buildings. In the building opposite to the Senate house I would propose a Vice-Chancellor's court, an appartment for the Librarian at the end towards the Library, and for the Register at the end towards St Mary's church. I must beg that you would give immediate attention upon an affair in which the ornament and conveniency of the university and my own credit are so much concerned[1].'

It will be noticed that the project thus outlined was far more ambitious than that put forward by Burrough; but it was not novel, as the erection of a building, parallel with the Senate house, had long been contemplated, and in 1738 a syndicate had been formed to negotiate the purchase of the site. Aware however that such an undertaking would be excessively costly, the Duke intended to proceed by degrees and to make a beginning with the Library front; but if he thought that the university would accept his proposal without demur, he was guilty of a bad error of judgment and forgot how easy it is to offend the pride of an architect. Burrough was not unnaturally much chagrined at having his design so lightly cast aside, and objected that the new Library front, as designed by Wright, was not uniform in style with the Senate house; and, as he was a popular character in the university[2], he found many sympathisers who were prepared to support him. There was consequently a danger of Wright's design being rejected by the Senate; but the Duke's friends at Cambridge took pains to preach the doctrine that the university 'might be hurt and disgraced by any behaviour upon this occasion which might have the

[1] Add. MS. 32733, f. 135.
[2] According to Cole, Burrough had no enemies, and any prominent person in an university, of whom this can be said, must be either singularly fortunate or remarkably amiable.

THE CHANCELLOR AND THE UNIVERSITY 225

appearance of rudeness and ingratitude[1]'; and when on 11th of June 1754 a Grace was submitted to the Senate, recommending that the syndicate appointed in 1738 should be entrusted with the execution of the Chancellor's plan for the new library front, it passed with only ten non-placet votes in the non-regents' house and six in the regents' house[2]. Burrough and ten other members of Caius college were among the non-placets, and as the controversy is said to have provoked 'a great deal of animosity and ill-temper in the university,' the Duke was lucky to have gained so easy a victory.

Immediately after the assent of the Senate had been obtained, building operations were begun. In September 1754 Newcastle visited Cambridge from Wimpole to inspect the trenches dug for the foundations, and in the following April he laid the foundation stone. Three years later the building was finished, and on July 3rd, 1758, was opened in state by the Chancellor[3]. General satisfaction was expressed with Wright's work which was described as 'extremely handsome,' though fault was found with the bookshelves which were said to be 'very beautifull and very inconvenient[4].' The whole cost amounted to about ten thousand, five hundred pounds, and it was not found at all easy to raise this sum. It had been arranged at the outset that an appeal should be made by the Vice-Chancellor for subscriptions; and Newcastle, realising that many would only give in the hope of receiving again, and that as a dispenser of the royal patronage he was favourably situated to ask for money, closely associated himself with the appeal.

'I desire Yonge' he wrote to Dr Keene in October 1753

[1] Add. MS. 32734, f. 320; see also f. 293.
[2] Add. MS. 32735, f. 431, f. 449; Add. MS. 5852, f. 136, f. 137.
[3] Add. MS. 5852, f. 145. [4] Add. MS. 32875, f. 75.

226 THE CHANCELLOR AND THE UNIVERSITY

'would, from the buttery books of the several colleges, send me up the names of the several peers, bishops, peers' sons, and persons of any distinction who have been at our university, that we may judge whereabouts our subscriptions will come. I desire also to have the names and sums given by the several persons upon the two last subscriptions in 1720 and 1724 or thereabouts[1].'

Dr Yonge was Vice-Chancellor when the subscription list was opened, and when he retired in November 1754, three thousand, six hundred and fifty pounds had been collected, of which sum the King had subscribed one thousand, and Newcastle five hundred pounds. Dr Thomas, Master of Christ's, who followed Yonge as Vice-Chancellor, raised another twelve hundred and seventy-one pounds; but after his retirement there was a serious falling off; and the three Vice-Chancellors who were in office from November 1755 to November 1758 only succeeded between them in raising a sum slightly less than that collected by Dr Thomas in a single year[2]. Thus when Dr Caryl became Vice-Chancellor in November 1758 between three and four thousand pounds were still needed; and encouraged and perhaps assisted by the Duke, he made an energetic appeal[3] and by the middle of May 1759 had reduced the debt to about two thousand, six hundred pounds[4]. This was still an embarrassingly large liability and Newcastle resorted to heroic measures. He added another five hundred pounds to his original donation, and arranged that the King should contribute another thousand pounds, thus considerably easing the financial situation[5]. By the middle of October 1759 only a sum of six hundred pounds remained to be paid[6], which was advanced out of the funds of the university.

[1] Add. MS. 32733, f. 135.   [2] Add. MS. 5852, f. 441.
[3] Add. MS. 32891, f. 88.   [4] Add. MS. 32891, f. 161.
[5] Add. MS. 32893, f. 3, f. 5.   [6] Add. MS. 32897, f. 213.

THE CHANCELLOR AND THE UNIVERSITY

'As the workmen have stayed so long for their money' wrote Dr Caryl to Newcastle on November 23rd, 1759 'I took a resolution to advance it to them out of the university stock, and have accordingly paid them all this morning, hoping that in two or three months I shall be enabled to replace it by the payment of such subscriptions as are already promised[1].'

It had clearly been very difficult to raise the necessary money, and the task might have been impossible but for the assistance given by the Duke. He and the King between them contributed more than a third of the total cost of the building; and it is possible that many subscribed because they knew that Newcastle was keenly anxious for the success of the scheme. 'Probably most of the clerical subscribers and possibly many of the laity' scribbled Cole in after years upon a list of subscribers 'put in here as into a lottery of the Duke of Newcastle's formation, Translations, places and preferments were what were fished for, and many succeeded to their heart's desire[2].' The difficulty he had found in collecting money was enough to convince the Duke that the completion of Wright's design must wait for another Chancellor; but he is deserving of our gratitude for what he actually achieved. It is not so easy to be grateful to him for the statue of George II which he presented to the university, and which now stands in the Library. Executed by Wilton, it is an ugly and cumbersome piece of work, lacking in any interest save as an indication of the taste of the age in statuary. George II was still on the throne when Newcastle announced his intention, expressing at the same time, a wish that the statue should be placed in the Library, 'as his Majesty has been so considerable a benefactor to it[3],' but it was not until 1766 that the statue was erected, and then

[1] Add. MS. 32899, f. 71.   [2] Add. MS. 5852, f. 441.
[3] Add. MS. 32911, f. 369; see also Add. MS. 32909, f. 278; Add. MS. 32912, f. 11.

not in the Library but in the Senate house[1]. The Duke himself was mainly responsible for the long delay by failing to make timely preparations for the composition of an inscription. 'You know' pathetically remarked Wilton in June 1763 'how much I want the inscription, and how many months I have waited for it to compleat the work[2].' Stirred at last into activity by this appeal, Newcastle sent instructions to Dr Caryl for an inscription to be written; 'His Grace' wrote the Duke's secretary 'thinks that there should be a good deal and something very handsome and proper said about the late King who was so great a benefactor, and something should also be said of the university and of himself with regard to his zeal for both[3].'

Newcastle however was not content to give general instructions, and he was not sparing of criticism on receiving a draft of the inscription in April 1764. He strongly objected to the words 'summa confidentia' being used with regard to his relations with George II, because they conveyed 'the sense of first minister which no man should say of himself'; and he also ventured to express an opinion on points of scholarship.

'I had some doubts' he told the Bishop of Norwich 'whether "quod volenti" was classical and sufficiently conveyed the sense, viz. because he did so. Lord Grantham assures me it is right and elegantly expresses the sense which is propter quod. Lord Grantham had himself some doubts, as I had, whether "ipsum per annos complures" is not at too great a distance from the conclusion to which it relates[4].'

[1] Add. MS. 32975, f. 91.   [2] Add. MS. 32949, f. 167.
[3] Add. MS. 32949, f. 263.
[4] Add. MS. 32958, f. 266. The final form of the inscription was as follows:

    Georgio Secundo
   Patrono suo, optime merenti,
    Semper venerando;
   Quod volenti Populo,

A few weeks later he returned to the charge, having in the interval consulted those of his friends who had kept up their classics.

'As to ipsum' he wrote to the Bishop of Norwich 'they were clear that there could be no objection to the distance, but one of them rather chose se or seipsum than ipsum alone; but, if ipsum will do, it is better alone. One of them had some doubts whether the verbs should not be in the subjunctive mood...but I believe it is better as it is. It has occurred to me, and to me only, whether four or five words might not be thrown in to heighten it; for example, something like this—in pace et in bello feliciter—and then another word of higher commendation. ...This is my own. Try it a little, and see whether it will do[1].'

The Bishop tried it and apparently came to the conclusion that it would do, for the words suggested appear in the final form of the inscription. The Bishop however upheld his use of *quod*, quoting as his authority 'the seventeenth section of Tully's *Fifth Philippic*,' and he preferred to drop the phrase 'ipsum per annos complures' rather than permit the introduction of se or seipsum. 'The reciprocal pronoun' he remarked 'is the most difficult thing to manage in the Latin language

          Justissime, humanissime,
          In Pace et in Bello,
          Feliciter Imperavit;
          Quod Academiam Cantabrigiensem
               Fovit, auxit, ornavit;
               Hanc Statuam
          Aeternum, faxit Deus, Monumentum,
             Grati Animi in Regem,
             Pietatis in Patriam,
             Amoris in Academiam,
          Suis Sumptibus poni curavit
               Thomas Holles
             Dux de Newcastle
          Academiae Cancellarius
              A.D. MDCCLXVI.

[1] Add. MS. 32958, f. 416.

and perhaps in the English too[1].' It is characteristic of Newcastle to have been so profuse of advice upon a question which might have been safely left to the experts, and typical of his whole attitude towards the university. He wasted his own and other people's time by continually interfering in matters which could easily have been arranged without him; and was ever seeking to assert his authority. Over his Chancellorship hangs an atmosphere of intrigue and wire-pulling for which he is largely responsible; and though he no more introduced jobbery and corruption into the university than he did into political life, it can hardly be denied that in both spheres of his activity he was not scrupulous as to the means he employed to win followers. Nevertheless he deserves to be remembered in the university for the love he bore it. His frequent professions of affection ring true; and it can at least be said of him that he strove, according to his lights, to promote the honour and glory of Cambridge.

[1] Add. MS. 32958, f. 427.

CHAPTER IV

THE CHANCELLOR AND THE COLLEGES

IF Newcastle had strictly confined himself to his prescribed duties as Chancellor it would have been unnecessary for him to concern himself with the domestic affairs of the various colleges, unless called upon to act in the capacity of visitor[1], and it would doubtless have conduced to the peace of mind, both of himself and the university, if he had restrained his activities. College politics are apt to be involved and tortuous labyrinths, perplexing enough to those who daily tread them, and quite bewildering to the uninitiated stranger. The political life of a small society tends to be fierce; and in a college, as in a city state, the balance of forces is never constant, parties are for ever forming and dissolving, and nothing is certain except an inexhaustible supply of contentious questions. Had Newcastle been born in a different station and passed his life as a Fellow of a college, his capacity for patient and industrious intrigue would not have been wasted; but, situated as he was, it was hopeless for him to attempt to control the affairs of sixteen separate societies. The task moreover was not only greater than any one man could perform; it was even more dangerous than it was difficult. Much as the Fellows of a college might cabal and intrigue against one another, bitter as might be their personal rivalries, they would certainly combine against the intruder from the outside; for college feeling ran high and the interference of a Chancellor would be bitterly resented.

[1] A few of the colleges had the Chancellor as their visitor.

Nevertheless Newcastle could not afford to be indifferent to college politics unless he was prepared very substantially to modify his conception of his part in academic business. His influence in the university depended in no small measure upon his influence in the various colleges, and that influence could best be gained and kept by the exercise of some sort of control over their internal politics. Moreover, with the exception of the Masters of Trinity, Jesus, and Magdalene, the Heads of Houses were elected by their Fellows; and, as the Heads wielded considerable power in the university, it was clearly to the Duke's advantage that they should be friendly to his interests.

Thus he might appear to be between the horns of a dilemma. If he intervened in college business he ran a serious risk of encountering a rebuff, and if he pursued a policy of strict non-intervention there was a real danger of his power in the university lacking foundation. The dilemma however was more apparent than real, since it was possible for a Chancellor, who knew his business, to exercise an influence in the colleges without too ostentatiously appearing to do so. It has already been mentioned that in his management of university business Newcastle depended to a great extent upon trusty friends at Cambridge who were aware of his wishes and worked for their accomplishment; and he pursued much the same method with regard to the colleges. Backhouse in Trinity, Talbot in Clare, Yonge and Caryl in Jesus, Green in Corpus, Rutherforth in St John's, and Marriott in Trinity Hall, were his agents in their respective colleges; and though it is only occasionally and when times are critical that we hear of their activities, it may fairly be assumed that they were constantly working to mould their colleges nearer to the Duke's desire. The work demanded uncommon tact and discrimination, and was by no means always successfully performed;

PLATE IV

LYNFORD CARYL
MASTER OF JESUS COLLEGE, CAMBRIDGE (1758-81)

THE CHANCELLOR AND THE COLLEGES

but if Newcastle had been denied such assistance, his hold upon the colleges, and consequently his hold upon the university, would have been very much less than it was.

It must not be imagined however that the system was completely organised, and that the Duke had a representative in every college. He does not appear to have ever established a foothold in either Caius or Emmanuel which were both reputed strongholds of toryism; and though it is perhaps not surprising that he failed to weaken the authority of Dr Richardson, the tory Master of Emmanuel, he might have been expected to be more successful in Caius where for a time his loyal supporter, Sir Thomas Gooch, Bishop of Ely, was Master. It seems however that Gooch, if he made the attempt, was signally unsuccessful in converting his Fellows to his own way of thinking; and it is significant that when he died in 1754 Newcastle apparently made no attempt to prevent the election into the mastership of James Burrough whom he regarded with profound suspicion. It is even still more significant that when Burrough died in 1764, at a particularly critical moment in the High Steward controversy, Newcastle seems never for a moment to have contemplated the possibility of influencing the election of the new Master. He doubtless realised that there was nothing to be done in a college which had only produced one vote in support of Lord Hardwicke's Grace; but his complete acquiescence in a policy of inaction vividly illustrates his impotence. Given a favourable opportunity he would not have hesitated to plant his banner in both Caius and Emmanuel; but he needed for the success of the operation a powerful ally within the gates, and was apparently unable to find him.

Caius and Emmanuel were not the only societies in which Newcastle had little or no influence; for we hear

234 THE CHANCELLOR AND THE COLLEGES

singularly little of his relations with Pembroke and St Catharine's, and it seems unlikely that he had a following in either of these colleges. The argument from silence is, however, admittedly dangerous, and inasmuch as Newcastle would prefer to remain in the background as far as possible, it is quite possible that his influence was most effective when it was least apparent. There is for instance no indication that when in 1754 Dr Rooke was succeeded in the mastership of Christ's by Hugh Thomas, the Duke intervened in any way; but it may well be that the Fellows of Christ's had been so carefully trained by Dr Rooke that they could be safely trusted not to elect a Master who would be displeasing to the Chancellor. Nor is there any evidence of external pressure upon the Fellows of Queens' when in 1760 they had to appoint a successor to Dr Sedgwick who had been their President for nearly thirty years. Newcastle was promptly informed that 'a major part of the society...are determined in favour of Dr Plumptre,...the junior of that name who is rector of Wimpole[1],' and it would have indeed been surprising if he had been unable to extend a cordial welcome to Lord Hardwicke's rector[2]. It is therefore possible that the Fellows of Christ's and the Fellows of Queens' were such loyal courtiers as to anticipate the ducal wishes; but, if so, they were exceptionable, and it certainly would be a great blunder to imagine that Newcastle disposed of masterships of colleges like places in the church or sinecure offices in the gift of the government. He naturally wished to have as many friends as possible among the Heads of Houses; but

[1] Add. MS. 32914, f. 60.
[2] A certain Mr Manning, an ex-Fellow of Queens', thought of standing for the Presidency against Plumptre, but quickly came to the conclusion that he would be unable even to put up a respectable fight. Add. MS. 32914, f. 116, see also f. 29, f. 58, f. 94.

he had to tread warily, and was well aware that the display of indiscreet activity would be the surest way of defeating the end he had in view.

It is indeed extremely difficult, if not impossible, to estimate with any accuracy the extent to which he interfered in the domestic affairs of the different colleges. There is good ground for thinking that the interference was occasional and for the most part confined to the elections to masterships; but it is dangerous to be more precise, and it is certainly not safe to lay down as a general rule that he never allowed the election of a Master to pass without his intervention. It is moreover quite certain that much must have happened of which we know little or nothing, and it would be idle to pretend that we have plumbed to their depths the subterraneous intrigues that were carried on. We know enough however to be perfectly sure that Newcastle was never indifferent to the choice of a Head of a House, and that on occasions he was prepared to go to great lengths to secure a suitable appointment. Sometimes his task was comparatively easy, as in the case of the mastership of Jesus which was in the gift of the Bishop of Ely, and was conferred in succession upon Dr Yonge and Dr Caryl, two of the most trusted of Newcastle's Cambridge supporters. Yonge was appointed by Sir Thomas Gooch, and, in view of the cordial relations between the Bishop and the Duke, it is probable that Yonge owed his good fortune to the favour he enjoyed with the Chancellor. But though this is no more than a surmise, we can at least be certain that Yonge's successor, Caryl, was deeply indebted for his advancement to Newcastle.

'I have the satisfaction of acquainting your Grace' he wrote to his patron on July 14th, 1758, 'that yesterday the Bishop of Ely[1] was so kind as to collate me to the mastership of Jesus

[1] Matthias Mawson, who had succeeded Gooch as Bishop of Ely.

college. My earliest and best thanks are due to your Grace for your kind and effectual recommendation of me to his Lordship[1].'

It was easy enough for Newcastle, especially when he controlled the distribution of the crown's ecclesiastical patronage, to influence the appointment to a mastership which was in the gift of a bishop; but the game was more intricate and success less certain when the electors were the Fellows of a college, jealous of their independence. Yet the stories of the election of Dr Green as Master of Corpus in 1750, and of Dr Law's election as Master of Peterhouse in 1754, suggest that, though the game was tricky, it was possible to play it with success. On the death of Edmund Castle, Master of Corpus in 1750, the Fellows were unanimous in wishing to elect Charles Skottowe, President of the society, as their Master, but Skottowe declined the honour, and as the Fellows could not agree upon any other candidate, a certain number of them appealed to Thomas Herring, Archbishop of Canterbury, to recommend them a suitable Master. It was quite natural that they should turn in their difficulty to the Archbishop who had been a Fellow and Tutor of the college and continued to take a friendly interest in its welfare; but it is at first sight somewhat surprising that the Archbishop should have advised them to go outside their own body and choose as their Master, John Green, Fellow of St John's and Regius Professor of Divinity[2]. As might have been anticipated, the suggestion was not received with favour, except by those Fellows who were responsible for the appeal, but, as they were the majority, Green was duly

[1] Add. MS. 32881, f. 317. On the occasion when Yonge was appointed Master, Newcastle wrote to the Bishop on behalf of Caryl; but it is likely that he also wrote on behalf of Yonge, and possibly gave him the preference. Add. MS. 32878, f. 397.
[2] The Archbishop's letter is printed in Nichols' *Illustrations of the Literary History of the Eighteenth Century*, VI, 794.

elected into the mastership. It is not improbable that the Archbishop's recommendation was inspired by Lord Hardwicke, and that, when the Fellows appealed to Lambeth, they were not acting on a sudden impulse but executing a carefully thought out scheme. Lord Hardwicke was intimate with Herring whose patron he had been in early days[1], and as he was also the patron of Green, it is not unlikely that he inspired the Archbishop's recommendation. And it may well be that the appeal was engineered with the sole object of securing Green's appointment. Many months before his death Castle was known to be in failing health; and a letter, written in 1749 by Edmund Pyle, whose son was a Fellow of Corpus, to the Archbishop, certainly suggests that an intrigue was on foot in which Herring was playing a leading part.

'I no sooner' wrote Edmund Pyle to the Archbishop 'received the great favour of your Grace's kind and good letter than I wrote to the person intimated therein, and deferred my dutiful answer to it no longer than till I was enabled to acquaint you with his truly filial reply that he should never find greater pleasure than that of complying with every desire of a father and the honourable friends of that father. Meantime, I am sorry for the ill state of my friend C—st—l which gives occasion to this affair[2].'

It can be taken for certain that the 'person intimated therein' was Pyle's son, the Fellow of Corpus, and it is not far fetched to assume that 'the truly filial reply' was a promise to obey the Archbishop's wishes in the event of the Mastership falling vacant.

There can be no doubt that Newcastle was privy to whatever intrigue there was, and that he and Hardwicke had agreed upon securing the mastership of Corpus for

[1] *Life of Lord Chancellor Hardwicke*, by P. C. Yorke, I, 422.
[2] Master's *History of Corpus Christi College*, with additional matter by John Lamb, p. 240, note A.

a friend whom they could trust. It is possible that Green was imposed upon the society with the express object of disciplining it in loyalty to the Chancellor and the whig faith; and, if so, the object was obtained, for nowhere in the university had the Duke greater influence than in Corpus. It has already been mentioned that when Green retired from the mastership in 1764, the Fellows, by previous arrangement, obediently elected in his place, Barnardiston, who could be relied upon to further the Chancellor's interests: and the ease, with which this transference of power was effected, is a tribute to the value of the work achieved by the retiring Master. The story of the election of Dr Law as Master of Peterhouse resembles in certain particulars the history of Green's introduction to Corpus, and provides a further illustration of the Duke's wishes being taken into account in the appointment of a Master. Dr Keene, Bishop of Chester, did not retire from the mastership of Peterhouse until 1754: but as early as 1752 he had already decided that his successor should be Edmund Law, Archdeacon of Carlisle, and was busily engaged in persuading his Fellows to pledge their votes beforehand. As Law had no connection with Peterhouse, having been an undergraduate at St John's and a Fellow of Christ's, he was not exactly a strong candidate: but Keene wanted the Archdeaconry of Carlisle for his brother in law, Venn Eyre, and, believing Law to be a sound whig who would be faithful to Newcastle, he decided to support him. But skill and management were needed to overcome the objection taken to Law as an alien, and it is possible that Keene intentionally delayed his resignation until he had made sure of his candidate's election.

'I have begun' he wrote to Newcastle on June 27th, 1752, 'to open the affair of my resignation to some part of the society, and find that it will be a more difficult matter than I expected.

The society is young and unacquainted with Dr Law, and the business of recommending a stranger is become very invidious since the affair of Benet college. It is natural for Mr Stuart, who is the principal person with whom I am to treat, to think that, having made one Master, should he be employed in making another, some douceurs are to be expected. And indeed, considering the part he has acted in overthrowing the old system of the college and establishing the new one, he is certainly deserving of favours. If your Grace will be so good as to continue your disposition to serve him with the living of Ashen in Essex, I would afterwards, as opportunity would offer to me, take him up[1].'

A few months after this letter was written, Stuart obtained a dispensation to hold the rectory of Ashdon with the vicarage of Steeple Bumpstead[2], and in 1754 Law was elected Master of Peterhouse, resigning the Archdeaconry of Carlisle which was conferred upon Venn Eyre.

It is noteworthy that Dr Law was appointed Master of Peterhouse and Dr Green was appointed Master of Corpus as the result of a college intrigue in which the Chancellor was not directly involved, though undoubtedly his wishes had great weight with the electors. On both occasions he had the good fortune to have a friend, upon whom he could implicitly rely, and who was in close touch with the Fellows; and there can be no question that from Newcastle's point of view such a method of procedure was ideal. He was saved the odium which would arise from intervention, and was able to secure the election he desired, without having to espouse the cause of one particular candidate and thereby cause offence to others who, rightly or wrongly, considered that they had an equal claim upon his favour. Indeed, when he could safely do so, he had every inducement to remain as much as possible in the back-

[1] Add. MS. 32728, f. 127. Charles Stuart had been elected to a Fellowship in 1740 and was a Tutor for several years.
[2] *Gentleman's Magazine* for 1753, p. 345.

240   THE CHANCELLOR AND THE COLLEGES

ground; and, if he had needed a lesson in the dangers of interference, he would have received it in the last years of his Chancellorship when he found himself compelled to take a hand in the election of a Master of St John's.

When Newcastle became Chancellor the Master of St John's was Dr John Newcome who was a loyal and enthusiastic supporter of the Duke, and had specially distinguished himself by his zealous opposition to the candidature of Frederick, Prince of Wales. As St John's was the largest college in the university, and had no rival in size or influence except Trinity, it was no small gain to Newcastle to have Newcome among his most fervent adherents, especially as his relations with Trinity were never from the first completely satisfactory, and became decidedly strained after the whig predominance in the state had been shattered by George III. It may be that it was impossible for a Chancellor to be on intimate terms with Trinity and St John's, so bitter was the feud between the two colleges[1]; but, if it was

[1] A letter from Dr Smith, Master of Trinity, to Newcastle, dated June 27th, 1751, affords a vivid illustration of the feelings of Trinity towards St John's. 'Last post' wrote the Master 'I received Mr Robinson's letter sent me from Cambridge by Dr Wilson, as your Grace had ordered him. I have not the honour to know much of Mr Robinson but surely he does me too great an honour to employ your Grace and Mr Pelham to sollicit me for a poor butler's place as he calls it. I am always ready, as I ought, to serve your Grace and Mr Pelham, otherwise it would be indifferent to me whoever is to be our butler, provided he be but a honest man. But your Grace may remember perhaps that St John's college always looked upon themselves as the rivals of Trinity, the next great college in the university. And the humour, I find, is still so prevalent among us that I much question whether the generality of my Fellows will not be very much averse to Mr Robinson's friend on that very account of his coming from St John's; and I am not sure whether some of the higher spirits among them would not sooner quarrel with their bread and butter than receive it from the hands of a Johnian butler.' Add. MS. 32724, f. 406.

THE CHANCELLOR AND THE COLLEGES 241

possible, the rôle was too difficult for the Duke to play, and he had to be content with fostering his influence in St John's through Dr Newcome. Hence it must have been with interest not unmixed with alarm that he heard in September 1758 that Dr Newcome was dangerously ill.

'I think it my duty to inform your Grace' wrote the Master of Christ's 'that the Master of St John's college has been indisposed for about a week. His disorder is the hickups which have in some fits held him ten or twelve hours. And last night they returned with some violence. This day his physician, Doctor Plumptre, finding the medicine he had prescribed did not take effect, and observing a kind of periodical return of the illness, has given him the bark which, according to the account which I received this morning at eleven o'clock, sits easy on his stomach. But if the bark should not succeed I should apprehend there will be danger in the case[1].'

The three most likely candidates for the mastership in the event of Dr Newcome's death were Dr Zachary Brooke, Dr Powell, and Professor Rutherforth. Brooke and Powell were the two Tutors of the college, and Rutherforth had held the same office from 1740 to 1751: but an ex-Tutor is comparable with a dead lion; and of the three candidates Brooke and Powell had far better prospects of success than Rutherforth. To secure election it was necessary to obtain the votes of at least more than half the number of Fellows; and as at this particular time there were forty-eight Fellows of the college, the candidate who could confidently count upon twenty-five votes was certain of election. Dr Brooke was apparently of the opinion that if the contest was only between him and Powell he could make sure of this necessary minimum[2]: and as he was a supporter of the Duke, and Powell was a leading member of the

[1] Add. MS. 32884, f. 51.
[2] Add. MS. 32884, f. 53, f. 73, f. 92.

242 THE CHANCELLOR AND THE COLLEGES

opposition party in the university, he not unreasonably expected to receive the Chancellor's assistance if the mastership fell vacant. He perceived however that his chance of success would be seriously diminished if Professor Rutherforth stood for election; for though Rutherforth had a scanty following in the college and was not at all likely to secure the mastership, there was a serious danger that, if he came forward as a candidate, he would secure a certain number of votes which would otherwise be given to Brooke, which might result in none of the three competitors securing the necessary minimum, in which event the appointment would lapse to the eight senior Fellows. It was clearly of great importance to Brooke that Rutherforth should not be a candidate; and he therefore appealed to Newcastle to dissuade the Professor from standing for election.

'I have, my Lord,' he wrote on September 20th, 1758, 'very carefully examined the state of my interest in the college upon a supposition that the mastership was now to be vacant: and, as far as I can judge, and I would not deceive your Grace or myself in this matter, I have nothing to apprehend from a competition with Dr Powell, provided my interest is not broke in upon from any other quarter. For out of forty-eight votes, the present number of electing Fellows, I have twenty-five that I can depend upon against him, and he has only sixteen that he can depend upon against me. And I can venture to say out of the remaining votes, which I consider at present as dubious, I have much the greatest likelyhood of a majority in my favour. As this is a true state of the case, my Lord, as far as I and my friends can determine from repeated surveys of the college, I shall hope for your Grace's countenance and favour. For that would put the affair out of all dispute[1].'

If the contest had only been between Brooke and Powell, Newcastle would not have hesitated between the candidates, for he certainly had no wish to see an enemy installed as Master of one of the most influential

[1] Add. MS. 32884, f. 92.

THE CHANCELLOR AND THE COLLEGES 243

colleges in the university. The situation however was unfortunately not quite so simple. Rutherforth, who from being an opponent had recently become an ally of the Duke, might presumably relapse into his former hostility if commanded to forego an opportunity of securing the mastership: and, if he stood for election, it would not be easy for Newcastle to discriminate between him and Brooke. Both were his friends and would expect his assistance; and the Chancellor might easily find himself in the position of Captain Macheath between Polly and Lucy. This situation never arose, for Dr Newcome made a speedy recovery; but while that recovery was still uncertain Newcastle had already indicated the policy he would probably pursue in the event of a fatal issue to Dr Newcome's illness. His main anxiety was to prevent at all cost Powell's election; and he therefore through Dr Yonge specially charged his true friends not so to 'differ amongst themselves as to let Dr Powell avail himself of their dissentions,' adding however that between Brooke and Rutherforth he desired to be neutral[1]. The Duke was clearly opposed to a three-cornered contest, fearing that it might result in Powell carrying off the prize, and as it was quite certain that Brooke had many more supporters in the college than Rutherforth, Newcastle's wishes, as expressed through Dr Yonge, were interpreted as a suggestion that Rutherforth should retire in favour of Brooke. Not only was Rutherforth told by some of the Newcastle party in the university that the Duke was in favour of his rival[2], but Brooke himself was assiduous in proclaiming the same fact.

'It was generally, I may say universally, understood' wrote Dr Yonge in after years 'that your Grace did actually take a part at that time and support Dr Brooke. He made no scruple to say so to everyone, and was perpetually with my Lord Kinnoull

[1] Add. MS. 32884, f. 88.　　[2] Add. MS. 32964, f. 343.

and me with his lists and his calculations. I have really forgotten (for it is four years ago if not more) how far your Grace did really support him. But I am sure the Professor believes you did most entirely, and so do all the university[1]'

It is probable that the Professor and the university were right, and that the Chancellor desired a straight fight between Brooke and Powell; but as Dr Newcome regained his health and continued Master, the Duke's plan of campaign was never fully revealed. It is not apparent that he could have steered any other course; but the incident affords an useful illustration of the difficulties which beset him when he had to play a part in college politics. In order to make certain of Powell's defeat Rutherforth's ambition had to be sacrificed: and, however sound the policy, the victim was not unnaturally a little sore. After the crisis was passed, Rutherforth in a letter to Newcastle contended that he would have certainly succeeded against Powell if Brooke had not stood, and that if the contest had been only between Powell and Brooke the former would have been victorious[2]: and though he was singular in this opinion, he may be excused for holding it and for believing that the Chancellor had acted with unbecoming partiality. Rutherforth indeed felt he had a grievance, and it was perhaps wise of Newcastle to refrain from replying to his letter[3]; but when on a sudden illness of Dr Newcome in December 1761, Rutherforth again appealed to the Duke and again received no answer[4], he must have felt that he was being very badly treated. It must have been difficult for him to realise that his patron had a difficult game to play and could not possibly allow personal considerations to influence his strategy; and it is to the credit of his

[1] Add. MS. 32964, f. 418.　　[2] Add. MS. 32886, f. 149.
[3] Add. MS. 32964, f. 343.
[4] Add. MS. 32964, f. 343; Add. MS. 32932, f. 445.

loyalty that in spite of these disappointments he remained an unswerving supporter of the Chancellor and actively supported Lord Hardwicke's candidature for the High Stewardship.

Such constancy was the more remarkable from being exceptional. When the acid test of the succession to the High Stewardship was applied, Dr Brooke showed his gratitude for the favours he had received by enlisting under the banner of Lord Sandwich, while an exactly opposite course was pursued by Dr Powell who forswore his hostility to the Duke and actively canvassed on behalf of Lord Hardwicke. It is possible that both men were influenced by the same well-founded belief that Dr Newcome, who was over eighty by that time, was not much longer for this life, and that therefore it behoved them to choose the patron most likely to advance their interests in the event of the mastership falling vacant. About August 1764 Powell seems to have definitely asked Newcastle to support his claims to the mastership, and received a most gratifying reply.

'I shall be extremely happy' wrote the Duke 'whenever I have an opportunity, to shew my grateful sense of the obligations I have to you, and I can never wish dignity and power to be placed in better hands than yours, and shall be always glad to contribute to it wherever and whenever I can[1].'

It was perhaps rather indiscreet of Newcastle to be quite so effusive over the repentant sinner; for it was by no means certain that Powell would prove himself as strong a candidate as he had been expected to be on a previous occasion. In 1761 he had relinquished his Tutorship and quitted Cambridge for London, and two years later had resigned his Fellowship; and though he still retained a considerable following in the college, his influence was presumably not quite what it had been. Newcastle moreover should have remembered the

[1] Add. MS. 32961, f. 269; see also f. 220.

claims of Rutherforth who had remained true to the whig cause when so many had deserted it, and it is possible that when he gave Powell an assurance of his support, he was not expecting a vacancy in the mastership in the immediate future, and was thinking more of saying the thing to please than of defining a policy. Yet by October 1764 it became fairly clear that Dr Newcome was nearing his end; and the old man, conscious of his growing incapacity, expressed the greatest anxiety to resign the Lady Margaret Professorship of Divinity which he had held since 1727. If he was permitted to execute this design, Newcastle would almost certainly find himself at a serious disadvantage when Newcome's death, which could not be far off, vacated the mastership. All doctors and bachelors of divinity were electors to the Lady Margaret Professorship, and as the divinity faculty was more strongly represented in St John's than in any other society, that college had come to regard the professorship as more or less its own possession[1]. In the event of the professorship being declared vacant, it was almost certain that Dr Law, Master of Peterhouse, and Dr Brooke would come forward as candidates, and whereas Brooke would look for support to his patron, Lord Sandwich, Law would appeal to Newcastle. There could be no doubt that Sandwich would use what influence he possessed on Brooke's behalf, and the fact that he supported a Johnian candidate would possibly gain him many fol-

[1] In November 1764 the number of electors to the Lady Margaret Professorship were 102, of which 36 were in St John's and 25 in Trinity, 12 in Queens', 7 in Emmanuel, 6 in Corpus, 4 in Clare, 3 in Christ's, 2 in King's, 2 in Caius, 2 in St Catharine's, 1 in Jesus, 1 in Magdalene and 1 in Sidney. Add. MS. 32963, f. 330. Writing on November 17th, 1764, to the Master of Corpus, an old Johnian, Newcastle remarks 'you gentlemen of St John's, having so many batchelors of divinity, look upon yourselves to have a right to that professorship.' Add. MS. 32964, f. 17.

lowers in St John's and enable him to intervene with telling effect when Dr Newcome's death necessitated an election of a new Master. Newcastle was in a very different and a far more difficult position. The Master of Peterhouse had undeniable claims upon his assistance, and his claims would certainly be favoured by many of the leaders of Newcastle's party in Cambridge[1]: but, though he had been an undergraduate of St John's, he had never been a Fellow of the college and had long ago severed his connection with it. Hence he could not be seriously counted as a Johnian candidate, and the Duke by supporting him would incur a serious risk of undermining his influence in St John's at the very moment when it was most important for him to foster it. Nor would the situation, as it affected the Duke, be much improved if, as would probably happen, another candidate appeared who was both a Johnian and an adherent of the Chancellor, for even if Newcastle decided to support such a candidate with a view of retaining his hold upon St John's, it was by no means certain that he would be able to persuade his friends to pursue a similar course, and it might therefore well happen that the appearance of a third candidate would rent the Chancellor's party in twain and throw the professorship into the hand of Dr Brooke.

In view of the extremely complicated and difficult situation which would thus arise, Newcastle was naturally anxious that Dr Newcome should not resign his professorship: and rightly believed that not only would a serious difficulty be thereby avoided but a positive advantage gained. The greatest disaster that could possibly happen would be for Dr Brooke to secure both the professorship and the mastership; and his chance of doing so would be very much diminished if both offices were simultaneously in the market. Indeed

[1] Add. MS. 32963, f. 328.

it was reasonable to assume that Dr Powell's prospects of obtaining the mastership would be materially improved if his candidature for that office coincided with an election to the Lady Margaret Professorship: for his most serious competitor, Dr Brooke, might possibly be bought off by being allowed to obtain the professorship.

'The election of a Margaret Professor and that of a Master of St John's' wrote Dr Powell in November 1764 'will certainly have great influence upon each other. And therefore I cannot but think myself somewhat interested in them. The resignation, which your Grace's letter prevented, would have hurt my expectations[1].'

It had only been with great difficulty that Dr Newcome had been prevented from resigning his professorship, and the success achieved was only partial. It is true that the Master was finally dissuaded from his intention by the Duke[2]: but he had been very insistent, and unfortunately had not kept his own counsel.

'His peace of mind, he says' Talbot informed the Duke on October 31st, 1761, 'depends upon its taking effect. I have plied him as closely as I could, but in the present low state of his spirits no reasoning has much influence upon him. I have also called into my aid, Miss Kirke, a relation of his who lives with him, and who has been a very faithful assistant to me in this difficult business[3]. She has done everything in her power and several times incurred his anger by steadily opposing his design. Yesterday, in spite of all her dissuasions, he enclosed his resignation of the professorship in a letter to the Vice-Chancellor and ordered his footman to carry it directly. Before the footman got out of the house she ventured to stop him, took the letter and put it into her pocket. In the evening she told him what she had done, and he bore it with less impatience than could be expected. At this time I called upon him, renewed my promise

[1] Add. MS. 32964, f. 25.
[2] Add. MS. 32963, f. 283, f. 344, f. 409.
[3] Talbot afterwards married Miss Kirke who was a co-heir with Richard Beadon of the bulk of Dr Newcome's fortune. Baker's *History of St John's College*, II, 1030.

of preaching his *Concio ad clerum,* rendering him any other service in my power, etc., and after about an hour and half left him in pretty good temper and spirits. Hitherto I had kept the secret of this design most religiously, even from your Grace's friends, but having learned from Miss Kirke that the Master had himself communicated it two (*sic*) of his Fellows, Dr Ogden and Mr Cardale (the Bursar)[1], I saw that concealment was no longer to be hoped for, and therefore this morning went to the Bishop of Lincoln[2] and imparted to him the whole affair. He was of the opinion that I should immediately tell it to Dr Law ...and Dr Law wished me to communicate it to his friend, the Dean of Ely[3]....Having gone thus far, I thought, and the Dean of Ely thought so too, that it would be right for me to tell it also to the Vice-Chancellor[4].'

Consequently it was quickly known all over the university that Newcome was anxious to resign his professorship; and by November 4th Dr Law, Dr Ogden, and Dr Brooke had announced their intention of standing for election in the event of a vacancy[5]. Thus, though the Duke had succeeded in persuading Dr Newcome to continue in his professorship, he failed to prevent the appearance of candidates for the succession. Ogden apparently contented himself with announcing his intention of standing and did not solicit votes, but the other two competitors were determined to waste no time, rightly calculating that, even if Dr Newcome did not resign, it could not be long before he died. Espousing Dr Brooke's cause, Lord Sandwich acted with promptitude and vigour; and it was reported that 'his applications on behalf of Dr Brooke are, if possible, warmer and stronger than those which he made for himself[6].' Nor was Dr Law behindhand, for he

[1] Joseph Cardale.
[2] Dr Green, who had recently resigned the mastership of Corpus.
[3] Dr Thomas, Master of Christ's.
[4] Add. MS. 32963, f. 134.   [5] Add. MS. 32963, f. 223.
[6] Add. MS. 32963, f. 344; Add. MS. 32964, f. 32.

appealed to Newcastle and Lord Hardwicke, sending them each a list of the electors, 'with some few of their connections[1],' and went about the university soliciting votes for himself[2]. It was certainly not to Newcastle's interest that this canvassing should continue, for he might be forced to take a side and thereby diminish his chances of being able to control the appointment of Dr Newcome's successor in the mastership. He could not support Dr Law without imperilling his influence in St John's, and by prematurely committing himself to Dr Ogden he would prevent himself from having a free hand to deal with the problem of the mastership when it came up for solution. He consequently played the waiting game, and, by persuading Dr Newcome to announce his intention of continuing to hold the professorship, must at least have succeeded in diminishing the activity of the canvassing. It was unlikely that many of the electors would commit themselves before it was absolutely necessary to do so; and though Dr Law's chances of securing the professorship were probably diminished by Newcome's resignation being deferred, Newcastle could not afford to weaken his position in the university and St John's in order to gratify one man's ambition[3].

[1] Add. MS. 35657, f. 213; Add. MS. 32963, f. 239, f. 328; Add. MS. 35657, f. 212.
[2] Add. MS. 32963, f. 409.
[3] In a letter to the Bishop of Lincoln Newcastle asserted that he had only advised the postponement of Newcome's resignation in order that Law should have a better chance of securing the professorship: but it is not easy to follow the reasoning. The main advantage arising from the elections to the professorship and mastership taking place concurrently was that a competitor for the mastership might be persuaded to forego his claims by being allowed to obtain the professorship; and as Dr Law was unlikely to be a candidate for the mastership, he had nothing to gain and something to lose by the resignation being delayed. Add. MS. 32964, f. 17.

THE CHANCELLOR AND THE COLLEGES 251

It was not however in Newcastle's power to prescribe the duration of Dr Newcome's life: and early in December it became perfectly clear that the old man's death was near at hand. The Duke therefore concluded that it was time to make preparations for securing a suitable successor to Newcome in the mastership, and though he was well aware that Professor Rutherforth was a possible candidate and would expect his support[1], he informed Dr Powell on December 13th that the Master of St John's was in a 'very declining way,' advised him to proceed to Cambridge without delay, and promised him the fullest measure of support:

'I think' he wrote 'no time should be lost in taking the necessary measures to secure your interest. I am ready to do whatever you yourself shall advise, for you cannot have your own interest more at heart than I have[2].'

Nor were these merely empty words. Powell had given him a list of certain Fellows of St John's, which showed that Mr Jenkin might be influenced by Lord Portmore, Mr Metcalfe by Lord Milton, Mr Todington by the Bishop of Ely, Mr Ashcroft by Mr Whichcot, Mr Loggan by Mr Jennings of Barkway, and Mr Horseman by the Duke of Grafton[3]; and furnished with these details the Duke at once began to discuss plans of action.

'Pray let me know to-morrow' he wrote to Powell on December 15th 'what your wishes are what I should do. In the meanwhile you should apply to everybody yourself, and that will help me in my applications. A letter from yourself to the Duke of Grafton will have more effect than one from me:

---

[1] See his letter dated November 5th, 1764, and addressed to the Bishop of Lincoln. Add. MS. 32963, f. 255.   [2] Add. MS. 32964, f. 283.

[3] Jenkin had acted as private tutor to Lord Milsington, Lord Portmore's eldest son; Metcalfe was vicar of Milton Abbas where Lord Milton had his country seat; and Horseman was curate at Houghton le Spring, of which the vicar was Richard Stonehewer whose son had been the Duke of Grafton's private tutor and afterwards became his secretary.

however an application from me shall not be wanting. I will answer for the Duke of Cumberland but I doubt whether he will be able to prevail, as Lord Portmore has just entered his son under Dr Brooke[1].'

In thus deciding to support Dr Powell with the whole weight of his influence, Newcastle was not acting on a sudden resolution but embarking on a carefully meditated plan of campaign. Nor moreover had he omitted to take the claims of Rutherforth into careful consideration. He was aware however that the Professor was unable to count upon many votes among the Fellows, that his chance of obtaining the mastership was very slender, and that the probable result of supporting him would be to give the victory to Dr Brooke. Rutherforth was clearly not a candidate to run: but it was not enough to refuse him support. He must be prevented from standing in order that Powell's success might be more certain; and, encouraged by the Bishop of Lincoln expressing an opinion that Rutherforth did not intend to be a candidate[2] the Duke determined to appeal to his supporter to sacrifice his ambition for the sake of the cause.

'The very sincere regard and esteem which I have for you and your merit' he wrote to Rutherforth on December 15th 'and the grateful sense I have of the many obligations which I have received from you, make me take the liberty to trouble you upon a subject which may probably soon come to be a great object of our attention. I mean the securing a good Master of St John's in case of a vacancy, the present Master, as I hear, being in a very declining way. My great object, and I hope that of all our friends, will be the preventing Dr Brooke from succeeding there, for which purpose my Lord Sandwich will exert his utmost endeavour and make use of all his force; but if our friends are so happy as to agree in the person, I hope they will be able in all events to exclude Dr Brooke, provided the person they are for be one who in all respects will fit that station with

[1] Add. MS. 32964, f. 301.   [2] Add. MS. 32964, f. 295.

THE CHANCELLOR AND THE COLLEGES

ability, integrity, and a pure zeal for our cause. There are certainly those of that college who will answer that character in every respect, and therefore the consideration is who is the most likely to succeed. As Dr Powell has been so lately Tutor there, and I believe has long had a view to the mastership, I doubt not but he has kept up such connections with his pupils and with the college as must give him a very fair chance of succeeding, provided we with all our force do assist him. If not, I should fear Dr Brooke might carry it, and then the three great colleges, St John's, Trinity and King's united, would undoubtedly fling the university absolutely into Lord Sandwich's hands, which I am sure nobody is more zealous to prevent than yourself. If for these considerations I should assist Dr Powell with any little credit I may have with any of the Fellows, I hope it would not be disagreeable to you[1].'

It is never easy to ask a man to play the part of a martyr, and it is not surprising that Newcastle found some difficulty in composing this letter[2]. Yet he performed a delicate task not ungracefully. Without definitely asking Rutherforth not to stand for election, he pointed out to him the path of duty: and if, as there can be little doubt, he was correct in assuming that it was not in Rutherforth's power to obtain the mastership, and that the utmost he could do would be to damage Powell's prospects, the sacrifice demanded was not too great. Everything had indeed been done to spare the feelings of the Professor, to whom Powell had also written, 'expressing' as he told Newcastle 'my respect and my hopes of his support and countenance in my view of the mastership if he has no thought of it for himself[3].' But the best laid plans often go sadly astray: and Rutherforth was found to be unwilling to immolate himself on the altar of duty. In a cool note addressed to the Duke he mentioned that his previous applications for the Chancellor's assistance had been left

[1] Add. MS. 32964, f. 303. [2] Add. MS. 32964, f. 301.
[3] Add. MS. 32964, f. 305.

unnoticed, that 'these discouragements have prevented me from endeavouring to keep up such an interest in the college as I otherwise might have done'; but that, having consulted his friends, he had been advised that his rank in the university and seniority in the college compelled him to stand for the mastership, and that he hoped, 'however your Grace may be disposed to favour Dr Powell in preference to me, you will not blame me if I have such a regard for my own family as to be a candidate[1].' To Powell Rutherforth wrote in a similar strain[2], and the Duke saw himself threatened by what he was most anxious to avoid, a contest between two of his friends.

'The meaning of my letters to Powell and Rutherforth' he declared 'was and is that the point to be agreed upon by common friends...should be to see which of the two, Powell or Rutherforth, is the most likely to carry it, and in plainer words whether Dr Rutherforth hath any chance at all to carry it. If that should appear, I cannot think Dr Rutherforth will be so weak and so unreasonable as to stand out, which must certainly bring in Dr Brooke[3].'

If Rutherforth, as he himself admitted, was able to count upon very few votes among the Fellows, his conduct may appear selfish and unreasonable: but it was not completely indefensible. He was doubtless very much influenced by the achievement of Dr Newcome who, after starting with only six certain votes among the Fellows, had in the end been elected Master[4]; and though Powell not unnaturally was emphatic in asserting that 'such a scheme can hardly take place twice in a century[5],' Rutherforth may be excused for hoping that history would repeat itself. Moreover, though he might have only a scanty following among the Fellows

[1] Add. MS. 32964, f. 343.
[2] Add. MS. 32964, f. 320.
[3] Ibid.
[4] Add. MS. 32964, f. 322.
[5] Ibid.

of the college, he was not without influential friends in the great world, among whom were the three uncles of the young Duke of Devonshire and Sir Anthony Abdy who was a member of the whig opposition party and an adherent of the Cavendishes[1]. It should further be noted that both Lord Hardwicke and the Bishop of Lincoln, who still retained considerable influence in his old college, St John's, informed Powell that they would assist him in his candidature if Rutherforth did not stand[2], thereby implying a preference for the competitor whom the Duke was so anxious to discourage.

Newcastle was undoubtedly much chagrined by the unfortunate course events had taken, and so was Powell who not only feared that he might be deserted by many of the Duke's friends[3], but began to suspect the loyalty of the Duke himself. It was in vain that Newcastle assured him that he certainly would not 'disoblige you and Mr Townshend[4] upon this occasion, whatever the consequences may be[5]': an unfortunate phrase in a letter of the Duke, which might be interpreted as meaning that he intended to be neutral between the two candidates, and the fact that he had delayed fulfilling his promise to write to certain of his friends on Powell's behalf, suggested to the angry man that he was being betrayed and forsaken. On the evening of Christmas Day the Bishop of Norwich had an interview with Powell and sought to dissipate his anger and alarm.

'I said what I could upon this occasion' wrote the Bishop to Newcastle, 'particularly that you had not designed writing till

[1] The Duke of Devonshire at this time was a boy of sixteen, having succeeded his father in October 1764. For details about Sir Anthony Abdy, whose sister was Rutherforth's wife, see Walpole's *Memoirs of the Reign of George III*, 1, 284; see also Add. MS. 32964, f. 311.
[2] Add. MS. 32964, f. 392.   [3] Add. MS. 32964, f. 365.
[4] For the connection between Powell and Charles Townshend, see ch. 11, pp. 71–72.
[5] Add. MS. 32964, f. 371.

you should have heard from Dr Rutherforth: that you expected Dr Rutherforth's letter would have been very different from what it was, that you was certainly cautious of offending the Cavenish (sic) family and Sir Anthony Abdy, that I myself, in my letter of last night to your Grace, had quite slighted what you said of a neutrality, having observed that it was not mentioned by your Grace with the force with which you expressed your determination to oblige Mr Townshend and him[1].'

The plea of the Bishop was apparently successful with Powell who two days later wrote a letter of reconciliation to Newcastle[2], but now the Duke in his turn displayed bad temper. 'I am weary' he told the Bishop of Norwich 'of writing to Dr Powell since I find I am not believed, as you must see by the forced unpolite terms of his letter to me this day[3]'; and he was probably not much comforted by being told by the Bishop of Norwich that the benefactors of mankind were proverbially the victims of gross ingratitude[4].

But, despite these ebullitions of temper, it was really out of the question for Newcastle and Powell to quarrel, for each was essential to the other. Newcastle had no intention of running any other candidate for the mastership, and Powell's position was not sufficiently secure to enable him to be indifferent to the Duke's influence. There was indeed no breach and Newcastle never contemplated deserting his candidate. After mature consideration he decided to leave Rutherforth's letter unanswered[5], and despatched notes to several friends, asking them to support Powell with all the influence they had[6]. In particular he urged the Bishop of Lincoln to assist Powell, in order to avert the catastrophe of

[1] Add. MS. 32964, f. 392.
[2] Add. MS. 32964, f. 416; see also f. 418.
[3] Add. MS. 32964, f. 438.   [4] Add. MS. 32964, f. 457.
[5] He wrote a draft of a reply which was not sent; Add. MS. 32964, f. 406, f. 438.
[6] Add. MS. 32964, f. 422, f. 424, f. 426.

THE CHANCELLOR AND THE COLLEGES 257

St John's falling into the hands of Lord Sandwich[1]; and though the Bishop in reply only undertook not to assist Rutherforth[2], Newcastle cannot be blamed for not achieving more in this particular quarter. He was doing his best and Powell had no valid ground of complaint.

Meanwhile Dr Newcome was rapidly dying, and towards the end became a victim to insane delusions. On January 8th, 1765, Talbot visited him and found him better; but there was no hope of any substantial improvement and the end was only a matter of days.

'He takes no food' reported Talbot 'but what is forced down, thinking it in his present unhappy state of mind to be a sin. He is very quiet at all times, save when this force is used upon him, and then he makes most piteous outcries: but when it is over he seems to retain no resentment against his attendants who are constrained to discharge this unpleasing office[3].'

Two days later death put an end to his sufferings, and the two great offices of Master of St John's and Lady Margaret Professor were thrown into the market to be scrambled for. But, as has been seen, the scramblers had anticipated the signal: and by the date of Newcome's death definite progress had been made. With regard to the Lady Margaret Professorship it was clear that though Dr Ogden still professed to be a candidate[4], he was not a serious one, and it was suspected that he was really aiming at the mastership, and hoped that, by setting up as a rival to Dr Law, he might induce Newcastle to purchase his withdrawal by adopting him as Newcome's successor in the mastership.

'I suspect' wrote the Master of Jesus on November 9th 'that he does not really aim at the professorship, but only, by making himself of consequence on this occasion, to secure some other point[5].'

[1] Add. MS. 32964, f. 440. [2] Add. MS. 32964, f. 451.
[3] Add. MS. 32965, f. 115.
[4] On January 10th, 1765, he asked Newcastle to support him. Add. MS. 32965, f. 141. [5] Add. MS. 32963, f. 328.

258 THE CHANCELLOR AND THE COLLEGES

It was also clear that Dr Law was not likely to be successful against Dr Brooke. His only hope of victory lay in winning a good number of votes in Trinity, and in the Johnian vote being divided between Brooke and Ogden, but there was really very little prospect of either of these things coming to pass. Though Law was for a time optimistic about Trinity[1], Dr Caryl, who was a more impartial judge and an exceedingly careful calculator[2], was far less sanguine[3]: and inasmuch as the electors in St John's were waiting until the situation with regard to the mastership was more certain before declaring themselves with regard to the professorship, it was impossible to forecast their action with any certainty. There was no doubt however that they desired to keep the professorship in the college, and that therefore there was little chance that they would play into Dr Law's hands by dividing their votes between two Johnian candidates.

'In respect to the Margaret professorship' wrote Talbot on December 23rd 'the difficulty of pronouncing anything certain is increased by the reserve in which the people of St John's (who make a third part of the electors) hold themselves. As the mastership and professorship are now likely to become vacant at the same time, their policy may not improbably be in the upshot to compromise their own differences by giving the mastership to one of their candidates and the professorship, if it can be managed, to the other[4].'

Law indeed had been playing an uphill game from the start, and a few days after Newcome's death Dr Caryl reported that Law and his friends 'are now convinced that it has been all along impracticable to effect such a division of St John's college as should make Dr Law's

[1] Add. MS. 32964, f. 81; Add. MS. 32965, f. 117.
[2] In a letter to Newcastle, Powell refers to Caryl's 'reckoning which is always exact.' Add. MS. 32965, f. 266.
[3] Add. MS. 32963, f. 328.   [4] Add. MS. 32964, f. 374.

THE CHANCELLOR AND THE COLLEGES

election sure[1].' If however Lord Sandwich's candidate was the favourite for the professorship, it was all the more important for Newcastle to make certain of the mastership for Powell, and the outlook in this direction was certainly promising. As the electors numbered forty-five[2], the successful candidate for the mastership must receive at least twenty-three votes; and as by the end of the year 1764 Powell believed that he could count with certainty upon twenty-one votes[3], he was not far off the necessary minimum[3]. Indeed Dr Brooke, though supported by all the influence that Sandwich could command, was proving a far less eligible candidate for the mastership than for the professorship; and though it is an adversary who says 'his character is such that his promotion to the mastership...can portend nothing but ruin to the college,' there is some reason to think that such an opinion was fairly common, and that Brooke was very unpopular[4]. Yet it was impossible to predict the result until the actual candidates were known. It was for instance by no means certain that, when it came to the point, Dr Rutherforth would stand[5]: for he stood no chance in a straight fight, and his only hope was that by intervening he might prevent any of the candidates obtaining a sufficient number of votes and thereby procure a lapse to the seniors. It was also believed in certain quarters that Dr Ogden would come forward as a candidate[6], and though it was scornfully remarked that on the first scrutiny he would only receive his own vote[7], any addition to the number of the

[1] Add. MS. 32965, f. 197.   [2] Add. MS. 32961, f. 220.
[3] Writing on December 30th Powell asserted that he was sure of twenty votes, and on the day following reported that Mr Todington had just promised him his vote. Add. MS. 32964, f. 459, f. 469.
[4] Add. MS. 32964, f. 374.
[5] Add. MS. 32964, f. 392; Add. MS. 32965, f. 205.
[6] Add. MS. 32963, f. 255.
[7] Add. MS. 32965, f. 205, f. 215.

competitors was a fresh complication and increased the
uncertainty of the issue. Dr Alvis, who had recently
been a senior Fellow, was also named as a possible
candidate, but the constantly changing character of the
situation is best illustrated by an important alteration
in the plans of the Sandwich party. It was soon clear
that Brooke was not proving himself a good candidate
for the mastership, and therefore it was agreed about
the end of the year 1764 that, while continuing to
stand for the professorship, he should resign his candidature for the mastership in favour of his assistant
Tutor, Thomas Frampton. The change was for the
better from the point of view of those who were endeavouring to overthrow the Newcastle interest; for
though Frampton was described as 'given to pleasure
and of little application,' he was believed to be a person
of some ability, and was certainly far more popular in
the college than Brooke[1].

The multiplication of possible candidates materially
added to the difficulties of Newcastle's task. He had
made up his mind to support Powell and was therefore
most anxious that others, with equal and possibly greater
claims upon his support, should not aspire to the mastership. It was awkward for him to withhold his favour
from Dr Ogden who had loyally supported him throughout the High Stewardship dispute: and he was much
annoyed by receiving on January 11th a letter from
John Skynner, announcing his intention of standing for
the mastership. 'I flatter myself' wrote Skynner 'that
I may still rely on your Grace's kind disposition to me,
and that you will not prefer the interest of any of the
candidates in prejudice to mine[2].'

Skynner was a Fellow of the college and a person
of some distinction in the university, having only
recently resigned the office of Public Orator which he

[1] Add. MS. 32965, f. 115.   [2] Add. MS. 32965, f. 147.

had held for ten years. Powell made light of the danger of his competition[1]; but Skynner himself believed that he could muster sufficient strength in the college to bring about a lapse to the senior Fellows upon whom he pinned his hopes[2]. If this belief was well founded he could successfully wreck Newcastle's scheme: and, even if the venture proved unsuccessful, it inevitably placed the Duke in a delicate situation. When in 1761 Dr Newcome was thought to be dangerously ill, Newcastle had encouraged Skynner to think of the mastership, and had apparently even gone so far as to discuss with him a plan of procedure. Therefore, when in reply to Skynner's announcement, the Duke declared his intention of warmly supporting Powell[3], he laid himself open to a cutting rejoinder.

'But when it was settled from the beginning' replied Skynner 'that I should procure such a number of votes only as would hinder any other candidate from a majority,...when the plan was approved by your Grace and you was so kind as to omit no opportunity of enquiring about the mastership whenever I had the honour of waiting upon you, I adhered to the resolution approved, not to stir till the Master's life became in extreme danger[4].'

Skynner indeed felt that he had a substantial grievance: and though Newcastle rightly pointed out that 'the state of the college and the candidates is much altered since that time[5],' it was impossible for him completely to gloss over the fact that he had discarded the candidate whom he had formerly encouraged.

Such was the situation when the death of Dr Newcome on January 10th, 1765, came as a call to arms. The election of a new Lady Margaret Professor was fixed

[1] Add. MS. 32965, f. 135.
[2] Add. MS. 32965, f. 207; see also f. 159.
[3] Add. MS. 32965, f. 167.   [4] Add. MS. 32965, f. 207.
[5] Add. MS. 32965, f. 167.

for Saturday January 19th, and of a new Master for Friday January 25th. Dr Law did not seem at all likely to get the professorship, and though Powell was almost certain to obtain more votes for the mastership than any of the other candidates, it was quite possible that he might fail to secure the necessary minimum, and that therefore the duty of appointing Dr Newcome's successor might devolve upon the seniors. The outlook was not free from anxiety, and that Newcastle was conscious of the need of exploring every avenue of assistance is shown by his letter to the Archbishop of Canterbury on January 18th.

'The most likely to carry it on our side' he wrote 'is Dr Powell, a very zealous friend and in every respect a most deserving unexceptionable man, was long and lately the first Tutor in the college, and has now a very good temporal estate of his own. I hope he will carry it, but the statutes of that college make it necessary for him to have a majority of the whole number of the Fellows or else there is a devolution, first to the senior Fellows, and afterwards to the visitor, the Bishop of Ely. But the seniors will scarce let it come there. I hear the bishops dine at Lambeth this day, and I wish your Grace would talk to the Bishop of Lincoln about it. Dr Murray, who was at Hamburgh, has a curate, one Mr Plucknett[1] who is a Fellow and has consequently a vote. I applied to Princess Amelia who had some knowledge of Dr Murray: Her Royal Highness told me she had not been able to serve Dr Murray and therefore had no pretence to ask a favour of him; but that your Grace had been so good as to take this Dr Murray (who is a very deserving man) under your protection, and that Her Royal Highness fancied your Grace would have more influence over him than anybody. If your Grace should think proper so far to interfere as to direct your chaplain to write to Dr Murray to influence his curate to vote for Dr Powell to be Master of St John's upon the present vacancy, I should be very much obliged to you. But if your

[1] William Plucknett was licensed to the curacy of Gainsborough in 1762. Dr Murray (or Murrey) was Vicar of Gainsborough from 1761 until his death in 1778.

THE CHANCELLOR AND THE COLLEGES 263

Grace thinks such an application would be improper, or has the least objection to it, I beg you would forgive the liberty I have taken in troubling you upon it[1].'

Dr Powell was also anxious and took a momentous decision on the same day that Newcastle wrote to the Archbishop. It had always been foreseen that the Fellows of St John's, in order to avert a contested election, might come to a friendly arrangement and agree upon a Professor and a Master: and in December 1764 a friend of Lord Sandwich had told Powell that his candidature for the mastership would not be opposed if he would undertake to support Dr Brooke for the professorship[2]. It would undoubtedly have been dishonourable of Powell to have promptly closed with this offer: for as an adherent of the Duke it was incumbent upon him to do his utmost to secure the professorship for Dr Law as well as the mastership for himself: but if, as the situation developed, it became clear that Law was not going to be elected Professor and that Powell was not certain of being elected Master, wisdom would dictate acceptance of the compromise offered by the Sandwich party. Therefore when a week before the election of a new Master, and a day before the election of a new Professor, Powell discovered that there was a certain majority against Law and not a certain majority for himself, he decided to compromise, and on January 18th there was peace in St John's. On that day it was arranged between Frampton and Powell that the former would not stand for the mastership and that the latter would support Dr Brooke for the professorship[3]: and on the following day Brooke was elected Lady Margaret Professor, prevailing over Law by a dozen votes. As the withdrawal of Frampton, and the support of the Sandwich interest in the college, made

[1] Add. MS. 32965, f. 242.   [2] Add. MS. 32964, f. 380.
[3] Add. MS. 32965, f. 244, f. 250, f. 252.

264 THE CHANCELLOR AND THE COLLEGES

Powell certain of securing the necessary minimum number of votes for the mastership, there was no point in any other candidate standing, and on January 25th, 1765, he was unanimously elected Master[1].

'The Lady Margaret, my Lord,' wrote Dr Ogden to the Duke on January 18th, 'as I apprehend, has made the Master[2]'; and Dr Ogden apprehended rightly. It is of course impossible to dogmatise upon what might have happened if there had been no compromise, but there is no reason to think that Powell was guilty of over-caution.

'I made no agreement' he told Newcastle on January 20th 'with Dr Brooke and Mr Frampton till Dr Caryl's reckoning, which is always exact, shewed me that the friends, who at my request were willing to remain neuter but not to vote against the interest of the college, were not able to turn the election in favour of Dr Law, nor would I have agreed even then if either Dr Rutherforth had declined or Dr Ogden engaged to vote for me. But without one or other of these things I could not be secure[3].'

Indeed the reproach of excess of caution can be levied more fittingly against Lord Sandwich and his advisers. It is possible that their intelligence department was inadequate, and that they failed to appreciate that Dr Brooke was safe for the professorship: for they certainly made a bad bargain and trumped their best card.

Newcastle however was disappointed, and, as was characteristic of him in moments of adversity, he was lavish in distributing blame.

'My friends at Cambridge' he wrote to Dr Caryl on January 16th 'are not so good managers of elections as I was formerly: and perhaps should still be if I knew as well how to go about getting an university (in which I have much miscarried) as in

[1] Add. MS. 32965, f. 292. Two days before his election he received 'a letter of compliments from Lord Sandwich.'
[2] Add. MS. 32965, f. 246.   [3] Add. MS. 32965, f. 266.

carrying a county. My first rule always was to think of the person that could carry it: that never comes into your thoughts (that is the thoughts of my friends at Cambridge). You only are afraid of disobliging everybody, and by that means will evidently let in the enemy. Had I had the sole management of these two elections, viz. the Margaret Professor and the Master of St John's, I would have forfeited anything if either Dr Brooke had been Professor, or Frampton, or any of his degree, Master[1].'

The Duke however exaggerated his own capacity and under-estimated the difficulties of the situation.

'It is now plain to everyone' replied Dr Caryl 'that, had we resolved upon carrying our point, we had no way for it but to have taken a candidate out of St John's: and I make no question but that many of us have seen it long: but as Dr Law had set his heart upon it ever since he returned to Cambridge and has been so firm to us, it was too delicate a point to confer upon, even among ourselves; and unless he could himself have seen the desperateness of his own case (which he hardly did at the last) and have given up in time, we could not act otherwise than we have done[2].'

Dr Law's persistence had indeed been the great difficulty. He had set his heart upon the professorship and had not sufficient detachment to realise that he could not be successful. He was not the candidate that Newcastle would have chosen, but he was too faithful an adherent to be thrown over.

The history of this double contest amply illustrates both the necessity which compelled the Duke to intervene in college politics and the difficulties he found in doing so. Unless he was prepared to sacrifice what influence and prestige remained to him in the university, he could not allow Lord Sandwich to appoint the Master of St John's, but all through the struggle he knew that he was treading on dangerous ground, and that by insisting overmuch on his own wishes he might easily alienate his friends and swell the number of his

[1] Add. MS. 32965, f. 227.   [2] Add. MS. 32965, f. 268.

266 THE CHANCELLOR AND THE COLLEGES

enemies. Possibly, when all was over and the bitterness of the struggle had been dimmed by time, he was able to see that he had at least attained his main objective, and that the mastership of St John's had been cheaply purchased by a divinity professorship; but he was not always so fortunate. There were occasions when he intervened in the domestic affairs of a college and did not even score a modified success: and, if at the close of his life he ever indulged in retrospection, it is probable that his two bitterest university memories were the election of Sir James Marriott as Master of Trinity Hall and the election of Dr Goddard as Master of Clare.

The election of Marriott as Master of Trinity Hall in 1764 was the culminating incident of a long story which cannot be understood without a knowledge of the constitution of the society with which it is concerned. In many ways Trinity Hall was unique among the Cambridge colleges. Of its twelve Fellows not more than two were usually in holy orders: and upon these two exclusively devolved the duties of maintaining discipline and education in the college.

'These men' wrote Gunning 'reside during the greater part of the year: they alone give lectures, they alone keep up the discipline of the college, and attend to the moral conduct of those in statu pupillari. The rest of the Fellows are laymen, generally lawyers, frequently members of parliament; they only reside during the twelve days of Christmas, the mornings of which they pass in auditing their accounts, and their evenings are devoted to the most splendid hospitality very generally extended[1].'

The Master was quite as much an absentee as the majority of his Fellows: and although such a practice would find little favour at the present time, it was in accordance with the traditions of the college and the

[1] Gunning's *Reminiscences*, II, 28.

THE CHANCELLOR AND THE COLLEGES 267

wishes of the Founder. Trinity Hall had been established as a 'perpetual college of scholars in the canon and civil law'; and it is therefore not surprising that the Master and Fellows of a college, devoted to one branch of knowledge, practised and presided in the various ecclesiastical courts, and were more commonly to be found at Doctors Commons than in Cambridge. But the inevitable consequence of this system was that the ordinary Fellow of Trinity Hall in the eighteenth century was far less 'donnish' and far more a man of the world than the Fellows of other colleges. Cambridge was not his home and academic interests did not preoccupy him. He knew the world, was conversant with affairs, and mixed on terms of equality with the great. A contemporary described the society as 'being always composed of people of the best families and fortunes[1]': and although, as the contemporary was a Trinity Hall man, this may be an exaggeration, it was not ludicrously untrue as it would have been if said of any other college.

As the Fellows were men of some importance in the world, and financially independent of what they drew from the college, they were apt to hold themselves in high esteem and to regard the Master as an equal and even as an inferior.

'In this college' wrote Marriott to the Duke in 1764 'the Master divides only as a thirteenth man, with small profits of absentees at Christmas, so that this Mastership or almost Fellowship is not better than that of one of our chaplains. He has not a vote at any election of a Fellow or Scholar, and it is a mere complaisance that he is permitted to name college servants[2].'

Yet the Master was not quite so powerless as this statement might seem to suggest. It is true that he had no vote in an election to a Fellowship, but no candidate could be elected unless a majority of the existing

[1] Add. MS. 32867, f. 417; see also Add. MS. 32871, f. 161.
[2] Add. MS. 32955, f. 134.

268 THE CHANCELLOR AND THE COLLEGES

Fellows voted for him, and in the event of all the candidates failing to obtain the requisite number of votes, the Master had the right of nominating whom he pleased to the vacant Fellowship[1]. If therefore the Master was a skilful politician it was within his power considerably to influence the composition of the society over which he presided; for, either by multiplying the number of candidates, or by persuading a few of the electors to observe a neutrality, he might render an election impossible and secure the exercise of his right of nomination. It is true that the Fellows regarded this privilege of the Master with considerable resentment, and in theory at least it was always possible for them to prevent him from exercising it[2]; but he was one and they were many, and by playing upon the jealousies of some and the indifference of others it was sometimes possible for him to combine the substance with the dignity of power.

When Newcastle became Chancellor the Master of Trinity Hall was Dr Edward Simpson who was already embarked upon a highly successful career in the ecclesiastical courts, having recently become Judge of the Consistory Court of London. His ambition lay outside Cambridge, and, anxious to advance in his profession, he wisely sought to obtain the protection of a powerful patron; for without some such support progress in the eighteenth century was apt to be tardy and uncertain. The patron he selected was Sir George Lee who, after being educated at Christ Church, Oxford, had been admitted an advocate at Doctors Commons, and quickly rose to great eminence, being appointed in 1751 Dean of Arches and Judge of the Prerogative Court of Canterbury[3]. The friendship of such a man was likely

[1] Add. MS. 32870, f. 186; Add. MS. 32871, f. 161.
[2] Add. MS. 32870, f. 186.
[3] Lee was not knighted until 1752.

THE CHANCELLOR AND THE COLLEGES 269

to prove of the greatest assistance to Simpson, especially as Lee was a person of some distinction in the political world. He had sat in parliament for several years and was an important member of the opposition party which, under the nominal leadership of Frederick, Prince of Wales, was engaged in relentless war against Newcastle and the government. The Leicester house party, as it was styled, continued in existence after the Prince of Wales' death, and the politics of Dr Simpson naturally took the same hue as those of his patron.

Newcastle could therefore at the outset of his career as Chancellor expect little support from the Master of Trinity Hall, and he was not much more fortunately situated with regard to the Fellows. It was remarked in 1750 that one of the most influential of the Fellows was Matthew Robinson who played a very leading part in the opposition to Newcastle's project of university reform, and in the June of that year Matthew Robinson still further increased his influence in the college by securing the election of his brother, John, to a vacant Fellowship.

'I am afraid' wrote Lord Dupplin on June 9th, 1750, 'Robinson will carry his point at Trinity Hall and bring in his brother to supply a vacancy which has lately happened. When the society is full there are twelve Fellows. The vacancy reduces the number to eleven. Professor Dickins never comes to college. Of the ten Robinson has five secure All measures that could be thought of have been taken to keep away Mr Mills of Canterbury. If he does not go there cannot be an election in favour of Robinson, for six must concur: otherwise the election devolves to the Master. Dr Monson, Pinfold and Salusbury (and Dale if he goes down) oppose Robinson strenuously. They have been for long inactive and have suffered him to get too much ground[1].'

Lord Dupplin's fears were justified. Either Mr Milles of Canterbury put in an appearance, or, which is more

[1] Add. MS. 32721, f. 91.

likely, one if not more of the Fellows opposed to Robinson preferred in the end to vote for his candidate rather than allow the Master to exercise his right of nomination; for John Robinson was duly elected and admitted a Fellow.

It is clear that whichever party prevailed in Trinity Hall Newcastle would not profit, for he could expect no assistance either from the Master or Matthew Robinson. In 1751 the Master's nephew, Francis Simpson, was elected to the Fellowship vacated by Salusbury: and, although we know no more than the bare fact, it is possible that the Fellows were of the opinion that Francis Simpson would be less amenable to his uncle's influence if he owed his Fellowship to their votes and not to his kinsman's nomination. Two years later however the Master was able to nominate to a vacant Fellowship, Peter Calvert, who had been recommended to him by Sir George Lee, and who had failed to secure the necessary minimum of votes among the Fellows; but, as a few months earlier in the same year, he had equally nominated to a Fellowship, George Carr, who had been an undergraduate at Jesus and was specially recommended for a Fellowship at Trinity Hall by Newcastle's friends, Dr Keene and Dr Caryl, 'as a proper person to manage and cultivate the whig interest in that society[1],' it might be thought that the Master was exercising his power with becoming impartiality. But appearances were deceptive. Carr, who was in holy orders, was nominated to one of the two tutorial Fellowships which could only be held by priests, and it may be surmised that, as a lawyer was out of the question, neither the Master nor Sir George Lee would take much interest in the appointment, that the Fellows would be equally indifferent, and that it would be comparatively easy for Dr Keene and Dr Caryl to utilise

[1] Add. MS. 32870, f. 123; see also Add. MS. 32866, f. 274.

THE CHANCELLOR AND THE COLLEGES 271

such a favourable opportunity of introducing a friend into Trinity Hall.

There were however only two such Fellowships, and if they were to be the only means by which Newcastle could influence the composition of the society, there was nothing for him but to abandon hope. Had it not been for the Master's nomination of Calvert the Duke might have acquiesced in his own exclusion, for he had a keener appreciation of the limitations of his power with regard to the colleges than with regard to the university; but the situation took on a different complexion when it became notorious that the Master was the obedient follower of Sir George Lee, and could be counted upon to exercise his privilege of nomination in accordance with Lee's recommendations. The Duke was always particularly fearful of any rival banner being planted in the university, but when that rival banner was that of an Oxford man and an avowed political opponent, the situation was desperate. It was essential that there should be a trial of strength, but it may well be that Newcastle would never have ventured upon such a dangerous undertaking if it had not been for the promptings of his friend and follower, James Marriott.

James Marriott, the son of a London attorney, had been admitted as a pensioner at Trinity Hall in 1746, and in 1751 had graduated as a bachelor of laws. After taking his degree he continued to reside in college[1], and, as he was contemplating a career in the church, he wisely sought to ingratiate himself with Newcastle. This venture was attended with signal success, for the Duke seems to have employed him in arranging his library, and on a later occasion Marriott was able to boast that he had 'been almost a domestic in your Grace's house[2].' It was therefore only right and proper that when the Chancellor visited Cambridge in April

[1] Add. MS. 32863, f. 298. [2] *Ibid.*

1755, to lay the foundation stone of the new library buildings, Marriott should present him with two poems in honour of the occasion; and he seems to have seized every possible opportunity of advertising the fact that he was under the special protection of the Duke. Doubtless Newcastle's patronage would have been of invaluable assistance to him if he had adhered to his original intention, but about the end of the year 1755 he abandoned his design of taking holy orders and determined to embark upon the profession of the civil law[1]. He was well fitted by his training and education for such a career, and could confidently count upon a certain amount of family influence[2].

This change of plan led him naturally enough to think of a Fellowship of Trinity Hall as a desirable acquisition, and he made up his mind to stand as a candidate at the next vacancy. But much to his disgust he discovered that he could expect no support from the Master who was under a promise to favour the claims of a certain Mr Andrews, a candidate recommended by Sir George Lee. He therefore turned to his patron for assistance.

'Being obliged for family reasons' he wrote to the Duke in November 1755 'to quit my design of going into orders, and having acquainted the gentlemen of Trinity Hall with my intention of offering myself a candidate for the next vacant Fellowship, the Master, Dr Simpson, does not give me so much encouragement as I hoped, Sir George Lee being desirous, I find, of recommending a gentleman who is greatly my junior, not having yet taken any degree, myself being of a doctor of laws' standing the next Commencement, and having had more than one junior put over my head already. I take the liberty therefore of desiring your Grace's favour to countenance me in this affair, and shall always esteem myself very happy to be honoured with the continuance of your Grace's patronage[3].'

[1] Add. MS. 32860, f. 465. [2] Add. MS. 32865, f. 368.
[3] Add. MS. 32860, f. 465.

THE CHANCELLOR AND THE COLLEGES

As there was no immediate prospect of a Fellowship falling vacant, it was not necessary for the Duke to do more than give words of kindly encouragement; but when in January 1756 Marriott wrote to say that Dr Pinfold was about to be appointed Governor of Barbadoes, and would almost certainly 'resign so small a thing as a Fellowship of Trinity Hall[1],' the Duke perceived that it was necessary to take some sort of action. What Marriott asked him to do was to request Dr Pinfold 'to make a circulation immediately in my favour[2]'; but as this was a direct invitation for him to intervene in the domestic affairs of the college, he might reasonably hesitate before risking such a hazardous adventure. He seems to have sent for Marriott and to have wisely advised him to approach the Master once more: but, though the counsel was prudent, when it was put into practice it only more fully revealed that Dr Simpson had completely sold himself to Sir George Lee.

'Since I had the honour of seeing your Grace' wrote Marriott on January 28th, 1756, 'and in consequence of what you pleased to say to me, I waited upon Dr Simpson who told me that he would not interfere in any election at Trinity Hall, and on my reminding him that the elections had of late devolved into his power solely and were likely to do so again, he answered that in such case he should be for Sir George Lee's man[3].'

What Marriott feared, and not unreasonably feared, was that the Master, despite his assertions, would interfere and scheme to secure the nomination to Pinfold's Fellowship when it was vacated. What Newcastle feared, and also not unreasonably, was that an influential Cambridge college would pass entirely under the influence of a political antagonist, and it is therefore extremely likely that when in March 1756 Marriott

[1] Add. MS. 32862, f. 151.   [2] *Ibid.*
[3] Add. MS. 32862, f. 269.

reported that Dr Keene, Bishop of Chester, had voluntarily offered to assist him and wanted Newcastle's permission to engage upon a canvass[1], leave was not refused. Too much was at stake for considerations of prudence to be overweighted, and Marriott, if elected to a Fellowship, could render invaluable service to the Duke who was without a friend among the Fellows of the college, and sorely needed one.

Yet when in June 1756 Dr Pinfold's Fellowship was declared vacant, it was obvious that Marriott was going to have a very uphill fight. Of the eleven electors three would certainly not come up to Cambridge to vote: and it was therefore necessary for Marriott to secure six votes out of the remaining eight. If he failed in this task the Master would nominate his own candidate to the Fellowship, and he had already announced his intention of obeying Sir George Lee and appointing Andrews. The dice were certainly loaded against Marriott. From the outset he had the support of Professor Monson who was one of the electors and greatly respected in the society[2], and it was a foregone conclusion that the Bishop of Chester would be able to engage Carr's vote[3]: but neither Thomas Ansell[4] nor Matthew Robinson had any reason to be prejudiced in favour of an adherent of Newcastle, and it seemed unlikely that William Wynne, who had been elected to a Fellowship in 1755, would take the trouble of making a journey from Wales, where he was living, in order to vote for Marriott. Moreover there was nothing to be expected from Francis Simpson, who was inclined to follow his uncle, or from Peter Calvert, who owed his Fellowship to the Master's nomination, and who, when indirectly approached by Newcastle, announced through his father that he was 'under great obligations to Sir George Lee

[1] Add. MS. 32863, f. 298.   [2] *Ibid.*
[3] Add. MS. 32865, f. 368.   [4] See ch. III, pp. 211–216.

THE CHANCELLOR AND THE COLLEGES 275

as well as to Dr Simpson, and cannot well refuse to act in concert with them at the next election[1].'

Nevertheless Marriott secured the necessary six votes and was duly elected into the Fellowship recently held by Pinfold. But he certainly did not owe his success to the labours of Newcastle and Dr Keene: for neither the Duke nor the Bishop were able to exercise any appreciable influence in Trinity Hall, and their sole contribution seems to have been Carr's vote. Marriott's victory was indeed mainly due to the mistakes made by his adversary, the Master, and to his own efforts. Dr Simpson was guilty of faulty strategy in making it too evident that he was working to obtain the nomination to the Fellowship. It was a point of honour with the Fellows to prevent the Master from exercising this privilege: and when it became clear that, unless they supported Marriott, there could be no election, Ansell and Matthew Robinson decided to swallow their prejudices and to vote for the Duke's candidate. Possibly moved by the same consideration, Wynne also decided to take a journey of two hundred miles and give his vote for Marriott, and thus, with Monson and Carr, Marriott was certain of five votes out of a possible eight. He needed one more vote however to defeat the Master's design; and of the three remaining electors, Calvert and probably Francis Simpson were pledged to support the Master. Only Dr Ridlington was left[2]: and as he had only recently come to an agreement with the Master and definitely refused to vote for Marriott, it looked for a time as if victory was to be missed by the closest of all possible margins. At the last moment, however, Ridlington was 'brought over by the rest through an expedient[3]'; and on

[1] Add. MS. 32866, f. 168.
[2] 'The three absent Fellows were Milles, Dale, and John Robinson.
[3] Add. MS. 32870, f. 186.

July 21st, 1756, Marriott was elected into a Fellowship[1].

It is obvious that his success was mainly due to the fact that there was no other candidate but Andrews whom nobody except the Master and Sir George Lee wanted, and that he owed little or nothing to the support he received from the Chancellor and his friends in the university. Marriott indeed was careful to point out to the Duke that the victory had been so unexpected, and achieved with so much difficulty, that it would be absurd to assume that the final battle had been fought and the Master's wiles defeated for ever. Indeed he inclined to the opinion that

Sir George Lee cannot easily be prevented, though an Oxford man, from having a society in the university of Cambridge... entirely at his disposal, and that this must be the consequence of those strange connections of the Master[2].

Newcastle however, believing that what had once been done could be repeated, and perceiving the importance of having for the first time a trusted friend among the Fellows of Trinity Hall, determined upon active steps for the eradication of Sir George Lee's influence. He instructed Marriott to confer with certain of his supporters upon 'the state of affairs at Trinity Hall[3],' and Marriott obeyed his patron's command.

'Agreeably to your Grace's desire' he wrote on October 28th, 1756, 'on my being down at Wimbledon with my good friend, the Bishop of Chester, I had a conference with him on the subject of Sir George Lee's interest at Trinity Hall and the late conduct of the Master. I have made his Lordship perfectly sensible of the difficulties which will arise in my endeavouring to prevent the influence which a person, who is at the head of

---

[1] For details, see Add. MS. 32865, f. 368; Add. MS. 32866, f. 168; Add. MS. 32867, f. 417; Add. MS. 32868, f. 466; Add. MS. 32870, f. 186.

[2] Add. MS. 32867, f. 417. [3] *Ibid.*

the civil law and pays great respect to all the members of that profession, must naturally have in such a society as ours. However, as there is reason to hope that I may possibly take the lead at the next election, and that the flying party, as they did lately, will range themselves with me, I have desired the Bishop and Dr Squire to take some measures, as far as they can, and when I go down to Cambridge at Christmas will neglect nothing myself that may be for your Grace's service. But in the meantime I must beg your Grace not to take any notice of what I have informed you, either to the Master, Dr Simpson, or to any other Cambridge people, for fear of the alarm being given and the Master's putting it into Sir George Lee's power to secure his interests betimes[1].'

We do not know what subterraneous intrigues Marriott carried on during the Christmas vacation: but when about the middle of February 1757 Dr Monson, a Fellow of the college and Regius Professor of Civil Law, was reported to be at the point of death, Marriott at once entered into close communication with the Duke. He was aware that in the event of Monson's death the Master would endeavour to redeem his pledge to Sir George Lee by nominating Andrews to a Fellowship: and, if this end was successfully attained, another Fellow would owe his place entirely to Lee's recommendation. To avert such a catastrophe Marriott strongly urged upon the Duke the claims of a certain Mr Crespigny, and was able to advance weighty arguments. He pointed out that he confidently hoped to persuade Ansell and Matthew Robinson to vote for Crespigny, that Dr Ridlington would probably vote the same way as Robinson, that the Master's nephew had engaged himself to support Crespigny, and that if

any one person more, either Carr, Wynne, or Calvert can be managed by any friends of your Grace or Mr Crespigny to vote the same way, then my voice will make the majority to throw out Sir George Lee's man this time, who, if he comes in

[1] Add. MS. 32868, f. 466.

278 THE CHANCELLOR AND THE COLLEGES

the next, must come in then by the immediate interest of your Grace and by no other[1].

It was clearly reasonable for Newcastle to support Crespigny if he was likely to be successful: and, if Carr's vote would ensure his election, the Duke was asked to perform an easy task. No sensible man is reluctant to back a winning horse, and, Monson having died in the interval, Crespigny was elected to a Fellowship on March 26th, 1757. But Monson's death also vacated the Professorship of Civil Law which was a crown appointment, and Dr Ridlington, one of the two Fellows in orders, was anxious to have the professorship. He had good reason however to fear the hostility of Newcastle, whom he had hotly opposed when the appeal question was dividing the university, and as the professorship was practically in the Duke's gift, Ridlington's chances were not of the best. Marriott however pointed out to the Chancellor that the situation was too serious to allow him to indulge his prejudices, and that not only had Ridlington acted as Monson's deputy, and was a very able man with influential friends, such as the Duke of Devonshire and Lord Exeter; but that as the only resident doctor of laws he was a perpetual member of the Caput, that, 'if obliged, can rivet this whole college in His Grace's interest beyond a possibility of a competition from any quarter,' and that 'therefore whether it is not for the Chancellor's interest to obtain the professorship for him, so as to lay him under an obligation[2].' In support of these arguments Marriott submitted to the Duke a letter written by Ridlington who declared that if he obtained the professorship, it would be his constant endeavour to display his gratitude to the Chancellor[3]. As Ridlington was probably the candidate with by far

[1] Add. MS. 3287c, f. 186. [2] Add. MS. 33061, f. 362.
[3] Add. MS. 32870, f. 191.

the strongest claims, it is possible that the amount of persuasion required was due to Newcastle's well-founded distrust of him: but Marriott carried the day, and Ridlington was appointed Professor of Civil Law.

'I hope' wrote Newcastle to the Lord Mayor of London on April 5th, 1757, 'Dr Ridlington acquainted your Lordship that I had promised him that he should have my recommendation for the professorship of civil law in our university, according to your desire: and I am extremely glad to have it in my power to shew my regard for your Lordship[1].'

Newcastle had good reason to be satisfied with the improvement in his relations with Trinity Hall. Seven years before he had been without a friend in the college: he could now rely upon the assistance of Carr and Marriott, and had some claim upon the loyalty of Crespigny and Ridlington. It might be thought that the time was now ripe for him to give the signal for the complete destruction of Lee's influence in the society: but he prudently refrained. The Fellows of Trinity Hall had not resisted the interference of the Master and Lee in order to facilitate the interference of Newcastle, and they would most bitterly resent such a consequence of their action. Further, in the course of the summer of 1757, Lee broke with the Dowager Princess of Wales, and Newcastle began to contemplate the possibility of entering into an alliance with him. Hence it was not to the Duke's advantage to offend Lee by waging open war against him at Cambridge: and Marriott was emphatic that, Newcastle's interest having been established, peace, not war, in the college was the right policy.

'Apprehending' he wrote on May 30th, 1757, 'your Grace's present footing with Sir George Lee, I would fain use all the early means necessary to secure your Grace's interest, without affronting him, upon a perpetual foundation in a society which,

[1] Add. MS. 32870, f. 366; see also f. 233.

280 THE CHANCELLOR AND THE COLLEGES

being composed of laymen and gentlemen, mostly of independent fortunes, is to be managed with more attention than has been usual, and with more delicacy than any other, the constitution of it giving the Master not the least shadow of power but in consequence of the majority not agreeing, which in such a society can never be your Grace's interest to foment, but rather to reconcile all parties to yourself under any one person with whom they may chose to act in concurrence, who as an equal will not give them either envy or jealousy[1].'

In giving this advice Marriott had doubtless one eye upon his professional prospects, for he was naturally unwilling to offend an eminent and influential civilian[2]: and he possibly under-estimated the difficulty of harmonising the interests of Lee and Newcastle in Trinity Hall. But the death of Sir George Lee in December 1758 relieved him of a task which might have proved impossible, and Newcastle of a rival who would always be in a position to cause trouble. From this time onward Dr Simpson, who succeeded Lee as Dean of Arches and Judge of the Prerogative Court of Canterbury, and received the honour of knighthood, became one of Newcastle's staunchest adherents in the university: and this was not the only consequence of Lee's death. The Duke's interference in the affairs of Trinity Hall had been mainly a defensive measure provoked by Lee's attack, and, now that the danger was over, he was ready to leave the college to manage its own concerns. There is no evidence that he played any part in

[1] Add. MS. 32871, f. 161; see also Add. MS. 32877, f. 130.
[2] In September 1756 Marriott, in a letter to Newcastle, expressed his fear that 'my very showing any inclination to traverse Sir George's interest will most certainly expose me to his severe resentment as a Judge which, to so young an advocate as I shall be, will do me an irrevocable prejudice for ever after. I must humbly hope therefore that your Grace's favour will set me in good time above that resentment by introducing and supporting me in Sir George's own court as the client of the Duke of Newcastle.' Add. MS. 32867, f. 417.

THE CHANCELLOR AND THE COLLEGES 281

the election in 1760 of Samuel Hallifax to the Fellowship vacated by George Carr, or in the election in March 1764 of Pedley to the Fellowship vacated by Crespigny; and this is not surprising if, as seems to have been the case, such interference on his part was the exception and not the rule. Nor can he be held to have suffered by thus withholding his hand. In the days of adversity which followed the accession of George III to the throne, the Master of Trinity Hall and five of the Fellows, Marriott, Wynne, Calvert, Francis Simpson, and Hallifax, supported the Newcastle interest in the university and voted for Lord Hardwicke as High Steward. The Judas of the society was Dr Ridlington who conveniently forgot his promises of eternal gratitude and enlisted under the banner of Lord Sandwich[1].

It is clear that the Duke had retired into the background as far as Trinity Hall was concerned, believing that Marriott and his other friends in the college would watch over his interests; but the death of Sir Edward Simpson on May 21st, 1764, forced him to emerge from his retreat. The times were too critical to permit him to be indifferent to the succession to Sir Edward Simpson in the mastership. The dispute over Lord Hardwicke's election was awaiting a decision in the law courts: and, as a fresh election might be ordered, it was of the greatest importance that the new Master of Trinity Hall, who might be the next Vice-Chancellor, should be a staunch supporter of the Duke and Lord Hardwicke. Yet at the outset Newcastle had little real cause for anxiety. The statutes of the college provided that no one could be elected Master unless he received the votes of at least seven out of the twelve Fellows, and that, in the event of no candidate receiving this necessary minimum, the Chancellor, as visitor of the college, should appoint to the mastership: and as

[1] Add. MS. 32957, f. 322.

282 THE CHANCELLOR AND THE COLLEGES

Newcastle believed that he could count upon the loyalty of at least five of the Fellows, and that at least one or two would not trouble to attend the election, it appeared to be within his power either to obtain the election of a friend or to secure a devolution of the appointment to himself.

'The first thing I beg of you' he wrote to the Bishop of Norwich on the day of Sir Edward Simpson's death 'is that you would see, as soon as you can, our friends of Trinity Hall, Dr Calvert, Dr Wynne, Dr Marriot (sic) and, I had forgot, Dr Simpson, and that you would shew them what I had written to the Archbishop in their favour, and that you would call upon the Archbishop yourself and talk over the affair with him[1]. But the most material of all is what relates to the mastership of Trinity Hall. I have no view but to have a good one, and I beg you would...speak to our friends at Doctors Commons and write immediately to Dr Halifax[2] (sic) to take care of it....Pray write to our Cambridge friends, Caryl, the Dean of Ely[3] and the Bishop of Lincoln about the mastership of Trinity Hall. I am amazed that none of you sent me word of the imminent danger this poor man was in[4].'

Newcastle, as was not unusual with him, was anxious and flurried, and undoubtedly what he most feared was that the Mastership might be secured by Dr Ridlington who would be supported by the whole weight of Lord Sandwich's influence. This was a catastrophe to be averted at all cost: but it is likely that at the opening of what was to be an arduous and unsuccessful campaign, the Duke believed that there was little danger of defeat. Confidently relying upon the votes of five of the twelve Fellows, he conceived that the Bishop of Norwich and

[1] This refers to the disposal of the civil law preferments vacated by Simpson's death; see Add. MS. 32959, f. 19.
[2] Dr Hallifax was chosen as one of the two tutorial and therefore resident Fellows: the other was Dr Ridlington.
[3] Dr Thomas, Master of Christ's.
[4] Add. MS. 32959, f. 24.

THE CHANCELLOR AND THE COLLEGES 283

his other friends at Cambridge, starting from such a position of advantage, might easily achieve victory. He knew however that time was of importance, and that Sandwich would prove himself a redoubtable and unscrupulous antagonist.

In his letter to the Bishop of Norwich Newcastle had emphasised that he was unprejudiced in favour of any one particular candidate and was solely intent upon meeting the wishes of his friends among the Fellows: and, had this indeed been the case, his task would have been far easier. There is good reason to think however that he was anxious for Dr Calvert to be elected[1]: for, apart from other considerations, it is otherwise somewhat inexplicable that, on hearing from the Bishop of Norwich that the gossip of Doctors Commons suggested Calvert as a likely Master, he should have decided at once to adopt him as a candidate. But as the Bishop also mentioned that neither he nor the Chancellor's other agents in the university were of any use in this emergency, as they knew 'none of the Fellows but the five who want not our solicitations[2],' Newcastle at once sent for Dr Marriott and on May 22nd conferred with him. His object in this interview was certainly to instruct Marriott to inaugurate a campaign on behalf of Calvert, and it is probable that he had never contemplated the possibility of resistance on the part of his faithful follower. Marriott however had not served Newcastle for naught, and he was unlikely to forget that he had served him far longer than Calvert. He consequently felt himself slighted, thus to be sent for merely to be

---

[1] He urged the Archbishop of Canterbury to appoint Calvert as Dean of Arches in place of Simpson, and gave as a reason that Calvert 'has two near relations, Mr John Calvert and Mr Nicholson Calvert, members of parliament and very zealous friends, who interest themselves extremely for him.' Add. MS. 32959, f. 19.
[2] Add. MS. 32959, f. 26.

instructed to promote the success of a colleague, and the interview was stormy. He told the Duke that he could not vote for Calvert as Master, that Dr Hallifax was equally unwilling to do so, and that, if Newcastle did not quickly adopt another candidate, Dr Ridlington would inevitably be elected Master. He seems also to have made fairly clear that he himself was the proper candidate for the Duke to adopt, though he dealt more fully with this point in conversation, a few days later, with John Roberts who was in Newcastle's confidence and had been Henry Pelham's secretary.

'He has already acquainted me' wrote Roberts on May 25th 'with his determination to be a candidate for the mastership of Trinity Hall himself, and he told me at the same time that he had been with your Grace at Claremont, made the same declaration to you, and had desired your assistance. He seemed to be much mortified at not receiving more encouragement from your Grace, and dropt to me obliquely that if he had not voted as Your Grace desired him, or should even now apply to those who are not your friends, he should not fail of reaping some advantage from the event of Dr Simpson's death[1].'

Marriott was angry and aggrieved, and not without justification. He probably was human enough to exaggerate the value of the services he had rendered: but he certainly had been of assistance to the Duke in the past, and not unnaturally resented being passed over. It was the old tale of the anger of the labourer, who had endured the heat and burden of the day, only to discover that he had done no better than the man hired at the eleventh hour: but it is Newcastle's apparent obtuseness and not Marriott's anger that constitutes the problem. It is of course possible that the Duke believed that his faithful follower was too well schooled and disciplined to think of the mastership unless it was his patron's will that he should have it; but this does not explain

[1] Add. MS. 32959, f. 79; see also f. 34.

the Duke's preference for Calvert. Certainty is out of the question, but there is some reason to think that his conduct was not quite so unpremeditated or without thought as it might superficially appear. From a stray remark in John Roberts' letter it appears that, subsequent to the accession of George III to the throne, Marriott had displayed an inclination to desert his patron and throw in his lot with those who were compassing the overthrow of the whigs; and, though he repented of his wrong doing and remained loyal to his party, a certain amount of pressure had been necessary to keep him in the straight and narrow path[1]. It is possible that the lesson had not been thrown away upon the Duke, and that he passed over Marriott for the very good reason that, though he used him, he distrusted him. It is at least suggestive that, after he was perfectly well acquainted with Marriott's ambition, he never contemplated supporting his candidature for the mastership.

But whether Marriott's rebellion was a risk which had to be incurred or was provoked by a blunder which might have been avoided, there is no doubt that it seriously deranged the Duke's plans. It was possible that Marriott was speaking the truth when he said that Calvert had no chance of securing election and that Hallifax would be loath to vote for him: and, if this were to prove the case, of the five votes which Newcastle had confidently counted upon for Calvert, only three would be left. But two or three days after Marriott had visited Claremont, even worse news came. It was reliably reported that Hallifax would not only not vote for Calvert but had pledged himself to vote for Ridlington, and that Ansell had also undertaken to support Ridlington who was confident of success[2]. Hence if Newcastle could count upon three votes for his candidate, Ridlington could count upon an equal

[1] Add. MS. 32959, f. 79.   [2] Add. MS. 32959, f. 81.

number for himself; and in such an evenly matched game it was impossible to foretell the winner. Moreover it was possible that the advantage lay with Ridlington, for it was rumoured that Mr Milles of Canterbury, who like John Robinson was a confirmed absentee, might attend the election and vote for Ridlington. 'I take him to be a humourist' wrote Calvert 'who seldom stirs out, but very able to travel if pressed, and they reckon him one of their number[1].'

The situation was undoubtedly very serious. As long as Newcastle had been able to rely upon five of the Fellows supporting him, and upon two being absent, he rightly assumed that, even if the candidate he favoured failed to secure the necessary minimum of votes, no other candidate could be more fortunate, and that it would fall to him as visitor to appoint the new Master. But if, as it appeared, he could only count upon the loyalty of Wynne, Calvert and Frank Simpson, and if Milles was going to emerge from his retreat at Canterbury, it was possible that Ridlington might dissuade Marriott from standing, and secure the seven votes which would give him the mastership. It was obvious that active measures were needed, and they were forthcoming. The Duke was prepared, if necessary, to drop Calvert as a candidate: but, before coming to a final decision on this point, he wrote on May 25th to both Dr Hallifax and Richard Milles, who was a nephew of Mr Milles of Canterbury, asking Dr Hallifax to reserve his vote for the mastership 'for such friend of ours as shall be thought most likely to succeed': and asking Richard Milles to persuade his uncle to do the same. 'The election or devolution to the Chancellor will depend' he urged Hallifax 'upon your vote[2].'

Richard Milles promised to write to his uncle in the sense indicated by Newcastle, but expressed the opinion

[1] Add. MS. 32959, f. 81.   [2] Add. MS. 32959, f. 83, f. 85.

that his kinsman's health was too infirm to permit of his undertaking a journey to Cambridge[1]. As he was likely, if he came, to vote for Ridlington, it was satisfactory to hear that he might be prevented from attending, for his absence would certainly assist the Duke in bringing about a devolution to himself. But from Hallifax came a reply which left no doubt that he was deeply pledged to support Ridlington, and his letter witnesses to genuine distress of mind.

'It is a cruel circumstance' he wrote 'to be thrown into a situation which makes it necessary for me either to violate the duties of friendship to one to whom I am under the greatest obligation, or seem to relinquish or neglect your Grace's interests in this university, which I feel myself bound by every tie of gratitude and honour to promote to the utmost of my power. When Dr Ridlington was informed of the death of our late worthy Master he applied to me for my vote and assistance. Considering the real services I had received from him when I was endeavouring to secure my own election at Trinity Hall, the intimate connexions that have since that time subsisted between us, being both of us jointly concerned in carrying on the business of the pupils, together with the readiness he has shown on all occasions to contribute to everything that might make my situation easy in the college, I thought he would have just reason to complain of unkindness from me, was I to refuse complying with his request, the first and the only request he ever made me. I told him therefore that my vote was at his service if he could make any use of it: at the same time giving it as my opinion that his being in orders would be an insuperable objection to him with the gentlemen at the Commons, and desiring him in that case, if he found he had no chance of succeeding himself, he would leave me at full liberty to assist any other person I pleased. This is the whole of the case between the Professor and me, and I own that I am exceedingly anxious that your Grace should consider my conduct on this occasion in a favourable light. I do assure your Grace that I have no oblique ends of my own to serve, no crooked politics to persuade me to

[1] Add. MS. 32959, f. 104.

swerve from the duty to which your Grace has the justest claim[1].'

The pathos of this letter was probably wasted upon Newcastle who must have been pre-occupied with the thought that Hallifax's vote was irretrievably lost if Ridlington stood for the mastership. Information from other sources also made clear that in no conceivable circumstances could Calvert secure election as Master: and that, as there was a strong prejudice in the society against allowing the visitor to appoint, it was probable that, if Calvert continued as a candidate, a sufficient number of the electors would rally round Ridlington to secure his election. Therefore, after a few days thought, the Duke decided to adopt Wynne instead of Calvert as his candidate: and there is no doubt that he was very well advised to make the change. It was possible that Dr Dale, Pedley, and even Milles, if he came, might be persuaded to vote for Wynne, Hallifax would certainly do so if Ridlington ultimately decided not to stand, and it was further discovered that if Marriott did not come forward as a candidate and was obliged to choose between Ridlington and Wynne, he would support the latter[2]. Therefore on May 30th the Duke informed Calvert that Wynne was to be the official candidate of the party, and Calvert loyally accepted the decision[3]. But Newcastle considered that something more was needed to be done in order to make as certain as possible of success, and he rose to the occasion.

'I find' he told Calvert 'most of the Fellows are afraid of a devolution, and that some of them may vote for Dr Ridlington, not out of regard to him but purely to prevent a devolution, and

[1] Add. MS. 32959, f. 148.
[2] Add. MS. 32959, f. 118, f. 146, f. 150, f. 172, f. 200, f. 227, f. 247.
[3] Add. MS. 32959, f. 200.

THE CHANCELLOR AND THE COLLEGES 289

that nothing would so effectually remove that objection as a previous declaration from me (not publick but to be understood) that, in case of a devolution to the Chancellor, I would appoint that person who should be the most agreeable to the majority of my friends in Trinity Hall[1].'

This 'previous declaration' was consequently made: but as the main objection of the society was to the principle of a devolution, it was unlikely to be very effectual. Early in June however a change came over the situation. Though supported by Lord Sandwich[2], Dr Ridlington discovered that being in orders was a fatal disability to a candidate for the mastership of Trinity Hall. He had successfully engaged the votes of Pedley and Hallifax: but Matthew Robinson refused to support him because he was a clergyman, and, as Robinson possessed considerable influence in the society, Ridlington wisely abandoned the contest[3]. Consequently Hallifax was now free to give his vote to Wynne[4], and Pedley also undertook to vote for Wynne against any other candidates except Ridlington, Ansell, and Matthew Robinson[5]. As Ridlington had decided to withdraw, and Robinson and Ansell had not yet appeared in the field, there was a reasonable chance of Pedley's vote being secured for Wynne who would thus be supported by five out of the twelve Fellows. But any reliable forecast was entirely out of the question, for the situation was constantly being modified, and it was impossible to foresee the events of the following day. For instance no sooner was it known that Ridlington would not stand than Marriott executed his threat and came forward as

[1] Add. MS. 32959, f. 200.
[2] 'I am informed' wrote Dr Burrell to Newcastle on June 4th 'Lord Sandwich tries every possible method to procure an election in favour of Dr Ridlington, and for that purpose sent a very extraordinary letter yesterday to one of the Fellows.' Add. MS. 32959, f. 254.
[3] Add. MS. 32959, f. 227.   [4] *Ibid.*
[5] Add. MS. 32959, f. 245.

a candidate for the mastership. He had bided his time, knowing perfectly well that if he and Ridlington both stood, they would so divide the votes that the appointment of a new Master would inevitably fall to the Chancellor; and he was certainly right to seize the opportunity afforded by Ridlington's withdrawal. He was able to count upon the support of Matthew Robinson, Ridlington, and Ansell, and, as it was understood that each candidate would vote for himself, he started his campaign with at least four votes in his favour. Lord Sandwich moreover adopted him as his official candidate[1]; and though Newcastle and his friends made light of his chance of success, it is possible that their optimism was more official than sincere.

Thus of the twelve Fellows, including the two candidates, five were ranged on the side of Wynne and four on the side of Marriott: and, unless there was a change in the situation, neither candidate could secure election. The three electors who had not yet declared themselves were Dr Dale, John Robinson, and Milles; and as it was correctly assumed that John Robinson would not attend, the interest centred round Dale and Milles. It was within their power, by voting for Wynne, to make sure of his election: but, as they were both unknown to Newcastle[2], it was unlikely that they would be prejudiced in favour of his candidate. But it did not necessarily follow that they would be in favour of Marriott. Dr Dale, who might be counted upon to attend, refused indeed to commit himself until he was better informed as to his own chance of securing the prize[3]; and though the 'humourist,' Milles, was worried by his nephew and possibly visited at Canterbury by Marriott and Matthew

[1] Add. MS. 32959, f. 304.
[2] It is significant that Newcastle communicated with Dale through Charles Yorke, and with Milles through his nephew.
[3] Add. MS. 32959, f. 284.

Robinson[1], he too was not to be drawn, and resisted the importunity of his suitors with the desperate courage of an invalid. In reply to the letter written by his nephew at Newcastle's request, Milles declared that he wished to remain at liberty to act as he thought best, and from this position he refused to budge[2].

There was however a general feeling that, when it came to the point, Milles would not break the habit of a lifetime by visiting his college, and if he and John Robinson were both absent, Newcastle fondly believed that a devolution to himself was inevitable, and that therefore Wynne would secure the mastership by his nomination[3]. But he soon discovered that the declaration he had made that he would 'appoint that person who should be the most agreeable to the majority of my friends in Trinity Hall,' had not been quite so effective as he had hoped. Though Calvert, Wynne and Simpson were prepared to go all lengths to thwart Marriott's ambition, there was a suspicion that Pedley, and much more than a suspicion that Hallifax, would, in the event of Wynne failing to secure the necessary minimum, rather vote for Marriott than allow no election to be held. Pedley indeed affirmed to Francis Simpson that he would rather 'see a devolution than vote for Dr Marriott[4],' and had promised Wynne that he would not vote for Marriott, 'though a lapse should be the consequence[5]'; but he was not regarded as absolutely safe, and considerable alarm was felt as to

---

[1] Add. MS. 32959, f. 254, f. 337, f. 367.
[2] Add. MS. 32959, f. 252, f. 282. For details concerning the situation at this stage, see Add. MS. 33061, f. 269; Add. MS. 32959, f. 235, f. 237, f. 272, f. 280, f. 306, f. 331, f. 351; Add. MS. 35640, f. 136.
[3] Add. MS. 32959, f. 237.
[4] Add. MS. 32959, f. 353; see also f. 337.
[5] Add. MS. 32959, f. 347.

the attitude he might ultimately adopt. He was justly suspected, for, unknown to his friends and in defiance of his promise, he had pledged himself to vote for Marriott rather than allow a devolution. Hallifax on the other hand acted with commendable frankness, quite definitely and openly stating that, if Wynne failed to secure election, he would vote for Marriott rather than allow the Chancellor to appoint the new Master[1]; and to this determination he adhered in spite of the admonitions of his old Master, Dr Caryl[2].

'I told him' Caryl reported to the Duke 'that there might be room for such apprehensions if there was any danger of a stranger being placed over them, but after what your Grace had been so good as to declare, he could not have a suspicion on that head[3].'

Even more emphatically did the Duke address the man who threatened to wreck the campaign.

'For God's sake, then, my good Sir' wrote Newcastle 'consider well what you are doing, and remember that by falling in with these people, under the very false notion of preventing a lapse,...you are adding weight to the very set of men you have been so strenuously and honourably opposing[4].'

But Hallifax was not to be moved by arguments or threats, and thus for a second time within a few days he played an ungrateful part. He was clearly an uncomfortable and most inconvenient ally: but he was able to give a reasoned defence of the position he had taken up.

'It has always been accounted' he wrote on June 13th 'so wrong a thing at Trinity Hall to suffer a lapse of any kind, and we are so plainly directed by our statutes to agree in an election, if it is possible, that I own I cannot reconcile it to the principles

---

[1] Add. MS. 32959, f. 245, f. 337, f. 347.
[2] Before his election to a Fellowship at Trinity Hall, Hallifax was a Fellow of Jesus.
[3] Add. MS. 32959, f. 347. [4] Add. MS. 32959, f. 369.

which I have been taught to entertain, to concur with any of the Fellows to make a lapse in the present instance. You seem to think that it all rests on me alone to make or prevent a devolution to the Chancellor. Give me leave to say, Sir, that you have been misinformed. There are, most undoubtedly, seven without me who have resolved at all adventures to have an election, and the names of the seven are these—Ridlington, Robinson, Ansell, Marriott, Pedley, Dale, and Dr Wynne himself who on all occasions, and more particularly on the present occasion, has declared repeatedly that he thought it of all things the wrongest to suffer a lapse, and that, as for his own part, in order to prevent it he would willingly go over with all his interest to any of the practising civilians at the Commons to make an election. Being asked to explain himself what he meant by the practising civilians, he answered Calvert, Simpson, Marriott, and himself....I believe it is an impracticable thing for Dr Wynne to secure his election, and therefore the next person at the Commons, on whom the society have turned their eyes, is Dr Marriott. I will freely own to you that Dr Wynne is the more eligible man of the two, and I am sure it was in compliance to what Dr Caryl told me would be agreeable to the Duke of Newcastle, that I went that very morning to Dr Wynne and promised him my second vote, and I have contributed all I could to gain others to his interests. But I cannot persuade myself to devote myself so entirely to Dr Wynne's cause as to go contrary to the sense of the society[1].'

Dr Hallifax's defence cannot be described as masterly. He admitted that Wynne would make a better Master than Marriott, and yet in certain circumstances was prepared to vote for the latter against the man he believed to be the better candidate. It is moreover impossible to believe that Wynne was opposed to a devolution which was indeed his only chance of obtaining the Mastership[2]. Yet, though the apologia is not very con-

[1] Add. MS. 32959, f. 381.
[2] On June 12th it was reported that Lord Sandwich was extremely angry with Wynne, because 'as Dr Marriott has six votes, he (Wynne) will not make the seventh.' Add. MS. 32959, f. 371.

vincing, it is unnecessary to assume that Hallifax was inspired by unworthy or corrupt motives. It is more probable that he was one of those exasperating politicians, the bane of the party to which they belong, who are for ever starting inconvenient scruples, and who wish the end without wishing the only means by which the end can be attained.

The election was fixed for Friday, June 15th, and on the eve of the decisive day the issue was still in doubt. It was known that neither John Robinson nor Milles would attend, and that of the remaining ten electors, five on the first scrutiny would vote for Wynne and four for Marriott, Dr Dale not having yet declared his vote. It was therefore certain that, even if Dale gave his vote for Marriott, no election could take place, and the appointment would lapse to the Chancellor unless on a second or later scrutiny two of the electors transferred their votes in order that there should be an election. Unfortunately for Newcastle, while there was no chance of any of Marriott's supporters voting for Wynne at any stage of the proceedings, it was certain that Hallifax would vote for Marriott rather than allow a devolution, and it became increasingly clear that Pedley, in spite of his promises and professions, would probably do the same[1]. Hence everything depended upon Dr Dale's vote. If he voted for Wynne and was prepared to face a devolution Marriott, even if both Hallifax and Pedley voted for him, could not be elected, but if Dale voted for Marriott it was within the power of Hallifax and Pedley, if they acted together, to make Marriott Master. Hence when two or three days before the election the rumour was spread that Dale had committed himself to Marriott, the greatest despondency prevailed among Newcastle's followers in the college. 'Nothing can save us' wrote Wynne on June 13th 'but another freak of

[1] Add. MS. 35640, f. 144; Add. MS. 32959, f. 379.

Matt Robinson[1],' but when, on the day following, the rumour was discovered to be untrue, a more cheerful view was taken of the situation[2].'

The rumour unfortunately proved to be an intelligent anticipation. When the Fellows met on the afternoon of Friday June 15th, Dale declared for Marriott, and thus on the first scrutiny each candidate received five votes, Wynne, Simpson, Hallifax, Pedley, and Calvert voting for Wynne, and Marriott, Matthew Robinson, Ansell, Ridlington, and Dale voting for Marriott. They then proceeded to a second scrutiny, but without however effecting any change in the distribution of votes. On the third scrutiny, however, Hallifax voted for Marriott who consequently now had six votes to Wynne's four. At this stage Pedley suggested that the election should be postponed until the following day: but the proposal was not accepted, and, after a brief adjournment for chapel, a fourth scrutiny was taken which again showed Marriott as having six votes and Wynne four. But on the fifth scrutiny Pedley, declaring 'that of the two evils he must chuse the least,' voted for Marriott who was consequently elected into the mastership and admitted on the following day[3].

It was a mortifying end to all Newcastle's labours, and all the more mortifying because the victor had been a faithful follower and dependent of the Duke. Marriott indeed was amply revenged for his claims upon the mastership having been slighted by his patron, and it was undoubtedly very fortunate for him that he found Lord Sandwich ready at hand to espouse his cause. To what degree the support of Sandwich contributed towards his success it is difficult to say[4]. It is certain

[1] Add. MS. 35640, f. 144.   [2] Add. MS. 32959, f. 407.
[3] Add. MS. 32959, f. 413, f. 421, f. 423, f. 425, f. 465; Add. MS. 35640, f. 146; Add. MS. 5852, f. 149.
[4] 'Lord Sandwich' wrote Caryl on 20th June 'I know values

that Newcastle would have won the battle but for the conduct of Hallifax and Pedley: but there is nothing to show that these two renegades acted under Lord Sandwich's influence. It appears that Hallifax had been persuaded by Ridlington, to whom he believed himself to be under a debt of gratitude, to give a pledge that he would prevent a devolution if he possibly could: and that 'the sense of his obligations to Dr Ridlington was the single principle upon which he acted through the whole contest at Trinity Hall[1].' It reflects little credit upon Dr Hallifax's intelligence that he failed to perceive that he could not serve both Newcastle and Ridlington, but there is not the slightest reason to think that he was inspired by a desire to serve Lord Sandwich. After the election he spared no pains to assure Newcastle that he was, as he had ever been, his faithful follower, and ready to obey his commands.

'As a proof of his sincerity' wrote Dr Caryl in October 1764 'he assures me that at this instant Dr Ridlington is willing to resign his professorship, and that Lord Hallifax (sic)[2] has signified to him (Dr Hallifax) that he may have it, but that he was absolutely determined to refuse it, because the consequence of his acceptance must be an expectation from him to joyn a set of people whose principles and measures he detests[3].'

Though Newcastle had been very angry with Hallifax, describing him in a letter to the Bishop of Norwich as 'this weak, ungrateful man[4]' he was touched by this manifestation of loyalty and penitence, and readily forgave him[5].

himself upon the countenance he afforded to Marriott's pretensions, but that he made him one vote I do not know.' Add. MS. 32959, f. 465.
[1] Add. MS. 32962, f. 249.
[2] Lord Halifax was one of the Secretaries of State, the other being Lord Sandwich.
[3] Add. MS. 32962, f. 249.   [4] Add. MS. 32959, f. 373.
[5] Add. MS. 32962, f. 297.

There is nothing to show that Pedley either asked for or received forgiveness: and perhaps he thought that he had sinned too deeply to hope for pardon. Like Hallifax he had pledged himself to prevent a devolution, but, unlike Hallifax, he had not only concealed his intention but had given lying assurances that he would never vote for Marriott.

'I cannot forgive Mr Pedley' wrote Francis Simpson 'who at the very time he promised me that he would not vote for Dr Marriott, even though a devolution should ensue, had actually given it under his (sic)[1] to the other party that he would vote for Marriott to prevent a devolution, which explains his meaning that of two evils he would chuse the least, for having verbally promised one party, and under his hand assured the other to vote for Marriott, he chose to adhere to his written promise rather than his verbal one[2].'

Yet inexcusable as was his conduct, it would be absurd to pretend that he had sinned against Newcastle, for he was not a follower of the Duke, and would have voted for either Ridlington and Ansell in preference to Wynne. It was for Wynne, whom he had basely deceived, and not for Newcastle, to give or refuse him pardon, and we do not know whether that pardon was ever given. Nor are we any wiser as to the motives leading Pedley to play this double game. It is possible that he was influenced by Sandwich: but it is quite as likely that he was influenced by resentment against such an obvious attempt to prevent an election being held.

Indeed, in dealing with the affairs of Trinity Hall and the other colleges, Newcastle was battling against eddies and currents completely unknown to him, and consequently he was often shipwrecked. On the other hand Marriott had not fostered the Duke's interest in the society without learning a great deal in the process,

[1] 'Hand' is probably the word omitted.
[2] Add. MS. 32959, f. 425.

and throughout the contest he had been fighting at an advantage. The victor and the vanquished were never reconciled[1], and it is impossible that Newcastle could have ever thought of his defeat with anything but bitterness. But his failure at Trinity Hall must have rankled far less deeply than the rebuff he suffered at his own college, Clare. For Clare and his old school, Westminster, he cherished a very particular affection: and, until he quarrelled with the college, it was at Clare that he always stayed when he visited Cambridge. Dr Wilcox, who was Master when the Duke became Chancellor, was his unswerving friend and ally, and it is probable that Newcastle was more at home in that society than in any other in the university. It is possible that he thought he could never be betrayed by a college upon which he had lavished so much affection: and, if such was his belief, he had towards the end of 1762 a very rude awakening.

'Our Master's state of health,' wrote on September 11th, 1762, William Talbot, who was a Fellow of Clare, 'has suffered so considerable a change within a few days past that it seems probable he cannot continue long. In case of a vacancy I know how much the society is bound to consult your Grace's judgment and good-liking in the choice of a new Master. Nevertheless I do not find that the present sett of Fellows are in general disposed to be duly attentive to this obligation, for out of seventeen Fellows, who have a right of voting on such occasions, I apprehend ten have by various arts been induced to engage their votes beforehand to Dr Goddard who has of late publickly boasted that he was certain of success. This intelligence, I doubt not, was sometime since communicated to your Grace by the Bishop of Norwich, to whom I opened the state of things here. As Dr Goddard is a man whom your Grace has little reason to approve

---

[1] Writing in June 1768, when Marriott was Vice-Chancellor, Newcastle remarks: "The present Vice-Chancellor will endeavour to pa : me by, as far as he can, and that I shall neither have power nor credit.' Add. MS. 32990, f. 224.

THE CHANCELLOR AND THE COLLEGES 299

of, I would be glad to do everything in my power in this conjuncture to exempt myself at least from the number of the ungrateful, and therefore beg leave to intreat the favour of your Grace's directions how I am to act[1].'

Dr Peter Goddard was of humble origin, probably being the son of a French barber settled in Cambridge. Admitted to Clare as a Sizar in 1721, he was elected to a Fellowship of the college six years later, and acted as tutor to Lord Lincoln, Newcastle's nephew, during his residence at Clare[2]. He was accordingly brought into close contact with the Duke, and, if his own account can be accepted, it was mainly due to his efforts that the Grace appointing Newcastle as High Steward was safely steered through the Caput[3]. He naturally put a high value upon the services he had rendered upon this occasion: and in 1751 reminded the Duke of his achievement and asked for preferment in the church, mentioning that he only held 'two livings, about £180 per annum, situated in a very pleasant but dear country, and therefore any addition, especially of a sinecure kind, would be extreamly acceptable[4].' His petition was either rejected or unanswered, and smarting under what he deemed a particularly base display of ingratitude, he determined to be the architect of his own fortunes and simultaneously to satisfy both his ambition and his spite. He made up his mind to be the next Master of Clare, and for ten years conducted a secret canvass of the Fellows of the college with the assistance of Richard Terrick, Bishop of Peterborough, who, as an ex-Fellow and distinguished prelate, was able to exercise considerable influence in the society[5]. From Talbot's letter

[1] Add. MS. 32942, f. 227.
[2] These details were kindly given me by Mr Wardale, Fellow of Clare.
[3] Add. MS. 32725, f. 382; see ch. 11. p. 37.
[4] *Ibid.*   [5] Add. MS. 32942, f. 269, f. 279.

we gather that by September 1762 Goddard had secured a majority among the electors: and, being of an arrogant and overbearing disposition, he began to boast of certain victory and to conduct himself as the destined successor to Dr Wilcox[1].

If he fulfilled his boast Newcastle's influence and prestige in his old college would be certain to decline and might easily disappear. It would be impossible to conceal the fact that Goddard had openly defied the Duke: and it was certainly not hopeful for his behaviour in the future that his two friends on the episcopal bench were the Bishop of Peterborough, who had thrown over Newcastle for Lord Bute, and Thomas Hayter who had recently been promoted to the see of London in direct opposition to the Duke's wishes. A man with such associates might well, as a Master of a college, be a particularly painful thorn in the Chancellor's side: but, though the outlook was black, Talbot did not give up hope. It was provided by the statutes of the college that a Master must be elected on the tenth day from the declaration of a vacancy, that no election was valid unless held in the presence of a majority of the electors, and that, if the tenth day passed without an election taking place, the right of nominating a Master passed to the visitor of the college who was the Chancellor[2]. As the month was September many of the Fellows were away from Cambridge and possibly in distant parts of England: and Talbot pointed out to the Duke that

it is not an improbable supposition that Goddard may not be able to collect together within the limited time nine determined men of his party, which number is requisite to constitute a majority of the whole society. In this case your Grace's friends, absenting themselves voluntarily on the day of the election, (which is the tenth day of the vacancy) it will be impossible for

[1] Add. MS. 32942, f. 227.   [2] Add. MS. 32942, f. 227, f. 269.

THE CHANCELLOR AND THE COLLEGES 301

them without us to proceed to an election. And no election being made on that day, the consequence will be a devolution to your Grace[1].

Before he heard of this proposal Newcastle had been carefully considering possible courses of action. As it was in the days before the university was rent in twain by the strife between him and Sandwich, which, while it lasted, coloured every academic controversy and divided almost every college, he had to beware of too openly interfering in what was a purely domestic affair: and he inclined to the opinion that, if Goddard was certain of a majority, it would be best for his supporters among the electors to acquiesce in the inevitable and vote for the man who had outwitted them. Yet he was not blind to the dangerous consequences of such a policy of submission, and he was prepared to consider, at least as an abstract proposition, the possibility of arranging for a devolution.

'I think I have a claim to some regard from them' he remarked with reference to the Fellows of Clare 'but as they think otherwise, or act as if they did, I think it would be by no means proper to give Dr Goddard any unnecessary disturbance, and therefore I wish that all our friends would shew a cheerful concurrence in his election, except any method could be found not to proceed to the election or make any that day, and then the appointment would devolve to the Chancellor, as it did in the case of Dr Grigg put in by the Duke of Somerset[2].'

Thus he dallied with the thought of working for a devolution, but when Talbot made a practical proposal he hesitated to sanction it:

'To be sure' he wrote 'I should wish it upon many accounts, but as I am so much concerned in the consequences of it, I must beg that I may not in the least appear in it, and that nothing may be done that would be liable to my just censure. For that reason I wish you would consult some of my friends, the Heads,

[1] Add. MS. 32942, f. 269.   [2] Add. MS. 32942, f. 271.

upon the subject, and any knowing men in the university upon whom you can depend[1].'

While the Duke was hesitating Dr Wilcox died, and the question of a policy at once became urgent. Talbot was anxious for a devolution to be attempted, and the Duke, after much hesitation, was prepared to sanction the scheme if the sole responsibility for it was shouldered by Talbot and his friends[2]. But Dr Goddard was not the man to throw away the labours of ten years by leaving anything to chance: and no sooner was the breath out of Dr Wilcox's body than he was sending for his friends among the electors to return to Cambridge post haste[3]. On September 23rd he was reported to have 'got such a number of his friends together that he is secure of his election[4],' and two days later he was elected into the mastership.

'As he had got together' wrote Talbot 'a clear majority, it was thought prudent that your Grace's friends should come into his election without any seeming reluctance. And I was the more attentive to this particularly for the sake of Mr Gould, a very ingenious and deserving young man who assists me in the care and instruction of my pupils, who, being in the junior part of the society, might have been exposed to some inconveniences from the resentments of a provoked Master. For my own part, though the signal discourtesies, that I have received from Dr Goddard and his abettors, would have justified my refusing to the last to concur in electing him, yet as the known relation I have the honour to bear unto your Grace as Chancellor of the university[5] might have induced a suspicion in some people that my conduct was framed according to your Grace's instructions, upon mature deliberation I resolved to come in with the rest, that no handle might be given for reflections of that sort. I cannot forbear mentioning to your Grace the names of Mr

[1] Add. MS. 32942, f. 285.
[2] Add. MS. 32942, f. 279, f. 296, f. 305.
[3] Add. MS. 32942, f. 287. [4] Add. MS. 32942, f. 330.
[5] Talbot succeeded Dr Squire as the Chancellor's university secretary.

Hagar, Mr Cay (who practises at the Bar) and Mr Gould as persons who are the ornaments of this society as well as of distinguished attachment to your Grace, and who are filled with the utmost indignation at the ungrateful treatment which your Grace have received from a sett of men here[1].'

Newcastle was quite as indignant as the gentlemen who were the ornaments of Clare, and he had good cause to be. He had identified himself more closely with Clare than with any other college in the university, and had taken particular pleasure in talking of himself as a Clare man: and he therefore the more bitterly resented the treatment he had received. A lengthy political experience however had taught him that few disasters are irretrievable: and, instead of brooding upon the wrong he had suffered, he was prepared to forgive his enemy who, after having achieved so notable a victory, might conceivably be ready to come to terms. He told Lord Hardwicke that he believed 'Goddard will act well enough[2]': and in his reply to the new Master's notification of his election, he tempered rebuke with forgiveness.

'You say very truly' he wrote 'that I have often expressed a very good opinion of you: I sincerely had it, and hope and believe that I shall never have any occasion to alter it. I own freely (for I will never disguise the truth) that some late connections which you had with one[3], who had acted a very ungrateful part to me who had been his chief if not only benefactor as to his publick preferments until just at last, could not be agreeable to me. And the manner in which the college has thought proper to proceed without taking the least notice of me, their Chancellor, their visitor, their friend, and, I may say, their benefactor, is so unusual in cases of the like nature that it did make a very strong impression upon me....However I rejoice to hear from yourself and Mr Talbot that your election was unanimous. I have had very strong assurances from my good

[1] Add. MS. 32942, f. 358. [2] Add. MS. 32942, f. 347.
[3] Thomas Hayter, Bishop of London.

304 THE CHANCELLOR AND THE COLLEGES

friend, the Bishop of Oxford, that your conduct will be agreeable to your old friends. I desire no more, and hope and don't doubt but you will endeavour to promote or to re-establish that union, friendship, and harmony in our college which has now subsisted for so many years, and that you will act in concert with those friends of the government in the university, with whom you were bred up, and upon those principles which I know are your own[1].'

Thus Newcastle made a magnanimous gesture, but Dr Goddard in his hour of triumph was not disposed to sue for forgiveness and replied to the Duke rather saucily. He pointed out that it was to Newcastle's nephew, Lord Lincoln, that he owed that connection with the Bishop of London for which he was blamed, and slyly contended that such a staunch friend of liberty as the Duke could not possibly condemn the Fellows of Clare for choosing 'without favour or affection that man for their Master whom they do in their consciences believe to be the fittest for that office[2].' Goddard indeed had not forgiven Newcastle for the neglect of former years, and though Talbot expressed a belief that he was anxious for a reconciliation[3], there was small foundation for optimism. There can be little doubt that the new Master was determined to free Clare from the Duke's influence, and his power for mischief would not be confined to the college as he became Vice-Chancellor within two months of his election as Master.

Formal hostilities between the Master and the Duke may be said to have begun on February 7th, 1763, when Dr Goddard deprived the Rev. Robert Hagar of his Fellowship on the ground that as Vicar of Hawnes he possessed an income exceeding that with which a Fellowship of Clare was tenable. Even if the action of the Master had been strictly in accordance with the

[1] Add. MS. 32942, f. 392. [2] Add. MS. 32942, f. 440.
[3] Add. MS. 32942, f. 442.

THE CHANCELLOR AND THE COLLEGES 305

college statutes, it would have been unfortunate that the victim should be one who was distinguished by his loyalty to Newcastle; but the incident took on a much worse complexion when it became clear that the Master had acted illegally. Supported by public opinion in the university, which was almost unanimously on his side[1], Hagar lost no time in appealing for redress to the Chancellor as visitor of the college[2]: and the Duke would have been more than human if he had not relished the prospect of humiliating the adversary who had rejected his forgiveness. Dr Goddard had indeed made a very bad blunder, and, realising his error, sought too late to extricate himself from a most unfortunate situation.

'Yesterday' wrote Talbot on March 6th, 1763, 'our Master began to think himself so much in the wrong that he sent for Mr Hagar and told him...he was now willing to give up that point, and, dropping the whole dispute, to permit Mr Hagar to enjoy his Fellowship as if nothing had passed. Mr Hagar's answer was to this effect, that your Grace as visitor of the college, having accepted the appeal and undertaken to hear and determine the cause, it seemed to be no longer in his (Mr Hagar's) power to let it drop. That he, (the Master) had thought good indeed to declare his Fellowship vacant: but to restore him, he apprehended, was beyond the limits of his authority. This, he believed, could only be done by the visitor[3].'

The Master was indeed trapped: and although in the presence of his Fellows he revoked his declaration of February 7th, and acknowledged that he had wrongfully dispossessed Hagar of his Fellowship[4], he failed to stop the proceedings which had been begun against him.

The case was heard on March 29th at Newcastle's town house in Lincoln's Inn Fields, the Duke having

[1] Add. MS. 32947, f. 188.
[2] Add. MS. 33061, f. 257; Add. MS. 32947, f. 39.
[3] Add. MS. 32947, f. 188.   [4] Add. MS. 33061, f. 257.

as assessors the Masters of Corpus and Trinity Hall, who had been appointed by the university in accordance with the college statutes. The proceedings were purely formal and the result a foregone conclusion. After various documents had been read, and Goddard and Hagar had spoken,

His Grace, the said visitor, with the advice and consent of his assessors, did pronounce for the appeal interposed in this behalf, and did pronounce, decree, and declare that the said Dr Peter Stephen Goddard, the Master of Clare Hall aforesaid, had proceeded wrongfully on the seventh day of February last in declaring the Fellowship of the said Robert Hagar void, and did therefore pronounce and decree the said declaration of the said Master null and invalid to all intents and purposes whatsoever, and did continue and confirm the said Robert Hagar in the quiet and full enjoyment of his said Fellowship with all the profits, benefits, emoluments, and advantages to the same belonging, in as full and ample manner as if the said declaration of the said Dr Peter Stephen Goddard, the Master, of the seventh day of February last had never been made, and did order and direct that this decree and the said declaration of the said Master, delivered this day and hereto annexed[1], be intimated to the said Master and Fellows, and that they be enjoined to register the same in the publick register of the said college, and that they do certify him, the said visitor, thereof under the seal of the said college, or under the hands of the Master and Fellows present in college, on or before the first day of May next ensuing. And the said visitor did further, by the advice and consent of his said assessors, at the petition of the said Robert Hagar, condemn the

[1] 'I, Peter Stephen Goddard, Doctor in Divinity and Master of Clare Hall in the university of Cambridge, do hereby declare that for want of proper information I did declare Mr Hagar's Fellowship void, contrary to the statutes, but that upon receiving further information I did publickly, in the presence of all the Fellows then in college, revoke the said declaration and acknowledge that he had by statute a right to hold his Fellowship with the Vicarage of Hawnes in the county of Bedford and diocese of Lincoln. And I do desire to have my said declaration of February 7th 1763 adjudged null and void by the visitor and his assessors.' Add. MS. 33061, f. 257.

THE CHANCELLOR AND THE COLLEGES

said Dr Peter Stephen Goddard in the sum of twenty pounds, in the name of costs, to be paid to the said Robert Hagar for and towards his charges and expenses in presenting this appeal[1].

Thus Goddard's attempt to assert his power as Master had woefully miscarried and only brought him humiliation; but even as he delivered his judgment the Duke knew perfectly well that, instead of crushing his enemy, he had only infuriated him. On the day before the appeal was heard, the Master of Corpus informed Newcastle that Goddard had 'expressed his desire to have some communication with your Grace to-morrow, if it might conveniently be, on the subject of an address from the university[2]'; and beneath the innocent appearance of this message was concealed an ugly menace. The Peace of Paris, which concluded the Seven Years' War, had recently been signed, and the occasion certainly demanded that the university should present a congratulatory address to the crown. It would fall to Goddard as Vice-Chancellor to draft the address, and he was acting perfectly correctly, and in accordance with a practice insisted upon by Newcastle, in wishing to consult the Chancellor before taking any steps in the matter. Yet the Duke was aware that the Master of Clare's civility was a sham. Driven from the ministry in 1762, Newcastle was now at the head of a small opposition party which had opened its attack upon the government of the day by an onslaught upon the Preliminaries of Peace. It was not therefore easy for him as Chancellor of the university to congratulate the crown upon what as a politician he had unsparingly condemned; but more than his reputation for consistency was at stake. He had been quick to see that his party could never prevail in a bribed and corrupted house of commons unless it possessed the confidence of the country, and that, tainted as it was

[1] Add. MS. 33061, f. 257.   [2] Add. MS. 32947, f. 341.

with that aristocratic exclusiveness which was the bane of whiggism, it was hopeless to expect the support of the nation unless it included the only really popular statesman of the day, William Pitt. To win Pitt had therefore been Newcastle's aim from the first. He had persuaded his friends to attack the Peace Preliminaries because he knew that Pitt disapproved of them; and there was no sacrifice he was not prepared to make to win the support of the man he deemed indispensable. But Pitt was not to be easily won. Though he unsparingly denounced the terms of peace when they came under discussion in the house of commons, he went out of his way to repudiate any connection with Newcastle and his friends, taking his stand as a man single and alone, contending for the right but unconnected with any party. Yet early in March 1763 it seemed that the union, so eagerly desired by Newcastle, was on the point of being achieved. Apparently discarding all his prejudices, Pitt closely associated himself with the opposition in an attack upon a cyder tax introduced by the ministry, professed to be firmly united with the men whose overtures he had recently scorned, and frequently conferred with them about the conduct of the parliamentary campaign. When on March 9th, 1763, he dined at Devonshire house in the company of the opposition leaders, the event was greeted as marking the beginning of a new political era; and his brother-in-law, Lord Temple, remarked to Newcastle that 'what he had been about unsuccessfully for six months, viz. the bringing Mr Pitt and us together, is now come about, as it were, of itself[1].'

Such was the political situation when the Master of Clare expressed a wish to consult Newcastle about an university address upon the Peace of Paris: and it is easy to appreciate the extremely difficult position of the

[1] Yorke's *Life of Lord Hardwicke*, III, 456.

THE CHANCELLOR AND THE COLLEGES 309

Duke. The university addresses the crown in the name of the Chancellor, Masters, and Scholars, and it was only too likely that Pitt, who was quick to take offence and regarded the Peace as a crime against the country, would be excessively angry if Newcastle associated himself with a public acknowledgment of the beneficial character of the treaty. It was by no means unlikely that he would vent his anger by severing his connection with the opposition, which would thus be deprived of the ally whom they had so laboriously won, and whom they were so anxious to keep. It was still more likely that Dr Goddard, who could not have been unacquainted with the political situation, would wreak his revenge by drafting an address extravagant in its praise of the Peace; and indeed so many were the difficulties that Newcastle would gladly have dispensed with an address altogether. This however was out of the question, for even his most loyal adherents at Cambridge would never have consented to exclude themselves from the royal bounty by so affronting the crown; and he consequently had to solve the problem of satisfying the needs of the university without giving offence to Pitt.

Before Goddard raised the question, Newcastle had sought advice from Lord Hardwicke and the Duke of Devonshire[1]. Apparently both these noblemen suggested that the language of the address should be moderate so as not to give offence to Pitt, which was doubtless most excellent counsel but not easy to put into practice. In view of their strained relations it is improbable that either Goddard or Newcastle showed his hand at their interview on March 29th when the former formally asked the Chancellor's permission to

[1] In a letter to the Master of Corpus, dated March 29th, 1763, (of which there is a copy in the Cambridge University Library) Newcastle mentions having consulted Hardwicke and Devonshire.

310 THE CHANCELLOR AND THE COLLEGES

draft an address. But on the same day Newcastle had an interview with Pitt who expressed the opinion that if the Duke was in

any way named or comprehended as Chancellor in an address upon the Peace, which must in any shape be some approbation of it, it will be laid hold of by the court and turned to my disadvantage all over the kingdom[1].

Sorely perplexed, the Duke, like many another commander in a difficulty, assembled a council of war. On March 30th the Bishop of Norwich, the Master of Corpus, and Thomas Townshend, who represented the university in parliament, conferred with him[2]; and the decision they reached was embodied in the following minute:

It is apprehended that the form and style of the university, inserting the name of the Chancellor in all addresses and acts of this kind, will not admit of any alteration in that respect. It is proposed that the measure should be that our friends should endeavour, as from themselves, to make the address as little liable to objection as possible; that the Chancellor should have no hand or concern in it; that the Vice-Chancellor should be the person to apply to the Secretary of State; that he (the Vice-Chancellor) should attend His Majesty with the address; and that the Chancellor should be then in town and by his non-attendance manifest his disapprobation of the measure and shew that he had no concern in it. It is also thought proper that the Chancellor should write a letter to the Vice-Chancellor when he comes to town, that he had heard the university had thought proper to address His Majesty upon the Peace; that he was sorry not to be able to attend the university in any mark which they may think proper to give of their respect and duty to the King, in which nobody would more readily concur than himself if his attendance upon that occasion did not appear to him inconsistent with the part he had already taken when that affair was under the consideration of parliament[3].

[1] In a letter to the Master of Corpus, dated March 29th, 1763.
[2] *Ibid.*; see also Add. MS. 32947, f. 347.   [3] Add. MS. 32947, f. 357

It will be noticed that, though the address was to be in the name of the Chancellor, Masters and Scholars of the university, Newcastle entirely dissociated himself from all the proceedings; and there is little doubt that he adopted this attitude of repudiation in order to placate Pitt. Lord Hardwicke indeed expressed the opinion that the Duke had protested over much, and pointed out that there was a great difference between 'what a man does in his private personal capacity and what he does as the head of a great body of men who are masters of their own actions[1]'; but Newcastle preferred to incur the charge of over-acting rather than run any risk of offending Pitt. But if he believed that he had surmounted his troubles, he had reckoned without Goddard who was not disposed to throw away such a golden opportunity for retaliation. He composed an address which opened with the declaration that

His Majesty, out of tender regard to his people, had concluded a destructive though successful war by a safe, honourable and most advantageous Peace that would for ever stand recorded and celebrated in our annals as an event the most glorious to our country;

and it is hardly uncharitable to assume that this flamboyant sentence was intended to pain and annoy. Pitt would certainly be chagrined at the war, which he had conducted, being described as destructive, and it would be intolerable for Newcastle if the university, over which he presided, described the Peace as the most glorious event in the annals of England.

An university address however had to be approved by the Heads and sanctioned by the Senate before it could be presented; and, anticipating the consequences of Dr Goddard's malice, Newcastle had arranged for his friends among the Heads of Houses to attempt to tone down the exuberance of the address. Consequently,

[1] Add. MS. 32948, f. 1.

when on April 2nd the Vice-Chancellor submitted his draft to a meeting of the Heads, the Master of Corpus took strong objection to the extravagant language about the Peace and the contemptuous reference to an overwhelmingly successful war.

'I was seconded' he reported 'by the Master of Pembroke, and my exceptions supported by several others, so that after a long debate and altercation it was carried by six to five to change the word "destructive" into "expensive," to leave out "most advantageous," and to alter the last flaming paragraph, "that would for ever stand recorded and celebrated" into "we trust would be attended with the greatest blessings, etc." The Vice-Chancellor was not very willing to submit to the alterations, but we insisted upon them and upon our right to make them as a majority. He threatened that he would not go up with an address that said so little in favour of the Peace; but it certainly says full enough, and I am apprehensive that your Grace will think it says too much. The Masters of Christ's, King's, Peterhouse, Jesus, Pembroke, and myself were for making these alterations; the Vice-Chancellor, Masters of Caius, Emmanuel, St John's, and Sydney were rather wishing it should pass as it first stood[1].'

The lesson was not thrown away upon Goddard. The customary procedure was for the Vice-Chancellor to submit the address to the Chancellor before bringing it before the Senate; but, aware that Newcastle would attempt still further to modify the fulsome language, the Master of Clare, wisely from his point of view, did not allow the Chancellor to see the address until it had been passed by the Senate[2]. Thus Newcastle was confronted with a document which he heartily disliked but which he could not alter; and his anger knew no bounds.

'I am amazed' he told Thomas Townshend 'that when we had a majority of the Heads who over-ruled the Vice-Chancellor

[1] Add. MS. 32948, f. 13. It is curious to find the Master of Pembroke, Dr Long, supporting, and the Master of St John's, Dr Newcome, opposing Newcastle.   [2] Add. MS. 32948, f. 15.

THE CHANCELLOR AND THE COLLEGES 313

in some things, that they could afterwards let such an address pass[1]'; and he told Lord Hardwicke that he was 'amazed that a serious religious body, as the university is or ought to be, and where there are so many worthy reputable men as there are there, should suffer...fulsome flattery, upon certain points to be made in their name[2].'

It was not enough for him to complain to his friends, and the letter, which he had originally intended to write when the Vice-Chancellor came to town, was dispatched at once.

'Reverend Sir' he wrote to Goddard on April 6th 'I received here yesterday the favour of your letter of the 4th, transmitting to me a copy of the address which the university have thought proper to make to His Majesty on occasion of the Peace. I am extremely sorry that anything should prevent my attending the university with their address to the King. Nobody can be more ready and desirous to show his duty and loyalty to His Majesty upon all occasions than myself; or, as far as in me lies, to promote and encourage those principles of steddiness and affection to the Protestant succession, happily established in His Majesty and His Royal Family, which now for many years I have had the pleasure to see so uniformly pursued and so warmly exerted there. I apprehend from several expressions in the address, which I own I cannot approve, and which I should have objected to if I had been previously consulted, that my attendance upon this occasion will not be consistent with the part which I and other Lords thought ourselves obliged to take when the consideration of the Preliminaries was before the parliament. I therefore hope that it will not be thought want of duty to the King or of respect to the university (in neither of which will I ever be guilty of the least failure) if I desire you, Sir, (as has been very frequently done in our late Chancellor's time) to acquaint the Secretary of State that the university has agreed upon an address to His Majesty, and that you desire to know

[1] A copy of the Duke's letter to Townshend, dated April 7th, is in the Cambridge University Library.
[2] Add. MS. 32948, f. 21. When the Duke wrote this letter to Hardwicke he had not seen the address, but he was aware from the Master of Corpus of its general tenor.

from his Lordship when you and the university may attend His Majesty with it[1].'

Though this letter was addressed to the Vice-Chancellor and circulated among the Heads of Houses, it was intended quite as much for Pitt as for the university. From the very outset Newcastle had been obsessed with fear of what Pitt would think; and, acting on a suggestion of the Bishop of Norwich[2], he lost no time in communicating his letter to his exacting ally. He must have been greatly relieved to find that it gave entire satisfaction: 'nothing' wrote Pitt 'can be more becoming or carry more propriety and dignity[3].' Thus if Goddard had hoped to rend in twain a political alliance recently concluded, he was disappointed, but he was probably well enough pleased by what he had actually achieved: it was enough for him that he had humiliated the Chancellor and demonstrated his loyalty to the crown. On April 14th he presented the address to the King, and, though unattended by the Chancellor, he was accompanied by a distinguished gathering which included several bishops, a sprinkling of peers and members of parliament, and about two hundred doctors and masters of arts[4]. As he surveyed the scene Goddard may have reflected that the last laugh is the best.

But though he had avenged himself, he did not wish for peace and harmony; and, as long as Newcastle lived, Goddard continued to wage war against him. His conduct with regard to Ragdale's application for a mandate degree was probably inspired by malice[5]; and into his farewell speech on resigning the office of Vice-Chancellor he introduced 'some strong expressions in favour of the Peace[6].' It was therefore quite natural that he should

[1] Add. MS. 32948, f. 13.   [2] Add. MS. 32948, f. 46.
[3] Add. MS. 32948, f. 84; see also f. 81.
[4] Cooper's *Annals of Cambridge*, IV, 326.
[5] See ch. III, pp. 166–171.   [6] Add. MS. 32952, f. 223.

THE CHANCELLOR AND THE COLLEGES 315

eagerly support Lord Sandwich's candidature for the High Stewardship; and, even when Newcastle had been many years in the grave, Goddard had not forgiven him for omitting to prefer him in the church. In 1781, shortly before his death, the Master of Clare published a volume of sermons which he dedicated to the then Duke of Newcastle, who as Earl of Lincoln had been his pupil; and he took the opportunity to recall his ancient grievance.

'You being one of my oldest pupils now living' he wrote 'as well as of the greatest dignity and consequence I ever had the care of, having been placed under my tuition at Clare Hall in the year 1737 by the late Duke of Newcastle, and not having received the least mark of favour either from him or yourself, (except that you have frequently acknowledged to my friends and others that I faithfully and conscientiously discharged my duty) though I am not conscious of any failure of a proper regard for you both on my part, I presume to present these sermons to you[1].'

Thus Goddard carried his grievance with him to the grave.

It must be admitted that Newcastle was equally unforgiving. 'It is indifferent to me' he wrote to Lord Hardwicke in August 1763 'what day the Vice-Chancellor comes, provided I know it time enough to avoid meeting him, for I am determined never to be in a room with him if I can avoid it[2]'; and his anger never lost its edge. Never again did he make Clare his headquarters; and when he visited Cambridge in the summer of 1766 he stayed at St John's[3]. Probably of the many disappointments he experienced in the course of a long life, he felt none more keenly than his treatment by Goddard. It was not so much vexation at the loss

[1] Wardale's *History of Clare College*, p. 163.
[2] Add. MS. 32950, f. 142.
[3] *Cambridge Chronicle*, July 5th, 1766.

of what had once been a stronghold of his influence at Cambridge, but sorrow and grief that he should have been repudiated by his own college, of which he had been so proud, and whose fidelity he had never doubted. Goddard indeed had been far more successful than he possibly realised: he had not only, like Marriott after him, outwitted the politician; he had wounded the man.

It must not be assumed however that, whenever Newcastle was unsuccessful in an election to a mastership, he made an enemy for life, for he was generally prepared to forgive and, if possible, to make a friend of a victorious adversary. It was clearly not to his interest to sow a crop of vendettas in the university, and though, when engaged in the contest, he was anxious to achieve success and not over-scrupulous of the means he used, he was generally ready to resume amicable relations when the battle was over and the issue determined. The history of his relations with Dr Sumner, Provost of King's, certainly supports the theory that, though an interfering, he was not an unforgiving Chancellor. When in 1756 the Provostship fell vacant through the death of Dr George, Dr John Sumner, who had been Headmaster of Eton from 1745 to 1754, and Dr John Ewer, who had been Lord Granby's private tutor, were the two candidates. As Dr Sumner was suspected of having the support of Lord Sandwich, Newcastle, ever jealous of a rival influence in the university, very readily agreed at Granby's request to support Dr Ewer[1]; and, even before Dr George was dead, Dr Yonge, the Duke's indefatigable agent, was busy in preparing for a canvass of the Fellows of King's[2]. Unfortunately we do not know the details of the contest; but there can be little doubt that it was vigorously waged on both sides, Newcastle admitting in after years that he had fought hard

[1] Add. MS. 32866, f. 109.
[2] Add. MS. 32866, f. 163, f. 165.

THE CHANCELLOR AND THE COLLEGES 317

for Dr Ewer[1]; and, as was perhaps inevitable, the vigour, with which the struggle was carried on, was productive of bitterness which was reflected in the strange reception accorded to the victor, Dr Sumner.

'I think it my duty' wrote Dr Yonge to the Duke on October 24th, 1756 'to acquaint your Grace with some circumstances which have attended the admission of the Provost of King's, as one of them very much concerns your Grace, and the others bear very hard upon some whose names are not mentioned, and who are, I hope, incapable of deserving the appellations given to them. The Provost was presented as usual to the Bishop of Lincoln[2] in a Latin speech which was made by Mr Upton, who, having said somewhat of the morals and learning of King's college, added "utcunque de nobis sentiant malevoli" or words to that purpose. In the college he was received (as usual likewise) with another Latin speech by Mr Read who mentioned the "nebulonum quorundam convicia in aulis potentium temere sparsa." What led Mr Upton to his reflection I know not, but the expressions of Mr Read may be accounted for from the Bishop of Lincoln's answer to the first speech, part of which, I am very well assured, was in sense as follows. "I am glad to hear so good an account of the college, I confess I thought otherwise of it, and imagined I had very good authority for my opinion; for the Chancellor of the university told me that the college, to which I was related as visitor, was the worst college in it." This affair gives great concern to those here who have the honour to be best known to your Grace, as they see what an effect it must have upon the gentlemen of King's college, who look upon themselves as charged with great immoralities and great want of literature. I am told that Mr Read, being asked whom he meant, made no scruple of mentioning Doctor Squire's name[3], but did not explain his using the plural number. Of this I am not certain, and although I am very clear in the other facts, which indeed are notorious, yet whether your Grace learning them from me should be a secret or not is a doubt with me, and I leave it entirely to your Grace's pleasure[4].'

[1] Add. MS. 32942, f. 233. [2] The visitor of the college.
[3] The Chancellor's university secretary.
[4] Add. MS. 32868, f. 410.

318 THE CHANCELLOR AND THE COLLEGES

It is clear from the above account that it was within Newcastle's power to join with the defeated minority in making war upon the newly elected Provost and his supporters; and it is therefore the more noteworthy that he pursued an entirely opposite policy. On discovering that

if the new Provost owed any share of his success to Lord Sandwich, (which I can scarce believe he did) he will yet certainly act in such a manner as to make it appear that he was ignorant of it, and that he is by no means connected with his Lordship[1],

Newcastle was quite prepared to bury the hatchet; and, as Sumner was equally conciliatory, the two antagonists established friendly relations which continued even after the Duke had been driven from the Cabinet by George III and Lord Bute. A few months after Newcastle had ceased to be a servant of the crown, he mentioned Dr Sumner as one who had remained faithful to him in the days of adversity[2], and although later on he had to mourn the desertion of the Provost who warmly supported Lord Sandwich for the High Stewardship, he had at least the consolation of knowing that he was in no way responsible for the breach. If he had failed to inspire Dr Sumner with a devotion proof against all temptations of worldly advantage, he had at least succeeded in winning and for several years retaining his friendship; and, considering how unpromising had been the beginning of their connection, this was no mean achievement.

Nor was Dr Sumner exceptionally fortunate in receiving this conciliatory treatment. When on June 9th, 1760, Dr Chapman, Master of Magdalene, died after a short illness, Newcastle was at once requested by several applicants to use his influence with Lady Portsmouth, in whose gift, as the owner of Audley End, the mastership lay. Dr Ogden expressed the hope that

[1] Add. MS. 32868, f. 352.   [2] Add. MS. 32942, f. 233.

'your Grace will promote a faithful servant and one whom your former bounty has already made your own[1]': Dr Berridge of Clare was careful to say that he was
more solicitous of the dignity and honour of this preferment through your influence than for its profits and emoluments, being, (I thank God), in such plenty of circumstances as can no way be thought necessitous[2];
while Mr Eliot, Tutor and Fellow of Magdalene, recommended himself on the ground that the society wished him to succeed Dr Chapman[3]. Without loss of time Newcastle instructed the Master of Corpus to consult a selected number of Heads of Houses as to the most suitable candidate for him to support, and wrote to Lady Portsmouth, politely requesting her
to suspend determining anything upon the vacancy of the mastership of Magdalen college...till I have the honour to lay before you the wishes and inclinations of the principal members of the university, who are the first friends of the government, and whose advice I am always desirous of having[4].
The Heads of Houses recommended Mr Eliot as 'a person of good principles and learning, zealously attached to His Majesty's family and government, very acceptable to your Grace's friends here, and much respected through the whole university[5]'; and Newcastle, if he had been given the opportunity, would certainly have recommended Eliot to Lady Portsmouth. But Lady Portsmouth had not waited for the death of Dr Chapman to decide upon the disposal of her patronage.

'I shall always be glad' she replied to Newcastle on June 11th 'to have it in my power to oblige your Grace, but, soon after I was in possession of Audely End, I promised the first vacancy of the preferment, and my engagement is so circumstanced that it is impossible for me to receed from it[6].'

[1] Add. MS. 32907, f. 141; see also f. 98.
[2] Add. MS. 32907, f. 100.   [3] Add. MS. 32907, f. 102.
[4] Add. MS. 32907, f. 137, f. 209.
[5] Add. MS. 32908, f. 209.   [6] Add. MS. 32907, f. 160.

320 THE CHANCELLOR AND THE COLLEGES

Lady Portsmouth's promise had been given to George Sandby who was rector of Denton in Norfolk and an Oxford man; and Newcastle was not unnaturally offended by the slight to Cambridge and Magdalene. 'I think' he wrote to the Master of Corpus 'my Lady Portsmouth does very unkindly by our university in not taking one of our body, especially when there is so very deserving an one at the college as Mr Elliott is[1].' But on learning that the new Master was the son of a zealous and orthodox whig, Newcastle welcomed him with open arms and warmly commended him to his friends at Cambridge[2]. Nor was Sandby unwilling to be won.

'Permit me to say' he wrote to the Duke in August 1760 'that there is not one amongst the warmest of our noble Chancellor's friends with whom your Grace's commands might be deposited with greater confidence, nor who would execute them, as far as my power and abilities will go, with more observance, caution, and punctuality than myself. My father was very zealous in the Revolution cause, and he always taught me by principle to succour that part which your Grace led the way in, and which he particularly engaged in himself under the counsel (*sic*) of poor Mr Pelham, when the times were perilous and the waste of money great. It was upon these accounts that your Grace, nineteen years ago, promised to give me a little fresh plumeage (*sic*) for all that which my father had destroyed; and when the disturbances in the house of commons rendered it inconvenient then to your Grace to do what you had designed, I soon afterwards saw my sorrowing father to his grave, and have sat down performing my best ever since. Providence has now thrown me before your Grace again, and, if it pleases your Grace to raise me up with any favour, it shall be received and held with every token of gratitude[3].'

Sandby moreover was as enthusiastic about his new university as he was about its Chancellor. 'I was once

---

[1] Add. MS. 32907, f. 351; see also f. 239, f. 282, f. 292.
[2] Add. MS. 32908, f. 152.   [3] Add. MS. 32909, f. 376.

THE CHANCELLOR AND THE COLLEGES

an Oxford man' he wrote a few months after his appointment as Master 'but am now all over Cambridge[1]'; and he proved himself a man of his word. Unlike the Provost of King's he did not desert to Lord Sandwich, and, if he erred, it was in excess of loyalty.

'I very lately made' he wrote to Newcastle in May 1765 'a domestick of Lord Rockingham's Fellow of Magdalen, and told him that, whenever his vote could be of use, I hoped he would remember that I helped to it. He promised that he would. I have likewise three bye Fellowships now vacant, and I intend keeping them so till within a year of the general election, that I may know the better how to dispose of them[2].'

Lady Portsmouth had indeed given the Chancellor a loyal supporter; but it is to the credit of the Duke that he was politic enough to welcome the intruder into the academic fold[3].

Enough has been said to show that if Newcastle quarrelled with a college it was only with reluctance and under great provocation; but his conciliatory tactics were not always successful. It was almost vital for his position in the university that he should be on friendly

[1] Add. MS. 32914, f. 221.   [2] Add. MS. 32966, f. 387.
[3] It should be mentioned that in October 1763 Newcastle was disturbed, though without adequate reason, about the Master of Magdalene. 'I send you an unpleasant letter' he wrote to the Bishop of Norwich 'which I have received from Dr Sandby. I generally guess pretty right when my friends, or those who call themselves so, begin to cool towards me. I have thought for some months that that was the case of the Master of Magdalene, and particularly from his not having sent me an edition of his Terence which he put out in August last, and which I saw at Wimple in that month, a present from the editor. I own it surprised me, and I spoke to Caryl about it. He has now sent me his Juvenal with some hints of dissatisfaction. Your Lordship is very good in your intentions about the Chancellorship and I hope you will, when vacant, determine it for Dr Sandby.' Add. MS. 32952, f. 47. The complaint was eminently characteristic of Newcastle, but Sandby profited, being appointed Chancellor of Norwich in July 1768. Add. MS. 32990, f. 336.

and intimate terms with Trinity which, as one of the largest colleges, wielded considerable power; and yet this proved more than he could accomplish. It is true that Trinity never became actively hostile until Lord Sandwich sought to establish his power in the university, and that even in those days a certain number of the Fellows remained loyal adherents of the Duke; but there is no disputing the fact that, even when his relations with the college were outwardly correct and superficially cordial, Newcastle was less sure of his ground in Trinity than in most of the colleges where he had established a footing. It was Trinity which led the opposition to his attempt to make the prolongation of the Vice-Chancellorship for a second year the rule and not the exception; and this was not the only occasion that the college adopted an independent line and proved unamenable to the Chancellor's influence.

The phenomenon is the more surprising from having no obvious cause. Trinity had warmly supported the Duke when he was a candidate for the Chancellorship, and until the accession of George III enjoyed the reputation of being 'the great strength of the whig interest[1]' in the university. The Duke moreover was unsparing in his flattery of a foundation which he once described as 'the finest college in England[2],' and there is no possible doubt that he was extremely anxious to have the support of a society which could, when it chose, play an important and often a decisive part in university politics. Yet he certainly failed, and it is probable that his failure was due to various and unconnected circumstances rather than to any one particular blunder. It has already been suggested that his intimacy with St John's would not plead in his favour with the rival college; and it also appears that certain of the Fellows of Trinity believed that the Duke, when he controlled

[1] Add. MS. 32724, f. 466. [2] Add. MS. 32908, f. 104.

THE CHANCELLOR AND THE COLLEGES

the crown's ecclesiastical patronage, had deprived them of their fair share of church preferment.

'Now these favours' wrote a member of the college in a periodical in 1764 'so great and singular, how have they been repaid? Nay sir, don't be so open-mouthed, I hear what you are saying, "by prebends, deaneries, and bishoprics." Nothing less I assure you; I hardly know of one man who has been preferred from that college[1].'

If this complaint was well founded, the college had an undeniable grievance against the Chancellor; and there is some reason to think that the influence of the Master, Dr Smith, was not often exercised to promote peace and goodwill. Though Dr Smith only became an avowed enemy of the Duke when there was nothing to be gained by serving him, he never appears to have been on more than terms of ordinary courtesy with him, and it is unlikely that Newcastle ever relied upon him to further his interests. It should not be assumed that Dr Smith was from the start actively working against the Duke, but there are indications that he adopted a neutral attitude, and resented as an encroachment upon his authority any attempt by Newcastle to establish his influence in the college.

But whatever were the reasons for the coolness, it is certain that Newcastle was very far from being hostile to the college, and that on the one occasion when he acted against its wishes he was the victim of an excusable error. In 1755 Mark Hildesley was promoted from the vicarage of Hitchin, a Trinity living, to the bishopric of Sodor and Man; and as at this date the sovereignty of the Isle of Man was vested in the House of Athol, it was at least an open question whether in the case of this particular see the crown could claim its usual right of presenting to a living vacated by promotion to a

[1] *The Scrutator*, April 12th, 1764.

324 THE CHANCELLOR AND THE COLLEGES

bishopric. Those who disputed the right of the crown contended that there was

'no instance of the crown presenting to any benefice upon a promotion to the see of Man, that there are instances where the private patrons have presented,...that in a case of a contest between the crown and a patron for the right of presentation to a living upon the promotion of a bishop, which was determined in favour of the crown and which is reported by Levinz, the judges rest their arguments very much upon the crown granting the temporalities,' and that 'no temporalities are granted to the Bishop of Man which distinguishes his case from that of other bishops[1].'

Acting however on the advice of Hildesley, who mentioned that in the opinion of some people the presentation to his living would lapse to the crown[2], the Master of Trinity petitioned Newcastle that a Fellow of the college should be appointed to the vicarage of Hitchin.

'The good Bishop of Sodor and Man, formerly one of my darling pupils,' he wrote on May 21st, 1755, 'having been pleased to apply to your Grace to desire that a Fellow of his own college may succeed him in the vicarage of Hitching, if your Grace be pleased to comply with the Bishop's request and will do us the honour to name the clerk or leave it to the Bishop or the Master and seniors to recommend one to your Grace, in any case it will be accepted by this society as a particular mark of your Grace's favour[3].'

Unfortunately the Master had dallied too long, and Newcastle had already pledged himself to give the living to Hildesley's curate, Mr John Jones, an Oxonian, whose claims were supported by the parishioners of Hitchin[4]. It is unlikely that the Duke would have thus committed himself if he had remembered that the living was in the gift of Trinity: but, having engaged himself to the curate, he could only politely refuse to comply with Dr Smith's request. There the matter might have

[1] Add. MS. 32858, f. 70. [2] Add. MS. 32860, f. 463.
[3] Add. MS. 32855, f. 94. [4] Add. MS. 32860, f. 463.

THE CHANCELLOR AND THE COLLEGES

ended if certain Fellows of the college had not raised the question of the right of the crown to present to a living vacated by a promotion to the bishopric of Sodor and Man.

'As soon as your pre-engagement was known in the college' wrote Dr Walker to the Duke in November 1755 'many of the Fellows came in a body to the Master and told him they were well advised that the presentation to Hitchin was in the college and not in the crown, and begged of him to let us try our right. After some deliberation it was agreed at first to enter a caveat, and to take time to consider whether we should proceed in the affair or no. Not long after we were informed from several knowing persons in such affairs that the preferments of Bishops of Mann did not lapse to the crown as in other bishopricks, upon which information the Master and seniors unanimously agreed to a conclusion to try the college right[1].' On July 7th, 1755, it was agreed by the Vice-Master and seniors, the Master consenting, 'that the college presentation to the vicarage of Hitchin be granted to Mr Morgan, and, if it should be contested, that our right of presentation be supported at the expense of the college[2].'

Thus the action of the crown or rather of Newcastle was definitely challenged, and the Master and Fellows of Trinity were set upon a fight to a finish. Encouraged by the Bishop of Lincoln[3], who sympathised with their attitude and in whose diocese Hitchin lay, they believed that they were in the right, and that their action would be upheld in a court of law. Nor was it only for a principle that they were contending, for the curate was objectionable as an Oxonian, and, as the Master explained, they had

very few livings in their gift for which a Fellow would quit his Fellowship, and that it was of little importance to the crown because the case of the Bishop of Sodor and Man is quite distinct from all other bishopricks[4].

[1] Add. MS. 32860, f. 463.
[2] Trinity College Conclusion Book.
[3] John Thomas.
[4] Add. MS. 32858, f. 70.

326 THE CHANCELLOR AND THE COLLEGES

On the other hand it was extremely difficult for Newcastle to retreat with honour from the position he had taken up, and indeed he could not do so without establishing a precedent against the crown which would certainly not be forgotten. He was advised by the crown lawyers not to abandon what they regarded as a legal right: and, if he had viewed the dispute exclusively from the point of view of the king's Prime Minister, he would probably have accepted the challenge of the college. But as the Chancellor of the university he could not forget that a quarrel with Trinity might seriously prejudice his position; and he therefore sought for a compromise, directing Lord Dupplin in August 1755 to propose to Dr Smith

to have the matter of right referred to any indifferent person or persons, and mentioned the Master of the Rolls as being one who could not be an unfavourable judge to his own college[1].

The Master however stubbornly refused arbitration, and Newcastle, probably because he was loath to offend Trinity, unconditionally surrendered and allowed the nominee of the college to remain in undisputed possession of the living[2].

As the college had been completely triumphant and

[1] Add. MS. 32858, f. 70.

[2] There is the following note on p. 356 of the Rev. Weeden Butler's *Memoirs of Dr Hildesley*: 'Mr Jones's expectation of obtaining the presentation to Hitchin must appear a little singular at first sight: as the patronage was in Trinity college, Cambridge, and Mr Jones himself belonged to Oxford. But the case was this: the king usually filling up such preferments as became vacant upon the appointment of a new bishop, it was supposed that the prerogative would have extended to the instance of Dr Hildesley's promotion, which it did not. The parishioners however petitioned the college in behalf of Mr Jones, not being aware of the informality of so doing: or that a society were not likely to dispose of the presentation to any one not a member of their body.' The parishioners may have petitioned the college but they certainly petitioned Newcastle through a certain Mr Plummer. Add. MS. 32860, f. 463.

Newcastle had completely cleared himself from any suspicion of malice, it is impossible to believe that the incident was productive of anything more than a temporary coolness: and there is no reason to think that, if it had never happened, the relations between Newcastle and the college would have been more cordial. The most fundamental factor in the situation was probably the lack of any friendly understanding between the Master and the Duke: and as the mastership of Trinity is in the gift of the crown, it was unfortunate for Newcastle that he never had, subsequently to his election as Chancellor, an opportunity of disposing of this particular piece of royal patronage. Dr Smith did not die until February 2nd, 1768, and by that date Newcastle was not only on the verge of the grave himself but shorn of his former greatness and out of favour with the court. Yet, though opposed to the government and without any appreciable political influence, he could not relinquish all idea of establishing a friend as Master of Trinity, and when his loyal supporter, James Backhouse, one of the Trinity Tutors, asked for his assistance, he was not deaf to the appeal. He could not have been sanguine of success, for he knew that the Prime Minister, the Duke of Grafton, was warmly in favour of Dr Hinchliffe, and that Grafton was entitled to advise the King as to the appointment: but, as on some previous occasion the Archbishop had 'recommended Mr Backhouse to the King, in case of a vacancy, for the mastership of Trinity[1],' it was to the Archbishop that Newcastle turned.

'I have had an account this day' he wrote on January 30th, 1768, 'that the Master of Trinity is so ill that he cannot last many days. Your Grace knows how much I have at heart Mr Backhouse's success. He is a very worthy man and has great merit from the long laborious part he has had of being a Tutor

[1] Add. MS. 32988, f. 125.

328 THE CHANCELLOR AND THE COLLEGES

with great reputation in a great college: and his services have been such as to give him just pretensions to the mastership when it shall be vacant....If Mr Backhouse should be Master and that college should join with St John's, we shall then have nothing to fear....The Bishop of Norwich has sent for Mr Backhouse to town, and intends that he shall wait upon your Grace as soon as possible after his arrival[1].'

Backhouse arrived in London on January 30th or perhaps before[2], and waited upon the Archbishop: but both his visit and the Duke's letter failed to produce the desired effect. The Archbishop, who was confined to his house, declined to write to the King on behalf of Backhouse, pleading that as his advice had not been sought by the crown, he was not justified in giving it: though apparently, if he had been able to attend at court, he would have been prepared to speak to the King in favour of Backhouse. He however suggested that the Bishop of London might say a good word to the King for Backhouse, but it is quite clear that he believed the enterprise to be hopeless; and the Bishop of Norwich reported that, when Backhouse returned from Lambeth, 'he thought from all he could collect from the Archbishop that all was over, and he said he would be the first to congratulate with Dr Hinchliffe, and would study to live upon the best terms with him at college[3].' It is possible that the Archbishop was franker with Backhouse than he was with the Duke: and the Bishop of London, if he interceded with the King, failed to persuade. Grafton had the royal ear and Dr Hinchliffe was appointed Master of Trinity.

Newcastle was not to live to see another Head of a House appointed, and before the year was out he was in his grave. It is obvious that he did not attain the power he coveted in the university, and that he was still

[1] Add. MS. 32988, f. 118.   [2] Add. MS. 32988, f. 122.
[3] Add. MS. 32988, f. 148; see also f. 124, f. 125.

THE CHANCELLOR AND THE COLLEGES

more unsuccessful in his excursions into college politics. Yet he can only be held to have failed if judged by the standard which he set himself. Few Chancellors can have played a more active and dominant part in university affairs: and the strongest testimony to his influence is that in the day of his greatest impotence in the State he was able to defeat Lord Sandwich who had the court and ministry behind him. As a politician and a servant of the State he would have been doubtless well advised not to toil so arduously in a field from which he could reap no adequate harvest: but, had he been wiser, we should have been poorer. Had he not so ceaselessly interfered and so carefully preserved the records of his campaigns, we should know far less about eighteenth century Cambridge and the way the academic game was played. And for that we owe him gratitude.

INDEX

Abbot, William, Fellow and Tutor of St John's, and the question of re-admissions, 82 n. 1

Abdy, Sir Anthony, brother-in-law of Professor Rutherforth, 255 and n. 1, 256

Adams, Judge, 18

Addresses, university, 153-159, 307-314

Alvis, Andrew, Fellow of St John's, and the election of a Master of St John's in 1765, 260

Amelia, Princess, 262

Andrews, a candidate for a Fellowship of Trinity Hall, 272, 274, 276, 277

Anglesey, Arthur Annesley, Earl of, High Steward of the University, 36

Ansell, Thomas, Fellow of Trinity Hall, and the dinner of the Westminster club, 211-212; proceedings against in the Vice-Chancellor's court, 213-216; and the right of appeal, 216-218; and the election of Marriott to a Fellowship of Trinity Hall, 274-275; and the election of Crespigny to a Fellowship of Trinity Hall, 277; and Marriott's election as Master of Trinity Hall, 285, 289-290, 293, 295, 297

Appeal, right of, 205-222

Armitage, Sir John, 23

Ashcroft, Thomas, Fellow of St John's, 251

Ashdon, Rectory of, 239

Ashton, Charles, Master of Jesus, 49

Athol, Dukes of, and the Isle of Man, 323

Audley End, and the Mastership of Magdalene, 318, 319

Ayscough, Francis, Chaplain to Frederick, Prince of Wales, 47

Backhouse, James, Fellow and Tutor of Trinity, his merits as a Tutor, 7, 15; and the new regulations, 209; and the Trinity Fellowship election in 1762, 14-15; and Lord Hardwicke's candidature for the High Stewardship in 1764, 69, 75, 77 n. 5, 95-96; and the conflict between the undergraduates and seniority in 1764, 117; and the election of the Caput in 1764, 126 n. 5; and the election of a Vice-Chancellor in 1764, 134; a candidate for the Mastership of Trinity in 1768, 327-328; relations with the Duke of Newcastle, 232

Bacon, of Gonville and Caius, 92

Balguy, Thomas, Fellow of St John's, and the question of the right of appeal, 220

Banson, John, Fellow of Trinity Hall, and the question of the right of appeal, 218

Barker, son of the Duke of Rutland's steward, 68

Barnard, Edward, Headmaster and afterwards Provost of Eton, supports Lord Hardwicke for the High Stewardship in 1764, 61, 73; and the election of a Vice-Chancellor in 1764, 134; and Dr Johnson, 73

Barnardiston, John, elected Master of Corpus in 1764, 130, 238; elected Vice-Chancellor in 1764, 130-137; and the examination for the Chancellor's medals, 223; and the election of the Duke of Grafton as Chancellor in 1768, 143

Barton, Captain, 68

Barton, of Clare, 94

Barton, Cutts, Dean of Bristol, 68

Bedford, John Russell, Duke of, and the Duke of Newcastle's candidature for the Chancellorship, 41-43,

INDEX

46; and Lord Sandwich's candidature for the High Stewardship, 59, 73
Bennet, 92
Bennet, Thomas, Esquire Bedell, 109
Bentley, Richard, Master of Trinity, 1, 4, 115 n. 3
Berridge, Charles, Fellow of Clare, and Lord Hardwicke's candidature for the High Stewardship, 64, 93; applies for the Mastership of Magdalene, 319; see also 150
Bickham, James, Fellow of Emmanuel, and the question of the right of appeal, 220
Biddle, Dr, and the election of a Vice-Chancellor in 1764, 134
Bigg, of Clare, 93-94
Birkbeck, Edward, Fellow of St John's, supports the candidature of the Duke of Newcastle for the Chancellorship, 45
Bowers, Thomas, Bishop of Chichester, and the Duke of Newcastle, 35 n. 1
Bristol, Bishop of, see Philip Yonge
Bristol, Dean of, see Barton
Brockett, 18
Brockett, Laurence, Fellow of Trinity and Regius Professor of Modern History, supports Lord Sandwich's candidature for the High Stewardship, 77, 113 n. 5; and the conflict between the undergraduates and seniority in 1764, 117 and n. 1
Brooke, Zachary, Fellow and Tutor of St John's, thinks of standing for the Mastership of St John's in 1758, 241-244; supports Lord Sandwich's candidature for the High Stewardship, 77, 113 n. 5, 245; elected to the Lady Margaret Professorship of Divinity in 1765, 246-266; a candidate for the Mastership of St John's in 1765, 247-269
Brown, James, Fellow and afterwards Master of Pembroke, and the dinner of the Westminster Club, 211-215
Boyce, William, sets the Duke of Newcastle's installation ode to music, 51
Buckden, 87 and n. 2
Bull, John, scholar of Christ's, 21
Burrel, see Burrell
Burrell, Sir William, and the election of a Vice-Chancellor in 1764, 134
Burrough, Sir James, Master of Gonville and Caius, and the Senate House and the Library East Front, 223-225, 223 n. 3; elected Master, 233; elected Vice-Chancellor, 28; and the address on the fall of Quebec, 156-157; knighted, 157; entertains the Duke of Newcastle, 150; and the address on the Peace of Paris, 312; and Lord Sandwich's candidature for the High Stewardship, 67, 77, 130 n. 4, 233; and the question of re-admissions, 97 n. 1; his popularity in the university, 224 and n. 2; Newcastle's distrust of, 233; death of, 131
Butcher, of Peterborough, 42, 44
Bute, John Stuart, Earl of, 318

Calvert, John, 283 n. 1
Calvert, Nicholson, 283 n. 1
Calvert, Peter, Fellow of Trinity Hall, nominated to a Fellowship, 270-271; and the election of Marriott to a Fellowship, 274-275; and the election of Crespigny to a Fellowship, 277; and Lord Hardwicke's candidature for the High Stewardship, 66, 281; and the election of Marriott as Master of Trinity Hall, 282-286, 288, 291, 293, 295; recommended to the Archbishop of Canterbury for the office of Dean of Arches, 283 n. 1; and the election of a Vice-Chancellor in 1764, 134
Canterbury, Archbishop of, see Thomas Herring, Matthew Hutton, Thomas Secker
Caput, method of electing, 30 and n. 1, 125; its powers, 30-32; and the appointment of the Duke of Newcastle as High Steward, 37; election of in 1764, 124-127

INDEX

Cardale, Joseph, Fellow and Bursar of St John's, 249 and n 1.
Carlisle, Dean of, see Charles Tarrent
Carlisle, George Howard, Earl of, 68
Carr, of Clare College, 94
Carr, George, Fellow of Trinity Hall, nominated to a Fellowship, 270; and Marriott's election to a Fellowship, 274–275; and Crespigny's election to a Fellowship, 277–278; supporter of the Duke of Newcastle, 279; vacates his Fellowship, 281
Carrington, James, undergraduate of Trinity, signs the Admonition in 1764, 118
Caryl, Lynford, Master of Jesus, and the new regulations, 209; and the East Front of the Library, 226–227; recommends Carr for a Fellowship of Trinity Hall, 270; appointed to the Mastership of Jesus, 235–236, 236 n. 1; elected Vice-Chancellor, 179; activities as Vice-Chancellor, 28–29; the Duke of Newcastle's agent at Cambridge, 147, 232; entertains the Duke of Newcastle, 150; and the address on the fall of Quebec, 155–156; and the election of Waring to the Lucasian Professorship of Mathematics, 195; and the address on the accession of George III, 157; and the address on the Peace of Paris, 312; and mandate degrees, 167–170; and Lord Hardwicke's candidature for the High Stewardship, 66–67, 69, 77, 85, 91–93; and the legal proceedings connected with Lord Hardwicke's candidature, 122–123; and the election of Marriott as Master of Trinity Hall, 282, 292, 293, 296; and the election of the Caput in 1764, 126 and n. 5; and the election of a Vice-Chancellor in 1764, 131, 134–137; and the elections to the Lady Margaret Professorship and Mastership of St John's in 1765, 257, 258, 264–265; and the statue of George II, 228; and the Duke of Grafton's election as Chancellor, 140, 143; see also 119

Carysfort, John Proby, Lord, supports Lord Sandwich's candidature for the High Stewardship, 80–81, 96; accompanies Lord Sandwich to Cambridge, 113
Castle, Edmund, Master of Corpus, appointed Dean of Hereford, 11; as Vice-Chancellor, 38, 40, 41; death of, 236–237
Castley, Thomas, Fellow of Jesus, 92 and n. 6
Cavendish, Lord John, 23
Cay, Fellow of Clare, 303
Chancellor of the university, 26, 27; method of appointment, 41; a member of the house of regents, 32 n. 1; installation of Duke of Newcastle as, 29; and university addresses, 153–154; and mandate degrees, 161–162, 170
Chancellor's medals, custom of giving begun by the Duke of Newcastle, 222–223; and Francis Maseres, 196
Chapman, Archdeacon John, dispute with the Master of Emmanuel over the precentorship of Lincoln, 77 n. 5
Chapman, Thomas, Master of Magdalene, and the election of Dr Green as Regius Professor of Divinity, 182, 185–186; and Duke of Newcastle's election as Chancellor, 47; and Duke of Newcastle's installation as Chancellor, 49–53; and the new regulations, 199, 209; and the question of the right of appeal, 220; and the prolongation of Dr Yonge's term of office as Vice-Chancellor, 173; author of a work on the Roman Senate, 5; his death, 8, 318–319
Charles II, and mandate degrees, 160
Chester, Bishop of, see Edmund Keene
Chesterfield, Philip Dormer Stanhope, Earl of, and the Prince of Wales' candidature for the Chancellorship, 40–41
Chevallier, John, Fellow and afterwards Master of St John's, supports Lord Hardwicke for the High Stewardship, 63 and n. 1

INDEX

Chichester, Bishop of, see Thomas Bowers

Christ's College, disturbance in, 20–23; Duke of Newcastle's relations with, 234; and Lord Hardwicke's candidature for the High Stewardship, 104; and the election of the Duke of Grafton as Chancellor, 143

Clare College, affection of Duke of Newcastle for, 11, 298; the Duke of Newcastle entertained by, 150; election of Dr Goddard as Master, 298–304; and Hagar's appeal, 304–307; the Duke of Newcastle's quarrel with, 315–316; and Lord Hardwicke's candidature for the High Stewardship, 104

Clive, Robert, Lord, 166–168, 170

Cole, William, and George Mounsey, 9; and Dr Newcome, 48; and Dr Chapman, 53; and Dr Keene, 58 n. 1; and the East Front of the Library, 227

Colson, John, Lucasian Professor of Mathematics, death of, 194

Constitution of the university, 25–33, 80–82, 80 n. 1

Cornwallis, Hon. Frederick, Bishop of Lichfield, 61 and n. 2

Corpus Christi College, election of a master in 1750, 236–238; election of a master in 1764, 130; supports Lord Hardwicke for the High Stewardship, 104; and the Duke of Grafton's election as Chancellor, 141

Cotterell, Sir Clement, Master of the Ceremonies at the Duke of Newcastle's installation, 51 n. 3

Courtail, John, Fellow and Tutor of Clare, and the new regulations, 209

Craven scholarship, examination for, 12–14

Crespigny, Claude Champion, Fellow of Trinity Hall, elected to a Fellowship, 277–279; and the Duke of Newcastle, 279; vacates Fellowship, 281

Crew, Samuel, Fellow of Trinity, and the dinner of the Westminster Club, 211–212; proceedings against in the Vice-Chancellor's court, 212–215

Cumberland, Duke of, 76 n. 2, 134, 252

Cumberland, Richard, 6–7

Dale, Robert, Fellow of Trinity Hall, and the election of John Robinson to a Fellowship, 269; and the election of James Marriott to a Fellowship, 275 n. 2; and Lord Hardwicke's candidature for the High Stewardship, 66; and the election of Marriott as Master, 288, 290 and n. 2, 293–295

Damerham, living of, held by Dr Ogden, 11

Dartmouth, William Legge, Earl of, 64

Davis, Henry, Fellow of Trinity, 117 and n. 1

Dawes, Richard, 4

De Grey, William, Solicitor General, and the legal proceedings connected with Lord Hardwicke's candidature for the High Stewardship, 123–124

Denton, 320

Devonshire, William Cavendish, fourth Duke of, 68, 89; and Dr Ridlington, 278; and the address on the Peace of Paris, 309 and n. 1

Devonshire, William Cavendish, fifth Duke of, 255 and n. 1

Dickins, Francis, Regius Professor of Civil Law and Fellow of Trinity Hall, 269

Disney, William, Regius Professor of Hebrew and Fellow of Trinity, supports Lord Hardwicke's candidature for the High Stewardship, 72

Divinity, Regius Professor of, disqualified for election as Vice-Chancellor, 27 n. 2; election of, 182–193

Doctors, Vice-Chancellor's authority over, 29; and the Caput, 30; right of voting in either house of the Senate, 31–32, 103–104, 104 n. 1

INDEX

Doctors' Commons, and the Fellows of Trinity Hall, 267, 282–283, 287, 293; see also 268

Draper, Colonel, afterwards Sir William, supports Lord Sandwich's candidature for the High Stewardship, 96

Drummond, Robert, Archbishop of York, supports Lord Hardwicke's candidature for the High Stewardship, 64, 71, 94

Dupplin, Thomas Hay, Lord, representative of the borough of Cambridge in parliament, 43–44; and the Duke of Newcastle's candidature for the Chancellorship, 43 and n. 6, 45–46, 47 n. 6; and the election of Dr Green as Regius Professor of Divinity, 185; and the new regulations, 208 n. 5; and the election of John Robinson to a Fellowship at Trinity Hall, 269; and the dispute with Trinity over the living of Hitchin, 326; see also 174, 243

Duquesne, 271

Edgecumbe, George Edgecumbe, Lord, 65

Egremont, Charles Wyndham, Earl of, 170

Ekins, Jeffery, Fellow of King's, 68, 69 and n. 2

Ekins, Rector of Barton in Northamptonshire, 68

Eliot, Fellow and Tutor of Magdalene, anxious for the mastership, 319, 320

Elkin, 19

Elkin, Rose, the "fair Jewess," 19 n. 4

Ellis, William, arranges to pair with Dr Berridge, 93

Elliston, William, Master of Sidney Sussex, elected Master, 61 and n. 7; and the address on the Peace of Paris, 312; supports Lord Hardwicke's candidature for the office of High Steward, 61, 64, 72, 77–79, 84, 86–90, 96–97, 99–102, 104–112; and the question of readmissions, 98–99; and Lord Sandwich's visit to Cambridge, 114; and the legal proceedings connected with the High Stewardship, 123–124; and his resignation of the Vice-Chancellorship, 127–129; see also 126

Ely, Bishop of, Mastership of Jesus in gift of, 235

Ely, Bishop of, see Sir Thomas Gooch and Matthias Mawson

Ely, Dean of, see Hugh Thomas

Emmanuel College, and the Duke of Newcastle's election as Chancellor, 48; and the election of a High Steward, 104 n. 2; little influence of the Duke of Newcastle in, 233

Esquire Bedell, 32 n. 1, 52, 109

Euston, Earl of, see Duke of Grafton

Evans, 92

Ewer, Rev. John, candidate for the Provostship of King's, 68 and n. 4, 316, 317

Exeter, Bishop of, see Frederick Keppel

Exeter, Brownlow Cecil, Earl of, and Dr Ridlington, 278

Eyre, Venn, and the archdeaconry of Carlisle, 238–239

Fellow-commoners, behaviour of, 17, 20–23; usual annual allowance for, 23 n. 2

Ferris, Thomas, Fellow of St John's, 95 and n. 3

Flitcroft, 150

Flitcroft, Henry, 150 and n. 2

Folkes, Major, 17–18

Folkestone, William de Bouverie, Viscount, 65

Forster, Ralph, Fellow of St John's, and Lord Sandwich's candidature for the High Stewardship, 106–110, 113 n. 5; 123; see also 125

Fountaine, Thomas, Fellow of Trinity, 15, 75

Frampton, Thomas, Fellow of St John's, a candidate for the mastership in 1765, 260, 263–265

Francis, Alban, given a mandate degree, 161

Francklin, Thomas, Fellow of Trinity and Regius Professor of

INDEX

Greek, and the dinner of the Westminster Club, 211–213; proceedings against in the Vice-Chancellor's court, 213–215

Frederick, Prince of Wales, a candidate for the Chancellorship, 38–49, 240; and the Leicester House party, 269

Fuller, John, and the Trinity Fellowship election in 1762, 14–15; see also 75 n. 1

Fuller, Rose, and the Trinity Fellowship election in 1762, 14

Gainsborough, Countess of, 94
Gainsborough, 262 and n. 1
Garnet, John, Fellow of Sidney Sussex, and the new regulations, 209
Gawthrop, William, Fellow of Trinity College, persuaded by James Backhouse to vote for Lord Hardwicke as High Steward, 95–96, 96 n. 1
George II, and the East Front of the Library, 226–227; statue of, 227–230; see also 35
George III, and Lord Sandwich's candidature for the High Stewardship, 56–59, 73, 112; see also 55, 240
George, William, Provost of King's, supports the candidature of the Duke of Newcastle for the Chancellorship, 44; and the election of Dr Green as Regius Professor of Divinity, 182–186; death of, 190, 316
Gisborne, Thomas, Physician in ordinary to the King, asked to vote for Lord Sandwich as High Steward, 73–74; and the election of a Vice-Chancellor in 1764, 134
Gisbourn, see Gisborne
Glynn, Robert, Fellow of King's, nominated for election to the Caput in 1764, 126 n. 5
Goddard, Peter Stephen, Master of Clare, and the appointment of the Duke of Newcastle as High Steward, 37, 299; applies to the Duke of Newcastle for church preferment, 37–38, 299; elected Master of Clare, 266, 298–304; elected Vice-Chancellor, 304; and the proceedings connected with Hagar's appeal, 304–307; and the address on the Peace of Paris, 307–314; and mandate degrees, 166, 168, 170–171, 314; supports Lord Sandwich's candidature for the High Stewardship, 77, 130 n. 4, 315; and the question of re-admissions, 80, 97; and the election of a Caput in 1764, 126; publishes a volume of sermons, 315

Godolphin, Francis Godolphin, Earl of, father in law of the Duke of Newcastle, 50 n. 2

Gonville and Caius College, influence of Tory party in, 46, 48; and the East Front of the Library, 225; and Lord Sandwich's candidature for the High Stewardship, 104; Lord Sandwich entertained at, 115; the election of Dr Smith as Master of, 131; little influence of the Duke of Newcastle in, 233

Gooch, Sir Thomas, Master of Caius and Bishop of Ely, and the Prince of Wales' candidature for the Chancellorship, 40–41, 44; and Dr Parris, Master of Sidney, 46; and the appointment of Dr Yonge as Master of Jesus, 235, 236 n. 1; and the question of the right of appeal, 207; a loyal supporter of the Duke of Newcastle, 233

Gould, Fellow of Clare, 302–303

Graces, method of passing, 31–32, 108, 110–111; see also, 26

Grafton, Augustus Henry, third Duke of, his good behaviour as a student at the university, 23; his acquaintance with Samuel Peck, Fellow of Trinity, 69; supports Lord Hardwicke for the High Stewardship, 69–71; suggested as a possible candidate for the High Stewardship, 100–101, 101 n. 3; and the election of a Master of St John's in 1765, 251 and n. 3, 252; appoints Dr Hinchliffe Master of Trinity, 327–328

INDEX

Grafton, Charles Fitzroy, second Duke of, visited by the Duke of Newcastle, 54

Granby, John Manners, Marquis of, 316

Grantham, Thomas Robinson, Lord, and the statue of George II, 229

Gray, Thomas, his opinion of Fellow-Commoners, 17; his account of the Duke of Newcastle's installation as Chancellor, 54; his contempt for the Duke of Newcastle, 149

Green, John, Master of Corpus Christi and Bishop of Lincoln, elected Regius Professor of Divinity, 184–189; elected Master of Corpus, 236–238; and the new regulations, 199 n. 3, 209; and the question of the right of appeal, 220; appointed Dean of Lincoln, 11, 190–191; and the admission of Dr Sumner as Provost of King's, 317; and the appointment of Dr Sumner as Vice-Chancellor, 177–178; elected Vice-Chancellor, 13, 179; and the Duke of Newcastle's policy of prolonging the tenure of the Vice-Chancellor's office, 179–180; and the election of Dr Rutherforth as Regius Professor of Divinity, 192–193, 193 n. 1, 194; and university addresses, 153, 155, 157, 158, 307, 309 n. 1, 310, 312, 313 n. 2; and mandate degrees, 165; supports Maseres' candidature for the Lucasian Professorship of Mathematics, 197 and n. 2, 198; and the examination for the Craven scholarship, 12–14; and the appointment of Sandby as Master of Magdalene, 319–320; appointed Bishop of Lincoln, 11; and Hagar's appeal, 306; and Lord Hardwicke's candidature for the High Stewardship, 61 and n. 1, 64–68 70, 77, 82, 86 n. 1, 87, 90–92, 91 n. 1, 99–101, 104 n. 1; and the question of re-admissions, 97; and Thomas Pitt's vote, 122; and the election of Marriott as Master of Trinity Hall, 282; resignation of Mastership, 129–130; and the election of a Vice-Chancellor in 1764, 128–130, 133; and the election of a Lady Margaret Professor in 1765, 249; and the election of a Master of St John's in 1765, 252, 255–256, 262; entertains the Duke of Newcastle, 150; the Duke of Newcastle's agent at Cambridge, 147, 232

Gremial, 183 n. 2 and n. 3

Grenville ministry, and Lord Sandwich's candidature for the office of High Steward, 56, 112

Grenville, George, and Lord Sandwich's candidature for the office of High Steward, 57–59, 89

Grigg, William, Master of Clare, 301

Gunning, Henry, 1, 8, 11; his account of Trinity Hall, 266

Hagar, Robert, Fellow of Clare, 303; deprived of his fellowship by the Master, 304; appeals against the Master, 304–307

Halifax, George Montagu Dunk, Earl of, and Lord Sandwich's candidature for the office of High Steward, 57–59; on friendly terms with the Duke of Newcastle, 59 n. 1; and Dr Hallifax, 296

Hall, supports the Duke of Newcastle's candidature for the Chancellorship, 44

Hallifax, Samuel, Fellow of Trinity Hall, elected to a Fellowship of Trinity Hall, 281; supports Lord Hardwicke's candidature for the High Stewardship, 281; and the election of Marriott as Master of Trinity Hall, 126 n. 2, 282 and n. 2, 284–289, 291–297; nominated for election to the Caput, 126 n. 2; his life threatened by an undergraduate, 19–20

Hamburgh, 262

Harding, supports the Duke of Newcastle's candidature for the Chancellorship, 44

338 INDEX

Harding, see Hardinge

Hardinge, George, an undergraduate of Trinity, 118–119

Hardwicke, Philip Yorke, first Earl of, and the Prince of Wales' candidature for the Chancellorship, 40; appointed High Steward, 54; admitted to the degree of Doctor of Laws, 149; and university addresses, 153, 154, 159, 309 and n. 1, 311, 313 and n. 2; and mandate degrees, 171; and the election of Dr Green as Regius Professor of Divinity, 188 and n. 2, 189; and the question of the right of appeal, 220; and the election of Dr Green as Master of Corpus, 237; and the election of Dr Goddard as Master of Clare, 303; death of, 55, 84–85; see also 150, 234, 315

Hardwicke, Philip Yorke, second Earl of, his character, 60; a candidate for the office of High Steward, 59–111; his attitude as a candidate, 60, 64, 78–79, 100, 138; interference in a Fellowship election at St John's, 95; opposes the suggestion that the Duke of Grafton should be a candidate for the High Stewardship, 100–101; and the legal proceedings connected with his candidature for the High Stewardship, 111–112, 120–124, 137; and the election to the Lady Margaret Professorship in 1765, 250; and the election to the Mastership of St John's in 1765, 255; a candidate for the Chancellorship, 139–144; see also 130–131

Hawnes, vicarage of, and Robert Hagar, 304, 306 n. 1

Hayter, Thomas, Bishop of London, 300, 303 and n. 2, 304

Heads of Houses, Vice-Chancellor appointed from among, 27–28; authority of Vice-Chancellor over, 29; as advisors to the Vice-Chancellor, 28–30; and the election of the Caput, 30; and the Duke of Newcastle's installation as Chancellor, 29; and university addresses, 29, 153–159; and mandate degrees, 161 and n. 1, 162

Henley, Lord, see Earl of Northington

Hereford, Dean of, see Edmund Castle

Herring, of King's, 71

Herring, Thomas, Archbishop of Canterbury, and the installation of the Duke of Newcastle as Chancellor, 50 n. 1; and the election of Dr Green as Master of Corpus, 236–237; and the new regulations, 200, 202 n. 3; and the question of the right of appeal, 220

Hertford, Francis Seymour, Marquis of, and the examination for the Craven scholarship, 12–14; and mandate degrees, 165

Hervey, 23

Hetherington, William, Rector of Dry Drayton, 42

High Steward of the university, Earl of Anglesey as, 36; appointment of the Duke of Newcastle as, 36–38; appointment of first Earl of Hardwicke as, 54; appointed by Grace of the Senate, 37, 83; contest for in 1764, 55–139

Hildesley, Mark, Bishop of Sodor and Man, 323–324, 326 n. 2

Hill, Samuel, of St John's, 94–95, 165

Hilton, Robert, Fellow of Trinity, 15

Hinchliffe, John, Master of Trinity, and the election of a Vice-Chancellor in 1764, 134; and the election of the Duke of Grafton as Chancellor, 142–143; appointed Master of Trinity, 327–328

Hitchin, dispute over appointment to living of, 323–326

Hooper, Francis, Fellow of Trinity, and the election of Dr Rutherforth as Regius Professor of Divinity, 193

Horseman, John, Fellow of St John's, 251 and n. 3

Houghton le Spring, 251 n. 3

House, of King's, 71

INDEX 339

Hubbard, Henry, Fellow of Emmanuel and Registrary of the university, 109
Hughes, of Queens', 61
Hume, John, Bishop of Oxford, 304
Humphreys, Thomas, given a mandate degree, 166–171
Huntingdon, Francis Hastings, Earl of, and mandate degrees, 166–168
Hurdis, Secretary to the Duke of Newcastle, 167–169
Hutton, John, and Dr Rooke, Master of Christ's, 20–23
Hutton, Matthew, Archbishop of York and afterwards Archbishop of Canterbury, 22 and n. 3, 50

Jacobs, Mrs, 19
James II, and mandate degrees, 161
Jenkin, Henry, of St John's, 251 and n. 3
Jennings, of Barkway, 251
Jenyns, Sir Roger, 134 n. 3
Jenyns, Soame, 134 and n. 3
Jesus College, and the appointment of Masters, 232, 235–236; and the appointment of a High Steward, 104; and the election of the Duke of Grafton as Chancellor, 143
Johnson, of St John's, 70
Johnson, James, Bishop of Worcester, 69 and n. 2
Johnson, Samuel, and Dr Barnard, 73
Jones, John, Curate at Hitchin, 324, 326 n. 2
Jones, Thomas, Fellow and Tutor of Trinity, his merits as a Tutor, 7; his writings and lectures, 7

Keene, Sir Benjamin, 58 n. 1
Keene, Edmund, Master of Peterhouse and Bishop of Chester, his character and early career, 58 n. 1, 21℃; appointed Bishop of Chester, 11; prolongation of as Vice-Chancellor, 172–173; and the riot in 1751, 17–18; and the election of Dr Law as Master of Peterhouse, 238–239; and the new regulations, 202–211; and the question of the right of appeal, 206–219, 221; and the East Front of the Library, 223,

225; recommends Carr for a Fellowship of Trinity Hall, 270; and the election of Marriott to a Fellowship of Trinity Hall, 274–275; consulted about establishing the Duke of Newcastle's influence in Trinity Hall, 276; and the election of Dr Rutherforth as Regius Professor of Divinity, 191–192; and Lord Sandwich's candidature for the High Stewardship, 58; and the election of a Vice-Chancellor in 1764, 135; and the election of the Duke of Grafton as Chancellor, 140; the Duke of Newcastle's agent at Cambridge, 147; see also 148 n. 1, 173, 177
Kelly, of Jesus, supports Lord Hardwicke's candidature for the High Stewardship, 74
Keppel, Frederick, Bishop of Exeter, 64
King's Bench, Court of, and the university, 115 n. 3, 123
King's College, Tory influence in, 48; and the new regulations, 208; and the election of Dr Sumner as Provost in 1756, 316–318; and Lord Sandwich's candidature for the High Stewardship, 104, 253; and the election of the Duke of Grafton as Chancellor, 143
King in Council, and the university, 113, 115 and n. 3
Kinnoull, Earl of, see Lord Dupplin
Kirke, Miss, and Dr Newcome, Master of St John's, 248 and n. 3, 249

Ladd, 17–18
Lady Margaret Professorship, election to, 246–266
Law, Edmund, Master of Peterhouse, elected Master of Peterhouse, 238–239; applies for the Deanery of Ely, 10; elected Vice-Chancellor, 175–177; activities as Vice-Chancellor, 28; and the election of Dr Rutherforth as Regius Professor of Divinity, 191–192; and university addresses, 153–156, 312; asked by Sir James Lowther

22—2

340 INDEX

to support Lord Sandwich for the High Stewardship, 73; supports Lord Hardwicke for the High Stewardship, 62, 67, 77; visited by Lord Sandwich, 114–115; a candidate for the Lady Margaret Professorship, 246–266; see also 5

Lee, Sir George, Dean of Arches, and the question of the right of appeal, 220; and Sir Edward Simpson, 268–269; and Fellowship elections at Trinity Hall, 270–279; death of, 280

Lee, Sir William, Chief Justice of the King's Bench, 220 and n. 3

Leicester House party, recruited from Whigs and Tories, 38; and Sir George Lee, 269

Library, University, erection of East Front of, 223–227

Lichfield, Bishop of, see Hon. Frederick Cornwallis

Lincoln, Bishop of, see John Green and John Thomas

Lincoln, Dean of, see John Green and James Yorke

Lincoln, Henry Pelham-Clinton, Earl of, and Dr Goddard, 299, 304, 315

Lipyeatt, Jonathan, and the question of the right of appeal, 205–206

Llandaff, Bishop of, see Richard Watson

Loggan, see Loggon

Loggon, George, Fellow of St John's, 251

London, Bishop of, see Thomas Hayter, Thomas Sherlock, Richard Terrick

Long, Roger, Master of Pembroke and Lowndean Professor of Astronomy, reported to be dying, 190; and the address on the Peace of Paris, 312 and n. 1; and Lord Sandwich's candidature for the High Stewardship, 64, 77, 129, 130 n. 4

Longmire, Daniel, Fellow of Peterhouse, and Lord Sandwich's candidature for the High Stewardship, 106–111; visited by Lord Sandwich, 114–115; and Thomas Pitt's vote, 122; and the legal proceedings connected with Lord Sandwich's candidature for the High Stewardship, 123; see also 125

Louisburg, fall of, 153

Lowther, Sir James, supports Lord Sandwich for the High Stewardship, 73, 115 n. 2

Lowther, William, 115 and n. 2

Ludlam, William, Fellow of St John's, a candidate for the Lucasian Professorship of Mathematics, 196–198; Dr Smith's high opinion of, 196–197; and the question of re-admissions, 82

Lushington, James Stephen, Fellow of Peterhouse, supports Lord Hardwicke for the High Stewardship, 74

Luther, John, 76 and n. 2

Magdalene College, Master of, not elected by the Fellows, 232; appointment of Dr Sandby as Master of, 318–320; and Lord Hardwicke's candidature for the High Stewardship, 104 n. 2

Man, Isle of, 323

Mandate degrees, 131–132, 160–171

Manning, and the election of a President of Queens' in 1760, 234 n. 2

Mansfield, William Murray, Earl of, and the legal proceedings connected with Lord Hardwicke's candidature, 124

Markham, William, Headmaster of Westminster School, 65

Markland, Jeremiah, 4

Marriott, Sir James, Fellow and afterwards Master of Trinity Hall, his early career, 271–272; elected to a Fellowship of Trinity Hall, 272–276; supports the interest of the Duke of Newcastle in Trinity Hall, 276–281; and the appointment of William Ridlington as Regius Professor of Civil Law, 278–279; agent for Newcastle at Cambridge, 232; supports Lord Hardwicke for the High Stewardship, 66–67, 281; deserts the Duke of Newcastle for

INDEX 341

Lord Sandwich, 129, 130 n. 4; elected to Mastership of Trinity Hall, 129, 130, 282-297, 316; and the election of a Vice-Chancellor in 1764, 130-132; and the election of the Duke of Grafton as Chancellor, 141; see also 267

Martyn, Thomas, of Sidney Sussex, 125

Maseres, Francis, awarded the first Chancellor's medal, 196; a candidate for the Lucasian Professorship of Mathematics, 196-198

Mason, William, composes the ode for the Duke of Newcastle's installation, 51

Masters of Colleges, see Heads of Houses

Mawson, Matthias, Bishop of Ely, and the appointment of Dr Caryl as Master of Jesus, 235-236; and Lord Sandwich's candidature for the High Stewardship, 115 n. 3; advocates the prolongation of Elliston as Vice-Chancellor, 180; and the election of Dr Powell as Master of St John's, 251, 262

May, of Pembroke, 71

Mease, Michael Driver, Fellow of St John's, 94

Meredith, Moore, Fellow of Trinity, 76, 117

Metcalfe, Thomas, Fellow of St John's, 251 and n. 3

Milles, Edward, Fellow of Trinity Hall, and the election of Marriott as Master, 286-288, 290 and n. 2, 291; see also 269, 275 n. 2

Milles, Richard, nephew of Edward Milles, 286

Milton, Joseph Damer, Lord, 251 and n. 3

Milton Abbas, 251 and n. 3

Moderator, George Mounsey, Fellow of Jesus, as, 9; Pretyman as, 19; and the house of regents, 32 n. 1

Monson, Henry, Fellow of Trinity Hall and Regius Professor of Civil Law, and the election of Marriott to a Fellowship, 274-275; death of, 277-278; see also 269

Montagu, Frederick, the first Fellow-Commoner to receive a mandate degree, 163

Morgan, John Pilkington, Fellow of Trinity, 325

Morgan, William, Fellow of Trinity, 6-7

Mounsey, George, Fellow and Tutor of Jesus, 9

Murhall, Thomas, Fellow of Christ's, 125

Murray, Dr, Vicar of Gainsborough, 262 and n. 1

Murrey, see Murray

Newbon, Richard, Fellow of Trinity, 117 and n. 1

Newcastle, Henry Pelham-Clinton, second Duke of Newcastle, see Earl of Lincoln

Newcastle, Thomas Pelham-Holles, first Duke of Newcastle, his character and ability, 35 and n. 1, 36, 145-146; his influence and interest in the university, 54-55, 66, 144, 152-153, 198-199, 230, 328-329; rebukes Dr Yonge, 148; appointed High Steward, 36-38; elected Chancellor, 38-47; installed as Chancellor, 49-54; resigns the office of High Steward, 53; anxious for Lord Hardwicke to succeed him as High Steward, 54; his use of ecclesiastical patronage, 10-12; and the examination for the Craven scholarship, 12-14; and a Trinity Fellowship election, 14-15; anxious to prolong certain Vice-Chancellors, 128, 171-180; founder of the Chancellor's classical medals, 222-223; and the statue of George II, 227-230; and the building of the East Front of the Library, 223-227; and the question of the right of appeal, 211, 213, 217, 220-221; and the new regulations, 199-211; his visits to the university, 148-152; and university addresses, 155-159, 307-314; and mandate degrees,

342 INDEX

160–171; and professorial appointments, 180–199, 278–279; his difficulties in controlling the colleges, 231–233, 235, 239; and Gonville and Caius, 233; and Emmanuel, 233; and Christ's, 234; and St Catharine's, 234; and Queens', 234; and Jesus, 235–236; and Corpus Christi, 236–238; and Peterhouse, 238–239; and St John's, 240–266; and Trinity College, 240 and n. 1, 322–328; and Trinity Hall, 268–298; and Clare, 298–304; and King's, 316–318; and Magdalene, 318–320; his dislike of Goddard, 315–316; and Hagar's appeal, 304–307; and Dr Sandby, 320–321, 321 n. 3; and Lord Hardwicke's candidature for the office of High Steward, 59–111, 138–139; and the legal proceedings connected with Lord Hardwicke's candidature, 111–112, 115 n. 3, 120–124, 137; and the appointment of Proctors and Scrutators in 1764, 125; and the election of the Caput in 1764, 124–127; and the election of a new Vice-Chancellor in 1764, 124–137; driven into parliamentary opposition, 307–308, 318; his death, 140, 142; see also 1, 11
Newcome, John, Master of St John's and Lady Margaret Professor of Divinity, his election as Master, 254; appointed Dean of Rochester, 12; supports the Duke of Newcastle's candidature for the Chancellorship, 39, 44, 47–48, 240; asks for ecclesiastical preferment for Birkbeck, 45; and the election of Dr Green as Regius Professor of Divinity, 182, 186, 187; and the election to the Lucasian Professorship of Mathematics, 197; and the address on the Peace of Paris, 312 and n. 1; and Lord Hardwicke's candidature for the High Stewardship, 61, 64, 77, 95 and n. 2; and the election of a Vice-Chancellor in 1764, 133; desires to resign the Lady Margaret Professorship, 246–250; and Dr Squire, 146; illnesses and death of, 241, 243, 244, 246–257, 261; see also 173
Non-Gremial, 52, 183 n. 2 and n. 3
Non-Regents, and the Caput, 30; and the passing of Graces, 31–32, 105
Northington, Robert Henley, Earl of, and Lord Sandwich's candidature for the High Stewardship, 73, 96; see also 77 n. 5
Norwich, Bishop of, see Philip Yonge
Norwich, Dean of, see Edward Townshend

Ogden, Samuel, Woodwardian Professor of Geology, his appetite, 8; Dr Johnson's opinion of his sermons, 8 n. 2; his epistolary style, 11; anxious to be appointed Master of Magdalene, 318–319; and Fellowship election at St John's in 1764, 95; and the election of a Vice-Chancellor in 1764, 134; a candidate for the Lady Margaret Professorship, 249–250, 257; and the Mastership of St John's, 257–259, 260, 264
Onslow, George, 75 n. 3
Ordinances of the university, 26
Oxford, Bishop of, see John Hume
Oxford, University of, Jacobite sentiment at, 199

Paris, Peace of, university address on, 307–314
Parris, Francis Sawyer, Master of Sidney Sussex, and the Duke of Newcastle's candidature for the Chancellorship, 41–43, 45–47
Peck, Samuel, Fellow of Trinity, and Lord Hardwicke's candidature for the High Stewardship, 69 and n. 3; appointed a Scrutator, 125
Pedley, Stanhope, Fellow of Trinity Hall, 281; and Marriott's election as Master, 288–289, 291, 293–297

INDEX 343

Pelham, Henry, and the Duke of Newcastle's candidature for the Chancellorship, 41, 44; see also 240 n. 1, 284, 320

Pelham, Henry, and the election of a Vice-Chancellor in 1764, 134

Pembroke College, Tories at, 48; and Lord Sandwich's candidature for the High Stewardship, 104; Duke of Newcastle's little influence in, 234

Peterborough, Bishop of, see Richard Terrick

Peterhouse, Tories at, 48; and Lord Hardwicke's candidature for the High Stewardship, 104; the Duke of Grafton replaces his name on the books of, 140 and n. 1; and the election of the Duke of Grafton as Chancellor, 141, 143; influence of Duke of Newcastle in, 238–239

Physicians, College of, and mandate degrees, 162

Pigott, John, Fellow of Trinity, 75 and n. 3

Pinfold, Charles, Fellow of Trinity Hall, 269, 273–275

Pitt, Thomas, afterwards Lord Camelford, 120 and n. 1, 121–122, 137

Pitt, William, afterwards Earl of Chatham, his reputation for financial disinterestedness, 35 n. 1; and the parliamentary opposition, 308; and the address on the Peace of Paris, 309–311, 314

Place, Marwood, Fellow of Trinity, 117 and n. 1

Plucknett, William, Fellow of St John's, 64, 262 and n. 1

Plummer, and the dispute over the living of Hitchin, 326 n. 2

Plumptre, Robert, President of Queens', election of as President, 234 and n. 2; and Lord Hardwicke's candidature for the High Stewardship, 77, 82–83, 94; offers to place Charles Townshend's name on the books of Queens', 80; and the election of a Vice-Chancellor in 1764, 134; and the election of the Duke of Grafton as Chancellor, 140–143; on intimate terms with the Yorke family, 78; see also 150

Plumptre, Russell, Regius Professor of Physick, attends the Master of St John's, 241

Politicians, interest in university of, 10–16, 34–36, 48–49

Porson, Richard, 4

Porteus, Beilby, Fellow of Christ's, 109

Portmore, Charles Colyear, Earl of, 251 n. 3, 252

Portsmouth, Lady, and the Mastership of Magdalene, 318–321

Powell, John, Fellow of Trinity, 117 and n. 1

Powell, William Samuel, Master of St John's, opposes Waring's election to the Lucasian Professorship of Mathematics, 197–198; anxious to become Master, 241–244; and Lord Hardwicke's candidature for the High Stewardship, 72, 88–89, 100, 245; and the legal proceedings connected with Lord Hardwicke's candidature, 124; election to the Mastership of St John's, 245–266; introduces annual college examinations, 25; and the election of the Duke of Grafton as Chancellor, 143

Pratt, Sir Charles, afterwards Earl Camden, 118–119

Pratt, Sir John, 115 n. 3

Prescot, Kenrick, Master of St Catharine's, applies for the Deanery of Ely, 10; and Lord Sandwich's candidature for the High Stewardship, 130 n. 4; and the question of re-admissions, 97; Lord Sandwich sups with, 115

Preston, William, Fellow of Trinity, and Lord Hardwicke's candidature for the High Stewardship, 75, 76 and n. 3

Pretyman, George, afterwards Bishop of Winchester, 19 and n. 1

Privy Council, and the Prince of Wales' candidature for the Chancellorship, 40

344 INDEX

Proctors, and the Caput, 30; and installation of the Duke of Newcastle, 51; and the regents' house, 31, 32 n. 1, 105–108; appointment of, in 1764, 124–125
Public Orator, and installation of the Duke of Newcastle, 51; Dr Yonge appointed, 183
Pyle, Edmund, and the election of Dr Green as Master of Corpus, 237

Quebec, fall of, 155
Queens' College, and Lord Hardwicke's candidature for the High Stewardship, 104; Duke of Newcastle's influence in, 234

Ragdale, given a mandate degree, 166–170, 314
Read, John, Fellow of King's, 317
Re-admission, question of, 79, 80 and n. 1, 81, 82 and n. 2, 96–99
Regents, and the Caput, 30; and Graces, 31, 105; see also 27 n. 1, 32
Regulations, the new, 199–211
Richardson, William, Master of Emmanuel, his Tory principles, 38, 233; and the Prince of Wales' candidature for the Chancellorship, 38, 41, 43, 47; and university addresses, 153–156, 312; and Lord Hardwicke's candidature for the High Stewardship, 77 and n. 5, 130 and n. 4; and the election of a Vice-Chancellor in 1764, 136 n. 3
Ridlington, William, Fellow of Trinity Hall and Regius Professor of Civil Law, his cure for the dropsy, 8–9; and the question of the right of appeal, 217, 278; and Fellowship elections at Trinity Hall, 275, 277; appointed Regius Professor of Civil Law, 278–279; and Lord Sandwich's candidature for the High Stewardship, 66 and n. 3, 281; and Marriott's election as Master of Trinity Hall, 282, 284–290, 293, 295–297; see also 282 n. 2
Roberts, John, secretary to Henry Pelham, 284–285
Robinson, 240 n. 1

Robinson, John, Fellow of Trinity Hall, 269, 270, 275 n. 2; and Marriott's election to the Mastership of Trinity Hall, 290–291, 294
Robinson, Matthew, Fellow of Trinity Hall, and Fellowship elections, 269–270, 274–275, 277; and the election of Marriott as Master, 289–291, 293, 295
Rochester, Dean of, see John Newcome
Rockingham, Charles Watson-Wentworth, Marquis of, and Lord Hardwicke's candidature for the High Stewardship, 67, 94; see also 321
Rooke, George Henry, Master of Christ's, and the Duke of Newcastle's candidature for the Chancellorship, 39, 44, 47 n. 5; and the election of Dr Green to the Regius Professorship of Divinity, 182, 184–189; appointed Prebendary of Lincoln, 189; and John Hutton, 20–23; and the new regulations, 203, 207–208; see also 234
Roper, Robert, 161 n. 1
Rose Inn, 102
Royal Letters, 26
Royston, Lord, see second Earl of Hardwicke
Rutherforth, Thomas, Fellow of St John's and Regius Professor of Divinity, and the Prince of Wales' candidature for the Chancellorship, 41, 43, 47–48; a candidate for the Regius Professorship of Divinity 1748–1749, 184–185, 187; reconciled with the Duke of Newcastle, 189–190, 245–246; anxious to be elected Lowndean Professor of Astronomy, 190; elected Regius Professor of Divinity, 190–194; and the examination for the Craven scholarship, 12–14; desirous of becoming Master of St John's, 241–244, 245–266; and Lord Hardwicke's candidature for the High Stewardship, 131, 245; and the election of a Vice-Chancellor in 1764, 131; and the election of the Duke of Grafton as Chancellor, 142 n. 3, 143; as agent

for the Duke of Newcastle at Cambridge, 232; see also 5

Rutland, John Manners, Duke of, 68

St Catharine's College, and Lord Hardwicke's candidature for the High Stewardship, 104; and the Duke of Newcastle, 234

St David's, Bishop of, see Samuel Squire

St John's College, state of parties in, 241–244; and Lord Hardwicke's candidature for the High Stewardship, 104 n. 2; Fellowship election at, 95; and the election of a Lady Margaret Professor, 246 and n. 1; and the election of a Master, 245–266; introduction of annual college examinations at, 25; Tories at, 48; the Duke of Newcastle stays at, 315

St Sepulchre's, 11

Salusbury, Thomas, Fellow of Trinity Hall, 269–270

Sandby, George, Master of Magdalene, appointed Master of Magdalene, 320; his enthusiasm for Cambridge, 320–321; relations with the Duke of Newcastle, 320, 321 and n. 3; appointed Chancellor of Norwich, 321 n. 3; his disposal of Fellowships, 321; and the university address on the accession of George III, 157–159; and Lord Hardwicke's candidature for the High Stewardship, 61 and n. 4, 62, 77, 109; and the legal proceedings connected with Lord Hardwicke's candidature, 112; and the election of a Vice-Chancellor in 1764, 133; see also 104

Sandwich, John Montagu, Earl of, and Dr Sumner, 316, 318; a candidate for the office of High Steward, 56–111, 138, 329; denunciation of John Wilkes, 56–57, 74; and nickname of Jemmy Twitcher, 57; and the question of re-admissions, 98–99; and the legal proceedings connected with his candidature, 112–115, 115 n. 3, 120, 137; and the election of

Marriott as Master of Trinity Hall, 129, 289 and n. 2, 290, 293 n. 2, 295–297; his visit to Cambridge, 113–115; and the election of the Caput in 1764, 125–127; and the election of a Vice-Chancellor in 1764, 131–137; and the election of a Lady Margaret Professor and a Master of St John's in 1765, 246, 249, 252, 253, 257, 259, 260, 263–266; see also 321

Scrope, Andrew, Provost of King's, 115 n. 3

Scrutators, and the election of the Caput, 30; and the house of non-regents, 31, 105–106; appointment of, in 1764, 124–125

Secker, Thomas, Archbishop of Canterbury, and Lord Hardwicke's candidature for the High Stewardship, 65; and the election of a Master of St John's, 262–263; and civil law preferments, 282 and n. 1, 283 n. 1; and the Mastership of Trinity, 327–328

Sedgwick, William, President of Queens', 45, 234

Senate, limitation of its power, 26; and the election of a Vice-Chancellor, 27; the two houses of, 27 n. 1, 31–32; and university addresses, 29

Senate House, erection of, 223 and n. 3

Shaftoe, Captain, 17–18

Sherlock, Thomas, Bishop of London, and Duke of Newcastle's installation, 50; and the new regulations, 200, 202 n. 3; and the question of the right of appeal, 220

Sidney Sussex College, and Lord Hardwicke's candidature for the High Stewardship, 104 n. 2

Simpson, Sir Edward, Master of Trinity Hall, his influence in the College, 66–67; and elections to Fellowships, 268–280; and the Duke of Newcastle, 280–281; and Hagar's appeal, 306; and Lord Hardwicke's candidature for the High Stewardship, 77, 109, 281; death of, 129, 281–282

346 INDEX

Simpson, Francis, Fellow of Trinity Hall, elected to a Fellowship, 270; and Fellowship elections, 274–275, 277; and Lord Hardwicke's candidature for the High Stewardship, 66 and n. 4; and Marriott's election as Master, 282, 286, 291, 293, 295–297; and the election of a Vice-Chancellor in 1764, 134

Skottowe, Charles, President of Corpus, declines the Mastership, 236

Skynner, John, Fellow of St John's, a candidate for the Mastership, 260–261

Smith, of King's, and the question of the right of appeal, 220

Smith, Dr, of Westminster School, 134

Smith, John, Master of Gonville and Caius, elected Master, 131, 233; created doctor of divinity by royal mandate, 131–132; and the election of a Vice-Chancellor in 1764, 131–137

Smith, Robert, Master of Trinity, and the Duke of Newcastle's candidature for the Chancellorship, 39, 44; and the election of Dr Green as Regius Professor of Divinity, 184–187; and the election of Dr Rutherforth as Regius Professor of Divinity, 193; and the election of Waring as Lucasian Professor of Mathematics, 195–198; and the Trinity Fellowship election in 1762, 14–15; and Lord Sandwich's candidature for the High Stewardship, 62, 74–77, 95–96, 103 and n. 1, 104, 108–109, 111, 130 n. 4; and the question of re-admissions, 97 n. 1; and Lord Sandwich's visit to Cambridge, 113, 115; his tyrannous treatment of his undergraduates, 116–119; and the election of the Caput in 1764, 126 n. 5; his opinion of Johnian examiners, 16; his relations with the Duke of Newcastle, 151, 152, 323–326; his death, 327; see also 5, 173, 240 n. 1

Sodor and Man, Bishop of, see Mark Hildesley

Somerset, Charles Seymour, Duke of, Chancellor of the university, 36, 38, 41; and mandate degrees, 162; appoints to Mastership of Clare, 301; his death, 41, 42, 45–47

Sondes, Lewis Watson, Lord, 94

Squire, Samuel, Bishop of St David's, supports the Duke of Newcastle's candidature for the Chancellorship, 44; as Chancellor's secretary, 146, 147 and n. 1, 148 and n. 1, 302 n. 5; and the question of the right of appeal, 221; and the admission of Dr Sumner as Provost of King's, 317 and n. 3

Statutes, Elizabethan, 26; and earlier, 26; and the question of the right of appeal, 206 n. 1

Steeple Bumpstead, Vicarage of, 239

Stonehewer, Richard, 251 n. 3

Story, of Magdalene, 95

Stuart, Charles, Fellow and Tutor of Peterhouse, 239

Summersham, Rectory of, and Regius Professorship of Divinity, 182

Sumner, John, Provost of King's, elected Provost, 28, 316–318; elected Vice-Chancellor, 28, 176–179; and the election of Dr Rutherforth as Regius Professor of Divinity, 178 n. 3, 192, 193 and n. 1; entertains the Duke of Newcastle, 150, 151 n. 1; asks for a bishopric, 10; and the address on the Peace of Paris, 312; relations with the Duke of Newcastle, 318; deserts to Lord Sandwich, 321; and Lord Sandwich's candidature for the High Stewardship, 61 and n. 3, 65, 77, 109, 130 n. 4; and the question of re-admissions, 97; Lord Sandwich dines with, 115

Talbot, William, Fellow of Clare, appointed the Chancellor's secretary for university business, 146, 147 and n. 1, 302 n. 5; and the election of a Master of Clare in 1762, 298–304; and Hagar's ap-

INDEX 347

peal, 305; and Lord Hardwicke's candidature for the High Stewardship, 93 and n. 2, 97, 102 and n. 2; and Thomas Pitt, 123; and Dr Newcome, 248 and n. 3, 249, 257; views on the Lady Margaret Professorship and the Mastership of St John's, 258; see also 232

Tarrent, Charles, Dean of Carlisle, 68

Tatham, John, scholar of Christ's, 21

Taxors, 32 n. 1

Taylor, Dr, 43

Temple, Richard Grenville-Temple, Earl, 308

Terrick, Richard, Bishop of Peterborough and afterwards Bishop of London, and Dr Goddard, 299–300; and Lord Sandwich's candidature for the High Stewardship, 73; and the Mastership of Trinity, 328

Thomas, Hugh, Master of Christ's, elected Master, 234; attempts to prolong his Vice-Chancellorship, 174 and n. 2; appointed Dean of Ely, 12; and the East Front of the Library, 226; and the election of the Provost of King's as Vice-Chancellor, 178; and the election of Dr Rutherforth as Regius Professor of Divinity, 191; entertains the Duke of Newcastle, 150, 151 n. 1; reports on the health of Dr Newcome, 241; and the address on the Peace of Paris, 312; and Lord Hardwicke's candidature for the High Stewardship, 77; and the question of re-admissions, 97; and the election of Marriott as Master of Trinity Hall, 282; and the election of a Lady Margaret Professor in 1765, 249; see also 173

Thomas, John, Bishop of Lincoln, and the living of Hitchin, 325 and n. 3

Three Tuns Tavern, and the Westminster Club, 211–212

Teddington, Thomas, Fellow of St John's, 251, 259 n. 5

Tomline, Sir George Pretyman, Bishop of Winchester, see Pretyman

Tories, influence of in university, 38; and Leicester House party, 38; and Duke of Newcastle's candidature for the Chancellorship, 46, 48; and the new regulations, 201; and the question of the right of appeal, 208

Townshend, Charles, second Viscount Townshend, 35 n. 1

Townshend, Charles, third Viscount Townshend, 90 and n. 1

Townshend, Charles, and Lord Hardwicke's candidature for the High Stewardship, 71 and n. 3, 72, 88–90, 91 and n. 1, 92 and n. 3, 96, 100, 111; and the election of Dr Powell as Master of St John's, 255–256

Townshend, Charles ("Spanish Charles"), and Lord Hardwicke's candidature for the High Stewardship, 71 and n. 3, 80, 81, 100 n. 5; and the election of a Vice-Chancellor in 1764, 134

Townshend, Edward, Dean of Norwich, 134–135

Townshend, George Townshend, fourth Viscount, and Lord Sandwich's candidature for the High Stewardship, 96, 108; a possible candidate for the High Stewardship, 100; visits Cambridge with Lord Sandwich, 113–115

Townshend, Thomas, university representative in parliament, 44 n. 1; and the Duke of Newcastle's candidature for the Chancellorship, 44, 46; and the address on the Peace of Paris, 310, 312

Townshend, Thomas, junior, and Lord Hardwicke's candidature for the High Stewardship, 92, 94, 96–97

Trinity College, and the installation of the Duke of Newcastle as Chancellor, 51–53; and the election of Dr Green as Regius Professor of Divinity, 182, 184, 187–188; and the new regulations, 208; and the Vice-Chancellor's term of office, 174–176, 178; and the election of the Provost of King's as Vice-Chancellor, 178; and the election of Dr Rutherforth as Regius Pro-

348   INDEX

fessor of Divinity, 191–193; and the dispute over the living of Hitchin, 323–326; Fellowship election at, 14–15; and Lord Sandwich's candidature for the High Stewardship, 62, 74–77, 104; and Lord Sandwich's visit to Cambridge, 113–115; disciplinary measures taken against undergraduates at, 116–119; the Duke of Newcastle and, 149–151, 192, 322–323; rivalry with St John's, 240 and n. 1, 322; appointment of Dr Hinchliffe as Master of, 327–328; see also 48, 232, 253
Trinity Hall, constitution of, 266–268, 279–281; Fellowship elections at, 269–281; election of Marriott as Master of, 129, 281–297
Twells, 70

Undergraduates, disorderly behaviour of, 16–23, 199 and n. 3; industry of, 23–25; and Lord Hardwicke's candidature for the High Stewardship, 104–106, 110; and the question of the right of appeal, 218–219
Upton, John, Fellow of King's, 317

Vane, Frederick, Fellow-Commoner of Peterhouse, 17–18, 212, 214–215
Vanneck, Sir Joshua, 94
Vernon, Lord Hardwicke's solicitor, 123
Vernon, James, Fellow-Commoner of Trinity, and the Westminster club 212, 215
Vice-Chancellor, method of electing, 27–28, 30 n. 1, 127–128, 131–133; and Heads of Houses, 28–29; judicial functions of, 29; and the Caput, 30, 31 and n. 1; a member of the house of regents, 32 n. 1; influence of in the election of a Chancellor, 42; prolongation of term of office of, 28, 128, 171–180; and university addresses, 153–159; election of in 1764, 124, 127–137; and rioting, 16–19; incapacity of Regius Professor of Divinity to serve as, 27 n. 2

Wadeson, Richard, Fellow of St John's, 64
Wales, Princess of, and Sir George Lee, 279
Walker, Richard, Vice-Master of Trinity, and Dr Green's election to the Regius Professorship of Divinity, 182, 184, 187–188; and the Vice-Chancellor's term of office, 174; and the dispute over the living of Hitchin, 325; and the Fellowship election in 1762, 14–15; and Lord Sandwich's candidature for the High Stewardship, 62; and William Preston, 75, 76 and n. 3; and the election of the Caput in 1764, 126 n. 5; death of, 9
Walpole, Sir Edward, 76 and n. 5
Walpole, Horace, and installation of the Duke of Newcastle, 49; and Edmund Keene, Master of Peterhouse, 58 n. 1
Walpole, Sir Robert, and Edmund Keene, Master of Peterhouse, 58 n. 1; see also 35, 37, 76 n. 5
Waring, Edward, Fellow of Magdalene and Lucasian Professor of Mathematics, election of as Professor, 194–198; see also 6
Warner, Dr, 65
Watson, Richard, Bishop of Llandaff, academic career of, 5–6, 16; his opinion of Fellow-Commoners, 23–24; his tribute to the industry of undergraduates, 23–24
Wentworth, Sir Thomas, 67
Westminster club, dinner of, 211–213
Westminster school, the Duke of Newcastle's affection for, 11, 298; and the Duke of Newcastle's candidature for the Chancellorship, 44
Weymouth, Thomas Thynne, Viscount, his good behaviour as a student at Cambridge, 23; and Lord Sandwich's candidature for the High Stewardship, 108
Whalley, John, Master of Peterhouse, 182
Whichcot, 251
Whigs, influence in Cambridge of, 37; and Leicester House party, 38;

INDEX 349

and the Duke of Newcastle's candidature for the Chancellorship, 46, 54
Whisson, Stephen, Fellow of Trinity, and the Fellowship election in 1762, 14–15; see also 119
Whiston, 90
White, Mr Serjeant, 97
Whitehall, James, Senior Fellow of Trinity, and the election of Dr Green as Regius Professor of Divinity, 182, 184, 187–188
Wilbraham, 121
Wilcocks, Joseph, 68, 69 and n. 2
Wilcox, John, Master of Clare, and the appointment of the Duke of Newcastle as High Steward, 37 and n. 1; and the question of the right of appeal, 219–220; and the Duke of Newcastle, 298; death of, 298, 302; see also 173
Wilkes, John, 56, 57, 74
Wilson, Dr, 240 n. 1
Wilton, Joseph, and the Statue of George II, 227, 228
Wimpole, 234
Winchester, Bishop of, see Pretyman
Worcester, Bishop of, see James Johnson
Wortham, of Royston, 95
Wright, Stephen, and the East Front of the Library, 223–225, 227
Wynne, William, Fellow of Trinity Hall, and Fellowship elections at Trinity Hall, 274, 275, 277; and Lord Hardwicke's candidature for the High Stewardship, 66, 281; and Marriott's election as Master, 282, 286, 288–297; nominated for election to the Caput, 126 n. 5; and the election of a Vice-Chancellor in 1764, 134

Yeoman Bedell, 52
Yonge, Philip, Master of Jesus, appointed Public Orator, 183; a candidate for the Regius Professorship of Divinity, 182, 183 and n. 2 and n. 3, 184–187; appointed Master of Jesus, 235, 236 n. 1; appointed Bishop of Bristol and afterwards Bishop of Norwich, 11–12; and the question of the right of appeal, 221–222; and the East Front of the Library, 225–226; and prolongation of as Vice-Chancellor, 173; and university addresses, 157, 310, 314; and mandate degrees, 163, 164; and the election of Dr Sumner as Provost of King's and Vice-Chancellor, 178, 316, 317; and the election of Dr Goddard as Master of Clare, 298; and Lord Hardwicke's candidature for the High Stewardship, 60, 61, 64, 66–70, 75–76, 79, 81, 82 n. 2, 83; and the legal proceedings connected with Lord Hardwicke's candidature, 120; and the election of Marriott as Master of Trinity Hall, 282–283, 296; and the election of a Vice-Chancellor in 1764, 134–135; and the Mastership of St John's, 243, 244, 255, 256; and the statue of George II, 228–230; and the Mastership of Trinity, 328; and the Duke of Newcastle, 147 and n. 1, 148, 232
York, Archbishop of, see Robert Drummond and Matthew Hutton
Yorke, Charles, relations with the university as Solicitor General, 29; and Dr Richardson, Master of Emmanuel, 77 and n. 5; and mandate degrees, 171; and Lord Hardwicke's candidature for the High Stewardship, 60, 100, 101 and n. 3; and the legal proceedings connected with Lord Hardwicke's candidature, 111, 112, 115 n. 3, 121; and the election of Marriott as Master of Trinity Hall, 290 n. 2; and the election of a Vice-Chancellor in 1764, 136 n. 3, 142 n. 3
Yorke, James, Dean of Lincoln, 92, 134 and n. 4
Yorke, John, 92, 134
Yorke, Philip, 23 n. 2, 24–25

Zouch, Thomas, Fellow of Trinity, 15